CONDUCTING RESEARCH ON GLOBAL ENVIRONMENTAL AGREEMENT-MAKING

Global environmental negotiations have become central sites for studying the interaction between politics, power, and environmental degradation. This book challenges what constitutes the sites, actors, and processes of negotiations beyond conventional approaches and provides a critical, multidisciplinary, and applied perspective reflecting recent developments, such as the increase of actor diversity and the digitalisation of global environmental meetings. It provides a step-by-step guide to the study of global environmental negotiations using accessible language and illustrative examples from different negotiation settings, including climate change, biodiversity, and ocean protection. It introduces the concept of 'agreement-making' to broaden understanding of what is studied as a 'site' of negotiation, illustrating how diverse methods can be applied to research actors, processes, and order-making. It provides practical guidance and methodological tools for students, researchers, and practitioners participating in global environmental agreement-making. It is one of a series of publications associated with the Earth System Governance Project: www.cambridge.org/earth-system-governance.

Hannah Hughes is Senior Lecturer in International Politics and Climate Change in the International Politics Department at Aberystwyth University. Hannah's central research concern is global environmental degradation and the forms of knowledge that inform the political response, as well as the necessary conceptual and methodological innovation to advance understanding of this. She has examined this through research on the Intergovernmental Panel on Climate Change (IPCC), and has published findings in *Nature Climate Change* and *Global Environmental Politics.* Hannah is co-investigator on the ESRC grant The Politics of Science in International Climate Cooperation and has a forthcoming book on *The IPCC and the Politics of Writing Climate Change*. Hannah and Alice began their collaboration in 2016 with the aim of initiating greater discussion on the study of negotiation sites through the concept of global environmental agreement-making, editing a special section in *Global Environmental Politics* and leading a multi-authored perspective piece in *Earth System Governance*.

Alice B. M. Vadrot is Associate Professor for International Relations, with a focus on Environmental Politics, at the Department of Political Science of the University of Vienna and Visiting Research Fellow at the Centre for Science and Policy (CSaP) of the University of Cambridge. Her work addresses the role of knowledge and science in global environmental politics. She has extensively researched the Intergovernmental Platform on Biodiversity and Ecosystem Services (IPBES) and developed the concept of 'epistemic selectivities'. As principal investigator of the five-year research project MARIPOLDATA, funded by the European Research Council (ERC), she develops and applies a new interdisciplinary methodology to study agreement-making and the interrelations between marine biodiversity politics and ocean science in practice. Vadrot is the author of *The Politics of Knowledge and Global Biodiversity* (2014) and editor of several special issues, research articles, and editorials in, inter alia, *Global Environmental Politics*, *Environmental Politics*, *Nature*, and *Marine Policy*.

The **Earth System Governance Project** was established in 2009 as a core project of the International Human Dimensions Programme on Global Environmental Change. Since then, the Project has evolved into the largest social science research network in the area of sustainability and governance. The Earth System Governance Project explores political solutions and novel, more effective governance mechanisms to cope with the current transitions in the socio-ecological systems of our planet. The normative context of this research is sustainable development; earth system governance is not only a question of institutional effectiveness, but also of political legitimacy and social justice.

The **Earth System Governance series** with Cambridge University Press publishes the main research findings and synthesis volumes from the Project's first ten years of operation.

Series Editor

Frank Biermann, *Utrecht University, the Netherlands*

Titles in print in this series

Biermann and Lövbrand (eds.), *Anthropocene Encounters: New Directions in Green Political Thinking*

van der Heijden, Bulkeley and Certomà (eds.), *Urban Climate Politics: Agency and Empowerment*

Linnér and Wibeck, *Sustainability Transformations: Agents and Drivers across Societies*

Betsill, Benney and Gerlak (eds.), *Agency in Earth System Governance*

Biermann and Kim (eds.), *Architectures of Earth System Governance: Institutional Complexity and Structural Transformation*

Baber and Bartlett (eds.), *Democratic Norms of Earth System Governance*

Djalante and Siebenhüner (eds.), *Adaptiveness: Changing Earth System Governance*

Behrman and Kent (eds.), *Climate Refugees*

Visseren-Hamakers and Kok (eds.), *Transforming Biodiversity Governance*

Biermann, Hickmann and Sénit (eds.), *The Political Impact of the Sustainable Development Goals*

Lamalle and Stoett (eds.), *Representations and Rights of the Environment*

Cover image: Pink Chicken Project by Nonhuman Nonsense, at UN CBD, COP-14. During the 14th Conference of the Parties (COP) to the Convention on Biological Diversity at Sharm El Sheik In November 2018, a large pink chicken appeared in the observer space of the negotiation room. The pink chicken was used as an artefact by the Pink Chicken Project during an activist campaign at COP 14 under the auspices of Nonhuman Nonsense, a 'research-driven design and art studio creating near-future fabulations and experiments somewhere between utopia and dystopia' (https://nonhuman-nonsense.com). The editors have chosen this image to identify how the conventional actors, sites and processes of environmental negotiations are being disrupted by non-state actors as they seek to challenge the reproduction of the social, political and economic order that is degrading the environment.

CONDUCTING RESEARCH ON GLOBAL ENVIRONMENTAL AGREEMENT-MAKING

Edited by
HANNAH HUGHES
Cardiff University

ALICE B. M. VADROT
University of Vienna

CAMBRIDGE
UNIVERSITY PRESS

CAMBRIDGE
UNIVERSITY PRESS

Shaftesbury Road, Cambridge CB2 8EA, United Kingdom

One Liberty Plaza, 20th Floor, New York, NY 10006, USA

477 Williamstown Road, Port Melbourne, VIC 3207, Australia

314–321, 3rd Floor, Plot 3, Splendor Forum, Jasola District Centre, New Delhi – 110025, India

103 Penang Road, #05–06/07, Visioncrest Commercial, Singapore 238467

Cambridge University Press is part of Cambridge University Press & Assessment, a department of the University of Cambridge.

We share the University's mission to contribute to society through the pursuit of education, learning and research at the highest international levels of excellence.

www.cambridge.org
Information on this title: www.cambridge.org/9781009179447
DOI: 10.1017/9781009179454

First published 2023

A catalogue record for this publication is available from the British Library.

ISBN 978-1-009-17944-7 Hardback

Additional resources for this publication at www.cambridge.org/9781009179447.

To Jonah, River, and Estelle

Contents

Figures, Tables and Boxes

Figures

Tables

Reflection Boxes

Method Boxes

Contributors

Hannah Hughes

International Politics Department, Aberystwyth University

Hannah is Senior Lecturer in International Politics and Climate Change in the International Politics Department at Aberystwyth University. Hannah's central research concern is global environmental degradation and the forms of knowledge that inform the political response, as well as the necessary conceptual and methodological innovation to advance understanding of this. She has examined this through research on the Intergovernmental Panel on Climate Change (IPCC) and published findings in *Nature Climate Change* and *Global Environmental Politics*, and a forthcoming book on *The IPCC and the Politics of Writing Climate Change* (Cambridge University Press, 2024).

Alice B. M. Vadrot

Department of Political Science, University of Vienna

Alice Vadrot is Associate Professor for International Relations and the Environment at the Department of Political Science of the University of Vienna and Visiting Research Fellow at the Centre for Science and Policy (CSaP) of the University of Cambridge. In 2018, she won an ERC Starting Grant for her project MARIPOLDATA. She has conducted extensive research on the Intergovernmental Platform on Biodiversity and Ecosystem Services (IPBES) and marine biodiversity negotiations, focusing on the Convention on Biological Diversity (CBD) and a new legally binding instrument for the conservation and sustainable use of biodiversity beyond national jurisdiction (BBNJ). Vadrot is the author *of The Politics of Knowledge and Global Biodiversity* (Routledge, 2014) and has published in *Global Environmental Politics*, *Environmental Politics*, *Nature*, and *Marine Policy*.

Jennifer Iris Allan

International Relations, Cardiff University

Jennifer Iris Allan is a senior lecturer in international relations at Cardiff University. Her research explores environmental and social movements, and how global rules are made and remade. Through contributing to the *Earth Negotiations Bulletin*, she has attended roughly fifty UN conferences on global climate governance, as well as chemicals and wastes management. Her publications in *Global Environmental Politics*, *Global Policy*, *Third World Quarterly*, and *Environmental Politics* and her book, *The New Climate Activism: NGO*

Authority and Participation in Global Climate Governance (University of Toronto Press, 2020), contribute to scholarship on NGO influence and state-based negotiations in global environmental politics.

Tracy Bach
Co-Focal Point, UNFCCC Research and Independent NGOs (RINGO)
Tracy Bach is a law professor who has taught and published on climate change, international environmental law and human rights, and health care and environmental health law. She earned degrees from Yale University (BA) and the University of Minnesota (JD and MA Public Affairs). Bach serves as the Co-Focal Point of the Research and Independent Non-Governmental Organizations (RINGO) constituency to the UNFCCC Secretariat, and is Visiting Professor at Washington University in St. Louis and an Affiliate Faculty Member at Moravian University.

Jennifer Bansard
Faculty of Economics and Social Sciences, University of Potsdam
Jennifer Bansard is an international relations scholar with a focus on climate change and marine biodiversity governance. Her previous scholarship mainly centres on the contribution of transnational city networks to climate change mitigation and the role of knowledge and science in environmental governance. In addition to her academic research, she works for the *Earth Negotiations Bulletin*, with which she has covered more than twenty international environmental conferences and gained extensive insights into the specificities of various multilateral environmental agreements and science-policy bodies.

Michele Betsill
Department of Political Science, University of Copenhagen
Michele Betsill is a professor of global environmental politics at the Department of Political Science, University of Copenhagen. As a scholar of global environmental governance, her research contributes to understanding the role of non-state and sub-national actors, and transnational forms of governance related to issues such as climate change, marine conservation, and natural resource extraction.

Lisa M. Campbell
Duke University Marine Lab, Duke University
Lisa M. Campbell is the Rachel Carson Professor of Marine Affairs and Policy in the Nicholas School of Environment at Duke University. A political ecologist, she studies oceans governance at a variety of scales, focusing on how science and non-state actors inform governance processes and outcomes. She has published on these themes in relation to protected areas, fisheries, marine spatial planning, marine protected areas, and tourism.

Pamela Chasek
Political Science Department, Manhattan College in New York
Pamela Chasek is Professor of Political Science at Manhattan College in New York. She is also the co-founder and executive editor of the *Earth Negotiations Bulletin*, a reporting service on United Nations environment and development negotiations. Her research focuses

on multilateral environmental negotiations and international environmental governance as a means for countries and non-state actors to address and resolve environmental problems at the international level. She is the author of numerous articles and books, including *Transforming Multilateral Diplomacy: The Inside Story of the Sustainable Development Goals* (Routledge, 2018), and *Global Environmental Politics* (Routledge, 2021, 8th ed.).

Catherine Corson

Department of Environmental Studies, Mount Holyoke College

Catherine Corson is the Miller Worley Associate Professor of Environmental Studies at Mount Holyoke College. As a political ecologist, Catherine Corson uses ethnography to explore questions of power, knowledge, and justice in case studies from rural villages to international policy arenas. Her research focuses on the rise of market-based environmentalism, popular resistance to it, the turn to technology in conservation, and associated shifts in governance.

Michelle David

University of Chicago Law School

Michelle David is a law student at the University of Chicago Law School, pursuing a career as a public interest attorney in environmental law with a focus on environmental justice. She studied political science and environmental policy as an undergraduate, where she was first trained in ethnography.

Noella J. Gray

Department of Geography, Environment and Geomatics, University of Guelph

Noella J. Gray is Associate Professor in the Department of Geography, Environment and Geomatics at the University of Guelph. A political ecologist, her research examines the politics of marine conservation and governance across scales. Her recent work focuses on knowledge conflicts in global environmental governance, governance of marine protected areas, and ocean territorialisation.

Rebecca L. Gruby

Department of Human Dimensions of Natural Resources, Colorado State University

Rebecca Gruby is Associate Professor in the Department of Human Dimensions of Natural Resources at Colorado State University. Her research focuses on contemporary transformations in ocean conservation and governance.

Kate Haapala

North Pacific Fishery Management Council, Anchorage, Alaska

Kate Haapala is a fishery analyst with the North Pacific Fishery Management Council in Anchorage, Alaska. Trained as a political scientist, she specialises in environmental policy and marine governance. Her work directly informs decision-makers on the impacts of management actions, with a focus on issues related to environmental justice, communities, and subsistence.

Shannon Hagerman
Faculty of Forestry, University of British Columbia
Shannon Hagerman is Associate Professor in the Faculty of Forestry at the University of British Columbia. She is interested in behavioural, institutional, and policy elements of managing social-ecological systems. Her current work focuses on climate change adaptation and transformation, knowledge politics at the science–policy–management interface, and the promise and pushback of targets-based environmental governance.

Arne Langlet
Department of Political Science, University of Vienna
Arne Langlet is a PhD student in the ERC Research Project MARIPOLDATA with a focus on the study of international institutions and regimes in current ocean governance. Methodologically, he is interested in quantitative methods and the application of network, and system analysis methods on international politics.

Timo Leiter
Grantham Research Institute on Climate Change and the Environment, London School of Economics and Political Science (LSE)
Timo Leiter is a PhD candidate at LSE and an independent consultant on climate change adaptation. Prior to joining LSE, Timo worked in the climate policy team of Germany's international development agency (GIZ). Timo's research and policy interest is the assessment of progress (monitoring and evaluation) of adaptation, i.e., whether countries and communities get better adapted to a changing climate.

Kimberly R. Marion Suiseeya
Department of Political Science, Northwestern University
Kimberly R. Marion Suiseeya is Assistant Professor in the Department of Political Science and Environmental Policy and Culture Program, Northwestern University. As a scholar of environmental justice, her research examines how Indigenous communities shape and are impacted by multilateral environmental agreements such as the UN Framework Convention on Climate Change.

Beth Martin
Environmental Studies, Washington University in St. Louis
Beth Martin is a teaching professor in Environmental Studies at Washington University in St. Louis, where she also serves as Director of the Climate Change Program. She teaches at the intersection of science, engineering, law, and policy and has taught in the schools of law, engineering, and arts and sciences. She serves as the co-focal point of the Research and Independent NGO constituency to the UNFCCC. Ms. Martin, a registered professional engineer, graduated from Birmingham-Southern College (BS) and Washington University in St. Louis (BSCE and MS).

Naghmeh Nasiritousi
The Swedish Institute of International Affairs and the Department of Earth Sciences, Uppsala University
Naghmeh Nasiritousi is an Associate Professor in Political Science, based at the Swedish Institute of International Affairs and the Climate Change Leadership unit at Uppsala University. Her research focuses on international climate change politics, issues of effectiveness, and legitimacy in global climate and energy governance, as well as the roles of non-state actors in environmental governance.

Matthew Paterson
Department of Politics, School of Social Sciences, University of Manchester
Matthew Paterson is Professor of International Politics and Director of the Sustainable Consumption Institute at the University of Manchester. His research focuses on the global governance, political economy, and cultural politics of climate change.

Silvia C. Ruiz Rodríguez
Department of Political Science, University of Vienna
Silvia C. Ruiz Rodríguez is a PhD student and sowi:docs Fellow at the Department of Political Science, University of Vienna. She is associated to the ERC project MARIPOLDATA. Her research contributes to understanding the role of different knowledge systems and digital multilateral diplomacy in negotiations for the conservation and sustainable use of marine biodiversity.

Ina Tessnow-von Wysocki
Department of Political Science, University of Vienna
Ina Tessnow-von Wysocki is a PhD candidate in the ERC project MARIPOLDATA, based at the University of Vienna, where she studies science–policy interfaces for ocean protection within the United Nations negotiations on the conservation and sustainable use of marine biological diversity of areas beyond national jurisdiction. With an academic background in international relations and professional experience in climate and foreign policy with the German development agency GIZ, as well as NGOs in several countries, she focuses on international cooperation on environmental issues.

Harriet Thew
School of Earth and Environment, University of Leeds
Harriet Thew (PhD) is a lecturer in Climate Change in the School of Earth and Environment and Priestley International Centre for Climate at the University of Leeds. Her research and teaching are dedicated to the inclusion and empowerment of young people in environmental governance, with particular focus on climate change education (CCE), youth participation in climate action, and social justice.

Valeria Tolis
School of Law and Politics, Cardiff University
Valeria Tolis is a lecturer in Politics at Cardiff University, School of Law and Politics. As a scholar of critical environmental politics, her research contributes to investigating

the mechanisms that govern status quo and change in the production of environmental knowledge and in the formulation of environmental policies.

Marcela Vecchione-Gonçalves
Centre of Advanced Amazonian Studies NAEA-UFPA
Marcela Vecchione-Gonçalves is an associate professor at the Centre of Advanced Amazonian Studies at the Federal University of the State of Pará (NAEA-UFPA), Brazil. She holds a postdoctoral research position at the Institute of Development Policy (IOB) at the University of Antwerp (2021–3), Belgium, as a member of the project Environmental Policy Instruments across Commodity Chains (EPICC).

Peter R. Wilshusen
Department of Environmental Studies and Sciences, Bucknell University
Peter Wilshusen is Professor of Environmental Studies and Sciences at Bucknell University. He is a broadly trained social scientist (human geography, cultural anthropology, environmental sociology, political ecology) with interests in international governance issues related to sustainability, environment, and development. His current research focuses on economistic (or 'market-based') approaches to transnational environmental governance efforts focused on biodiversity conservation.

Yulia Yamineva
Centre for Climate, Energy and Environmental Law, University of Eastern Finland
Yulia Yamineva is a senior researcher, holding the title of Docent in Climate Law and Policy at the Centre for Climate, Energy and Environmental Law, University of Eastern Finland. She has published widely on international climate and environmental law and governance in leading academic journals. She has been participating in the UN climate negotiations in various capacities for more than a decade. Yamineva holds a PhD in International Studies from the University of Cambridge and previously worked for the UN Climate Change Convention Secretariat and the International Institute for Sustainable Development.

Laura Zanotti
Department of Anthropology, Purdue University
Laura Zanotti is a Professor in the Department of Anthropology, Purdue University. As a scholar that prioritises feminist political ecology, Indigenous rights, and media sovereignty, her research contributes to amplifying the experiences of Indigenous Peoples and local communities at sites of local to global environmental governance.

Preface

We (Hannah and Alice) first met during a workshop in Brussels in 2015. Hannah presented her research on the Intergovernmental Panel on Climate Change (IPCC) and Alice gave a talk about her study on the emergence of the Intergovernmental Science-Policy Platform on Biodiversity and Ecosystem Services (IPBES), commonly perceived as the 'IPCC for biodiversity'. It was Steven Bernstein who commented on our research, drew out key similarities between our cases, and encouraged us to collaborate. During weekly Skype calls, we noticed how similar the assessment practices of IPBES and IPCC were and how much they resembled the negotiation practices of other global environmental meetings. From participant observation that we did at UNFCCC and CBD COPs, we learned how relevant our research objects – IPCC and IPBES – were for these conventions, but also discovered the importance of multilateral negotiation practice for global environmental knowledge production. 'Weighted concepts' and the struggle over environmental knowledge travel between conference sites and matters beyond the assessment and intergovernmental approval processes where the appearance is first contested. We wanted to test the significance of these observations and also initiate a broader discussion on the need for conceptual and methodological innovation in the study of global environmental politics. To do this, we began to organise and host a series of workshops and conference panels that could identify and bring together scholars that shared this interest in methodological innovation.

After our first co-authored article and co-edited special section (with Kimberly Marion Suiseeya) in *Global Environmental Politics* on 'Methodological Innovation in the Study of Global Environment Agreement Making', we decided that we needed to go further. We wanted to create a guide for the next generation of scholars that would enable them to advance conceptual and methodological innovation for the critical study of negotiation processes, and to bring together scholars that were pioneering understanding and study of global environmental meeting sites to achieve this. In 2018, Alice won an ERC Starting Grant Project funded by the European Research Council (financed under the European Union's Horizon 2020 research and innovation programme under grant agreement No 804599) for a period of five years, which included the objective to train PhD students in studying marine biodiversity negotiations collaboratively. The so-called BBNJ negotiations (Biodiversity Beyond National Jurisdiction) provided an excellent additional case and entry point for catalysing scholarship during a workshop hosted by the MARIPOLDATA team in Vienna in September 2019. We invited some of the most important contributors in the field to participate in our ambition to broaden what is conventionally understood as the *site* of global environmental negotiations and to develop what we felt we were missing when we started to conduct this research: a practical and methodological guide.

This book is a product of the concept papers and discussions presented at the Vienna workshop, alongside a perspective piece that we collaboratively wrote and published in *Earth System Governance* in September 2021. To ensure that each chapter and the book as a whole provides the most comprehensive content in terms of practical and methodological guidance and responds to and initiates new directions in the field, we organised a series of workshops and conference panel events between 2019 and 2021. Due to the COVID-19 pandemic, two of these events were held virtually: an innovative panel discussion on 'How do practitioners view our work?' during the 2020 Virtual Earth System Governance Conference, and a second author workshop in August 2021. The book is a product of these collective discussions, as well as the careful and thoughtful comments and feedback provided in person and on subsequent drafts by all members of the author team.

Acknowledgements

We would like to first thank our distinguished colleagues and authors of this book. This has been a remarkable journey of learning and sharing, and the book is the product of the expertise and experience of an extraordinary group of scholars.

To the authors: many of you have participated in and researched global environmental meetings for years and we are grateful for the knowledge, expertise, and experiences that you shared, for your critical questions and remarks, and for your continuous support and belief in this project. Your involvement and the diverse perspectives you provided were not only critical for us but provided the group of PhD researchers involved in the project with important guidance and research perspectives. We would like to specifically thank Jennifer Allan, Michele Betsill, Pamela Chasek, Noella Gray, Mat Patterson, and Kim Marion Suiseeya for reviewing and commenting on the Introduction, Starting, Concepts and Adapting chapters (Chapters 2, 4, and 14, respectively). We would like to offer a particular thank you to the authors of the reflection boxes for broadening the perspectives. From the outset, we wanted to engage early career scholars in the making of the book, and we would like to thank Arne Langlet, Timo Leiter, Ina Tessnow-von Wysocki, Harriet Thew, Silvia Ruiz-Rodríguez, and Valeria Tolis for taking part in this experiment, for reflecting on your own research practices, and for providing the authors with the feedback necessary to identify and address early career scholars' requirements. Thank you also to the three anonymous reviewers of the book proposal for their constructive feedback and suggestions.

Many of us have learned from 'being there' and from engaging with state and non-state actors participating in global environmental negotiations and agreement-making. We would like to thank those that have helped us to access and attend the events we have studied, including the International Studies Association (ISA), which provided access to Alice and her team for all BBNJ negotiations, to Gabriele Obermayr for facilitating access to Alice for attending IPBES and CBD meetings as part of the Austrian delegation, to Mike Hulme and Tyndall Centre who supported Hannah to observe an IPCC plenary, to the many IPCC actors who have supported her research, and for the Secretariats of IPCC, IPBES, UNFCCC, UNCLOS (UNDOALOS), and CBD for answering many questions and facilitating observer status. More importantly, we would like to thank all those who were willing to be interviewed, share their knowledge, and invest themselves personally in our research. Special thanks go to Thomas Loidl, who supported MARIPOLDATA from the beginning and was willing to share his insights on multilateral environmental diplomacy and the Law of the Sea.

This book would not have been possible without the remarkable work of Phoebe Fuhrmann from the MARIPOLDATA team, who assisted us in finalising the manuscript of the book, and Sarah Lambert from Cambridge University Press, who supported us with advice and guidance. Thank you both for your patience. Thanks also to Emmanuelle Brogat, who did a brilliant job in organising the kick-off workshop in Vienna in September 2019.

We would also like to thank those institutions and funding schemes that have believed in our project ideas and supported our work financially. The book has significantly benefited from financial support by the European Research Council, which awarded an ERC Starting Grant Project to Alice Vadrot in 2018 (ERC Starting Grant project MARIPOLDATA of Alice Vadrot, financed under the European Union's Horizon 2020 research and innovation programme under grant agreement No 804599). Thanks also go to the Austrian Science Fund (FWF) for supporting Alice Vadrot's research from 2015 to 2018 with an Erwin Schrödinger Fellowship, the Centre for Science and Policy (CSaP), and the University of Vienna that hosted Alice. Hannah would like to thank the School of Law and Politics at Cardiff University for her first permanent post as a lecturer, which enabled her to conduct this research and financially supported workshops on the special issue and travel for the Vienna workshop for herself and colleagues. She would also like to thank the International Politics Department at Aberystwyth University for the support and encouragement they have already provided.

When you take on a project like this everyone in the family knows about it and is impacted in some way, whether we are physically away for a workshop or mentally distracted by thoughts of a chapter and a growing 'to do' list. Thus, most importantly, we would like to thank our families (especially José and Michael), which grew during the making of the book! Hannah gave birth to River in November 2019, just after the first book workshop, and Alice gave birth to Estelle in August 2021, just after the second book workshop. We hope that in some small way this book contributes to helping us become better collective stewards of the planet and making it a less degraded home for you, all peoples of your generation, and future generations.

Abbreviations

ABNJ	Areas beyond national jurisdiction
AC	Adaptation committee
ACE	Action for Climate Empowerment
ADP	Ad Hoc Working Group on the Durban Platform for Enhanced Action
AFB	Adaptation fund board
APA	Ad Hoc Working Group on the Paris Agreement
BA	Biennial assessment
BBNJ	Biodiversity Beyond National Jurisdiction
BINGO	Business and industry non-governmental organisations
BMZ	German Federal Ministry for Economic Cooperation and Development
CAN	Climate Action Network
CBD	Convention on Biological Diversity
CDM	Clean development mechanism
CEE	Collaborative event ethnography
CGE	Consultative group of experts
CITES	Convention on International Trade in Endangered Species of Wild Fauna and Flora
CMA	Conference of the Parties Serving as the Meeting of the Parties to the Paris Agreement
CMP	Conference of the Parties Serving as the Meeting of the Parties to the Kyoto Protocol
COICA	Coordinadora de las Organizaciones Indígenas de la Cuenca Amazónica
COP	Conference of the Parties
COP10	Tenth Conference of Parties to the Convention on Biological Diversity
COVID-19	Coronavirus Disease 2019
COY	Conferences of youth
CRP	Conference room paper
CTCN	Climate Technology Centre and Network

ECOSOC	Economic and Social Council (of the United Nations)
ENB	*Earth Negotiations Bulletin*
ENGO	Environmental non-governmental organisations
ERC	European Research Council
ERGM	Exponential random graph models
FWG	Facilitative working group
GAP	Gender action programme
GCF	Green Climate Fund
GDPR	General Data Protection Regulation
GEF	Global environmental facility
GEG	Global environmental governance
GEP	Global environmental politics
GHG	Greenhouse gases
GIZ	Deutsche Gesellschaft für Internationale Zusammenarbeit (GIZ) GmbH
GRULAC	Group of Latin America and the Caribbean
HLPF	High-Level Political Forum on Sustainable Development
ICT	Information and communication technology
IGC	Intergovernmental conferences
IGO	Intergovernmental organisation
IO	International organisation
IP	Indigenous people
IPBES	Intergovernmental Science-Policy Platform on Biodiversity and Ecosystem Services
IPCC	Intergovernmental Panel on Climate Change
IPO	Indigenous peoples' organisations
IR	International relations
ISA	International Studies Association
ISA	International Seabed Authority
ISE	International Society of Biology
IUCN	International Union for the Conservation of Nature
KCI	Katowice Committee of Experts on the Impacts of the Implementation of Response Measures
KP	Kyoto Protocol
LCIPP	Local Communities and Indigenous People's Platform
LDC	Least developing countries
LDCF	Least developed countries fund
LEG	Least developed countries expert group
LGMA	Local government and municipal authorities
LMDC	Like-minded developing countries
MARIPOLDATA	The Politics of Marine Biodiversity Data (ERC project)
MEA	Multilateral environmental agreements
MOP	Meetings of the parties

MPA	Marine protected area
NCP	Nature's contribution to people
NDC	Nationally determined contribution
NGO	Non-governmental organisations
OE	Operational entity
OECD	Organisation for Economic Co-operation and Development
OWG	Open working group
PA	Paris Agreement
PAICC	Paris Agreement Committee to Facilitate Implementation and Promote Compliance
PCCB	Paris Committee on Capacity Building
PI	Principal investigator
RFMOs	Regional fisheries management organisations
RINGO	Research and independent non-governmental organisations
SB	Subsidiary body
SBI	Subsidiary body for implementation
SBSTA	Subsidiary Body for Scientific and Technological Advice
SBSTTA	Subsidiary Body for Scientific, Technical and Technological Advice
SCCF	Special Climate Change Fund
SCF	Standing Committee on Finance
SDGs	UN Sustainable Development Goals
SNA	Social network analysis
SPM	Summary for policymakers
TEC	Technology executive committee
TEEB	The Economics of Ecosystems and Biodiversity
TUNGO	Trade union non-governmental organisations
UN	United Nations
UNCLOS	United Nations Convention on the Law of the Sea
UNDOALOS	UN Division on Ocean Affairs and the Law of the Sea
UNDP	UN Development Programme
UNEP	UN Environment Programme
UNFCCC	United Nations Framework Convention on Climate Change
UNGA	United Nations General Assembly
WCC	World Conservation Congress
WGC	Women and Gender Constituency
WIM	Warsaw International Mechanism on Loss and Damage
WPC	World Parks Congress
YOUNGO	Youth non-governmental organisations

1

Introduction

A Broadened Understanding of Global Environmental Negotiations

HANNAH HUGHES AND ALICE B. M.VADROT

In the past three decades, global environmental conferences have emerged as major events assembling a growing community of actors interested in the diverse aspects of environmental protection. These events establish a routine and practice for state actors to negotiate the future of the environment and the social, political and economic modes of organization that are degrading it. This has made environmental meetings critical sites for all actors invested in challenging world order to protect the environment, including researchers. While critics point to the limitations of multilateralism, and as COVID-19 postponed and disrupted the meeting cycle, the pandemic highlighted the continued importance of these events in crafting and maintaining a collective response to the environmental crisis. As this crisis deepens, however, the landscape of global environmental action grows more crowded and complex as new issues and interlinkages emerge and actors, activities and processes are created in an attempt to address these. The critical nature of global environmental degradation and the order-making in its name mean that scholarship must keep pace with, document, analyze and illuminate this expanding field of global environmental activity.

In this book, we aim to contribute to how we undertake this vital research by offering a reconceptualization of these spaces, their purposes and the stakes involved as global environmental agreement-making, and by providing a range of methodological tools for the study of negotiations in all their forms. We define global environmental agreement-making as the multiple actors, sites and processes through which environmental agreements are made, and the new sets and arrangements of actors, sites and processes that are created by any specific agreement, which have the potential to reinforce or reorient the global political order.

The global environmental conference, be it a summit, a conference of the parties (COP) or a smaller intergovernmental meeting, is the nucleus of agreement-making. Once you collect your badge and walk down the gray-carpeted, slightly bouncy floor of the temporary structure into the main artery of a negotiation venue, or have ridden up the elevator through a glassy high-rise and arrived at the floor of your intergovernmental meeting, you are greeted with more human interactions and forms of activity than it is possible to document. Beyond the formal informals and informal informals with delegates focused on particular agenda items and decisions, there are the in-between spaces of the conference: the side events, the booths, the coffee cart, the press conference, as well as the social media platforms where all of this is captured, framed and shared. The history, struggle and order-making that animate much of this action occasionally rupture to the surface when time and pressure builds, becoming audible as huddled negotiations, verbal outbursts and ignored requests and pleas from the chairs of the meeting. But, more often or not, this is masked behind layers of diplomatic conventions that can feel as impenetrable as a wall.

This activity and its contestations radiate outwards from the meeting venue, as illustrated by protests on the streets and simultaneous events, meetings and exhibitions that overflow in the parks, surrounding hotels and other city sites. Intergovernmental meetings are shaped by complex connections across space and time, most tangibly through the negotiations and agreements reached at previous sessions. Each decision (or nondecision) made at any sized meeting has the potential to create new sets of activities and interactions that will shape future meetings. As agreements shape practice, these decisions ripple out from the meeting site into the conduct of national policies and domestic societies, and further outward to interconnected organizations and new processes, actors, partnerships and initiatives. This is the significance of global environmental agreement-making.

The aim of this book is to render these complex processes, their multiple layers and their interconnections easier to study. We offer a guide and a methodological toolkit for the study of global environmental negotiation sites, in their multiple forms, which can be assembled and put to different research questions and problems designed to increase our understanding of agreement-making and its products. We do this by offering a new framework for conceptualizing and analyzing the multiple actors, sites, processes and order-making constitutive of global environmental agreements, and by providing the building blocks for designing and conducting research into and of these events. Building on existing scholarship, we offer this reconceptualization to further shift the study of collective environmental action in five related directions:

1. To broaden the conceptualization of global environmental agreements to the actors and sites beyond formal negotiations and their outcomes.
2. To focus on the processes of agreement formation alongside the outcomes, with particular sensitivity toward the historical forces shaping the present and the future actors and activities created by agreements.
3. To pay greater attention to how global political order shapes agreement formation and how final decisions *reflect* and have the potential to *remake* this global political order of relations.
4. To call for greater reflection on the situation of research and researchers within these agreement-making processes in order to confront and counter academic and cultural dominance.
5. To encourage the use and combination of, as well as innovation with, different methods and data collection techniques on and off site.

While we offer agreement-making as a framework to deepen understanding of the opportunities and challenges that collective action offers for ensuring the health of the planet, our reader is not bound by it. This approach is offered as a way to organize, spatialize, situate and connect diverse forms of scholarship into, around and related to negotiation sites and their products. As such, it is relevant for many other nonenvironmental issue areas where collective action is at the core, such as global health, nuclear nonproliferation, security and trade. Before we unpack *how* to study global environmental negotiations and related sites as *agreement-making*, however, it is important to explore *why* there is so much scholarly interest in these processes, and how the conceptualization and study of these has changed over time.

1.1 Why Study Global Environmental Agreement-Making?

Global environmental meeting venues have not always been popular sites with researchers, and few observed the 1992 Earth Summit in Rio de Janeiro. During the 1990s, in the early phase of the climate change and biodiversity conventions, COPs were smaller, nongovernmental organization (NGO) participation marginal, side events almost nonexistent and communication pre-digital (see Reflection Box 1.1). Researchers were mostly interested in analyzing the outcomes of summits rather than as objects of study in themselves, with some important exceptions (e.g., Constantinou 1998). However, in recent years this has changed dramatically, with more and more universities seeking accreditation and sending delegations to UN climate change and biodiversity negotiations in particular. What explains this growth in research interest and participation?

Reflection Box 1.1 How global environmental meetings have changed

By Pam Chasek

Pam Chasek is a scholar of global environmental politics and editor of *Earth Negotiations Bulletin*. She attended her first United Nations meetings in the period leading up to the Earth Summit in Rio de Janeiro in 1992. Here she reflects on five major changes since this time:

1. NGO participation in the work of multilateral environmental agreements (MEAs) and other UN environmental conferences has grown exponentially. Thousands of NGOs entered the space at the Earth Summit in Rio, which opened the door to greater participation and, since then, increasing numbers of nonstate actors began participating in these meetings.
2. Side events emerged from the UN Commission on Sustainable Development to continue to engage nonstate actors in sustainable development after the Earth Summit. This practice quickly expanded to the MEAs, creating a trade fair atmosphere and dozens of events during lunch breaks and the evening hours. These side events provided a place for discussion on new and emerging issues and an opportunity to hold governments to account.
3. Technology has changed dramatically. The Earth Summit was the first meeting of the mobile phone era. The World Wide Web further opened these processes: suddenly anyone with an internet connection could read the documents, see what was being discussed and, once digital photography advanced, see photos from the meetings. More recently, the advent of Web 2.0 and social media platforms such as Facebook, Twitter, Instagram, TikTok and SnapChat have given everyone a chance to comment, share photos and videos, and invite the world into the conference sites.
4. As the urgency of responding to environmental problems has increased, so too have the political and economic implications. Where once COPs and other meetings took place in

relative obscurity, increasingly governments are seeing these issues through economic, political and national security lenses, which has ramped up interest at the governmental level and increased the size of many delegations, especially from developed countries.

5. Finally, the MEA meeting calendar has exploded, especially before COVID-19. Not a week goes by without a major subsidiary body meeting, constituted body or a COP or meetings of the parties (MOP) from one MEA or another. In pre-COVID times, this led to exhaustion as some government delegates who cover multiple MEAs and other environmental bodies (UN Environment Assembly, High-Level Political Forum on Sustainable Development, etc.) found themselves criss-crossing the globe from meeting to meeting, with limited time at home. The COVID-19 pandemic slowed the meeting schedule considerably. However, the use of online meeting platforms has led to a new kind of exhaustion: screen fatigue.

Perhaps the simplest and most important reason for studying global environmental meeting sites is because we care deeply about the state of the planet and want to understand and contribute to how environmental degradation is collectively addressed. The stakes in global environmental politics scholarship are high. The environment is degrading at an unprecedented rate (UN Environment Programme 2019). The Intergovernmental Panel on Climate Change (IPCC) 1.5 °C report highlights the impacts and risks of warming beyond this temperature target and emphasizes that the window to achieve it is rapidly closing (IPCC 2018). The Sixth Assessment Report documents the continued rise in global greenhouse emissions, with the last decade recording the highest average increase on record (IPCC 2022). In 2019, the extent of biodiversity loss was highlighted when it was reported that "of an estimated 8 million animal and plant species (75 percent of which are insects), around 1 million are threatened with extinction" (IPBES 2019, 13). At the same time, concerns over the effects of plastic pollution are mounting, with the great Pacific garbage patch fed by approximately 1.15 to 2.41 million tons of plastic entering the ocean annually (Lebreton et al. 2017).

While global environmental assessments agree that human activities are responsible for this planetary degradation, not all societies are equally polluting, and the impacts and benefits of an exploitative global economic system are not evenly distributed. Furthermore, the global community's response to environmental problems can exacerbate and deepen existing social injustices (Tauli-Corpuz et al. 2020). Over the past century, and as illustrated in Figure 1.1, the international community has increasingly attempted to respond to this emerging array of environmental issues through MEAs. Despite this extensive treaty-making and recognition of the need to differentiate between parties based on level of responsibility and capability, the planet continues to degrade at unprecedented rates and, as it does, inequalities become further entrenched.[1]

The failure to redress some of the most pressing environmental issues that humanity faces can in part be understood through the issues themselves and the process that has

[1] Work by Farias and Roger indicates that some form of developing country differentiation relates back to the early 1960s, but that nearly 75 percent have appeared since the 1990s (Farias and Roger 2023), and even then only 6 percent of agreements contain some form of differentiation.

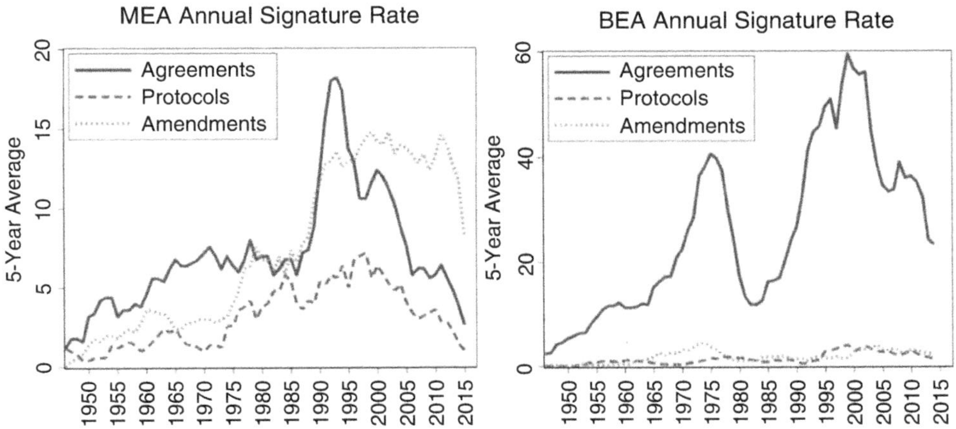

Figure 1.1 Rates of successfully completed MEA negotiations.
Source: Mitchell et al. 2020.

emerged to address them, but, more profoundly, the difficulty lies in changing the social, political and economic practices that are degrading the planet. Each discrete environmental issue has unique physical characteristics and political complexities, the full implications of which often only become apparent over time. Most environmental issues, including ozone depletion, climate change and biodiversity loss, have emerged progressively as scientific knowledge of the causes and consequences increased (see, for example, Litfin 1994; Paterson 1996; Vadrot 2014). Once an issue is scientifically accepted, there is a process of translating and presenting this knowledge to policymakers in order to build the necessary momentum and support for a multilateral response (Haas 1992a). Even in cases where scientific uncertainties remain, the precautionary principle has guided the political response (Haas 1992b; Litfin 1994).

Organizationally, these issues have been addressed through the creation of institutions with shared principles and practices. This includes the establishment of a secretariat, scientific and technical advisory arrangements, and a decision-making body, such as a COP, to negotiate and agree the terms of action. This process of establishing MEAs, from the early treaty-making stage to ratification, institutionalization and implementation, takes time, political will and resource mobilization. While this has led to successes – for example, ozone depletion over Antarctica is beginning to recover (Strahan and Douglass 2018) – building an effective multilateral response to other pressing environmental problems has proven challenging.

It has become apparent that the environmental degradation that the international community is attempting to address is generated by a dominant economic system and mode of organizing life that have human and environmental extraction at its core (Brand and Wissen 2021; DiMuzio 2015; Moore 2015; Yusoff 2018). If redressing social organization were not sufficiently challenging, entrenched interest groups – which do not want to relinquish the social position, power and resources they have accumulated through this model – continue to make every effort to confuse, detract and stall collective environmental efforts

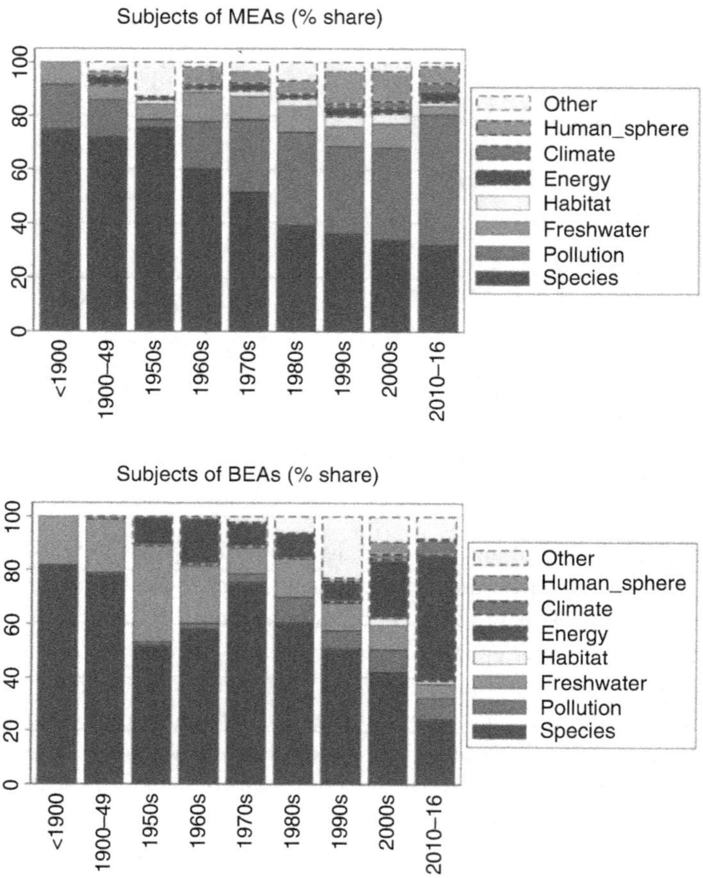

Figure 1.2 Subjects of MEAs. Figures 1.1 and 1.2 show the increasing numbers of MEAs and increasingly diverse subjects they cover, where one-third of MEAs "address species, one-third address pollution and energy, and the remaining third cover an array of other issues" (Mitchell et al. 2020, 106).
Source: Mitchell et al. 2020.

and prevent change (Dunlap 2013; Newell and Paterson 2010; Oreskes and Conway 2012; Purdue 1996; Shiva 1993). The struggles this engenders play out differently depending on the issue area and the site of contestation. For climate change, the focus is on the world's dependence on fossil fuels, common but differentiated responsibilities, the unequal impacts and capacities to adapt, and compensation for loss and damage. For biodiversity loss, the conflicts have centered around ownership of land and natural resources to be protected, demands for access to and benefit-sharing of genetic resources to prevent biopiracy, the rights of Indigenous People and local communities, and the multiple and often conflicting values associated with biodiversity, capacity building and technology transfer.

Despite the broad array of existing MEAs covering a wide range of issue areas, emerging environmental concerns continue to create new treaty negotiations. These become sites for the emergence of new struggles between governments over the establishment of and form of the MEA, as well as, relatedly, sites for the continuation of deeply entrenched division between the South and North over the distribution of resources and the right to continued development. Recent examples include negotiations on a new, legally binding instrument for the conservation and sustainable use of marine biodiversity beyond national jurisdiction (Vadrot 2020). The distinct focus of this new treaty-making process on areas beyond national jurisdictions (compared with the Convention on Biological Diversity [CBD]) has become an emergent site of struggle around existing global inequalities in exploring and exploiting marine ecosystems (Vadrot et al. 2021a).

In order to better understand and analyze the complexities and challenges of creating successful multilateral action, increasing numbers of scholars have sought to access and observe interstate negotiations and their outcomes. Growing participation, however, is not just a trend among researchers, as the ensuing scholarship reveals; these events have become a focus point for a diverse range of nonstate and substate actors interested in and seeking to shape environmental action (Bulkeley and Newell 2015). As documented, NGOs (Allan 2020; Betsill and Corell 2001; Corell and Betsill 2001), business actors (Falkner 2005; Newell 2006; Maxwell and Briscoe 1997), cities (Hoffmann 2011), Indigenous and marginalized groups (Ciplet et al. 2015; Marion Suiseeya 2014; Marion Suiseeya and Zanotti 2019; Schroeder 2010; Witter et al. 2015; Vadrot et al. 2021a), scientists (Tessnow-von Wysocki and Vadrot 2022; Vadrot 2014) and youth movements (Thew 2018) congregate at global environmental conferences and, within these events, create new sites of agreement-making. Actors participate and use these sites for different strategic purposes, including as one site in historical and multilevel struggles for recognition (Brysk 2000; Picq 2018; Vecchione-Gonçalves 2009), to connect to other social issues (Allan 2020) and to promote particular governing modes, such as targets, goals and market-based instruments (Campbell et al. 2014; Kanie and Biermann 2017; MacDonald and Corson 2012).

The growth in the number, variety and motivations of actors congregating at global environmental meetings means that these venues provide the researcher with unparalleled opportunities to observe and interact with the diversity of actors and networks that assemble around the governance of an issue in a single setting (Campbell et al. 2014). These events "put on display" the varied discourses, practices and institutional dynamics constituting the politics of an issue within a clearly delimited time and space. It is hardly surprising that researchers strive to access these events to observe, question and analyze these activities and interactions as they unfold at key moments in global environmental agreement formation. Organizing study and making sense of observations and other forms of data collected at these events requires the right methodological tools. How we situate environmental negotiations and the actors that participate in them within broader patterns of global environmental governance and critically evaluate their effectiveness in the response to environmental degradation depends on existing ideas and theories that inform the research. Therefore, in the next section, we review some of the most influential concepts and methods that have informed the study of MEA processes and the events and sites of their making, and outline what distinguishes the agreement-making framework from these.

1.2 Concepts and Methods in the Study of MEAs

Historically, the most important approach for organizing study of collective environmental action has been the concept of an international regime. Pioneered within international relations (IR) by John Ruggie (1975) and popularized by Keohane and Nye's *Power and Interdependence* (Keohane and Nye 1989, 257), the regime-focused research agenda was advanced by a common working definition of a regime as the principles, norms, rules, procedures and programs around which expectations converge on a given issue (Krasner 1982). Proponents of regime theory have sought to question the conditions of formation, the regulative function and the effectiveness of given regimes in solving the collective action problems that arise through environmental degradation (Levy et al. 1995). This approach focused scholarship on the behavior of state actors and the design of institutional arrangements that bound state parties in a shared response to a particular issue, and those contributing to the regime research agenda deploy both quantitative and qualitative techniques to explore these cooperative arrangements (Underdal and Young 2004). Oran Young has provided some of the most detailed descriptions of the development of international environmental regimes and his research has contributed to the conceptualization of the emergence, evolution and effectiveness of institutions designed to protect the environment (Young 1989; 2010).

The regime research agenda led to many important insights, including improved understanding of the role of scientific knowledge and transnational communities of experts in regime formation (Haas 1989). The epistemic community model identifies the role that scientists play in helping states to identify their interests in a collective problem, particularly where there is scientific uncertainty, through framing the issue for debate, proposing specific policies and identifying salient points for negotiation (Haas 1992, 2). This approach has illuminated the role of transnational communities of scientists in informing the multilateral response to marine pollution in the Mediterranean Sea (Haas 1989), ozone depletion (Haas 1992) and climate change (Paterson 1996). However, the regime approach has been criticized for its focus on interstate and supranational arrangements (Levy and Newell 2005), which results in overlooking and "black boxing" the wide variety of environmental actors, forms of authority and institutional configurations constituting today's global environmental governance landscape (Bauer 2006; Okereke, Bulkeley and Schroeder 2009).

New scholarly accounts of global environmental negotiations and negotiation sites have emerged through ethnographic methods and scholarly embeddedness within the "black boxes" which provide deeper insight into and understanding of the actors and organizational dynamics of treaty-making processes (Campbell et al. 2014; Chasek 2001; Depledge 2004; Jinnah 2014). This research has challenged state-centric ideas in the study of IR through documenting the role and influence of previously disregarded actors on agreement formation, such as secretariats and chairs (Biermann and Siebenhüner 2009; Depledge 2007). While revealing power asymmetries within and between actors, this scholarship illuminates the different forms of authority that operate alongside state power (Bauer 2006; Jinnah 2014; Marion Suiseeya and Zanotti 2019). It also identifies how nonstate actors have contributed to the transformation of spaces considered outside the conventional negotiating site, including side events and exhibits (Hjerpe and Linnér 2010; Schroeder and Lovell 2012), press conferences, corridors and even virtual spaces, resourcefully creating "new" sites of negotiation to raise issues and exert pressure with measured effect (Betsill and Corell 2001; Marion Suiseeya and Zanotti 2019). Jennifer Bansard identifies and describes the myriad spaces that exist beyond the recognized and formal sites of negotiation in Chapter 7.

As a wider variety of public and private nonstate actors have become invested in treaty-making and the response to global environmental degradation, the sites of action and forms of activity have evolved beyond interstate treaty formation and the events and organizations that support these. New concepts have emerged to try to capture these proliferating sites and interactions and determine their role in responding to environmental degradation, including regime complex and the notion of transnational and multilevel governance (Abbott 2012; Bulkeley et al. 2012; Keohane and Victor 2011). The concept of "regime complex" still remains largely focused on interstate relations (Abbott 2012), but looks beyond conventional sites of multilateralism to denote the decentralized, diffuse and seemingly unstructured institutional landscape that has emerged to address complex environmental issues such as climate change (Keohane and Victor 2011). The concept of "transnational governance," on the other hand, looks beyond interstate interactions in order to capture and analyze the wide variety of actors, partnerships, networks and initiatives that have emerged and operate within and across multiple levels to govern environmental change (Bulkeley et al. 2012; Bulkeley and Newell 2015; Hoffman 2011).

The Earth System Governance Project has provided an important overarching research framework and impetus to much of the scholarship exploring the governance of environmental issues and the myriad actors shaping the societal response (Biermann 2007; Biermann et al. 2010; Burch et al. 2019). The project offers a shared conception of Earth System Governance which retains key elements of the regime approach while spatially expanding the focus beyond the state and interstate interactions to capture the transnational nature of environmental governance. Earth System Governance is defined as "the sum of the formal and informal rule systems and actor-networks at all levels of human society that are set up in order to influence the co-evolution of human and natural systems in a way that secures the sustainable development of human society" (Biermann 2007, 329).

While new conceptions of governance have broadened the relevant actors, sites and activities of global environmental politics, intergovernmental meetings and conferences have remained and have grown as the locus of governance and its scholarship. As such, there has been an attempt to zoom in on these sites and to situate them within these broader patterns of governing arrangements. Methodologically, this has led scholars to think in terms of networks, complexity and assemblages (Corson et al. 2019; Orsini et al. 2020; Pickering 2019). Scholars have conceptualized meetings as single nodes within a network (Campbell et al. 2014), as sites where networks assemble (Corson et al. 2019) and as sites embedded in complex governance structures (Pickering 2019). The increased use of network analysis and the conduct of team ethnography have been important research methods for enabling new conceptualizations of the broader role that intergovernmental meetings play in global environmental governance.

As outlined earlier, scholarly observation and embeddedness within negotiating processes played a critical role in shifting understanding of the actors and forms of authority constitutive of negotiating sites and illuminated how the focus on interstate interactions is misleading. In Chapter 10, Kim Marion Suiseeya and Laura Zanotti introduce the reader to ethnography as an approach to the study of global environmental agreement-making, offering insights and practical guidance through their own experiences. However, a limitation to this approach to date has been connecting observations and analysis across vast conference sites and multiplying venues. Collaborative event ethnography (CEE) attempts to overcome this by conducting *team* ethnography and, as explored in Chapter 11 by Noella Gray et al. establishes a shared methodological practice to underpin this collaborative undertaking (Campbell et al. 2014; Corson et al. 2019; Gray et al. 2020). This makes it possible to spread a team of researchers across conference venues and follow multiple processes simultaneously, which has increased the evidence for acknowledging the myriad sites of negotiation *within* a venue and the range of strategies mobilized by nonstate actors to influence treaty-making proceedings *across* venues over time (Doolittle 2010; Marion Suiseeya et al. 2021; Scott et al. 2014; Witter et al. 2015).

Social network analysis (SNA), on the other hand, has made it possible to connect venues and organizations by following actors through their participation and interactions *between* and *beyond* the formal treaty-making event. Thus, the increased use of network perspectives and related metaphors has arisen in part because of the apparent fit of this imagery with the density of actors and interactions observable at negotiation sites, and in part because of the increased use of SNA to capture, connect and analyze these interactions across a wider range of meeting sites (Allan 2020; Hadden 2015; Paterson 2019). In Chapter 12, Matthew Paterson explores this further, reviewing the application and development of SNA within global environmental politics scholarship and indicating its potential for the study of agreement-making. Thus, both CEE and SNA have provided important evidence for expanding the study of collective environmental action beyond the actors, sites and processes formally associated with treaty-making, and thereby opened space for reconceptualizing the field and multiple processes of global environmental action as the study of agreement-making.

1.3 Global Environmental Negotiations and Meeting Sites as Agreement-Making

The term "agreement-making" emerges out of, captures and aims to advance key conceptual and methodological developments in the study of global environmental governance. The chapter offers a framework for understanding that builds on existing scholarship and expands the study of global environmental agreements to encompass the actors, sites, processes and order-making that is constitutive of collective attempts to address global environmental degradation. Expanding out from a treaty text and its negotiation in time and space opens up the framing and analysis of agreement-making in four related ways.

First, to the wide variety of governmental and nongovernmental actors invested in global environmental action and the myriad sites at which they are operating within conference venues and during, between and after these events, as identified and analyzed in the literature reviewed. This research has evidenced how nonstate actors create and mobilize an array of sites, strategies and media within and outside the conference venue to raise issues, perspectives and concerns and have their views represented in the final text, including through handouts and flyers, side events, press conferences, protests and virtual sites (Ciplet, Roberts and Khan 2015; Corell and Betsill 2001; Hjerpe and Linnér 2010; Marion Suiseeya et al. 2021; Schroeder and Lovell 2012; Vadrot et al. 2021b). Alongside this role in agreement formation itself, nonstate actors are at the forefront in the creation of new partnerships, networks and initiatives to monitor and enhance the collective response in a given issue area (Betsill and Bulkeley 2004; Bulkeley et al. 2012; Hoffman 2011).

Further evidence for the need to broaden the sites of agreement-making from recognized locales at global environmental conferences has come from study of the knowledge bodies informing the negotiating processes. As described in Reflection Box 1.2, participant observation and CEE of the Intergovernmental Platform on Biodiversity and Ecosystem Services (IPBES) and the IPCC have highlighted the similarity in actors and processes between the scientific advisory arrangements and the agreements they are designed to inform in the CBD and United Nations Framework Convention on Climate Change (UNFCCC) (Hughes and Vadrot 2019). Global environmental agreement-making captures these advances in knowledge, and, while acknowledging power asymmetries (Vadrot 2014), highlights that all actors interested and invested in an issue have the potential to "exert a force" in shaping how it is constructed and acted upon (Wacquant 1989, 36; Hughes 2015).

Reflection Box 1.2 Expanding the site of negotiations

One of the most important rationales for expanding agreement-making sites beyond formal negotiation venues came from studying the IPCC and the IPBES. Two of the most popular concepts for studying and understanding how science informs international environmental action are the epistemic community model (Haas 1989) and the notion of a boundary organization. In both of these approaches, knowledge bodies such as the IPCC and the IPBES are situated outside of formal negotiation processes, even while the political importance of these sites and the entanglement in the knowledge products is accepted (Lidskog and Sundqvist 2015). However, once you undertake observation of both the knowledge body and the negotiating process, the separation conceptualized between sites becomes difficult to uphold. This is easiest to illustrate through the approval of IPCC and IPBES Summary for Policymakers (SPM) documents.

The IPCC and the IPBES produce global assessments of the science and impacts of climate change, biodiversity loss and related environmental issues, as well as special and technical reports at the request of member governments and/or the negotiating bodies they inform. These assessments are authored by appointed scientists and others with relevant expertise, as guided by the elected bureau and government-approved report outline. In order for these scientific assessments to have a wider impact on policymaking, the key findings are compiled in a shorter summary document that is subject to line-by-line approval by member governments. At a dedicated intergovernmental session, usually held over four days and often through the night, this summary for policymakers is essentially negotiated word by word between its authors and member governments (De Pryck 2020; Fogel 2005; Hughes and Vadrot 2019; Kouw and Petersen 2018).

During the approval sessions, heated debate often breaks out over particular terms, figures or sentences that are perceived to have implications for or the potential to shape negotiations. This can lead to text and figures being removed from the SPM (De Pryck 2020), and new concepts and terms, if they do remain in the text, being tightly defined (Hughes and Vadrot 2019). This is what we observed with the struggle over biocultural diversity in the IPBES SPM approval process for the special report on Pollinators, Pollination and Food Production (IPBES 2016), and why we conceptualized the term as "weighted" (Hughes and Vadrot 2019). What is critically important and what we aim to illuminate through the notion of weighting is that this struggle is not generated by the concept per se, but by the potential that the concept has to shape multilateral environmental negotiations, in this case within the CBD. Furthermore, this struggle and contestation is often related to or has the potential to impact upon deep-seated tensions between the Global South and North over the distribution of resources and the related social and political orders (Vadrot 2014, 2020).

Second, by understanding agreement-making as a process rather than a single outcome, this approach aims to focus scholarship on the ongoing formation of global environmental agreements. This situates the moment under analysis within past struggles and contestation, particularly between the global South and global North, which condition the present and have the potential to re-open and shape future negotiations even once final agreement is reached (Hughes and Vadrot 2019; Miller 1995). Thinking in terms of process keeps the researcher attentive to the historical forces that are shaping the present as well as orientated toward the future, sensitizing study toward the new sets of actors, sites and processes that are created by and emerge from any decisions, non-decisions and other outcomes written into or out of an agreement (Vadrot et al. 2021a).

Third, the agreement-making framework aims to emphasize that the stakes in all global environmental agreements is global order and, for some, including Indigenous actors, life itself (see Chapter 5). As we explore in Chapter 4 through the use of concepts, the order of relations at agreement-making sites – the actors that are recognized as knowledgeable, authoritative and have the greatest power over the text – is closely coupled to the global distribution of economic resources and the investment in agreement-making processes these enable. These resources, brought in from outside the conference venue, shape who is able to gain access and to which sites, the levels of know-how and expertise available to represent views, the human resources to cover simultaneous negotiations and, ultimately, the capacity to be heard and have interests reflected in the final agreement reached. A central aim of the book is to deepen the scholarly focus on and analysis of the intertwinement between the global economic order and the order of relations within any given negotiation venue at the multiple sites and scales that agreement-making takes place. At the same time, the stakes in agreement-making are not homogenous: while some actors seek to secure an economic order, others are fighting to preserve threatened lifeways and the lands that gave rise to them. Identifying the stakes in global environmental agreement-making is critical to challenging and re-ordering politically degrading relations and to securing any chance of preserving the lifeways from land already lost (Beier 2009; Lightfoot 2016; Watts 2013).

Fourth, to the situatedness of the researcher and knowledge production within global patterns of order and the ordering force of global environmental agreements. The expanded field of action encompassed by the term "agreement-making" situates the researcher and knowledge production within the remit of study and demands greater reflexivity on individual and collective research practices (Corson et al. 2019; Gray et al. 2020; Hughes et al. 2021). Researchers have the potential to shape the field of agreement-making in at least two ways: first, through the knowledge produced on the issue and, second, through the relations cultivated in generating that knowledge. The chapters in this book are sensitive to the potential stakes of knowledge production processes and offer reflections on the ethics of how a researcher engages and cultivates relations both with participants and other scholars in collaborative research.

In Chapter 5, Marcela Vecchione-Gonçalves explores how working with Indigenous groups in the negotiations has shaped what constitutes her research practice, as she supports participants with translation and other tasks through the negotiations, and her participants interests and concerns, in turn, shape her research questions and methods. In Chapters 11 and 13, Harriet Thew describes how she generated trust with the UK climate youth movement, by continually re-visiting the power relations between herself and her participants as she engaged in the process alongside them. And in Chapter 11, Noella Gray et al. identify ways to challenge neo-liberal academic practices of ownership and output through collaboration. Even the interview creates relations of reciprocity, as explored in Chapter 9, and, as Yulia Yamineva highlights, offers the opportunity to cultivate the interview participant's interest in the research and a recipient for its outputs. Each of these accounts highlight that there is not one way to relate to and conduct ethical research on negotiations, but rather an individual process that the researcher embarks on in relation to the questions and issue areas that they study.

This new approach for studying the myriad actors, sites, processes and ordering forces of agreement-making is not theoretically or methodologically prescriptive. The chapters of the book are authored by a diverse group of scholars from multiple disciplines, informed but not confined by the disciplines of anthropology, geography, IR, political ecology, political science, law, science and technology studies and sociology. Rather than providing a single theory or approach, the authors offer their reflections on what they have done and why. In Chapter 3, for example, Michele Betsill and Naghmeh Nasiritousi recount their experiences with developing and adapting theoretical frameworks to enable readers to take from this what is most relevant to their own research journey. One of the central aims of the book is to make it possible to better connect existing quantitative and qualitative studies that provide empirical insight on any aspect of agreement-making, however theoretically informed, to further knowledge and spur the next generation of scholarship. It is, however, an ethically laden approach to the study of environmental negotiation processes, the agreements that are in the making and the worlds these have the potential to build. This is an approach for scholars that have a deep concern for the state of the planet and the state of global relations, and who want in some small way to contribute to building fairer, more inclusive environmental treaties that better steward the Earth.

1.4 Do We Need to "Be There" to Study Agreement-Making?

A theme that reoccurs throughout the book is whether studying agreement-making requires us to "be there" (O'Neill and Haas 2019) – on site – to observe and cultivate relations with the actors and processes that we are studying, or whether this kind of research can be done virtually and from a distance? As noted earlier, many of the advances in scholarship that have facilitated a reconceptualization of global environmental agreements have come from scholars that have "been there" – become close to, worked alongside and gained an insider perspective on the actors and organizations constitutive of these processes. However, this does not mean that all future knowledge of agreement-making needs to be built in the same way; as is clear from Pam Chasek's reflections (see Reflection Box 1.1), the practices of agreement-making are ever evolving. COVID-19 made the shift online a necessity, thus it is in the virtual realm that some of the greatest shifts in practicing collective action are currently taking place, and so, therefore, must the study.

Alongside the shifts wrought by a pandemic, the environmental impact of traveling to global environmental conferences has become an increasingly important concern for scholars to address (Hughes et al. 2021). The question of whether the research can be conducted virtually is considered from the start. In Chapter 2, we put this question at the top of the list when puzzling and planning research into and on agreement-making processes. The virtual resources available on treaty websites, combined with *Earth Negotiations Bulletin* (*ENB*) and photographs of the sessions, means that you can trace the evolution of a text and get a feel for the process even if you are not there to observe its negotiation because you want to save on air travel. Jennifer Allan and Pamela Chasek provide important insights into the possibilities and limits of using the different textual resources available, and how to compile and analyze these, in Chapter 8. Documents are not the only important research resources to be found on the treaty secretariat's website, however; many opening and closing sessions are live-streamed and archived, which makes it possible to gain a sense of the proceedings and the layout of the room even if you are unable to be on site. As Tracy Bach and Beth Martin indicate in Chapter 6, some UNFCCC-constituted bodies had developed this capacity for virtual participation even before COVID-19, and these captured meeting resources continue to expand.

The authors of the book identify many strategies and avenues for getting to know the processes and to follow the actors central to agreement-making virtually. As Yulia Yamineva describes in Chapter 9, researchers can gain valuable insight through virtual interviews and forge relations that better connect the researcher and the knowledge produced to those that are informing it. Social network analysis is another key method and research tool in this regard; as demonstrated in Chapter 12, the scholar can draw connections and infer relationships between actors across multiple sites and venues through readily available participant lists that do not require data collection in person. And while ethnography has traditionally been a physical immersion in the space of negotiation and treaty-making, in Chapter 10 Kim Marion Suiseeya and Laura Zanotti explore how the researcher can also follow and connect with actors through virtual platforms, such as Twitter and Facebook. This highlights the importance of adapting research methods to the study of an evolving field of practice, which, as described by Alice Vadrot in Chapter 14, includes adapting our collaborative practice to span these physical and virtual spaces. What these chapters aim to make clear, is that it is not necessarily the types of research methods or in-person versus virtual presence that gives us better knowledge and understanding of agreement-making. What is critical is how the researcher mobilizes, combines and innovates with these methodological tools in order to address the challenging questions, problems and puzzles that redressing global environmental degradation collectively pose.

1.5 A Practical and Methodological Guide to the Study of Agreement-Making

Through the chapters in this volume, we aim to translate the agreement-making framework into a practical approach for the empirical study of global environmental collective action. The chapters provide methodological tools to guide the design and conduct of study at the multiple physical and virtual sites constitutive of global mega-events, conferences and intergovernmental meetings. The book does this by breaking down the research process into four stages: Part I: Developing a Methodology; Part II: Navigating Sites; Part III: Collecting and Analysing Data; and Part IV: Implementing and Adapting. Within each chapter there are also reflection boxes, wherein guest writers reflect on how they have applied and tested the content of the chapter through their own research. These boxes are written by authors that have recently finished or are in the middle of postgraduate research projects on varied aspects of agreement-making, which makes their reflections particularly valuable to the reader just beginning a research journey or grappling with methodological issues.

Part I of the book begins by preparing the researcher for study at and on these sites (Chapter 2) and by unpacking how analytical frameworks (Chapter 3) and concepts (Chapters 4 and 5) can inform, organize and help construct the research problem. By recounting their own experiences, the authors of these chapters highlight that identifying the right theoretical approach and assembling the necessary conceptual tools is not always a linear and straightforward process, but one where the researcher keeps moving back and forth between the problem and the approach. The experiences of the authors indicate the importance of allowing the empirics to inform the theory as much as the theory informs the methods and types of data collection. The accounts given in Chapters 4 and 5 also highlight how particular starting points condition the knowledge produced and aim to sensitize the reader to reflect on what order of relations is transmitted into the research project, including the types of questions asked and the sites and actors chosen through the theories and concepts adopted.

In Part II of the book, the researcher is "made ready" for conducting research at the multiple sites of global environmental agreement-making. Chapter 6 equips the reader with the basic governance arrangements and structures of MEAs as well as the different spaces and formats of intergovernmental negotiations. While this chapter is useful for the researcher to be able to quickly orient themselves on site, it also provides essential guidance on how to locate the research at an event and identifies preparations that can be undertaken beforehand to manage the often frenzied nature of conducting research at these venues. Chapter 7 is also essential reading for familiarizing the reader with the multitude of different spaces that exist between and beyond the formal negotiation spaces. The chapter identifies the opportunities these different spaces offer for conducting research and connecting to different sets of actors at conference sites, as well raising important research questions that remain to be addressed about the roles and functions that these sites have in agreement formation.

Part III of the book turns to methods of research, exploring different approaches to collecting and analyzing data and questions that can be addressed through texts (Chapter 8), interviews (Chapter 9), ethnography (Chapter 10), collaboration (Chapter 11) and SNA (Chapter 12). The chapters do not prescribe a single approach for collecting data at or on negotiations, but rather offer a range of insights on how to conduct research and collect, analyze and evaluate the data and experiences gained from observing and participating in negotiating processes. Critically, the chapters highlight what is to be gained from using particular forms of data and methods, and equip the reader with this knowledge to apply to their own research questions.

In Part IV of the book, the authors take a closer look at their own experiences at applying the methods in the preceding section and identify how they adapted these to their own research projects. The authors of Chapter 13 are perhaps best placed to evaluate and provide relevant advice on the application of these approaches as they are most closely immersed in the research of either undertaking or recently completing a PhD. While Chapter 13 lays out some of the ideal conditions for conducting research at and on negotiation sites, Chapter 14 helps the reader navigate the research process when things do not go as planned. By describing the challenges that the author encountered in her own research, the chapter is able to identify how all research projects can be adapted to the often uncertain and rapidly changing environment of agreement-making sites and processes.

Finally, the Conclusion looks back and identifies the key themes that have emerged across the chapters relevant to the study of global environmental agreement-making, and emphasizes the role that reflexivity plays in advancing methodologies and knowledge of this critical field of study. The chapter also looks forward, identifying future directions for expanding knowledge and the practical utility of global environmental politics scholarship to help redress international relations that degrade the planet.

Further Reading

1. Hughes, H. and Vadrot, A. B. M. (2019). Weighting the World: IPBES and the Struggle over Biocultural Diversity. *Global Environmental Politics* 19, 14–37.

Evidence for expanding sites of negotiation to the intergovernmental science bodies that inform these processes came from collaborative research that brought together observations from across sites, as presented in the cited article.

2. Hughes, H., Vadrot, A., Allan, J. I. et al. (2021). Global Environmental Agreement-Making: Upping the Methodological and Ethical Stakes of Studying Negotiations. *Earth System Governance* 10, 100121.

This collective piece authored by the contributors to this book introduces the term "agreement-making" and calls for methodological innovation and greater reflection on the ethical stakes of research on global environmental negotiations. The piece resulted from a workshop funded and organized by MARIPOLDATA in Vienna in September 2019.

3. Vadrot, A. B. M. (2020). Multilateralism as a "Site" of Struggle over Environmental Knowledge: The North-South Divide. *Critical Policy Studies* 14(2), 233–245.

This article discusses agreement-making sites as "sites of struggle over environmental knowledge." It argues that CEE is crucial for studying the multiple and contested roles of science in global environmental negotiations, but needs to be combined with the social study of the scientific field, as exemplified by the European Research Council MARIPOLDATA project (www.maripoldata.eu).

References

Abbott, K. W. (2012). The Transnational Regime Complex for Climate Change. *Environment and Planning C: Politics and Space* 30(4), 571–590.

Allan, J. I. (2020). *The New Climate Activism: NGO Authority and Participation in Climate Change Governance*. Toronto: University of Toronto Press.

Bauer, S. (2006). Does Bureaucracy Really Matter? The Authority of Intergovernmental Treaty Secretariats in Global Environmental Politics. *Global Environmental Politics* 6, 23–49.

Beier, J. M., ed. (2009). *Indigenous Diplomacies*. London: Palgrave Macmillan.

Betsill, M. M. and Bulkeley, H. (2004). Transnational Networks and Global Environmental Governance: The Cities for Climate Protection Program. *International Studies Quarterly* 48(2), 471–93.

Betsill, M. M. and Corell, E. (2001). NGO Influence in International Environmental Negotiations: A Framework for Analysis. *Global Environmental Politics* 1(4), 65–85.

Biermann, F. (2007). "Earth System Governance" as a Crosscutting Theme of Global Change Research. *Global Environmental Change* 17, 326–337.

Biermann, F. and Siebenhüner, B. (2009). *Managers of Global Change: The Influence of International Environmental Bureaucracies*. Cambridge, MA: MIT Press.

Biermann, F., Betsill, M., Gupta, J. et al. (2010). Earth System Governance: A Research Framework. *International Environmental Agreements: Politics, Law and Economics* 10(4), 277–298.

Brand, U. and Wissen, M. (2021). *The Imperial Mode of Living: Everyday Life and the Ecological Crisis of Capitalism*. London: Verso Books.

Brysk, A. (2000). *From Tribal Village to Global Village: Indian Rights and International Relations in Latin America*. Stanford, CA: Stanford University Press.

Bulkeley, H. and Newell, P. J. (2015). *Governing Climate Change*. 2nd ed. London: Routledge.

Bulkeley, H., Andonova L., Bäckstrand, K. et al. (2012). Governing Climate Change Transnationally: Assessing the Evidence from a Database of Sixty Initiatives. *Environment and Planning C: Government and Policy* 30(4), 591–612.

Burch, S., Gupta, A., Inoue, C. Y. A. et al. (2019). New Directions in Earth System Governance Research. *Earth System Governance* 1, 100006.

Campbell, L. M., Corson, C., Gray, N. J., MacDonald, K. I., and Brosius, J. P. (2014). Studying Global Environmental Meetings to Understand Global Environmental Governance: Collaborative Event Ethnography at the Tenth Conference of the Parties to the Convention on Biological Diversity. *Global Environmental Politics* 14(3), 1–20.

Campbell, L. M., Hagerman, S., and Gray, N. J. (2014). Producing Targets for Conservation: Science and Politics at the Tenth Conference of the Parties to the Convention on Biological Diversity. *Global Environmental Politics* 14(3), 41–63.

Chasek, P. S. (2001). *Earth Negotiations: Analyzing Thirty Years of Environmental Diplomacy*. Tokyo: United Nations University Press.

Ciplet, D., Roberts, J. T., and Khan, M. R. (2015). *Power in a Warming World the Global Politics of Climate Change and the Remaking of Environmental Inequality*. Cambridge, MA: The MIT Press.

Constantinou, C. (1998). Before the Summit: Representations of Sovereignty on the Himalayas. *Millennium* 27, 23–53.

Corell, E. and Betsill, M. M. (2001). A Comparative Look at NGO Influence in International Environmental Negotiations: Desertification and Climate Change. *Global Environmental Politics* 1(4), 86–107.

Corson, C., Campbell, L. M., Wilshusen, P. and Gray, N. J. (2019). Assembling Global Conservation Governance. *Geoforum* 103, 56–65.

De Pryck, K. (2020). Intergovernmental Expert Consensus in the Making: The Case of the Summary for Policy Makers of the IPCC 2014 Synthesis Report. *Global Environmental Politics* 21(1), 108–129.

Depledge, J. (2004). *The Organization of Global Negotiations: Constructing the Climate Change Regime*. London: Routledge.

Depledge, J. (2007). A Special Relationship: Chairpersons and the Secretariat in the Climate Change Negotiations. *Global Environmental Politics* 7, 45–68.

DiMuzio, T. (2015). *Carbon Capitalism: Energy, Social Reproduction and World Order*. Lanham, MD: Rowman & Littlefield International.

Doolittle, A. A. (2010). The Politics of Indigeneity: Indigenous Strategies for Inclusion in Climate Change Negotiations. *Conservation & Society* 8(4), 286–291.

Dunlap, R. E. (2013). Climate Change Skepticism and Denial: An Introduction. *American Behavioral Scientist* 57(6), 691–698.

Falkner, R. (2005). The Business of Ozone Layer Protection: Corporate Power in Regime Evolution. In D. Levy and P. Newell, eds., *The Business of Global Environmental Governance*. Cambridge, MA: MIT Press, pp. 105–134.

Farias, D. B. L. and Roger, C. (2023). Differentiation in Environmental Treatymaking: Measuring Provisions and How They Reshape the Depth-Participation Dilemma. *Global Environmental Politics* 23(1).

Fogel, C. (2005). Biotic Carbon Sequestration and the Kyoto Protocol: The Construction of Global Knowledge by the Intergovernmental Panel on Climate Change. *International Environmental Agreements: Politics, Law and Economics* 5(2): 191–210.

Gray, N. J., Corson, C., Campbell, L. M. et al. (2020). Doing Strong Collaborative Fieldwork in Human Geography. *Geographical Review* 110(1–2), 117–132.

Haas, P. M. (1989). Do Regimes Matter? Epistemic Communities and Mediterranean Pollution Control. *International Organization* 43(3), 377–403.

Haas, P. M. (1992a). Introduction: Epistemic Communities and International Policy Coordination. *International Organization* 46(1), 1–35.

Haas, P. M. (1992b). Banning Chlorofluorocarbons: Epistemic Community Efforts to Protect Stratospheric Ozone. *International Organization* 46(1), 187–224.

Hadden, J. (2015). *Networks in Contention: The Divisive Politics of Climate Change.* Cambridge: Cambridge University Press.

Hjerpe, M. and Linnér, B. O. (2010). Functions of COP Side-Events in Climate-change Governance. *Climate Policy* 10(2), 167–180.

Hoffmann, M. J. (2011). *Climate Governance at the Crossroads: Experimenting with a Global Response after Kyoto.* Oxford: Oxford University Press.

Hughes, H. (2015). Bourdieu and the IPCC's Symbolic Power. *Global Environmental Politics* 15(4), 85–104.

IPBES (2016). The Assessment Report of the Intergovernmental Science-Policy Platform on Biodiversity and Ecosystem Services on Pollinators, Pollination and Food Production. Secretariat of the Intergovernmental Science-Policy Platform on Biodiversity and Ecosystem Services, Bonn, Germany.

IPBES (2019). *Summary for Policymakers of the Global Assessment Report on Biodiversity and Ecosystem Services of the Intergovernmental Science-Policy Platform on Biodiversity and Ecosystem Services.* Bonn: PBES Secretariat.

IPCC (2018). Summary for policymakers. In: An IPCC Special Report on the Impacts of Global Warming of 1.5°C above Pre-industrial Levels and Related Global Greenhouse Gas Emission Pathways, in the Context of Strengthening the Global Response to the Threat of Climate Change, Sustainable Development, and Efforts to Eradicate Poverty. World Meteorological Organization, Geneva, Switzerland, p. 32.

IPCC (2022). Summary for Policymakers. In: Climate Change 2022: Mitigation of Climate Change. Contribution of Working Group III to the Sixth Assessment Report of the Intergovernmental Panel on Climate Change. Cambridge: Cambridge University Press.

Jinnah, S. (2014). *Post-Treaty Politics: Secretariat Influence in Global Environmental Governance.* Cambridge, MA: The MIT Press.

Kanie, N. and Biermann, F., eds. (2017). *Governing through Goals: Sustainable Development Goals as Governance Innovation.* Cambridge, MA: MIT Press.

Keohane, R. O. and Nye, J. S. (1989). *Power and Interdependence.* 2nd ed. Northbrook, IL: Scott Foresman and Co.

Keohane, R. O. and Victor, D. G. (2011). The Regime Complex for Climate Change. *Perspectives on Politics* 9(1), 7–23.

Kouw, M. and Petersen, A. (2018). Diplomacy in Action: Latourian Politics and the Intergovernmental Panel on Climate Change. *Science & Technology Studies* 31(1), 52–68.

Krasner, S. D. (1982) Structural Causes and Regime Consequences: Regimes as Intervening Variables. *International Organization* 36(2): 1–21.

Lebreton, L., van der Zwet, J., Damsteeg, J. W. et al. (2017). River Plastic Emissions to the World's Oceans. *Nature Communications* 8, 15611.

Levy, D. L. and Newell P., eds. (2005). *The Business of Global Environmental Governance.* Cambridge, MA: MIT Press.

Levy, M. A., Young, O. R. , Zürn, M., and Levy, M. A. (1995). The Study of International Regimes. *European Journal of International Relations* 1, 267–330.

Lidskog, R. and Sundqvist, G. (2014). When Does Science Matter? International Relations Meets Science and Technology Studies. *Global Environmental Politics* 15, 1–20.

Lightfoot, S. (2016). *Global Indigenous Politics: A Subtle Revolution.* Oxfordshire: Routledge.

Litfin, K. (1994). *Ozone Discourse: Science and Politics in Global Environmental Cooperation.* New York: Columbia University Press,

MacDonald, K. I. and Corson, C. (2012). "TEEB Begins Now": A Virtual Moment in the Production of Natural Capital. *Development and Change* 43(1), 159–184.

Marion Suiseeya, K. R. (2014). Negotiating the Nagoya Protocol: Indigenous Demands for Justice. *Global Environmental Politics* 14(3), 102–124.

Marion Suiseeya, K. R. and Zanotti, L. (2019). Making Influence Visible: Innovating Ethnography at the Paris Climate Summit. *Global Environmental Politics* 19(2), 38–60.

Marion Suiseeya, K. R., Zanotti, L., and Haapala, K. (2021). Navigating the Spaces Between Human Rights and Justice: Cultivating Indigenous Representation in Global Environmental Governance. *The Journal of Peasant Studies* 49, 604–628.

Maxwell, J. and Briscoe, F. (1997). There's Money in the Air: The CFC Ban and DuPont's Regulatory Strategy. *Business Strategy and the Environment* 6(5), 276–286.

Miller, M .A. L. (1995). *The Third World in Global Environmental Politics*. Buckingham: Open University Press.

Mitchell, R. B., Andonova, L. B., Axelrod, M. et al. (2020). What We Know (and Could Know) About International Environmental Agreements. *Global Environmental Politics* 20, 103–121.

Moore, J. (2015). *Capitalism in the Web of Life: Ecology and the Accumulation of Capital*. London: Verso Books.

Newell, P. (2006). *Climate for Change: Non-state Actors and the Global Politics of the Greenhouse*. Cambridge: Cambridge University Press.

Newell, P. and Paterson, M. (2010). *Climate Capitalism: Global Warming and the Transformation of the Global Economy*. Cambridge: Cambridge University Press.

Okereke, C., Bulkeley, H. and Schroeder, H. (2009). Conceptualizing Climate Governance Beyond the International Regime. *Global Environmental Politics* 9(1), 58–78.

O'Neill, K. and Haas, P. M. (2019). Being There: International Negotiations as Study Sites in Global Environmental Politics. *Global Environmental Politics* 19, 4–13.

Oreskes, N. and Conway E. M. (2012). *Merchants of Doubt: How a Handful of Scientists Obscured the Truth on Issues from Tobacco Smoke to Global Warming*. London: Bloomsbury.

Orsini, A., Le Prestre, P., Haas, P. M. et al. (2020). Forum: Complex Systems and International Governance. *International Studies Review* 22(2), 1008–1038.

Paterson, M. (1996). *Global Warming and Global Politics*. London: Routledge.

Paterson, M. (2019). Using Negotiation Sites for Richer Collection of Network Data. *Global Environmental Politics* 19(2), 81–92.

Pickering, J. (2019). Deliberative Ecologies: Complexity and Social–Ecological Dynamics in International Environmental Negotiations. *Global Environmental Politics* 19(2), 61–80.

Picq, M. L. (2018). *Vernacular Sovereignties: Indigenous Women Challenging World Politics*. Tucson: The University of Arizona Press.

Purdue, D. (1996). Hegemonic Trips: World Trade, Intellectual Property and Biodiversity. *Environmental Politics* 4(1), 88–107.

Ruggie, J. G. (1975). International Responses to Technology: Concepts and Trends. *International Organization* 29(3), 557–583.

Schroeder, H. (2010). Agency in International Climate Negotiations: The Case of Indigenous Peoples and Avoided Deforestation. *International Environmental Agreements* 10(4), 317–332.

Schroeder, H. and Lovell, H. (2012). The Role of Non-Nation-State Actors and Side Events in the International Climate Negotiations. *Climate Politics* 12(1), 23–37.

Scott, D., Hitchner, S., Maclin, E. M. and Dammert B. J. L. (2014). Fuel for the Fire: Biofuels and the Problem of Translation at the Tenth Conference of the Parties to the Convention on Biological Diversity. *Global Environmental Politics* 14, 84–101.

Shiva, V. (1993). *Monocultures of the Mind: Perspectives on Biodiversity and Biotechnology*. London: Bloomsbury.
Strahan, S. E. and Douglass, A. R. (2018). Decline in Antarctic Ozone Depletion and Lower Stratospheric Chlorine Determined from Aura Microwave Limb Sounder Observations. *Geophysical Research Letters* 45(1), 382–390.
Tauli-Corpuz, V., Alcorn, J., Molnar, A., Healy, C., and Barrow, E. (2020). Cornered by PAs: Adopting Rights-Based Approaches to Enable Cost-Effective Conservation and Climate Action. *World Development* 130, 104923.
Tessnow-von Wysocki, I. and Vadrot, A. B. M. (2022). Governing a Divided Ocean: The Transformative Power of Ecological Connectivity in the BBNJ Negotiations. *Politics and Governance*, 10(3).
Thew, H. (2018). Youth Participation and Agency in the United Nations Framework Convention on Climate Change. *International Environmental Agreements* 18, 369–389.
UN Environment Programme (2019). *Global Environment Outlook – GEO-6. Healthy Planet, Healthy People.* Nairobi.
Underdal, A. and Young, O. R., eds. (2004). *Regime Consequences: Methodological Challenges and Research Strategies*. Dordrecht: Kluwer Academic.
Vadrot, A. B. M. (2014). *The Politics of Knowledge and Global Biodiversity*. London: Routledge.
Vadrot, A. B. M., Langlet, A. and Tessnow-von Wysocki, I. (2021a). Who Owns Marine Biodiversity? Contesting the World Order Through the "Common Heritage of Humankind" Principle. *Environmental Politics* 31(2), 226–250.
Vadrot, A. B. M. Langlet, A., Tessnow-von Wysocki, I. et al. (2021b). Marine Biodiversity Negotiations during COVID-19: A New Role for Digital Diplomacy? *Global Environmental Politics* 21(3), 169–186.
Vecchione-Gonçalves, M. (2009). Between the Leader of Virtù and the Good Savage. In J. M. Beier, ed., *Indigenous Diplomacies*. New York: Palgrave Macmillan, pp. 133–154.
Wacquant, L. (1989). Towards a Reflexive Sociology: A Workshop with Pierre Bourdieu. *Sociological Theory* 7(1): 26–63.
Watts, V. (2013). Indigenous Place-Thought and Agency Amongst Humans and Non-Humans (First Woman and Sky Woman Go on a European World Tour!). *Decolonization: Indigeneity, Education & Society* 2(1), 20–34.
Witter, R., Suiseeya, K. R. M., Gruby, R. L. et al. (2015). Moments of Influence in Global Environmental Governance. *Environmental Politics* 24(6), 894–912.
Young, O. R. (1989) The Politics of International Regime Formation: Managing Natural Resources and the Environment. *International Organization* 43(3), 349–375.
Young, O. R. (2010). *Institutional Dynamics: Emergent Patterns in International Environmental Governance*. Cambridge, MA: MIT Press.
Yusoff, K. (2018). *A Billion Black Anthropocenes or None*. Minneapolis: University of Minnesota Press.

Part I

Developing a Methodology

2

Starting

Practical and Ethical Considerations

ALICE B. M. VADROT AND HANNAH HUGHES

2.1 Introduction

Conducting research on global environmental agreement-making requires time for preparation. The scope of a research project may range from a PhD thesis, where a single researcher starts to become familiar with the research process and techniques (see Chapter 13), to a large-scale collaborative project involving several scholars with sometimes diverging disciplinary backgrounds and research interests (see Chapter 11). Regardless of this, researchers will be faced with the challenging task of developing a research methodology that is both intellectually provoking and feasible. Feasibility in this context covers two important issues: first, the development of your methodology – that is to say, the broader framework that justifies the selection and application of certain concepts and methods; and second, the practicability and implementation of conducting this research. The latter involves several tasks, ranging from gaining access to the field to employing a data collection method in a complex, and often overwhelming, research environment.

Agreement-making sites can be used for various research purposes. Scholars with different, or even contradictory, ontological and epistemological assumptions (about what is and how it can be comprehended) can use the same negotiation site to address widely dissimilar research questions or apply distinct research methods to a shared problem. For example, an ethnographer who views the negotiation site as a "relational space" (see Chapter 10) and a scholar who understands global meetings in terms of social networks (see Chapter 12) might both use participant observation, but their intellectual purposes, research questions, and theoretical assumptions will not be the same. While each data collection method comes with its own unique challenges – sometimes implying the need to adjust one's methodology throughout the research process to respond to unforeseen circumstances (see Chapter 14) – studies conducted on-site do share specific features as regards both challenges and opportunities. This chapter addresses these by providing the reader with a step-by-step guide to getting started with research in the specific setting of global environmental agreement-making.

Global environmental negotiations vary in size and purpose (Chasek 2001). Different on-site conditions necessitate different forms of conduct from the researcher to carry out the research while complying with both scientific and ethical standards. A conference of the parties (COP) held under the United Nations Framework Convention on Climate Change (UNFCCC), which assembles tens of thousands of people at a large and specially organized conference venue, has its own rules regarding access and poses unique challenges (see Chapters 6 and 7). This is particularly the case for solo researchers, who may find it difficult to capture processes and actors across the whole site and duration of a "mega-event" where the individual is submerged in a multitude of people. In comparison, research during intergovernmental conferences (IGCs) organized in the United Nations' Headquarters in New York City, as exemplified by the BBNJ (Biodiversity Beyond National Jurisdiction) treaty negotiations (see Reflection Box 6.1), requires careful and restrained behavior (e.g., when approaching interview partners or participating in "informal informals") in order not to become too conspicuous, and a disrupting factor, during a relatively small event. Online meetings and hybrid events further expand the sites of agreement-making and create a new set of challenges for the researcher (see Chapters 10, 11, and Reflection Box. 14.2)

Regardless of the size and purpose of a global environmental meeting, the preparatory phase, on-site research, and processing and analyzing of data can be organized in a step-by-step way. The aim of this chapter is to guide the researcher through key elements of this by breaking it down into the following components: (1) Methodological: how to develop a research project (Section 2.2); (2) Ethical: how to reflect on and comply with ethical standards (Section 2.3); (3) Legal: how to protect, manage, and store data (Section 2.4); and (4) Organizational: how to prepare research on-site (Section 2.4). Starting with the development of your research methodology and ethical and legal issues in the first part, the chapter describes practicalities that need to be considered before, during, and after fieldwork at negotiation sites in the second part. It will assist the reader in preparing research on-site and will address key crosscutting issues relevant to all chapters of the book, including research ethics, data management, and the central question of how to decide whether you need to be on-site to answer your research question and advance the state of the art on global environmental agreement-making or whether you can conduct your research virtually.

2.2 How to Develop a Research Project

Any research starts with curiosity and questioning, but this has to be developed into a researchable problem. Once we find an area of interest, we immerse ourselves in the topic by reading the existing literature, by searching for the most recent research findings (e.g., in university libraries or on the web through Google Scholar, Research Gate, or the Web of Science, etc.), or by approaching experts in the field. Global environmental politics has become part of the public and political debate: the UNFCCC COPs, in particular, have turned into prominent events that the whole world seems to watch. They are broadcast (at least partly), reported on, and their actors, processes, and sites are recorded through many audiovisual and textual media, most prominently the *Earth Negotiations Bulletin* (*ENB*) (see Chapter 8), all of which can be used to inform and transform your curiosity into a research question or puzzle. Attending a global environmental negotiation – on the basis of desk research – is another valuable way to locate the research interest by providing the opportunity to observe and identify relevant actors, sites, and processes of global environmental agreement-making, which can then inform the construction of the research problem and the project to address this.

In this book, and as is most fitting with the agreement-making framework, we view methodology as including: (1) the conceptual basis that informs how we approach our object of study – in this case a broadened understanding of what constitutes negotiations, global environmental events, and agreement-making; (2) how this is constructed as a research problem to be located at specific sites, by engaging relevant actors, observing particular processes, documenting power relations on-site; and (3) the appropriate methods to gain information and knowledge on these in order to address the research question or puzzle. The research itself does not necessarily unfold from (1) to (3) in a linear manner. In fact, you may not be able to give a clear account of your project's methodology until after you have finished the research and are writing up, which is the point at which you may need to describe how the chosen theory and/or concepts have informed how you constructed, analyzed, and have come to understand your research problem. Chapters 4 and 5 describe this process as it unfolds through different research journeys, which indicates the divergent pathways that this process takes. Nevertheless, there are steps or stages to the process of "building" a research project that we try to distill here (see Table 2.1).

Table 2.1 *A step-by-step approach for developing your methodology*

Step 1: Identifying your research area, interests, and research question

a. Reading, reading, reading
b. Literature review to assess state of the art and situate your research interest within the field
c. Conversation with peers
d. Attend and observe relevant meeting
e. Watch webcast negotiations
f. Ask questions (what, who, when, where, why, how)
g. Develop your research question/hypothesis

Step 2: Developing your conceptual and theoretical framework (see Chapters 2 and 3)

a. Reading, reading, reading
b. Literature review to assess how your or similar research questions have been addressed (using what theories and methods) by other scholars
c. Conversation with peers
d. Identify concepts/theories that you are interested in and that are suitable for your research purposes
e. Apply to empirical material (iterative process)

Step 3: Selecting your research methods and tools

a. On-site vs./and off-site
b. Single researcher/collaboration (Chapter 11)
c. Acquaint yourself with research materials, tools, and methods, and select yours
   a. Text (Chapter 8)
   b. Interviews (Chapter 9)
   c. Surveys (Chapter 3, Box 3.1)
   d. Ethnography (Chapter 10)
   e. SNA (Chapter 12)
d. Test your methods

Step 1: Identifying Your Research Area, Interests, and Research Question

In addition to acquiring knowledge about the area and object of study, one should become familiar with the kind of research that has been conducted and published so far. What do we already know about global environmental agreement-making, what research questions have scholars addressed so far, what methods have they employed, and what concepts or theories have they used to explain their observations and research findings? Assessing the state of the art (i.e., listing all relevant publications on the basis of categories such as focus of study, research question, method, or conceptual and theoretical framework) enables a researcher to learn, develop their curiosity, and situate their own research interest. Positioning your research within existing work and clarifying how you intend to advance specific aspects of the state of the art is a cornerstone of scientific practice. Many chapters of this book include literature reviews and examples of the kind of research that has already been conducted on the topic, as well as some of the gaps and questions that remain to be addressed (see Chapter 7).

Conversation with peers, attendance at relevant events, and looking up online material (such as recorded negotiation sessions) are useful strategies that will help you avoid erroneous research directions and misunderstandings. Reach out to experts in an issue area, theory, or methods that you are interested in; these could include practitioners, government representatives, nonstate actors, journalists, or any other participant that is willing to share their experiences on certain aspects of their work and involvement in agreement-making. Exploratory interviews are a good methodological tool in this regard because they require careful preparation and help structure early research ideas (see Chapter 9). The same is true for attending events related to the negotiation site under question. Scholars interested in a Convention on Biological Diversity (CBD) COP may wish to attend a meeting of the Subsidiary Body on Scientific, Technical and Technological Advice (SBSTTA) or a preparatory event first (see Chapters 2 and 13). A SBSTTA meeting will allow you to acquaint yourself with negotiation practice and specific actors, conflict lines, emerging issues, and so on, and enable you to meet future attendants of the event. Meetings are increasingly webcast and made publicly available (see Chapters 5 and 13); this provides interested researchers with digital material that can be used as an additional source during the preparation of the research questions and design (Vadrot et al. 2021).

The development of a research question is an iterative process, where you bounce back and forth between what you would like to know, what is already known, and how you can locate and "get at" your research interest. One way to find out what you do not know about your topic of interest is to ask obvious questions, for instance about the specific outcome of a negotiation, important actors, central conflicts, and power asymmetries. It is also useful to ask the standard journalistic questions: who, what, when, and where, although it is highly recommended to focus on how and why (Booth et al. 2008). Thus, while asking the first set of questions will allow you to reconstruct a given aspect of a negotiation (such as the inclusion of specific wording in the final negotiating text), analytical questions enable us to ask why and how certain actors have succeeded in promoting specific words or deleting bracketed text, which might have altered the meaning of the agreement in a way that would have weakened their position in world politics (e.g., Hughes and Vadrot 2019;

Vadrot et al. 2021). Other analytical questions include those about the history, composition, categorization, and values of a research topic (Booth et al. 2008) – for instance: when, why, and how the "ecosystem services" concept entered biodiversity negotiations during the CBD COPs; who promoted it and who opposed it; and the effects it had on environmental protection, actor constellations, and global environmental discourses.

Step 2: Developing Your Conceptual and Theoretical Framework

The formulation of a research question goes hand in hand with the development of a methodology and theoretical framework to guide the research. There are several possible approaches regarding the order of these tasks, depending on the principles that inform our reasoning. While some scholars develop theories that are based on empirical data (*induction*), others use observations to validate or falsify specific theories (*deduction*). In the social sciences, and in our attempts to make sense of empirical phenomena and generalize mechanisms, we often find ourselves "constructing theory" – that is to say, "engaging in creative attempts to generalize mechanisms, particular cases, or links between causal statements (Abend 2008, 177–79; Gross 2009) in ways that provide better traction for understanding observations they work with and possibly anticipate observations in other cases" (Timmermans and Tavory 2012, 167). The process of theory construction understood in this way (grounded theory, abduction) is often perceived to be an iterative, pragmatic process of "puzzling out," implying a "dialectic between data and generalization to account for empirical findings" (Timmermans and Tavory 2012, 167). These different approaches to conceptual and theoretical development are explored extensively in the first section of this volume. In Chapter 3, the authors recount the steps they undertook in developing and adapting their analytical frameworks for studying nongovernmental organization (NGO) influence, Chapter 4 examines the role that different thinkers (Bourdieu and Foucault) and concepts (e.g., habitus, discourse, epistemic selectivities) can play in research construction and analysis, and Chapter 5 identifies how concepts can emerge through the ethnographic process.

Step 3: Selecting Your Research Methods and Tools

The selection of methods in the context of studying agreement-making will depend on whether a researcher plans to attend an intergovernmental meeting and in what form (physically or digitally, see Chapter 13). The decision of whether to include fieldwork at negotiation sites in your research design is part of your methodology. In contrast to *methodology*, *methods* may be defined as research tools and procedures for collecting data, including quantitative and qualitative methods (e.g., interviews, participant observation, surveys). Ethnography, for instance, can be both a method for collecting data through participant observation (e.g., field notes or audiovisual material) and a research lens attributing meaning to the observer (how they are situated within the field site) and the specific community under study (see Chapters 10 and 11).

While any research will start with getting your methodology right, thinking about techniques for conducting the research, and developing a comprehensive overview of the tools and instruments to be used, the methods themselves will be developed at a later stage. Methods imply identifying the actual tools and steps of data collection and analysis. The latter entails experimenting, testing, and adjusting your methods if the circumstances of your research change (see Chapter 13). While it may appear that agreement-making as a field of study is more attuned to qualitative methods, this is certainly not the case. Being on-site also offers many opportunities for collecting quantitative data (e.g., survey data, network data, textual data) or combining qualitative and quantitative methods (see Chapter 13 [this volume]; Vadrot et al. 2021). In contrast, research off-site can draw on participant lists, iteration of texts, and *ENB* reports (see Chapters 8 and 12).

On-Site Versus Off-Site

Attending intergovernmental negotiations as part of your research project is appealing for many reasons, including beyond the actual research work: It enables you to study agreement-making in practice, acquaint yourself with multilateral environmental diplomacy, and meet key state and nonstate actors from all over the world that may become important connections in your future academic or nonacademic work. Growing scholarly interest in attending environmental meetings can partly be explained by their attractiveness as sites for data collection. Even if the researcher has no interest in text-based negotiations and other areas and procedures of the event as such (e.g., side events, exhibition halls, or activism; see Chapter 7), they may use the time on-site to approach potential interviewees, collect material (e.g., leaflets, books, and brochures) on specific issues, or network with like-minded people. The sheer number of participants – one could say that some of the most significant actors in the community are there – promises easy access to a large sample of contacts and potential interviewees in a short time.

Research into environmental negotiation processes and practices has strongly benefited from scholar participation in those events. Studies that draw on "insider perspectives" (including diplomats reflecting on their experiences and *ENB* reporters; see Chapter 8) might reveal negotiation dynamics, including bargaining behind closed doors (which may be problematic from an ethical point of view, as will be outlined in Section 2.3).

However, this does not mean that there is no valid research on environmental agreement-making using methods that do not involve on-site participation and data collection. *ENB* reports and other textual material, including the protocols of meetings, compilations of decisions and so-called nonpapers (see Chapter 8), interviews conducted after a meeting (with respondents identified thanks to meeting participant lists; see Chapter 9), press releases, audiovisual material, statements uploaded by state and nonstate actors, and webcast sessions all allow off-site researchers to pursue their research interests and conduct valid, reliable research on diverse aspects of the negotiation at hand, including intersessional periods and other relevant meetings and events (see Chapter 6). Gradually, virtual sites and digital spaces (e.g., social media, webcasts, and video recordings of sessions) have emerged; not only do they provide additional opportunities for collecting data, but as such they also constitute important new sites for agreement-making. They have continued to expand, especially in light of the COVID-19 pandemic and the UN's ambition to become environmentally sustainable (see Chapters 6 and 14).

Participant Observation

While almost the same methods can be used for off-site and on-site research, participant observation and ethnography (except for digital ethnography; see Chapter 14) tend to be reserved for those researchers who strive to collect data and find an answer to their research question by "being there." While ethnography can – as mentioned earlier – be employed as a data collection technique as well as a methodology and a heuristic (see Chapter 10), participant observation entails specific research tasks, such as observing a group of people and taking field notes on diverse aspects (for instance: specific actions, speech patterns, habitual strategies, or moments of contestation). Our emphasis on the "participant" in participant observation during negotiations is justified insofar as it implies that the researcher becomes part of the group and gains a deeper understanding of the events, actors, and patterns of interaction at the negotiation site.

As Baker points out, participant observation is

> a complex research method because it often requires the researcher to play a number of roles and to use a number of techniques, including her/his five senses, to collect data. In addition, despite the level of involvement with the study group, the researcher must always remember her/his primary role as a researcher and remain detached enough to collect and analyze data relevant to the problem under investigation. (Baker 2006, 172)

To be a participant is a process in two ways. On the one hand, the social researcher should increasingly participate in and gain access to the field – and to the persons in the field. On the other hand, the researcher's observations have to become gradually more concrete and condensed with regard to the research question and the unit of analysis (Flick 1995, 158). These challenges need to be reflected upon even before a selection of the methods for data collection and analysis is made.

Participant observation is associated with many practical problems, such as "how to gain access to the field" (i.e., the political terrain, informal negotiation processes, the people, etc.), as well as ethical and methodological problems. The mere fact that access to the site is conditioned by obtaining a badge that you have to wear during your stay (see Section 2.5) and taking on a formal role (e.g., observer, NGO, government, media) revealed by the color of the badge to all other conference participants does not allow for any "objective" detached observation without becoming an involved part of the whole. Correspondingly, the participant observer needs to be aware of challenges encountered during the research process by engaging in critical self-reflection throughout their research practice (Bourdieu 2003).

2.3 How to Reflect on and Comply with Ethical Standards

Reliable research on negotiation sites has two important ethical aspects: reflexivity and positionality, and compliance with ethical standards. First, researchers have a duty to reflect on (and carefully manage) their position in the field, any potential biases and privileges, how they relate to their "research objects" and the field, and what stakes they have or support. This is especially important if you decide to be an ethnographer (see Chapter 10) or if you participate as part of a group of actors that has a specific stake in the negotiations (e.g., with an NGO or a national delegation; see Chapter 13, or accompanying local and Indigenous People; see Chapter 5). As outlined in Chapter 10, conference sites are "relational spaces" and the way people relate to you will depend on the institution that you represent, your reason for being at the conference, and the way you enter into relationships with other participants.

As described in Chapter 5 and in Hughes et al. (2021), researching negotiations implies having a stake, and not being disconnected from the effects of agreement-making on world order or from the impacts of certain negotiation dynamics and outcomes on vulnerable groups, marginalized actors, and society–nature relationships. The latter includes a critical reflection of our own mobility and consumption practices, our carbon footprint, and whether the benefits of traveling to a conference outweigh the environmental damage. In addition, issues such as collaboration with other researchers (including a division of labor before, during, and after on-site research), along with data sharing and authorship, should follow ethical standards as described in Chapter 11.

Secondly, reliability implies compliance with ethics in terms of codified research standards and obligations. Depending on your research institution and the funding agency that finances your work, your project may have to undergo evaluation and approval by a research ethics committee. Criteria may vary depending on the country and institution where you are based, but your ethics declaration should generally include a list of measures that ensure (1) the protection of the rights of your research participants (e.g., how you identify, approach, and inform research participants about the purpose of the study and their rights), and (2) compliance with data protection laws (e.g., how you protect your data/data subjects by safely storing, managing, regulating access and ownership, anonymizing, and pseudonymizing your data).

Research ethics generally aim to protect research participants; in the case of research at negotiation sites, these are the people attending the meeting that you observe. In the negotiation context, they are not considered to be vulnerable persons because they are function owners. This implies that the data you collect is not sensitive per se; however, you should develop measures to ensure (1) that the privacy and rights of each participant are protected, and (2) that research participants are not exposed to any risk greater than the risk they are exposed to by attending the meeting. Box 2.1 contains a standard clause that you may use in an application to an ethics commission.

Box 2.1 Standard clause for application to ethics commission

Participants of *project x* are not vulnerable persons. Research participants will be function owners (state representatives, experts, public servants, scientists, NGO representatives) attending *meeting* y in their professional capacity representing their institution (government, IGO, or NGO). The project is exclusively interested in collecting nonsensitive data respecting the privacy of each participant. Participants will not be exposed to any risk that exceeds the risk that they expose themselves to by participating in international negotiations and/or working in their work environment, where they will be interviewed/observed. *Project x* will not collect or process any sensitive data, and will respect the privacy of each participant by following the principle of confidentiality and implementing related technical, organizational, and security measures.

2.4 How to Protect, Manage, and Store Your Data

Each university should have established technical, organizational, and security measures, such as access control to workplaces, access control to data-processing systems, and control of databases and data alteration. In the European Union context, research institutions must comply with the General Data Protection Regulation 2016/679 (GDPR) and employ a data protection officer who can inform you of the kinds of measures that your institution has put in place to comply with data protection laws. One example of this is that any processing activities performed on personal data must be recorded in what is called "a record of processing activities." This might mean that you must centrally record and document all applications (even small-scale applications, such as simplifying a quote) that can process personal data.

For the purpose of collecting data at international negotiation sites, it is often necessary to clarify beforehand how you will identify and recruit research participants for interviews, surveys, focus groups, and so on; how you will inform them about their rights and the measures that you have put in place to protect their privacy, which is usually via a project information sheet and informed consent form; how you will protect the data once collected and stored (for instance, through anonymization and pseudonymization, see Section 2.3); and how you will analyze and use the data. Table 2.2 gives some guidance on how to ensure confidentiality when you identify and recruit your research participants, and how to practice informed consent. Table 2.3 includes guidance on how to protect the data and privacy of your interviewees.

Table 2.2 *Measures to protect the privacy, rights, and data of research participants*

1. Clarifying how you identify and recruit research participants
   Research x involves ethnographic research/participant observation/fieldwork at intergovernmental negotiations during *conference y*, conducting *type of* interviews.
   - Procedures/criteria for identification of research participants:
     - Before including participants in a study, you have to identify who is eligible to participate. For example, the research participant must be a national delegate (head of delegation, delegate responsible for x in negotiation y, delegate specializing in x), expert, public servant, or researcher.
     - Before fieldwork, previous participant lists and official websites of ministries and international organizations can be consulted and potential interviewees identified, which will yield a list of potential interviewees.
   - Procedures/criteria for recruitment of research participants:
     - As a first step, an email can be sent to the secretariat of the convention or organization concerned, informing them about the research project, its objectives, and the data to be collected. An information sheet summarizing the project and an informed consent form should be attached to the email. The secretariat should be asked to inform participants about the study. Additionally, information material (leaflets) can be made available at an information desk on site.

Table 2.2 (*cont.*)

- As a second step, potential interviewees can be contacted before the fieldwork; you should inform them about the study and ask for an interview that can either take place before, during, or after the negotiations. Additionally, potential participants can be contacted on the basis of the snowball principle and during the fieldwork itself. The Principle Investigator (PI)/researcher in charge should contact potential interviewees while respecting their privacy (do not approach them in front of toilet facilities; preferably approach them during breaks when they are sitting in the negotiation room; be careful when approaching them outside of the negotiation room).
- Before each interview, the researcher in charge (PI or team member) should explain the research project and inform the person about her/his rights. The researcher should hand an information sheet to the interviewee, including an "informed consent form," which first should be explained, then be signed by both the research participant and the researcher.

2. Clarifying how you inform research participants: Informed consent
   The PI or the researcher in charge should inform the participant about the objectives of the project, the rights of the participant, and the interview procedure, duration, and contents.
   - The participant should be informed both verbally and in written form that participation in the study is voluntary and that they can refuse to participate at any time without having to give a reason, or withdraw their agreement to participate once the study has already started; there will be no negative consequences for them if they refuse to participate or withdraw from the study after it has started.
   - The researcher in charge will ask the participant to take time to read the information provided in the consent form carefully and to feel free to ask any questions. The researcher in charge will inform the participant about the fact that they should only sign the declaration of consent
     - o if they have fully understood the type of study and procedure to be followed,
     - o if they are willing to consent to participate, and
     - o if they are aware of her/his rights as a participant in this study.
   - The research participant will be informed about the interview duration.
   - The research participant will be informed that the researchers do not anticipate any risks to be associated with her/his participation, but that they have the right to stop the interview or withdraw from the research at any time.
   - The research participant will be asked to sign the form and will be provided with the contact details of the PI should any queries arise, or information be needed about the data and its use/ the project results/the deletion of data.

Table 2.3 *Data protection: Interview data*

- Register your data/all interviews and produce an identity database, e.g., by using an Excel sheet including the name of the interview, date and time, name and contact details of the interviewee, and keywords (it is best to do this on site). Make sure you save this identity database in a folder separate from the folders containing (1) raw data, (2) transcripts.
- Transcribe your interviews and confirm that no sensitive data was collected.
- If some sensitive data was collected (e.g., when an interviewee refers to her/his family, personal values, or preferences), this data should be deleted and you should only transcribe parts of the interview that contain information relevant to the project and not where interviewees share sensitive data.

Table 2.3 (*cont.*)

- In order to protect the rights and privacy of interviewees, data should be anonymized and pseudonymized. Because interviewees are function owners, it might sometimes be difficult to anonymize the data (e.g., there is only one head of delegation of the US).
- Records, transcripts, and registers should be stored separately and various anonymization and pseudonymization techniques should be used to protect the privacy and rights of interviewees.

Anonymization techniques: First, determine the release model for each anonymized dataset. Second, data attributes should be classified and unused data (sensitive data, which the project should not collect) removed: (1) Attributes in the dataset should be classified as direct identifiers, indirect identifiers, or nonidentifiers; (2) Any attribute that is clearly not required in the anonymized dataset should be suppressed; (3) Direct and indirect identifiers should be anonymized, through (a) attribute suppression, (b) character masking.

Pseudonymization techniques: The attribute values [name] should be replaced by made-up values [numbers such as: 111267]. For instance, pregenerate a list of made-up values, and randomly select from this list to replace each of the original values. The made-up values should be unique, and should bear no relationship to the original values (to avoid deriving original values from the pseudonyms: e.g., initial date of interview). The identity database should be securely kept and stored separately from the data. The identity database should only be used by the PI and the researcher in charge to resolve any specific queries (the number of such queries will be controlled).

2.5 How to Prepare Research On Site

Given the complexity of global environmental meetings, a careful preparation of fieldwork, including the production of the aforementioned project documents and forms, is essential. Regardless of the research purpose and data collection method, practical tasks can be divided into three phases: before fieldwork, at the site, and after fieldwork. We will describe these phases in Sections 2.5.1–2.5.3, taking a step-by-step approach (see Table 2.3), and signpost where in the book you can find detailed information on the individual steps.

2.5.1 Before Fieldwork

Once you have developed your research methodology, it is recommended to start collecting information on upcoming events. Conferences may be held annually (UNFCCC COPs) or every two years (CBD COPs), while meetings of subsidiary bodies in between COPs sometimes take place twice a year. Treaty negotiations preceding the establishment of a multilateral environmental agreement (MEA) and its decision-making body may be scheduled in quick succession: In the BBNJ case, four IGCs were scheduled within two years. Collecting all available information on the meeting you wish to attend is the first step in preparing your research stay and a precondition for refining your research methodology (depending on access conditions, topics on the agenda, access to specific meeting sites, etc.), planning your research stay (travel to the meeting town, accommodation, and venue), and creating a cost estimate and schedule. Chapter 6 provides an illustrative example of how you might prepare a schedule for yourself at a climate COP (see Section 6.4.1: Prior to the Event).

A research stay can be costly, and both the cost and research environment vary significantly depending on the region, country, and institutions studied (see Table 2.4). If your research project is funded by a university or funding institution, make sure you include travel expenses in your application. In the case of the European Research Council (ERC) project MARIPOLDATA, the budget included several field trips for a team of researchers, which meant that the funding was already in place for the successful PhD candidates. However, if you do not have funding available through your research project or studentship, it is advisable to start looking for funding opportunities as early as possible. You may have access to funds from your faculty or department, or you can search the funding available for travel support and fieldwork from relevant funding agencies or academic associations. Depending on the location of the meeting that you wish to attend and the length of your research stay, the fieldwork may cost anything between EUR 500 and 5,000. Attending the UNFCCC COP26 in Edinburgh (United Kingdom) as a UK-based scholar would obviously have been easier and less expensive to arrange than participating in the CBD COP10 in Nagoya, Japan. However, even finding and booking accommodation and travel within the United Kingdom for COP26 was more challenging than usual

Table 2.4 *Checklist: Preparation for research stay*

- Find a meeting you wish to attend
  - Where and when does the meeting take place?
  - What information is already available (preparatory documents, draft agenda and decisions, *ENB* reports)?
- Check funding sources available
  - Does your university/institution provide funding?
  - Is the travel covered by your grant/a project you are working on?
  - Ask your supervisor for possible sources of funding.
  - Check with associations, foundations, and other institutions with an interest in environmental meetings.
- Registration/accreditation process
  - What are the conditions for access?
  - Contact secretariat and familiarize yourself with accreditation process.
  - Check out specificities (COP: trading badges)
  - Reach out to your head of department (you may need a signature to approve the trip).
  - In what role will/can I attend?
  - How long do I want to stay?
  - Do I need a visa?
- Cost estimate and travel plan
  - Travel arrangements to the meeting town/city
  - Accommodation (conference hotel vs. other accommodation)
  - Travel arrangements from accommodation to meeting venue

due to limited availability and significant cost increases; thus, it is advisable to arrange this as early as possible.

Regarding accommodation, you will have several options. Each conference host offers a selection of conference hotels within different price ranges. Depending on the conference, shuttle buses between hotels and the venue or public transport passes may be available. Staying in a conference hotel offers the opportunity to meet other participants during breakfast or while using organized transportation to and from the venue. Many attendees wear their badges at breakfast time so that you can identify them easily. At the CBD COP14 in Sharm El Sheikh, for instance, the conference location could only be reached by using the shuttle buses between the hotels and the venue; the bus trip took twenty to thirty minutes, which could be used to network, reach out to participants, arrange an interview appointment (or even conduct an on-the-spot interview), or informally talk about ongoing negotiations. Staying at conference hotels may be expensive, hence some researchers prefer to share accommodation (see Chapter 11).

One precondition to be able to participate in a global environmental conference is to register and become accredited. Contact your university or research institution and check whether they are admitted to attend meetings of the convention you wish to attend. If you seek to participate in a UNFCCC COP, participation can be complicated because the conference sets a limit on the number of participants from various groups.[1] In other cases, such as the CBD, it is easier to attend and you may even be able to accredit your institution by asking the head of your department to register your university and provide you with a nomination letter. While selecting and finding an institution through which you can be registered can be a burden and may seem bureaucratic in the first instance, the choice that you make will significantly affect your participation and on-site research. Being part of a national delegation, for instance, may offer valuable insights into dynamics within national delegations and decision-making, but may impact your research in three important ways: first, you may have to fulfill specific tasks on behalf of your government, which leaves less time for research; second, your schedule will be strongly impacted by your delegation's schedule, which will make you less flexible in terms of the meetings you would like to follow; and, third, other participants will identify you as a national delegate and may relate either positively or negatively to your position (see Chapter 13).

Before your departure, make sure that you have gathered all the documents (research documents, draft agenda, draft decisions, etc.) and devices needed for conducting your research on site (see Table 2.5). You should prepare a folder holding printed documents and, additionally, save all documents on your laptop, tablet, or mobile phone. Usually, conference venues offer computer rooms and printers where you can print or copy any material needed. It is advisable to bring your own laptop or tablet, one or two USB sticks, and a recorder, and to think beforehand about your field note-taking technique and the devices needed for it (see Chapters 10 and 11).

[1] COP26 of the UNFCCC limited the number of government representatives to 10,000, and allowed up to 7,000 observers, including civil society, per week, and 300 media representatives.

Table 2.5 *Checklist: Before your departure*

- Assemble all documents (virtually and physically)
  - Everything you need for travel, accommodation, access to site
  - Information sheets about your project
  - Informed consent forms
  - Interview guide
  - Any other research material
- Be aware of dress code
  - Business casual/smart casual
  - For receptions: business/informal
- Check research material and devices
  - Computer/tablet
  - Mobile phone
  - Voice recorder
- Start networking and reaching out to other participants
  - Other research groups
  - Interviewees
  - Other contacts

While the clothes you wear will depend on the climate at the conference location and on individual choice, our experience shows that it is sensible, first, to pay attention to your dress code and, second, to be prepared for cold air-conditioned meeting rooms and extreme conditions at the conference venue, including hot and humid cities. Your choice of clothes may also depend on the actors that you follow and their dress code, but if you feel unsure we suggest "business casual" or "business informal."

Reaching out to other participants can facilitate your research stay in several ways. Some conferences assemble a large number of researchers, giving you the opportunity to connect with other individuals and groups that share similar interests and concerns. When attending a conference for the first time, making contact with others can help you to navigate and gain insight on the present and past meetings, and research collaborations might emerge (see Chapter 11). Ask your supervisor or colleagues who might know other researchers that are observing. There may also be dedicated events, such as the daily Research and Independent Non-Governmental Organization (RINGO) constituency meeting at climate COPS or side events that provide the perfect opportunity to meet others, share research interests, network, and collaborate on data collection for the meeting (see Chapter 6). It is also advisable to identify and contact interview participants before the event as well, to save time and to ensure that your participant can fit you into their schedule once you arrive on site (see Table 2.3).

2.5.2 During Fieldwork

When should you arrive at the negotiation site? This will depend on the meeting you attend and what you aim to observe there: for example, if you follow a particular issue or item, you may want to search the schedule to identify dedicated days and relevant side events (see Chapter 7 for an example on gender). UNFCCC and CBD COPs often set up a dedicated desk in the arrival zone at the airport, offering information on the event and free transit from the airport to the conference site and hotels. You thus get a chance to meet other participants before the conference has started and to become part of the community before having accessed the conference venue. Large conferences extend to the public and create new "material geographies" (Craggs and Mahony 2014). Hosting large-scale conferences often brings about changes in host cities, both temporary and permanent. Such events are part of city marketing campaigns and civic boosterism, while placing restrictions on residents and guests. As discussed in Chapter 7, surveillance, police, and a military presence, which are common around meeting venues, can sometimes extend to the city, which becomes securitized (Craggs and Mahony 2014).

Regardless of the kind of research you plan to conduct, you should aim to make yourself familiar with your research site as quickly as possible. Chapters 6 and 7 introduce the reader to the ways in which venues are organized and explain how to navigate the site and conference schedule. Follow the maps and explore the site, the negotiation and meeting rooms, areas where side events and exhibitions take place, and the food courts and computer and print areas. Preparing yourself by exploring the site as well as internalizing the venue's structure and conference schedule is especially important to avoid getting lost when things get busy. The better you know the venue and schedule, the better you will be able to adjust to unforeseen developments, especially as a solo researcher with fewer capacities to cover sprawling negotiation dynamics.

Once you are familiar with the site, you should start to establish a routine and research practice that will organize your day-to-day participation in the event. While it is advisable to start thinking about this routine (including a schedule) beforehand, you may have to adjust it once you are on site and are familiar with the physical and organizational structure of the meeting. It takes a while to internalize where to find everything and to estimate how long it takes to travel to the venue, pass security, and be at a specific place at the conference, or to know where to find quiet areas suitable for conducting an interview or taking field notes without being interrupted by noise or other participants.

Irrespective of the size and type of the meeting, your routine will quickly resemble the day-to-day practices of participating state and nonstate actors. You will arrive at the meeting in the morning (eventually by using conference transportation); pass security; immerse yourself in various meetings, conversations, or activities; walk a lot; observe a lot; take notes; arrange interviews; meet other people; eat quickly in order not to lose too much time; and so forth. Chapter 10 provides an example of what your research schedule might look like (see Box 10.2). When traveling back to their hotels, many participants are exhausted, especially toward the end of the conference, when evening and night negotiations become more common. If you are ready and willing to immerse yourself into the dynamics and drama of the meetings (Death 2011), you may feel the same excitement and exhaustion as those that you observe and interview. Capturing the performative aspects of a conference and how it affects you as a researcher may be more relevant if you are an ethnographer; even if you are not, it might still be useful to reflect on these dynamics and how they shape your on-site research and the conditions for data collection (see Chapter 10 for guidance on this).

In this regard, field notes are an important technique that can be used by researchers even if they do not conduct any participant observation or ethnography in the narrow sense. Field notes may be considered a data collection technique but may also be useful to record important observations and thoughts of the researcher regarding the application of methods, the formulation of assumptions, or interesting preliminary findings. As a data collection technique, field notes can provide a record of observed negotiation dynamics, general conflict lines, individual positions of parties, or the statements and roles of individual actors and actor groups within the negotiation process. There are several types of field notes: methodological, observational, and analytic.

2.5.3 After Fieldwork

After fieldwork, and before you start analyzing your material and writing up your results, you should make sure that your data travels safely home, as well as contacting participants with a follow-up and a "thank you" note.

Taking your data home entails a variety of tasks depending on the kind of data you collected. If you collected artifacts on site (e.g., leaflets, brochures, decision texts, etc.), make sure that you have enough space in your luggage and are able to carry the material with you. After a two-week COP, for instance, you may well have to carry several kilograms of material. In order to avoid extra charges on your luggage if you are flying back, try to leave space when you pack for the trip. Alternatively, you can send the material by post or – if you carried out the research collectively – distribute the material among all researchers. Once you arrive home, it is advisable to archive the material by making back-up copies that can be saved in a folder together with other digital material and collected data, including interview recordings, pictures, videos, and field notes. You can either develop your own data archive, use an existing data archive or digital infrastructure, or use specific software, such as the Qualitative Data Analysis and Research Software ATLAS.ti, which can be used to analyze the material as well.

If you conducted interviews, make sure that you have all recordings, related field notes, informed consent forms, and contact details of your interviewees. In order to protect their data and privacy, you should save the recordings, transcripts, and informed consent forms in separate folders (see Table 2.3). It is best not to wait too long after fieldwork before writing up your observations, preliminary interpretations, and explanations of what you researched at the site. Regardless of the type of data collected, once you have registered and organized your data, you should start writing up your thoughts against the background of the research question that you had in mind, and of the concepts and theoretical framework that guided your on-site research. As outlined in Chapter 11, organizing writing-up meetings straight after fieldwork can facilitate the process of data aggregation and preliminary analysis, especially if you attended a meeting as a team. Ethnographers who aim to develop thick descriptions of the community and site of fieldwork – descriptions of observed actor behavior, negotiation dynamics, etcetera, including a record of subjective interpretations, explanations, or meanings – will especially profit from writing-up sessions shortly after fieldwork. When describing negotiation dynamics and the research object at hand, your writing style should be adapted to the type of data collected, so make sure that you follow the writing standards of your specific discipline.

2.6 Conclusions

This chapter introduced the reader to the general features of conducting research on and at global environmental negotiations and agreement-making. It closes with three main takeaways: First, the ethical, legal, and organizational aspects of this kind of research are as important as the conceptual and methodological work that prepares scholars for data collection and participant observation on site. We propose a three-step approach for developing a methodology, which we understand as an iterative rather than a linear process, as further illustrated by Chapters 3 and 4 of this book. Second, cross-cutting issues, such as access, funding, and data protection, need to be addressed early in the research and should be reflected on regularly at different stages of the process. Third, regardless of the research puzzle and methodology, conducting research on and at negotiations will always imply a high degree of reflexivity and preparedness. This theme runs through several chapters of the book, and you will learn more about how to use and adapt a methodology and specific method based on illustrative examples and insider perspectives in each of the book's chapters.

Further Reading

1. Chasek, P. S. (2001). *Earth Negotiations: Analyzing Thirty Years of Environmental Diplomacy*. Tokyo: United Nations University Press.

This book is a standard work that gives an overview over thirty years of global environmental negotiations, how they work, and how they have changed over time. It is a key source for scholars new to the field and illustrates what negotiation sites look like from an insider perspective.

2. Mitchell, R. B., Andonova, L. B., Axelrod, M. et al. (2020). What We Know (and Could Know) About International Environmental Agreements. *Global Environmental Politics* 20, 103–121.

This article introduces the International Environmental Agreements Data Base (IEADB) cataloging the texts, memberships, and design features of over 3,000 multilateral and bilateral environmental agreements. The authors have created a comprehensive review of the evolution of international environmental law, including how agreements have changed over time.

References

Abend, G. (2008). The Meaning of "Theory." *Sociological Theory* 26, 173–199.

Baker, L. M. (2006). Observation: A Complex Research Method. *Library Trends* 55 (1), 171–189.

Booth, W. C., Colomb, G. G. and Williams, J. M. (2008). *The Craft of Research*. Chicago, IL: University of Chicago Press.

Bourdieu, P. (2003). Participant Objectivation. *Journal of the Royal Anthropological Institute* 9, 281–294.
Craggs, R. and Mahony, M. (2014). The Geographies of the Conference: Knowledge, Performance and Protest. *Geography Compass* 8 (6), 414–430.
Death, C. (2011). Summit Theatre: Exemplary Governmentality and Environmental Diplomacy in Johannesburg and Copenhagen. *Environmental Politics* 20 (1), 1–19.
Flick, U. (1995). *Qualitative Forschung. Theorie, Methoden, Anwendung in Psychologie und Sozialwissenschaften*. Reinbek: Rowohlt.
Gross, N. (2009). A Pragmatist Theory of Social Mechanisms. *American Sociological Review* 74, 358–379.
Hughes, H. and Vadrot, A. B. M. (2019). Weighting the World: IPBES and the Struggle over Biocultural Diversity. *Global Environmental Politics* 19 (2), 14–37.
Hughes, H., Vadrot, A., Allan, J. I. et al. (2021). Global Environmental Agreement-Making: Upping the Methodological and Ethical Stakes of Studying Negotiations. *Earth System Governance* 10, 100121.
Timmermans, S. and Tavory, I. (2012). Theory Construction in Qualitative Research: From Grounded Theory to Abductive Analysis. *Sociological Theory* 30 (3), 167–186.
Vadrot, A. B. M., Langlet, A., Tessnow-von Wysocki, I. et al. (2021). Marine Biodiversity Negotiations During COVID-19: A New Role for Digital Diplomacy? *Global Environmental Politics* 21 (3), 169–186.

3

Frameworks

Developing and Working with Analytical Frameworks

MICHELE BETSILL AND NAGHMEH NASIRITOUSI

3.1 Introduction

Making sense of agreement-making in a systematic way does not come with a clear guide. The process of developing a coherent research project can often be messy rather than following linear steps, especially because different research traditions offer various research design options and methodologies. Many research projects begin with questions such as "what is going on here" and "why doesn't the theory explain this phenomenon?" A key step is to develop or apply an analytical framework to guide the empirical work to answer these questions.

An analytical framework is a set of ideas that structures analysis by specifying core concepts and relationships to be explored. Analytical frameworks help the researcher to organize thoughts on what is important to focus on by guiding the selection of methods, data collection and analysis, and interpretations of research findings. The research process can be overwhelming, especially in the context of multilateral agreement-making processes. A carefully crafted framework can help the researcher make informed choices about whether to attend meetings in person, how and where to spend their time at these meetings, whom to talk to, what types of questions to ask, and what types of data to collect. Analytical frameworks allow the researcher to think creatively about the types of data that can speak to the elements of the framework and about how to leverage different sources of data (Yin 2015). At the same time, an analytical framework can help the researcher know when it might be time to change direction. If the framework isn't working, the scholar can spend some time seeing if it can be revised. Even if the framework is ultimately abandoned, it has served its purpose as an initial organizing tool.

In this chapter, we share our own experiences of developing and adapting a particular analytical framework to study the influence of nonstate actors in agreement-making. We address a common set of questions to offer insight into the value of analytical frameworks as well as the more detailed processes of developing, revising, and adapting a framework. Thus, rather than a step-by-step guide, this chapter presents different experiences of working with and developing analytical frameworks and draws out similarities and differences between the two processes in the conclusion. While our own work has focused on the range of actors and forms of agency in international environmental negotiations (specifically the climate regime), we hope to provide guidance and inspiration for scholars conducting research on all aspects of agreement-making.

3.2 Michele's Reflections

My contribution focuses on developing and revising an analytical framework with Elisabeth Corell to study the influence of nongovernmental organizations (NGOs) in international environmental negotiations (Betsill and Corell 2001, 2008; Corell and Betsill 2001).[1] In brief, what came to be known as the "Betsill–Corell" framework identifies two dimensions of NGO influence: participation in international negotiations and subsequent effects on the behavior of other actors (e.g., states). The framework calls for gathering data on these two dimensions from multiple sources, including documents, interviews, and participant observation (if possible). Researchers can then use process tracing and counterfactual analysis to identify whether and how NGOs shaped the negotiation process (e.g., through issue framing, agenda-setting, or shaping the position of key states), as well as the final outcome as reflected in the final treaty text. In considering the range of possible effects NGOs may have, scholars can make qualitative assessments of their overall influence on negotiations.

I became interested in the role of NGOs in international environmental negotiations after working for an environmental NGO that was involved in negotiating the elephant ivory trade ban under the Convention on International Trade in Endangered Species and in talks leading up to the 1992 Rio Earth Summit and Agenda 21. For my PhD, I wanted to research whether and how NGOs influenced multilateral treaty-making processes given that such negotiations were seen as operating in the realm of states. My dissertation examined environmental NGO influence on negotiations related to climate change in the period 1988 to 1997.

My collaboration with Elisabeth began when we met at an International Studies Association (ISA) conference and realized that we were doing similar dissertation research (she was working on NGO influence in the desertification negotiations). As we moved through the dissertation process, we had many conversations about how to measure "influence." At the time, we were both struggling to find a strong analytical foundation in the existing literature. This was in the late 1990s, when the study of NGOs/nonstate actors was re-emerging in the field of international relations (IR) after having received some attention in the 1970s through the concept of complex interdependence (Keohane and Nye 1972). While many scholars claimed that NGOs were influencing global politics, we found that they rarely defined what they meant by "influence" and frequently conflated the concepts of power and influence (Betsill and Corell 2001). Moreover, much of the literature was focused on NGOs as "activists" using "outsider" strategies such as consumer boycotts and public awareness campaigns. We were both studying NGOs that were engaging with state actors in formal negotiation spaces and in a highly professionalized manner. Informed by our ongoing discussions, Elisabeth and I developed our own individual approaches appropriate to the specific types of questions we were asking in our respective dissertations.

[1] This discussion represents my personal recollection and reflection on our collaborative process.

Why Did You Feel the Need to Develop an Analytical Framework?

The "Betsill–Corell" framework was a hybrid of our individual dissertation approaches. After completing our degrees, Elisabeth and I found ourselves with postdoctoral fellowships in the same city. By then we had become friends and thought it would be fun to write a paper together comparing our respective dissertation findings. As noted, there was a lack of analytical guidance on the topic of NGO influence in the existing literature, and we thought we could make a contribution. We developed the framework to facilitate the comparison between our two cases. Initially, we did not anticipate applying the framework beyond our analyses of NGO influence in the climate change and desertification negotiations.

How Did You Go About Developing Your Analytical Framework?

We quickly realized that we would need a common framework to allow for a systematic comparison of our cases since we had taken different approaches to analyzing NGO influence in our respective dissertations. My research looked at NGOs as norm entrepreneurs while Elisabeth focused on NGOs as providers of expert knowledge. While I examined NGO influence on the negotiation process (e.g., how issues were framed), Elisabeth's study traced NGO influence on the final treaty text. We spent many hours revisiting literature on power and influence and debating the merits of different strategies for understanding and operationalizing their relationship.

Finding a common analytical framework was far more challenging than we had anticipated. We were trying to find a middle ground that allowed us to retain and highlight the unique qualities and rich detail of our individual case studies while facilitating systematic comparison and lesson drawing. We also were constrained by the fact that we had collected different types of data for our dissertation research, as we wanted to draw on our existing data for the comparative analysis. For example, Elisabeth had a much richer set of participant observation data as she had attended most of the negotiating sessions for the desertification convention as a reporter for the *Earth Negotiations Bulletin*, while I only attended one conference of the parties of the United Nations Framework Convention on Climate Change (UNFCCC). This was a highly iterative process that involved moving back and forth between versions of the analytical framework and our empirical data, and countless attempts to visualize what we were trying to do.

After many months of working through these issues, a breakthrough came when we arrived at a shared definition of "influence," indicating the central importance of concepts in developing an analytical framework (see Chapter 4). Drawing on Knoke (1990, 3), we argued that influence involves the intentional transmission of information to other actors who subsequently alter their behavior compared to what they would have done in the absence of that information (Betsill and Corell 2001). This focus on influence through information fit nicely with the types of data we had collected for our dissertations and thus allowed for systematic comparison between our two cases. This conceptual definition then guided the development of our framework's methodological approach.

This approach called for collecting and analyzing evidence related to two different aspects of influence: (1) the intentional transmission of information (e.g., what did NGOs do?), and (2) changes in behavior in response to that information (e.g., what was the effect of what NGOs did?). We emphasized the value of triangulating many different sources of data (interviews, primary and secondary texts, participant observation) to provide this evidence (see Chapters 8 and 9) and using process tracing and/or counterfactual analysis to analyze the causal relationship between NGO activities and effects (Box 3.1). We felt we had two important contributions: the new analytical framework, which we hoped could be helpful to other scholars interested in questions of NGO influence in multilateral negotiations, and the comparative analysis using the framework. We managed to convince the editor of *Global Environmental Politics* to allow us to submit both papers simultaneously, and ultimately to appear together in a single issue after further refinement through the review process (Betsill and Corell 2001; Corell and Betsill 2001).

As ambitious early-career scholars who enjoyed working together, we decided to continue this work by designing a new project to analyze NGO influence in other multilateral environmental negotiations. We reached out to colleagues who were already working in this area and invited them to apply our framework to their own research. We organized

Box 3.1 Triangulation, process-tracing, and counterfactual analysis

Triangulation refers to the use of multiple types of data drawn from diverse sources using different methodologies: "Triangulation is supposed to support a finding by showing that independent measures of it agree with it or, at least, do not contradict it" (Miles and Huberman 1994, 66). For example, one might draw on interview data, media accounts, and notes from participant observation to see if they tell a common story about what NGOs were trying to achieve in a particular negotiation process. We found triangulation useful for making sure that we were not only looking at instances where NGOs succeeded in influencing negotiation while ignoring failures. Triangulation allows scholars and their readers to have greater confidence in research findings.

Process tracing is "the analysis of evidence on processes, sequences, and conjunctures of events within a case for the purpose of either developing or testing hypotheses about causal mechanisms that might causally explain the case" (Bennett and Checkel 2015, 7). The Betsill–Corell framework suggested process tracing as a way to construct a causal chain connecting NGO activities and communication to responses of other actors. If targeted actors were unaware of an NGO proposal and/or did not consider the proposal as politically viable, then the researcher must question whether influence occurred. Contributors to the *NGO Diplomacy* book (Betsill and Corell 2008) conducted process tracing through detailed narratives organized around propositions specific to the individual cases.

Counterfactual analysis requires the analyst to consider what *might* have happened in the absence of a key variable or process in a chain of events (Biersteker 1995). We encouraged users of the Betsill–Corell framework to consider whether the negotiation process and/or outcome might have been different without the participation of NGOs. While rigorous counterfactual analysis can be quite challenging (George and Bennett 2005), we found counterfactual reasoning to be helpful in ruling out alternative explanations and in strengthening claims of NGO influence when combined with other methods, such as process tracing.

a couple of ISA panels and convened a workshop for authors and commentators. Along the way, we continued to revise the analytical framework based on feedback from our contributors as they applied the framework to their respective cases and related to changes in our own thinking about the central concept of NGO influence. For example, rather than focusing solely on the intentional transmission of information, we expanded our definition of influence as occurring "when one actor intentionally communicates to another so as to alter the latter's behavior from what would have occurred otherwise" (Corell and Betsill 2008, 24). We found that our previous focus on information as the primary tool of NGO influence was too narrow and that "communication" better captured the range of resources deployed by NGOs in their efforts to influence international environmental negotiations (e.g., technical information, claims of legitimacy, or threats to use "naming and shaming" strategies). Despite objections from our editor, we included an explanation of our reasoning for making these changes in our edited volume, *NGO Diplomacy: The Influence of Non-Governmental Organizations in International Environmental Negotiations*, because we thought it was important to be transparent about how the research process really works (Corell and Betsill 2008).

What Was the Relationship Between Your Analytical Framework and Empirical Analysis?

It is important to emphasize that we developed and revised our framework to allow for the use of data that had already been collected. Throughout this process, we were always moving between theory and our existing data, reflecting an "abductive" approach to analysis (Timmermans and Tavory 2012). As discussed earlier, being clear about our theoretical understanding of core concepts was especially important (see Chapter 4). We spent a lot of time reflecting on the relationship between power and influence. Informed by the work of Cox and Jacobson (1973), we came to view power in terms of resources or capabilities and influence as an emergent property of a relationship between actors that is shaped, but not determined, by power. We also were influenced by methodological debates of the time, especially King, Keohane, and Verba's (1994) book on inference in qualitative research. This directed our attention to the "observable" implications of NGO influence in international environmental negotiations that could be identified through analysis of negotiation processes (e.g., agenda-setting and issue framing) and outcomes (e.g., final treaty text). More recent work using ethnographic approaches has made advances in making visible some of the subtler ways in which NGOs and other nonstate actors affect change in multilateral negotiations (e.g., Witter et al. 2015; Chapter 10).

Empirical knowledge informed the development and evolution of the framework throughout the process of doing comparative analysis. In the book project, for example, Steinar Andresen and Tora Skodvin (2008) found that domestic politics figured prominently in their case of the whaling negotiations. This prompted extensive discussions among contributors that involved looking at the role of domestic politics in other cases. In the end, we revised the analytical framework and expanded our understanding of the pathways through which NGO influence occurs. We recognized that the study of agreement-making involves looking beyond what happens in the context of formal treaty negotiation sessions. The book project also revealed that there were limits to how far our framework could "stretch." Elisabeth and I had developed the framework based on our own research on discrete sets of negotiations leading up to a specific treaty. As discussed in the conclusion to *NGO Diplomacy* (Betsill 2008), we learned that it was much more difficult to use the framework to analyze negotiation processes over longer periods of time or to examine the evolution of ideas.

What Did Your Framework Help You to Capture That You Would Not Have Discovered Otherwise?

First, our analytical framework allowed for more robust claims of NGO influence in individual case studies of international environmental negotiations by systematically linking evidence of what NGOs did to their effects on negotiation processes and outcomes. Importantly, our focus on triangulating multiple types of data along with causal analysis through process tracing and counterfactual analysis enabled researchers to identify both NGO successes and failures, overcoming a tendency to focus on successes in the literature. Second, our framework made it possible to arrive at qualitative judgments of different levels of NGO influence that could subsequently be used as the basis for comparative work and exploration of conditioning factors to explain differences across cases. We concluded *NGO Diplomacy* by identifying eight possible conditioning factors that might shape NGO influence in international environmental negotiations and called for more carefully designed empirical research to look at these factors in greater detail (Betsill 2008). We hoped this could provide a starting point for other researchers interested in these types of questions.

What General Advice Do You Have for Scholars New to the Study of Multilateral Environmental Negotiations and Interested in the Study of Agreement-Making Processes?

Today, there are many different analytical frameworks available in the literature to study multilateral environmental negotiations and agreement-making processes. While it can be tempting to apply an existing analytical framework to one's research, doing so requires caution. Recall that analytical frameworks are always developed for a specific purpose, so it is important to reflect on what this means in terms of applying a framework in a new context or answering slightly different questions (see Section 3.3). Elisabeth and I were explicit that our analytical framework was created for the purpose of studying NGO influence in the context of multilateral negotiations and argued that it "should not be read as a definitive statement of NGO influence in all areas of political activity" (Corell and Betsill 2008, 24). We were frustrated when the framework was criticized because it did not help explain NGO influence in other contexts such as domestic politics or intra-NGO relations in global civil society. Scholars wishing to work on such questions may need to adapt the framework to reflect the unique qualities of these arenas and/or develop new frameworks. We were also clear that our approach would be most useful "to scholars coming from a liberal institutionalist or pluralist perspective who wish to assess the influence on NGOs in the development of specific policies" (Betsill 2008, 182). The framework may not be as helpful for scholars starting from a different theoretical vantage point or interested in long-term effects related to the evolution of ideas or changing power relations.

The world of multilateral environmental agreement-making has changed dramatically since the mid-1990s when I began my dissertation research. At that time, these meetings were first and foremost about negotiating the treaty text. Today there is much more going on at multilateral meetings, raising important questions about other ways that NGOs and other nonstate actors may be shaping global environmental governance beyond their influence on treaty-making. Elsewhere, I have written about how NGOs have become global governors in their own right and may be involved in developing alternative governance instruments through side events and other gatherings organized in parallel to the formal treaty negotiations (Bernstein et al. 2010; Betsill 2015; Chapter 7). There is a need to examine how these activities in the transnational political sphere interact with multilateral governance institutions (Betsill et al. 2015), which requires a more sophisticated and nuanced theoretical understanding of "power" and "influence" than what we originally proposed in our analytical framework. NGOs that are still focused on formal treaty negotiations have more tools and strategies at their disposal. Similarly, scholars can incorporate data on social media content and conduct social network analysis to reveal the less visible ways in which NGOs operate and shape treaty-making processes and outcomes.

On the question of whether one needs to attend negotiations in person, my answer is "it depends." I was only able to attend one negotiating session for my dissertation research, but I found this to be enormously helpful in understanding the dynamics of the process and the informal ways in which negotiations take place. I also was able to identify key informants for subsequent interviews, wherein I asked them to provide detailed information on what happened at sessions that I was unable to attend (see Chapter 9). As it is not always feasible to attend negotiations in person due to timing or resource constraints, it is important to ask "What am I missing by not being there?" and to look for ways to draw on other data sources to fill in gaps. While I relied heavily on interviews, media sources, the *Earth Negotiations Bulletin*, and negotiation documents (see Chapter 8), today one could also look to social media feeds and even recordings of negotiations and side events available on treaty secretariat websites (see Chapter 6). I would strongly encourage reaching out to other scholars who have experience with doing research in and on these spaces. They can provide feedback on the viability of your research questions and/or the likelihood that you can collect the data you need to answer those questions. They also can offer insight on the necessity of attending negotiations in person. If you are able to attend a meeting, they can provide orientation on the physical layout of the venues, norms about interacting and engaging with participants, and ways to develop networks with other researchers (see Chapter 6).

3.3 Naghmeh's Reflections

My reflections focus on how my PhD thesis was inspired and informed by the work of Michele Betsill and Elisabeth Corell and how their analytical framework served as a stepping-stone to develop one about governance profiles and the ways in which governance profiles relate to nonstate actor agency. The concept of governance profiles was developed in one of the first papers of my thesis, which consisted of a set of articles on the roles of nonstate actors in climate governance (Nasiritousi 2016). Governance profiles serve as an indication of nonstate actors' agency across governance activities. It refers to the combination of governance activities that a category of nonstate actors has gained recognition for (Nasiritousi et al. 2016). This idea grew out of the observation that different types of nonstate actors often play different roles and have competitive advantages in certain governance activities. It also builds on literature that shows that recognition by other actors is an important indication of agency (Dellas et al. 2011). By developing the concept of governance profiles and an analytical framework to guide this research, the paper sought to contribute to the literature on nonstate actors' agency and unpack some of the key categories of nonstate actors to show variations in governance activities across groups of nonstate actors.

In writing my thesis, I decided to focus not on the influence but rather on the roles of nonstate actors in global climate governance. This interest in the roles of nonstate actors had developed during an internship with ICLEI – Local Governments for Sustainability. During my work there, I observed how such an NGO is involved in many different processes of governing toward sustainability at many levels. In other words, while they attend multilateral negotiations and seek to influence the negotiation outcome, their work spans many other types of governance activities that would be difficult to understand if only focusing on their influence at multilateral negotiations. In addition, while attending multilateral negotiations, nonstate actors can also use their participation to advance their work outside the intergovernmental arena even if they do not influence the negotiation outcome. Thus, similar to the agreement-making framework that is broader than a focus on direct influence, my dissertation sought to capture the many roles that different types of nonstate actors can play in climate change governance.

Why Did You Choose to Develop an Analytical Framework Based on Betsill and Corell's Work?

My PhD thesis (Nasiritousi 2016) was very much inspired by Michele Betsill and Elisabeth Corell's book *NGO Diplomacy: The Influence of Nongovernmental Organizations in International Environmental Negotiations* (Betsill and Corell 2008). I was interested in finding out more about the roles of nonstate actors in global climate change governance, and in particular how different types of nonstate actors can play different roles. As the book itself highlights, influencing intergovernmental negotiations is a very important role that nonstate actors can play, but it's far from the only one. By the time I started my PhD, I had been fortunate to participate in two UNFCCC COPs as an observer, and it fascinated me how many different types of nonstate actors there were at these conferences. By observing their activities and listening to their statements, it became clear that these actors were there for different reasons, and not all had a primary aim of influencing the texts produced by negotiators. I therefore turned to the literature to see how these different roles of nonstate actors were explained. What I found was mainly case studies and piecemeal evidence that different nonstate actors fulfill different roles in global governance. I decided to piece this literature together into an analytical framework that allowed for a more systematic comparison of the roles of various nonstate actors in global climate change governance.

How Did You Go About Developing Your Analytical Framework?

I read the works of Michele Betsill and Elisabeth Corell thoroughly and started thinking about the advantages and disadvantages of their approach. It was clear that they had made a significant contribution to the literature through their analytical framework, as well as through their novel methodological and empirical contributions. This is why I decided to follow their framework, though I felt that the scope of their operationalization of influence, which focused on direct influence among a set of actors, could be further elaborated and widened. I wanted to develop a broader framework that could help us understand the different roles of nonstate actors outside the formal negotiations.

To that end, I went through the previous literature to learn more about different approaches to characterizing nonstate actors and how they act in international politics more broadly. What I found was a lack of systematic studies on the roles of different nonstate actors. While differences in the nonstate actor category were often acknowledged in the literature (not least in Betsill and Corell's work), I found no comparative work to understand how different types of nonstate actors could be seen in global governance. To develop my framework, therefore, I went through different strands of literature – e.g. on negotiations, policy cycles, agency (i.e., Albin 1999; Dellas et al. 2011; Keck and Sikkink 1999), to draw up a framework that highlighted differences in types of nonstate actors and their agency across different roles played in global governance. Thus, by combining these different strands of literature, and with the help of my PhD supervisors, Björn-Ola Linnér and Mattias Hjerpe, we came up with the concept of "governance profiles" to facilitate analysis of how agency differs across nonstate actor categories.

Our analytical framework outlined why different types of nonstate actors may have a comparative advantage across the policy spectrum, how this advantage may be recognized by others, and how this can shape their governance profiles and, ultimately, their agency. The development of this framework was not a straightforward process; rather, it took several turns before the different parts came together. The initial framework required refinement and clarification before it was accepted by reviewers for publication. An important step in the research process is thus to gain critical feedback from colleagues (either at workshops/conferences or through a review process) in order to improve and strengthen the framework.

What Was the Relationship Between Your Analytical Framework and Empirical Analysis?

Our framework was developed to be able to understand differences in agency across nonstate actor groups. To this end, we focused on some of the major constituency groups involved in global climate change governance: business and industry groups, research organizations, environmental NGOs, municipalities and local authorities, trade unions, intergovernmental organizations, and Indigenous Peoples' organizations. Based on previous literature on agency, we noted that agency is a relational concept that builds on perceptions (Dellas et al. 2011). In other words, while different types of nonstate actors have various sources of power, their agency ultimately hinges on gaining recognition by other actors. Inspired by the work of Michele Betsill, Elisabeth Corell, and others, we settled on a mixed-methods approach, whereby we studied both self-perceptions through submitted documents as well as the perceptions of others on particular groups of nonstate actors through questionnaires (Box 3.2). Thus, the question of what empirical material to use was answered with the help of the analytical framework, since it placed focus on self-perceptions as well as recognition by other relevant audiences. Through the *International Negotiations Survey*, a survey distributed yearly by Linköping University researchers at UNFCCC COPs, we gathered the perceptions of a large set of actors involved in global climate change governance. This approach allowed us to compare how self-perceptions differed from perceptions held by other actors.

Moreover, while previous research had focused on the differences between state and nonstate actors, we were able to offer a comparative picture across a cross-section of nonstate actors. While acknowledging the heterogeneity of organizations within the constituency groups, our results nevertheless found distinct governance profiles for each group. For example, we found that environmental NGOs were perceived as particularly strong in raising awareness; business NGOs in influencing decisions; research NGOs in providing expertise, evaluating consequences, and proposing solutions; local governments in taking action, particularly in the field of climate adaptation; intergovernmental organizations in influencing the agenda; and Indigenous Peoples' organizations in representing marginalized voices. The governance profiles also indicate where recognition is low and where agency may not be strong. Except for environmental NGOs, which were found to have a relatively strong governance profile in most activity categories, the results show that most governance profiles show strength in roles associated with either (1) influence and action, (2) ideas and expertise, or (3) awareness-raising and representation, but not all three combined (Nasiritousi et al. 2016).

Box 3.2 Questionnaires

Questionnaires are a useful research method if you need to obtain answers from a large set of respondents. Questionnaires are valuable for obtaining structured information about peoples' knowledge, beliefs, attitudes, and opinions (Bryman 2016; Creswell and Creswell 2017; Oppenheim 2000). It is possible to obtain information from a broad set of respondents who can answer questions either online or in paper form. However, questionnaire design is important and, in the context of studying international negotiations, it is vital to think about who your respondents are.

As outlined in the methods chapter of my dissertation (Nasiritousi 2016), the International Negotiations Survey administered by Linköping University exists in two versions: one that follows a quota sampling approach in the conference venue, and a second that is distributed to participants at selected side events during the UNFCCC COPs. This means that the former is better at capturing the views of the average COP participant (i.e., including COP participants who do not attend side events) while the latter better captures the views of the average side-event participant. Fewer negotiators, particularly from the developed world, attend side events, meaning that this sample underrepresents negotiators compared to the COP sample and over-represents observers. Nevertheless, the two questionnaires produce similar answers to the same question, and because our studies were more interested in the differences between actor types than absolute figures, the questionnaires provide a sound basis for such analysis. The survey has the advantage of obtaining many responses each year (around 400 for each questionnaire) and produces more reliable results than other studies that send out the questionnaire via email lists since the on-site collection of questionnaires ensures that we have an informed view of who the respondents are and produces a higher response rate. The International Negotiations Survey is paper based, meaning that a group of researchers hand out questionnaires (and pens) to COP participants and collect the questionnaires on site. While it is time-consuming to enter the collected data into a database after a COP, the paper-based format is generally appreciated by respondents as it is easy and convenient to fill out.

The questions were designed based on readings of the academic literature on nonstate actors and tailored to the specific research questions of the thesis. The same survey questions were repeated over at least two years to reduce sampling biases resulting from the location of the conference, as participation (particularly by nonstate actors) can differ depending on the region where the conference is held. It is thus important to keep in mind some of the drawbacks of using questionnaires as the sole research method. Because of its short format and need to keep questions simple so as to be understood by people from different backgrounds, the questionnaire cannot provide in-depth answers and there is a risk that questions may be misinterpreted by some. Moreover, it is less effective in capturing the views of constituencies with few representatives or where language barriers prevent participation in the questionnaire; in these cases, targeted interviews might be a better option. Therefore, qualitative methods can be useful to complement the survey data.

What Did Your Framework Help You to Capture That You Would Not Have Discovered or Identified Otherwise?

The perceptions of the roles of nonstate actors in our study indicate the level of recognized authority across governance activities for different nonstate actor groups. The framework helped us show that certain activities are strongly associated with one particular nonstate actor category, but that no single category of nonstate actor is strong across all governance activities. It thereby provided us with a tool to map the different roles of nonstate actors in climate change governance, which contributes to a better understanding of patterns of cooperation and competition over policy space. Overall, the findings suggest that power asymmetries among nonstate actors are not only based on access to financial resources or structural inequalities at the organizational level, as often highlighted in previous literature, but may also be dependent on different governance profiles (Nasiritousi et al. 2016). Since this study was published, other researchers have adopted the framework and applied it in different ways (e.g., Thew 2018) – something which is great to see, and which indicates the usefulness of the framework.

Moreover, we conducted our questionnaire study not only at UNFCCC COPs but also at the Rio+20 conference on sustainable development to examine whether the governance profiles differed much when comparing actors in climate change governance to broader sustainable development governance. Interestingly, the governance profiles were remarkably robust. Of course, this could be because both fields (climate change and sustainable development) involve similar actors with similar roles, but it is still telling that the governance profiles fit even in a different governance arena (Nasiritousi 2019). The framework itself could certainly be developed and improved further, but I leave that to a new generation of researchers!

Do You Have Any General Advice to Scholars New to the Study of Multilateral Environmental Negotiations and Interested in the Study of Agreement-Making Processes?

If possible, make sure that you observe at least one of the negotiations that you are interested in on site in order to get a feel for the actors and processes. While there are great descriptions of various negotiations in previous literature, and through *Earth Negotiations Bulletin* (see Chapter 8) and mass-media and social-media reports, attending in person is a valuable experience and provides an updated picture of where the dynamic negotiations stand. By attending the negotiations, it is possible to obtain insights into the networks of actors propagating different viewpoints (Chapter 12), and to observe what happens outside the negotiations, such as in corridors or restaurants where more informal discussions often take place. Negotiations under the COP are also great venues for networking, both with fellow researchers but also with other stakeholders. Finally, side events are helpful to attend in order to learn more about different actors and topics (see Chapter 7).

In terms of being a site for empirical work on agreement-making, the decision to attend in person or virtually may depend not only on resources but also on the method used. The type of paper-based questionnaires that were described in Box 3.2 are ideal for on-site fieldwork at large multilateral negotiations. However, if you conduct in-depth interviews as part of your research, intersessionals or online interviews are recommended over COPs due to the availability of respondents (see Chapter 8). For scholars who do not have the option to attend negotiations, following the conference website and watching recordings of the plenary sessions is recommended. In addition, by signing on to researchers' networks in connection with the negotiations (e.g., the research and independent nongovernmental organizations (RINGO) network of the UNFCCC), scholars can gain access to notes and presentations from other researchers who are present on site. Finally, the list of participants can be a useful source to consult when considering whom to interview.

3.4 Conclusion

Developing and working with analytical frameworks is an exciting part of the research process. This is where you can think creatively about how you can contribute to previous literature by building on existing scholarship and addressing research gaps. It requires deep thinking about key concepts (see Chapter 4) and their relationships in order to guide your empirical analysis. While starting off with literature and theories, you also need to think about the larger research design questions for how to apply your framework. Sometimes, as described in Michele's reflections (Section 3.2), you will already have empirical material to apply it to. Other times, as described in Naghmeh's reflections (Section 3.3), you will need to develop an approach to capture the data that your analytical framework requires. In either case, the development of the analytical framework will usually be an iterative process wherein the framework will be refined over the course of the research. Inspiration can often come from existing analytical frameworks, but it is important to revise or develop them when applied to new cases or slightly different questions. Your framework can also be determined by whether you are working alone or working with others in a collaborative process where you have to negotiate the boundaries for making comparisons. It is important for the researcher to think about the advantages and disadvantages of particular analytical frameworks as they all produce trade-offs in terms of what is included in the analysis and what is left out. Your framework will determine how concepts and relationships are defined, ordered, and operationalized. By thinking of analytical frameworks as an organizing tool for the rest of the research process, it becomes clear that spending some time on the analytical framework can facilitate later parts of the research process as it helps guide the work and assists in bringing out the research findings' contributions to previous literature.

Further Reading

1. Powner, L. C. (2015). *Empirical Research and Writing: A Political Science Student's Practical Guide*. Los Angeles: Sage/CQ Press.

This book provides a concrete guide to planning, conducting, and writing up empirical social science research.

2. Timmermans, S., and Tavory, I. (2012). Theory construction in qualitative research: From grounded theory to abductive analysis. *Sociological Theory*, 30(3), 167–186.

This article outlines a pragmatic approach to moving between theory and empirical data to generate conceptual innovation in social science research.

3. Yin, R. K. (2015).*Qualitative Research from Start to Finish*. New York: Guilford Publications.

This book provides an excellent overview of the various choices that scholars make in the practice of conducting qualitative research, including the question of whether and how to integrate theoretical concepts into the research design.

References

Albin, C. (1999). Can NGOs enhance effectiveness of international negotiation? *International Negotiation*, 4(3), 371–387.

Andresen, S. and Skodvin, T. (2008). Non-state influence in the International Whaling Commission, 1970 to 2006. In M. Betsill and E. Corell, eds., *NGO Diplomacy: The Influence of Nongovernmental Organizations in International Environmental Negotiations*. Cambridge, MA: The MIT Press, pp. 119–148.

Bennett, A. and Checkel, J. T. (2015). Process tracing: From philosophical roots to best practice. In A. Bennett and J. T. Checkel, eds., *Process Tracing: From Metaphor to Analytical Tool*. Cambridge: Cambridge University Press, pp. 3–37.

Bernstein, S., Betsill, M. M., Hoffmann, M. J. and Paterson, M. (2010). A tale of two Copenhagens: Carbon markets and climate governance. *Millennium: Journal of International Studies*, 39(1), 161–173.

Betsill, M. M. (2008). Reflections on the analytical framework and NGO diplomacy. In M. Betsill and E. Corell, eds., *NGO Diplomacy: The Influence of Nongovernmental Organizations in International Environmental Negotiations*. Cambridge, MA: The MIT Press, pp. 177–206.

Betsill, M. M. (2015). NGOs. In K. Bäckstrand and E. Lövbrand, eds., *Research Handbook on Climate Governance*. Cheltenham: EE Elgar, pp. 251–261.

Betsill, M. M. and Corell, E. (2001). NGO influence in international environmental negotiations: A framework for analysis, *Global Environmental Politics,* 1(1), 65–85.

Betsill, M. M. and Corell, E., eds. (2008). *NGO Diplomacy: The Influence of Nongovernmental Organizations in International Environmental Negotiations*. Cambridge, MA: The MIT Press.

Betsill, M. M., Dubash, N., Paterson, M. et al. (2015). Building productive linkages between the UNFCCC and the broader global climate governance landscape. *Global Environmental Politics*, 15(2), 1–10.

Biersteker, T. J. (1995). Constructing historical counterfactuals to assess the consequences of international regimes. In V. Rittberger, ed., *Regime Theory and International Relations*. Oxford: Clarendon Press, pp. 315–338.

Bryman, A. (2016). *Social Research Methods*, 5th ed. Oxford: Oxford University Press.

Corell, E. and Betsill, M. M. (2001). A comparative look at NGO influence in international environmental negotiations: Desertification and climate change. *Global Environmental Politics,* 1(1),86–107.

Corell, E. and Betsill, M. M. (2008). Analytical framework: Assessing the influence of NGO diplomats. In M. Betsill and E. Corell, eds., *NGO Diplomacy: The Influence of Nongovernmental Organizations in International Environmental Negotiations*. Cambridge, MA: The MIT Press, pp. 19–42.

Cox, R. and Jacobson, H. K. (1973). The framework for inquiry. In R. Cox and H. Jacobson, eds., *The Anatomy of Influence: Decision Making in International Organization*. New Haven, CT: Yale University Press, pp. 1–36.

Creswell, J. W. and Creswell, J. D. (2017). *Research Design: Qualitative, Quantitative, and Mixed Methods Approaches*, 5th ed. Thousand Oaks, CA: SAGE Publications, Inc.

Dellas, E., Pattberg, P. and Betsill, M. (2011). Agency in earth system governance: Refining a research agenda. *International Environmental Agreements*, 11(1), 85–98.

George, A. L. and Bennett, A. (2005). *Case Studies and Theory Development in the Social Sciences*. Cambridge: Cambridge University Press.

Keck, M. and Sikkink, K. (1999). Transnational advocacy networks in international and regional politics. *International Social Science Journal*, 51(159), 89–101.

Keohane, R. O. and Nye, J. S. (1972). *Transnational Relations and World Politics*. Cambridge, MA: Harvard University Press.

King, G. , Keohane, R. O. and Verba, S. (1994). *Designing Social Inquiry*. New Haven, CT: Princeton University Press.

Knoke, D. (1990). *Political Networks: The Structural Perspective*. New York: Cambridge University Press.

Miles, M. B. and Huberman, A. M. (1994). *Qualitative Data Analysis*, 2nd ed. Thousand Oaks, CA: SAGE.

Nasiritousi, N. (2016). *Shapers, Brokers and Doers: The Dynamic Roles of Non-State Actors in Global Climate Change Governance* (published PhD dissertation, Linköping University Electronic Press).

Nasiritousi, N. (2019). NGOs and the environment. In T. Davies, ed., *Routledge Handbook of NGOs and International Relations*. London: Routledge, pp. 329–342.

Nasiritousi, N., Hjerpe, M. and Linnér, B.O. (2016). The roles of non-state actors in climate change governance: understanding agency through governance profiles. *International Environmental Agreements*, 16, 109–126.

Oppenheim, A. N. (2000). *Questionnaire Design, Interviewing and Attitude Measurement*, 2nd ed. London: Continuum International Publishing Group Ltd.

Thew, H. (2018). Youth participation and agency in the United Nations Framework Convention on Climate Change. *International Environmental Agreements*, 18, 369–389.

Witter, R., Marion Suiseeya, K. R., Gruby, R. L. et al. (2015). Moments of influence in global environmental governance. *Environmental Politics*, 24(6), 894–912.

4

Concepts

Selecting, Applying and Innovating Concepts

HANNAH HUGHES AND ALICE B. M. VADROT

4.1 Introduction

In this chapter, we want to unpack the use of concepts. One of the ways that we study the social world is through engaging with social theory and theorists. Frequently, these scholars have become popularized in the discipline for their original approach and insights into how and why social actors function as they do and the forms of power, control and domination that accepted institutions and cultural practices produce. Pierre Bourdieu and Michel Foucault are two scholars whose work has illuminated historical patterns of power asymmetry and their effects on the present, and they have provided a range of concepts that have been taken up by diverse forms of scholarship, such as discourse, biopolitics and governmentality (Foucault), and habitus, capital and fields (Bourdieu). Many of their concepts have been applied to issues within environmental politics to shed light on how social asymmetries persist and are remade through global interactions designed to address environmental degradation (Death 2010; Epstein 2008; Hughes 2015; Luke 1995; Oels 2005; Okereke et al. 2009; Pettenger 2007; Vadrot 2014a). The aim of this chapter is to explore the processes of identifying, applying and adapting concepts to the study of global environmental agreement-making.

Sites of global environmental negotiations are characterized by diverging interests, power asymmetries and struggles over the extent to which these imprint on the final text and the environmental actions the text creates. If we start by visualizing negotiations between state parties it quickly becomes apparent that the difference in resources available to identify and represent national interests is stark. The most well-resourced countries, with clearly defined interests in the issue area, arrive at the annual conference of the parties (COP) or other intergovernmental meeting sites with large, well-prepared delegations to cover the parallel sessions, which includes their own legal and other relevant technical expertise. The least resourced parties have much smaller delegations (perhaps only one or two state negotiators), often cover multiple environmental conventions and may rely on nongovernmental and secretariat legal and technical advice and support. The level of resources available to a state during an environmental negotiation depends in large part on the economic wealth of the state and, relatedly, their position in world order, which in turn has been shaped by historical processes of colonization and human and environmental exploitation (Gilio-Whitaker 2019; Yusoff 2018). Thinking in these terms makes apparent why we need critical analytical tools that can help us to connect the present with the past, economic resources to negotiating capacity, and state interests and investment in an issue area to use and degradation of the environment.

However, thinking in terms of agreement-making also means that, as researchers, we do not limit ourselves, conceptually or analytically, to state actors and conventional sites of negotiation. The nongovernmental organization and secretariat actors supporting smaller state delegations may also need to be considered as shaping the object of study. As such, the research site itself may need to be expanded or shifted to the corridors, coffee carts, side events and booths where the conversations between these actors are taking place (see Chapter 7), and potentially beyond the negotiation site to the offices and buildings of these actors. This makes clear why concepts are needed to guide the researcher in identifying actors that are relevant to the question or problem and to aid in delineating the sites of field research, as Valeria Tolis discusses in relation to Lacanian concepts (see Reflection Box 4.1).

It is vital to confront from the outset that theory selection has effects. In this chapter, we explore concepts and analytical approaches developed by three very influential white, French men. The need to open up the study of international relations (IR) and global environmental politics to more diverse "global" perspectives and from starting points originating from different lifeworlds is increasingly recognized (Acharya 2016; Anderl and Witt 2020; Inoue 2018; Sharma 2021). In Chapter 5, Marcela explores indigenizing methodologies and the ethics for engaging with diverse actors, sites and processes of agreement-making. However, the approaches discussed in this chapter are a product of our institutional and disciplinary encounters – the interests of those that taught us and the influence of scholars we encountered. We attempt to lay these bare and, as part of our interrogation of concepts, delve into their influence on our thinking, how we have attempted to engage and deploy these critically, and how and when to recognize their limits so that we can move beyond them, which may require embracing new epistemological starting points. By doing this, we acknowledge that these theories and concepts have been "constitutive of our worlds" and the knowledge we have built on it (Inoue 2018, 27). Through the "self-reflection and dialogue" of this chapter we hope that we situate its products in time and space (Inoue 2018, 27), although we acknowledge this is only the first step in revealing what is hidden by the concepts we have used to look into other worlds.

We initiate our exploration of concepts with the reading process, reflecting how we draw out and identify relevant concepts, how we start to think through and problematize these and how they inform the construction, analysis and write up of research. Exploring how we have identified and applied concepts in our own research allows us to demonstrate that this is often a messy process, but useful concepts can guide us through the back and forth between theory and empirics and help us to make sense of the often complex and confusing realm of global environmental agreement-making. We also discuss how to recognize the limits of a concept's capacity to explain our observations, and from this point, how we develop new concepts to explain and deepen our understanding of political processes conducted in the name of the environment.

4.2 Which Theorist? Which Concept?

Some theorists become popular and have a significant impact across disciplines, and Michel Foucault is perhaps the most notable in this regard. His conception of governmentality, for example, has had notable influence on the study of environmental governance (Bäckstrand and Lövbrand 2006; Death 2010; Lövbrand, Stipple and Wiman 2009; Methmann 2013; Rutherford 2007; Stripple and Bulkeley 2013). In this chapter however, we focus on Foucault's conception of discourse. In Foucault's understanding, a discourse represents a historically contingent social structure. This structure produces knowledge and meaning based on practices that form the objects spoken about (Foucault 1969). Staying within a discourse implies being "in the truth" – that is, talking about an object in a specific way and in line with the rules of a specific (scientific) discipline and logic (Foucault 1971, 36). One of these logics is the efficiency logic of the political economy, the latter being inherent to political rationality and the concept of "governmentality." Foucauldian-inspired studies of discourse shifted epistemological understanding toward the social construction of environmental problems and provided inspiration for new approaches to identify the social structures shaping how issues are known and acted upon. Scholars influenced by Foucault and borrowing and adapting his notion of discourse have revealed that issues such as climate change, acid rain, ozone depletion and biodiversity loss are not simply discovered by science and acted on by politics; they undergo a process of social construction, with prevailing actors, institutions and knowledges influencing the outcome (Hajer 1997; Litfin 1994; Pettenger 2007; Vadrot 2014a). The work of Karen Litfin and Maarten Hajer made significant contributions to this. Both scholars developed their own Foucauldian-informed discursive frameworks and applied them to different issue areas: the emergence of ozone depletion (Litfin 1994) and acid rain (Hajer 1997). Reviewing these enables us to explore how each author has taken up Foucault's conception of discourse differently and designed analytical frameworks that fit their specific research problem.

Karen Litfin (1994) developed a discursive approach to explore the role of scientists and scientific knowledge in treaty-making processes and to identify other actors and influences on the framing of ozone depletion. Litfin describes the concept of discourse as a set of linguistic practices and rhetorical strategies embedded in a network of social relations (Liftin 1994, 3). Through her empirical research into the actors shaping ozone discourses, Litfin revealed how knowledge of ozone depletion was not solely a source of power for the scientists: "once produced, knowledge becomes something of a collective good, available to all who want to incorporate it into their discursive strategies" (Litfin 1994, 37). The analytical approach that Litfin developed, alongside in-depth empirical study, revealed that discursive power does not necessarily lie with those who produce knowledge; it can also empower those who *make use* of it: interpreting and manipulating it in their frame of the problem. From this observation, Litfin was able to develop her own conceptual innovation by identifying a new set of actors, which she termed *knowledge brokers*. Knowledge brokers acted as intermediaries between the scientists producing knowledge and the policy-makers consuming it and were influential in shaping the discourse on ozone depletion and the resulting Montreal Protocol.

Also informed by Michel Foucault, Marten Hajer (1997) developed a different conception of discourse in his research on how emergent environmental discourses constrain political action and enable social change. Hajer conceived of politics as a struggle for discursive hegemony, whereby actors try to convince others of their definition of reality (Hajer 1997, 59). He illuminates this struggle by developing an analytical framework in which discourse is defined as "a specific ensemble of ideas, concepts, and categorizations that are produced, reproduced, and transformed in a particular set of practices and through which meaning is given to social and physical reality" (Hajer 1997, 44). In Hajer's approach, the institutional context is as important as language because it "codetermines what can be said meaningfully" (Hajer 1997, 2). Through this discursive approach, Hajer explores how the conceptualization of environmental problems has changed since environmental degradation first emerged on the international political agenda in the 1970s. At this time, pollution was not considered a structural problem, but something that could be controlled and contained through quality control targets and abatement strategies (Hajer 1997, 25). Hajer provides a genealogy of environmental discourses that came to challenge this way of thinking and describes how different strands of environmental discourses converged with the institutional practices of international policy-forming organizations, such as the OECD and UN Environment Programme (UNEP). According to Hajer, the historical roots of the dominant ecological modernization discourse lie in this convergence between discursive and institutional forces, which produced a discourse that made continued development compatible with environmental care (Hajer 1997, 101–102).

While Litfin and Hajer were both informed by the work of Michel Foucault, they conceptualized discourse differently and developed analytical approaches tailored to their distinct research puzzles. Valeria Tolis provides another illustration of this in her reflection box on how she used a Lacanian theory of discourse to study the EU's climate action (see Reflection Box 4.1). These examples illustrate how we can draw inspiration, understanding and conceptual tools from the theorists that we engage with, while not necessarily remaining bound by them. Theorists have their own motivations and concerns which their conceptual apparatus is shaped by and for, and we need to do the same when adapting it to our problematic. Litfin and Hajer's conceptual innovations demonstrate that this is not a static process, but one where we tailor the approach to our research question and, when this leads to new insights and observations that our concepts do not explain, we further adapt concepts and/or develop new concepts. But how do we do this?

Concepts are embedded in particular ontologies and epistemologies, which are connected in a way that makes it difficult to extract or disentangle single elements and which are sometimes overwhelming to apply in their entirety. How do we know which concepts are most relevant to our research? Can we extract a single concept or do we need to apply all of an author's thinking? In the following two sections, Hannah explores these questions in her research on the IPCC, which was informed by the sociological thinking and conceptual apparatus of Pierre Bourdieu. Hannah attempted to comprehensively apply several of Bourdieu's concepts to identify who had power within the organization and what constituted it. However, in other instances, where strong criticism of a particular theorist or concept exists, where we need to overcome gaps in the theory or where a concept needs to be tailored to our research problem, we may combine the work of different scholars. In Section 4.4, Alice explores how she developed her conceptual framework of "epistemic selectivities" in order to go beyond Foucault and explore how discourses and institutions change.

Reflection Box 4.1 The EU's climate change mitigation action: The social link unfolded

By Valeria Tolis

The aim of my PhD was to reflect on *how* the EU's climate mitigation action is constituted and on the possibility of change in relation to scientifically informed climate warnings.

To study this I made use of Jacques Lacan's theory of discourse, wherein discourse is the social link – an overarching sociolinguistic structure that allows the speaking beings to establish and maintain their intersubjective societal relations (Lacan 2007; Lacan et al. 1998). This theory of discourse retains a more active role of the subject: the subject presupposes this structure and inevitably resorts to language to create sense, but the speaking activity creates an excess of meaning, perceived as a loss in the enunciation, as the sociolinguistic order can never fully complete the subject (Stavrakakis 1999). Conclusive and full meaning is then constantly deferred and – by virtue of this dual mechanism – fractures emerge in the discourse that leave room for a paradigm shift.

A Lacanian perspective made me appreciate the field as the sites where I can observe this dialectical relationship between discourse and subject. The EU's climate action manifests itself as a multi-institution, multistakeholder and multilevel process which includes how EU officials work in their offices and interact with actors inside and outside the European headquarters. Hence, any document produced, as well as the inter-departmental or interinstitutional negotiations that inform these policy documents, can be conceptualized as societal climate relations that are made possible by an overarching sociolinguistic structure and are presupposed as "what needs to be done" to organize and maintain given climate policies. Likewise, the EU representatives, their stakeholders or even the citizens as Lacanian subjects are the speaking beings that, in the pursuit of given climate objectives, are caught in a signifying machine determining the climate relations available to them along with the excess of meaning thereby produced – which a Lacanian-inspired discourse analysis helps to identify and explain.

The EU climate policymaking at the European headquarters intertwines with UNFCCC climate governance, where the EU is both a negotiator and is presented in ad hoc side events. Hence, finding suitable sites of observation at the start of my fieldwork activity was not a straightforward process. When I attended COP23, my aim was to "follow the EU" and learn how to navigate the series of accessible official negotiations, contact groups, plenaries and informal consultations. However, as the Paris Agreement leaves parties to determine their decarbonization policies, I soon realized that the UNFCCC – despite being an instance of the Lacanian social link unfolding – was not an ideal site for understanding the EU's specific climate policies and strategies. As a result, I decided to extend my observations to the EU headquarters in Brussels so I could do a qualitative investigation of the EU's mitigation strategy taking shape.

When I arrived, I found myself in the middle of an important policymaking process: the finalization of the 2030 Clean Energy Package and the preparatory work of the 2050 long-term decarbonization strategy (COM(2018)773 final), which later became the EU Green Deal (COM (2019) 640 final). The policy tools of *energy efficiency*, *renewables*, and *the circular economy* became the case studies of my project. These concepts played a key role in both the 2030 Clean Energy Package and the 2050 long-term strategy and allowed me to identify the role that desire plays in Lacan's theory. As apparently desirable solutions, these tools are potential change carriers, as no one would argue against equipment and devices that save energy, use energy generated from renewable sources, or are recycled and remanufactured. Hence, the policy tools established by these strategies provided me with the empirical data to answer my research question about status quo and change. I concluded that except for a few potentially disruptive elements that leave room for a true rupture and possible change, the EU's current climate mitigation action appears more as a fictitious change than as a real transition.

4.3 Hannah Hughes: Learning to Analyze Power with Pierre Bourdieu

I was observing a plenary of the Intergovernmental Panel on Climate Change (IPCC). A developing country delegate stood up and made his intervention, the room fell silent, he sat back down and his words were lost as the proceedings carried on as if nothing had been said. This moment stuck with me, but at the time I did not know how to explain its significance. This is where the concepts we apply and the analytical approach that we develop from these can help us. The right concepts aid with problematizing research interest, guide how we build and design a project to study this, and then support analysis and the account developed to bring new insights to the study of global environmental politics. In this section, I aim to unpack this process by drawing on my experience of learning with Pierre Bourdieu.

Before I started the PhD, I had been studying the UK government's role in constructing climate change as an international issue through the usage of security. By the end of the master's dissertation, I realized that the United Kingdom was only one actor in a multisited, multilevel struggle to define and control the implications of climate change. I wanted to explore this global struggle and to identify who ultimately had the power to determine the meaning of this issue and what constituted this power. The IPCC seemed an ideal site to address this question because of its status as the intergovernmental body responsible for producing up-to-date knowledge of climate change to inform the global response. When I arrived at the International Politics department at Aberystwyth University in 2008, I was looking forward to starting the PhD but I had no idea *how* I was going to conduct this research.

It was in a research seminar that I first learned of Pierre Bourdieu's sociology. At the time, Bourdieu was rising in popularity in IR and several scholars in the department were working with his concepts (Jackson 2008; Williams 2007). The seminar introduced the notion of habitus, and I was immediately struck by its fit with what I called "the social veil" – the way myself and others change to fit the social setting. In Bourdieu, I saw the possibility of learning things that I was interested in, as well as a way to practically study the IPCC, with the added bonus that he was becoming a "fashionable" scholar.

I was encouraged by my supervisor to read as much Bourdieu as possible. At first, I struggled with how deeply intertwined Bourdieu's analytical tools were with his research objects, such as the university (Bourdieu 1988), education system (Bourdieu and Passeron 1977) and French society (Bourdieu 1986). I felt unsure of how to disentangle individual concepts from the disciplinary context and "apply" them to a study of the IPCC. I was also nervous about writing these ideas in my own words. In this early reading stage, two bodies of literature were invaluable. The first was reflective accounts coauthored by Bourdieu, sometimes in interview style, wherein he described his work in a way that was easier to apply (Bourdieu and Wacquant 1992; Wacquant 1989). The second was the work of other IR scholars who had already used key Bourdieu concepts (e.g., Leander 2002, 2005; Huysmans 2002; Jackson 2008; Williams 2007).

Many IR scholars are selective in their usage of Bourdieu, applying one or two concepts. However, Bourdieu's concepts of habitus, interest, field, capital and symbolic power appeared so interrelated that I did not know how to disaggregate them or to choose which would be most appropriate. The concepts also seemed inseparable from Bourdieu's theory of the social world and the scholarly ethos of reflexivity. I thus found myself attempting to work with all of it, albeit at different moments in the research process and in an iterative manner. In order to illustrate how this worked in practice, it is easiest to describe how and when I applied different concepts to illustrate how each informed my methodology.

4.3.1 Constructing the IPCC As an Object of Research

Bourdieu's concepts of field and interest were initially the most useful in helping to construct the IPCC as an object of study. Bourdieu describes field as a particular "space of social forces and struggles" generated by the objects of interest that motivate action within that field (Bourdieu and Wacquant 1992, 102). Thinking of field and interest in their simplest terms helped to situate the IPCC in the field of climate politics and made me attentive to how political and scientific interests in climate change shape the organization (Hughes 2015). Interest and field were also useful for thinking about the actors that participate in the IPCC: what motivated their participation and how participation shaped them and their knowledge production. This influenced my interview questions, which aimed to identify what motivated participation and the social, scientific and political rewards – or capital – earned through this. Field also helped to situate actors in the professional sphere that qualified them to participate (science, diplomacy, policymaking, international organization), and to consider how these fields of action shaped IPCC participants and the assessment practice, and, in turn, whether participants' interest in the IPCC shaped these domains.

To address the question of who gets to write the reality of climate change and what constitutes their power, I also needed to get to know the assessment practice. To begin with, I drew most heavily on the notion of habitus because it helped me to think about social order, how hierarchy is generated, the traces and signs of it and the mechanisms of its reproduction. Social hierarchy in the IPCC is most obvious when observing intergovernmental interactions and when listening to authors discuss their research and the expertise and contribution of others. However, as I described the delegate who spoke with seemingly no effect, I also needed a way to connect the mechanisms of social ordering inside the IPCC with broader global patterns of political and economic order beyond. For that, I needed Bourdieu's notion of economic capital.

One of the things that I want to illustrate through this account is that the concepts learned through the reading of a scholar may guide and inform research in a way that we are not completely aware of until later. This happened to me during the write up. Through my interviews and observations, I learned about the IPCC's intricate practices for producing an assessment of climate change. I came to learn that governments had a far greater influence over the production of reports than was documented in the literature, and that this influence was concentrated in the hands of a few in a manner that was also connected to the authorship and administration of the reports. As I mapped the intricacies of the IPCC's assessment practice, I became aware of the time and human resources required to meaningfully participate in the IPCC, and thus how active participation was dependent on economic resources. It was at this moment that I realized I would need economic capital to make an empirical connection between the social order within the IPCC and the economic order beyond.

Bourdieu's notion of capital makes it possible to map locations in social space: the social order. The structure of a field is determined by the distribution of capital. All fields and all actors within the field possess a "definite configuration of properties," specific to the field and actors in question (Bourdieu and Wacquant 1992, 107). These properties, or forms of capital, are what enable or qualify actors to enter the field and determine their relative position in the social order of the field. It is an actor's position in social space that generates a particular point of view on the field, as internalized in habitus, a description that highlights the coupled relationship between the different concepts. The species of capital – the resources that have an effect – are specific to the research object and are only identifiable through the research process. There are three principal types of capital: 1. economic capital – material wealth and financial assets; 2. cultural capital – knowledge, skills, technical qualifications and titles; and 3. social capital – the resources accrued by virtue of membership in a given group (Wacquant 1998, 221). There is also symbolic capital, which is an acknowledgment of an actor's status in the field (or misrecognition at the arbitrariness of the field's values on which this status depends). These attributes distinguish actors and permit them to yield a particular power, or force, in and over the conduct of the IPCC.

The concept of capital gave me the analytical means to identify actors' capacity to influence the organizational form of the IPCC and its assessments of climate change, and to connect symbolic power in the organization, and over its products, to global economic order. This is how the concept that I initially thought would play the smallest part in my study came to play the biggest. Capital allowed me to reveal why some delegates stand up, say something and have no effect, while other delegates stand up, speak and have their views reflected in the text. In order to shape the IPCC process in practice, you have to be able to justify changes to the text in terms of language, procedure or science. The best justifications for revisions are made by long-standing delegates that have been deeply invested in the IPCC since the beginning or have inherited that knowledge from their predecessors (cultural and symbolic capital). These actors tend to have good working relations with other members of the panel, secretariat and bureau through the relations they have cultivated and maintained over time (social capital). Many of these delegates will have a degree in science and are also likely to be part of the national delegation to the UNFCCC (cultural capital). As the national focal point to the IPCC, these actors oversee the author nomination process and the review of draft reports, which gives them a relationship to the report's authors (social capital) and knowledge of the report's content and procedures for its compilation (cultural capital). These forms of cultural and social capital are built through and are dependent upon economic investment in IPCC participation and its resource intensive activities (economic capital). It is through this dependent relationship that it becomes possible to connect the social order within the IPCC, and who is the most powerful in the writing of climate change, to the distribution of economic resources globally.

4.4 Alice Vadrot: Going Beyond Foucault with the "Epistemic Selectivity" Concept

When I started my PhD in 2009, I was intrigued by the idea that science and political power are bound and that they are mutually constitutive. At that time, I was already interested in debates over creating an "IPCC for biodiversity." I participated in COP9 of the CBD in 2008, wherein the idea of a new global assessment body for biodiversity was advocated by scientists and policymakers alike. When states envisaged meetings to negotiate the Intergovernmental Science-Policy Platform on Biodiversity and Ecosystem Services (IPBES), I saw this as THE opportunity to study how science and political power are bound and become mutually constitutive throughout the negotiation and institutionalization of a new global knowledge body. It was clear from the first moment I entered into the negotiation room that I wanted to use this opportunity to answer some theoretical questions I had in mind, inspired by Foucault.

Although fascinated by the work of Michel Foucault, I found it difficult to understand how and why discourses emerge, how they materialize, how they change and under which conditions. Sitting in the negotiation room, with multiple actors exchanging views on complex legal text and using clauses that I had never heard of, I had a hard time detecting what was meaningful and what wasn't, and how to identify and delimit relevant discourses based on my observations of what was happening in the negotiation room. I struggled with how to conceptualize individual action and the emergence of common interests of different actors within relatively stable politico-institutional and discursive settings.

For Foucault, it is a matter of being "in the truth" ("dans le vrai") in the sense that propositions (statements) can only be heard and considered if they are formulated within the rules of a specific (scientific) discipline and logic (Foucault 1971, 36) that is itself aligned with the *authority of the truth* and the efficiency logic of the political economy, which are inherent to the concept of "governmentality" introduced by Foucault to describe the techniques, rationalities, and mentalities governing subjects (Foucault 2004). I was aware that in order to apply Foucault to the case of IPBES I had to conduct a careful analysis of the policymaking process and the negotiations, inter alia to further understand the role and impact of both scientific and nonscientific knowledge in biodiversity politics and the IPBES establishment. I expected that an analysis of the IPBES negotiation process would allow me to better understand how this coconstitution actually "works" on the ground, why, by what means it is dialectical, and how it can be strategic, interest-driven and discursively structured at the same time. In order to clarify these issues, I developed the concept of "epistemic selectivity."

First, I started to engage with the structure–agency debate discussed in sociology (e.g., Archer et al. 1998) and IR (e.g., Wendt 1987). I had to make ontological and epistemological choices: what do I consider to be "real" when I observe negotiations (what are my units of analysis?), and how can I develop knowledge about what I assume exists and is real? I was struggling with empirical realism that "treats the world as consisting of observable atomistic objects, events, and regularities among them, as if objects had no structure or powers, and in particular, no unobservable qualities" (Sayer 2000, 11). Instead, I found the assumptions of critical realism convincing. Critical realism acknowledges the existence of real causal mechanisms that influence events and are manifest through these events. Critical realism does not assume that our social world is based on universal laws or structures that are intelligible and empirically observable (Bhaskar 1998). However, by observing specific "events," we can detect regularities, patterns and reasonably stable relationships organizing the social world.

I considered "events" to be specific moments in the IPBES negotiations, when dominant knowledge about the policy issue at hand becomes contested and implicit conflicts become explicit. For me, the negotiations provided "the setting within which social, political and economic events occur and acquire meaning" (Hay 2002, 94). Thus, I was looking for "events" and important moments of conflict in the negotiations that I could use to study the making of the IPBES and the underlying "epistemic selectivity." The idea behind the concept of "epistemic selectivity" was that actors within the negotiation room tend to reproduce the structural context within which they act by selecting those kinds of discursive strategies and narratives that promise the success of their action. However, these strategies often reproduce the dominant meaning and knowledge associated with the policy issue under negotiation. They do this based on their knowledge of and insights into the context that is discursively mediated and institutionally reflected (Hay 2002, 382). The epistemic selectivity concept assumes that actors' knowledge of the context within which they act, and the policy issue at hand, is selective and incomplete. Actors reproduce the selectively structured context and knowledge to realize their interests, but by doing so they create "habitual strategies" and reproduce the logic of negotiating and knowledge of a specific environmental problem. Epistemic selectivity explains why the politico-institutional and discursive settings within which we negotiate environmental problems are relatively stable but open to contestation and conflict (Vadrot 2014b, 2017).

4.4.1 Using the "Epistemic Selectivity" Concept to Study the Institutionalization of IPBES

Early in the IPBES negotiations, I expected conflicts over the term "ecosystem services," which became a central pillar of the conceptual framework of the new body. I assumed that state and nonstate actors would discuss the kind of knowledge and approaches that would feed into the assessments and thought that such debates could figure as important "events" and data for my study. However, it seemed that actors agreed on the economic framing of biodiversity and its inclusion in the text. In 2011, during a meeting taking place at the UNEP headquarters in Nairobi, things changed. In the middle of the meeting, the representative of the Plurinational State Bolivia, speaking on behalf of GRULAC, took the floor and expressed – for the first time – concern:

> The notion of ecosystem services is mentioned quite often in the text. These concepts are not clear to us … Biodiversity has many functions and many values; you cannot only look at the monetary value. Biodiversity has to be analysed in its diverse meanings. Social values need to be taken into account … We should not base the discussion on nature on economic vision and market values. Documents should be reviewed and references, which are made to the market use of biodiversity, should be stroked out.[1]

The room was silent. A Belgian delegate sitting next to me shook his head and seemed irritated. As I was sitting in the first row, I did not see the reaction of others, but when the chair gave the floor to the United States, I turned around, assuming that a heated debate would follow. To the contrary: The US delegate made a long, detailed statement that did not refer to Bolivia's statement at all. Same for the next speakers; the participants simply ignored Bolivia's statement. A few days later, when the chair asked for approval of the protocol of the meeting, Bolivia refused to consent to the document because its statement was not included. The chair tried to calm the situation and asked Bolivia to submit a paragraph summarizing the statement, which the delegate did.

During the note taking I was already trying to make sense of my observation and immediately thought of Foucault and his notion of being "in the truth." I deduced that Bolivia's statement did not follow the disciplinary rules or the logic behind them. The statement was simply not part of how others in the room talked about or conceived biodiversity and the kind of framing that the majority considered appropriate to guide the assessment work of IPBES. After the negotiations I asked my Belgian neighbor about Bolivia's intervention. He said, "Well, he does that always, in all environmental meetings and it's just annoying."

I was puzzled by my observation. Shouldn't negotiations openly address questions on the kind of value that we as humans attribute to nature and what these values imply for the policies guiding environmental protection? How can I make sense of this? My previous data indicated a strong prevalence of the narrative "Measuring and valuing biodiversity" as a (the?) key driver for the desire to create a new body and little contestation over its validity. The "event" when Bolivia took the floor and insisted on the inclusion of its statement revealed the existence of implicit conflicts – conflicts that are embedded within the context in which actors act and that may become explicit and reveal its selectivity.

Conceptualizing biodiversity in terms of ecosystem services is, indeed, only one way to understand the diversity of life and became popular in intergovernmental circles after 2005, when the Millennium Ecosystem Assessment was released. Several subsequent international initiatives turned their attention to the economic costs of environmental change,

[1] From notes taken by Alice Vadrot.

including the Stern Report for Climate Change and The Economics of Ecosystems and Biodiversity (TEEB). International actors such as the World Bank and UNEP contributed to such efforts and took part in a process that changed the discourses and "stories" about why we should care about nature (Vadrot 2014a). Many of my interviewees interpreted this shift in meaning as a "window of opportunity" for an "IPCC for biodiversity," because they assumed economic framings to resonate with the logic of policymakers and political economy. Referring to the need to understand the relationship between biodiversity and ecosystem services and the economic value of biodiversity became a "habitual strategy" during the IPBES meetings employed by many IPBES supporters. The repetitive nature of such statements created a context that was less permeable for alternative conceptualizations of biodiversity and which reinforced "epistemic selectivity" (Brand and Vadrot 2013; Vadrot 2014a, 2014b)

Yet, as my observation in Nairobi showed, this does not mean that no alternative meaning or knowledge exists, and it is especially during intergovernmental negotiations that we need to be sensitive to what is not being said. Moments of contestation, as demonstrated earlier, equip us with the possibility to analyze events, when implicit conflicts become explicit and allow us to study both the selectively structured context within which actors act and the way in which such selectivities guide political action. In the case of IPBES, the first concerns regarding the concept of "ecosystem services" and the economic framing of biodiversity turned out to be decisive for the future of IPBES and its conceptual framework (Vadrot 2020). The body went through several stages wherein it had to adapt to critical voices and acknowledge alternative concepts such as Pachamama and Buen Vivir, which informed the current notion of "Natures' contributions to People" (NCP).

The development and application of the "epistemic selectivites" concept has helped me to fulfill what, in my mind, social scientists are conditioned to do: reveal, analyze and explain regularities and disruptions in the way in which societies govern and know themselves, especially those regularities that lead to inequity or exclusion, and those disruptions or "windows of opportunity" that enable political and social change.

4.5 Creating New Concepts

As we undertake empirical research – guided by theories, concepts and the analytical frameworks that we develop from these – we may gain new insights and make novel observations that are not accounted for in the approach that we are applying or the existing literature. While these observations may have been enabled by the scholars that inspired and shaped how we initially constructed the study object, they cannot be adequately captured or explained by these, and this may signal the need for conceptual innovation. This was the case in the development of the "weighted concept," which we introduced to explain observations made in our studies of the IPCC and IPBES (Hughes and Vadrot 2019). The social theories of Pierre Bourdieu and Michele Foucault, which informed our observations of these two bodies, highlighted the role of language in the social construction of reality and the struggle this initiates as actors attempt "to define what the social world is" (Wacquant 1989, 34). They directed our analytical focus to the contestation that takes place among member governments over IPCC and IPBES documentation, particularly during the approval of an assessment report's Summary for Policymakers (SPM). However, they did not provide an explanation for or conceptualize the effects of the struggles that we observed through extended study of these bodies.

One observation that puzzled and intrigued us was the repetition in proceedings and party interventions. We found that delegates objected to the same word or concept each time it appeared in the text, which often sparked an equally repetitive reaction from other parties. We might expect some repetition within the IPCC as this is a long-standing body, but as Alice's account of the Belgian delegate's annoyance at Bolivia's intervention on ecosystem services indicates, repetition was also observable in the newly forming IPBES. We conceptualized the objects – words, concepts and terms – that triggered this repetition as weighted because of the struggle they initiated, but also because of the origins of or motivation for this struggle. Through observation of both assessment bodies – IPCC and IPBES – and the negotiating processes – UNFCCC and CBD – that they inform, we became aware of the similarity in proceedings and the fact that many delegates were active in both forums. Far from being distinct sites, as conceptualized in the literature, these knowledge bodies appeared more as the continuation of the negotiations, and in fact, the site where negotiation over new concepts began or was successfully deterred (Hughes and Vadrot 2019). Identifying the IPCC and IPBES as the sites where the negotiation of some objects began was key in the development of the agreement-making framework. Alongside other research that had identified the range of actors informing negotiated outcomes, it supported expanding the sites and processes that are considered constituent of global environmental agreements.

Interpreting observations and attempting to conceptualize them in order to identify their significance, and to enable other scholars to study and expand knowledge of them, is an ongoing process. Through continued observation of the same process or observation at a new site it is possible to test the initial ideas and understandings that inform the conceptualization. Thus, we came to realize that once the definition of an object has been accepted it is hard to reopen – struggle can be reactivated and often identified by the repetition, but the agreement reached is again put in place to resolve controversy and prevent further contestation. The *weighting* that struggle initiates is driven by deep-seated differences and contestations over the distribution of economic, social and cultural resources – political order. While the definition of a particular object may be resolved, these deeper North–South divisions and struggles over the economic resources and cultural values are not, and they simply move on to the next word, term or concept that has the potential to reshape global order and the economic relations that it rests upon.

4.6 Conclusion

In this chapter we have attempted to break down the process of identifying, applying and developing concepts in the study of global environmental agreement-making. We have done this through recounting our own experiences of identifying and applying concepts from the work of Michel Foucault and Pierre Bourdieu. From these concepts, we built analytical approaches to study the questions and organizations that we were interested in. When we found that these concepts could not explain all the observations that they directed we had to innovate and create new concepts, which we describe through the weighted concept.

Our own work has benefited from theoretical engagement with white, French, male philosophers, which has enabled us to develop critical analyses of different constituent elements of agreement-making. However, we also recognize that conceptual starting places can (and should) vary. The starting point will be imbued in the work that develops from it, even if it is critical. As other scholars have identified, if we are to overcome Western dominance (and its reproduction in the knowledge we produce) then we must have "concepts and theories that are derived from other societies and cultures" (Acharya 2016, 6). That is why it is essential that we explore different methodological starting points and Chapter 5, on "Stakes," offers precisely that.

Further Reading

1. Inoue, C. Y. A. (2018). Worlding the Study of Global Environmental Politics in the Anthropocene: Indigenous Voices from the Amazon. *Global Environmental Politics* 18(4), 25–42.

Inoue challenges us to think hard about our methodological starting points in the study of global environmental politics, and it is increasingly important to engage with this from the outset.

2. Litfin, K. (1994). *Ozone Discourse: Science and Politics in Global Environmental Cooperation*. New York: Columbia University Press.

This is an excellent study of the role of science and scientists in treaty making and an example of how Foucault's notion of discourse can inspire a new approach that results in further conceptual development.

References

Acharya, A. (2016). Advancing Global IR: Challenges, Contentions, and Contributions. *International Studies Review* 18(1), 4–15.

Anderl, F. and Witt, A. (2020). Problematising the Global in Global IR. *Millennium* 49(1), 32–57.

Archer, M., Bhaskar, R., Collier, A., Lawson, T. and Norrie, A. (1998). *Critical Realism: Essential Readings*. London: Routledge.

Bäckstrand, K. and Lövbrand, E. (2006). Planting Trees to Mitigate Climate Change: Contested Discourses of Ecological Modernization, Green Governmentality and Civic Environmentalism. *Global Environmental Politics* 6(1), 50–75.

Bhaskar, R. (1998). Philosophy and Scientific Realism. In M. Archer, R. Bhaskar, A. Collier, T. Lawson and A. Norrie (eds.), *Critical Realism: Essential Readings*. London: Routledge, pp. 16–47.

Bourdieu, P. (1986) *Distinction: A Social Critique of the Judgement of Taste*. London: Routledge & Kegan Paul.

Bourdieu, P. (1988). *Homo Academicus*. Translated by Peter Collier. Cambridge: Polity Press in association with Basil Blackwell.

Bourdieu, P. (1990). *The Logic of Practice*. Cambridge: Polity Press.

Bourdieu, P. (1991). *Language and Symbolic Power*. Cambridge: Polity Press.

Bourdieu, P. and Passeron, C. (1977). *Reproduction in Education, Society and Culture*. Translated by Richard Nice. London: Sage Publications.

Bourdieu, P. and Wacquant, L. J. D. (1992). *An Invitation to Reflexive Sociology*. Cambridge: Polity Press.

Brand, U. and Vadrot, A. B.M. (2013). Epistemic Selectivities Towards the Valorization of Nature in the Nagoya Protocol and the Making of the Intergovernmental Science-Policy Platform on Biodiversity and Ecosystem Services (IPBES). *LEAD: Law, Environment and Development Journal* 9(2), 202–222.

Death, C. (2010). *Governing Sustainable Development: Partnerships, Protests and Power at the World Summit*. London: Routledge.

Epstein, C. (2008). *The Power of Words in International Relations: Birth of an Anti-Whaling Discourse*. Cambridge, MA: The MIT Press.

European Commission. (2018). "A Clean Planet for all: A European Strategic Long-Term Vision for a Prosperous, Modern, Competitive and Climate Neutral Economy" (COM (2018) 773 final). Brussels: European Commission https://eur-lex.europa.eu/legal-content/en/TXT/?uri=CELEX%3A52018DC0773 (last accessed July 2022).

European Commission. (2019). "Communication": The European Green Deal (COM (2019) 640 final). Brussels: European Commission. https://eur-lex.europa.eu/legal-content/EN/TXT/?qid=1591201354409&uri=CELEX:52019DC0640 (last accessed July 2022).

Foucault, M. (1969). *L'archéologie du savoir*. Paris: Gallimard.

Foucault, M. (1971). *L'ordre du discours*. Paris: Gallimard.

Foucault, M. (2004). *Naissance de la biopolitique: cours au Collège de France (1978–1979)*. Paris: Gallimard & Seuil.

Gilio-Whitaker, D. (2019). *As Long as Grass Grows: The Indigenous Fight for Environmental Justice from Colonization to Standing Rock*. Boston, MA: Beacon Press.

Hajer, M. A. (1997). *The Politics of Environmental Discourse: Ecological Modernization and the Policy Process*. Oxford: Clarendon Press.

Hay, C. (2002). *Political Analysis: Contemporary Controversies: A Critical Introduction*. New York: Palgrave Macmillan.

Hughes, H. (2015). Bourdieu and the IPCC's Symbolic Power. *Global Environmental Politics* 15(4), 85–104.

Hughes, H. and Vadrot, A. B. M. (2019). Weighting the World: IPBES and the Struggle over Biocultural Diversity. *Global Environmental Politics* 19(2), 14–37.

Huysmans, J. (2002). Shape-Shifting NATO: Humanitarian Action and the Kosovo Refugee Crisis. *Review of International Studies* 28(3), 599–618.

Jackson, P. (2008). Pierre Bourdieu, the "Cultural Turn" and the Practice of International History. *Review of International Studies* 34(1), 155–181.

Lacan, J. (2007). *The Seminar, Book XVII. The Other Side of Psychoanalysis*. New York and London: W. Norton.

Lacan, J., Miller, J. A and Sheridan, A. (1998). *The Four Fundamental Concepts of Psycho-Analysis*. New York: Norton and Company.

Leander, A. (2002). Do We Really Need Reflexivity in IPE? Bourdieu's Two Reasons for Answering Affirmatively. *Review of International Political Economy* 9(4),601–609.

Leander, A. (2005). The Power to Construct International Security: On the Significance of Private Military Companies. *Millennium: Journal of International Studies* 33(3), 803–25.

Lövbrand, E., Stripple, J., and Wiman, B. (2009). Earth System Governmentality: Reflections on Science in the Anthropocene. *Global Environmental Change* 19, 7–13.

Luke, T. W. (1995). On Environmentality: Geo-Power and Eco-Knowledge in the Discourses of Contemporary Environmentalism. *Cultural Critique* 31, 57–81.

Methmann, C. (2013). The Sky is the Limit: Global Warming as Global Governmentality. *European Journal of International Relations* 19, 69–91.

Oels, A. (2005). Rendering Climate Change Governable: From Biopower to Advanced Liberal Government? *Journal of Environmental Policy & Planning* 7(3), 185–207.

Okereke, C., Bulkeley, H. and Schroeder, H. (2009). Conceptualizing Climate Governance Beyond the International Regime. *Global Environmental Politics* 9(1), 58–78.

Pettenger, M. E., ed. (2007). *The Social Construction of Climate Change: Power, Knowledge, Norms, Discourses*. Aldershot: Ashgate Publishing.

Rutherford, S. (2007). Green Governmentality: Insights and Opportunities in the Study of Nature's Rule. *Progress in Human Geography* 31, 291–307.

Sayer, A. (2000). *Realism and Social Science*. London: Sage.

Sharma, A. (2021). Decolonizing International Relations: Confronting Erasures through Indigenous Knowledge Systems. *International Studies* 58(1), 25–40.

Stavrakakis, Y. (1999). *Lacan and the Political*. London: Routledge.

Stripple, J. and Bulkeley, H. (2013). On Governmentality and Climate Change. In H. Bulkeley and J. Stripple (eds.), *Governing the Climate: New Approaches to Rationality, Power and Politics*. Cambridge: Cambridge University Press, pp. 1–24.

Vadrot, A. B. M. (2014a). *The Politics of Knowledge and Global Biodiversity*. Routledge studies in biodiversity politics and management. London: Routledge.

Vadrot, A. B. M. (2014b). The Epistemic and Strategic Dimension of the Establishment of the IPBES: Epistemic Selectivities at Work. *Innovation: The European Journal for Social Science Research 27*(4), 361–378.

Vadrot, A. B. M. (2017). Knowledge, International Relations and the Structure–Agency Debate: Towards the Concept of "Epistemic Selectivities." *Innovation: The European Journal of Social Science Research* 30(1), 61–72.

Vadrot, A. B. M. (2020). Building Authority and Relevance in the Early History of IPBES. *Environmental Science & Policy* 113(11), 14–20.

Wacquant, L. J. D. (1989). Towards a Reflexive Sociology: A Workshop with Pierre Bourdieu. *Sociological Theory 7*(1), 26–63.

Wacquant, L. J. D. (1998) Pierre Bourdieu. In R. Stones (ed.), *Key Sociological Thinkers*. London: Macmillan Press, pp. 335–370.

Wendt, A. E. (1987). The Agent-Structure Problem in International Relations Theory. *International Organization 41*(3), 215–229.

Williams, M. C. (2007). *Culture and Security: Symbolic Power and the Politics of International Security*. London: Routledge.

Yusoff, K. (2018). *A Billion Black Anthropocenes or None*. Minneapolis: University of Minnesota Press.

5

Stakes

Conducting Relational Research with Indigenous Peoples

MARCELA VECCHIONE-GONÇALVES WITH HANNAH HUGHES

5.1 Introduction

There are multiple ways of researching and looking at global environmental negotiations. This wide array of possibilities stretches from the choice of which international issue area to study and which conference of the parties to attend, down to the choice of a specific agenda item to chase during a conference to follow the crafting of a draft, a decision or an article in an Accord. Within the study of negotiations, Indigenous Peoples' participation in and relationship to agreement-making is distinct. It requires thinking about the source of the political and the politics of worlds coming together – at times colliding and in friction – and always in negotiation. To study, observe and understand Indigenous politics at negotiation sites requires adjusting scholarly thinking and expectations as to what constitutes a negotiation and where this negotiation begins and ends. At present, scholarship and practice often do not reflect, nor take seriously, that the world – including the world of negotiations – is a **system of many worlds** (de la Cadena 2015; de la Cadena and Blaser 2018).

In this chapter, I describe how my research with Indigenous Peoples[1] has informed my understanding and conceptualization of what could constitute an ethical research with Indigenous negotiators, representatives and researchers at environmental negotiations so that other non-Indigenous researchers may gain from these experiences in reflecting on the role of Indigenous politics in agreement-making. I imagine that it could take us through a path of dialogue with other political worlds and, consequently, to different trajectories of becoming political and making politics in environmental agreement-making. I describe and reflect on Indigenous participation at negotiations, and during a given meeting, as both a **political place** and a **political event**, which brings different worlds into relation with one another: the world of multilateralism and the world of territories and pluriversal life projects.

[1] I use the term "Indigenous Peoples" to characterize more generally Indigenous groups (as a People) I am working with. In the text, relations where this terminology is used will be related both to issues of domestic and international politics and negotiations and to issues related to constitutional and land rights. The term "Indigenous groups" will be used when talking about the stories and the construction of a politics for becoming political in the connection between territorial and environmental negotiation sites drawing the relation of building a political subjectivity with building a political place that allow political recognition and participation while reassuring the group identity as a specific People, such as the Ashaninka or the Guarani. Consequently, as I introduce the particular stories, I will use the Indigenous groups' names as a form to narrate their particular ways of becoming political. By the same token, when telling these stories I will often use the term "'Indigenous persons' in order to give credit to particular persons" stories about being in an Indigenous group and becoming part of the category "Indigenous Peoples" by the way of going through different forms of experiencing resistance, endurance and participation in negotiations. To use their group names and their particular stories as references throughout the text is a way of reassuring agency and Indigenous diplomacies.

I consider negotiations as a **process event**, which neither begins nor ends at the conference observed or with the agenda item followed. Negotiations are important events to analyze for understanding the nature, power relations and actors involved in agreement-making, and Indigenous politics-making in environmental negotiations is fundamental for grasping how Indigenous Peoples craft their participation in this process. As such, thinking about global environmental negotiations as a *process* is key to trace an ethical methodology of research with Indigenous Peoples and groups, and to make oneself available as an ally within the power assemblage of environmental negotiations. This way of thinking and of taking position (positionality) allows the researcher to explore the ways in which Indigenous groups relate to each other during the environmental negotiations, but also the ways they relate to other political actors, such as diplomats, international organizations, NGO actors and activists.

The process of relating to – which, for epistemological, methodological and ethical purposes, the Indigenous scholar Linda Tuhiwai Smith (1999) calls relationality – happens not just at a specific negotiation but across meeting sites and negotiations, as captured by the agreement-making framework. More importantly, as I aim to explore in this chapter, such a process starts before the recognized site of negotiation; it starts in Indigenous territories, with the daily challenges faced due to environmental transformations caused by the expansion of global extractivism into their territories. For this reason, it is important to understand what is being shaped as a political problem (and why) to be *taken* to the negotiation. Oftentimes, it happens before negotiations and across different places where Indigenous politics plays out. As I have argued elsewhere, the political mobility of Indigenous Peoples is in the bringing of being from one site of living to the other, or representing and performing a political position in foreign political sites. This is a way of making place – as a political and social territory – through places, in the sense of building affective connections as related to one group's own cosmology (Vecchione-Gonçalves 2014). This is the political mobility of a people, as represented by persons of the group traveling to spaces of global negotiation, such as the climate or biodiversity conference of the parties (COP), and a way of constantly making them as "a people" connected to a territory that is land, materially speaking, but also a place relational to past, present and future stories **projected as collective permanence of life**, or, in other words, **life projects** (Vecchione-Gonçalves 2009).

The concepts that I identify and describe from my research in this chapter are informed by and from this understanding, and may help in providing some avenues for engagement with Indigenous Peoples and groups participating in negotiations. The concepts were assembled through research alongside the life projects and political practices of Indigenous groups that I have engaged with. In methodological terms, to take these concepts seriously is also to engage with this politics seriously. Frequently, this makes it possible to engage (with) different kinds of Indigenous People participating at different levels and positions in negotiations, even when not being at the negotiations per se. Certainly, the way we approach an Indigenous group or participants we are working with is likely to be different from how you might approach other actors in global environmental politics, such as state delegates or scientific experts. Remembering relationality and political mobility,

Indigenous groups have distinct stakes in this process as they are actively taking care of the continuation of their worlds in the here and now, as they have already lost many of what these worlds used to be.

These stakes, the continuation of worlds, mean that we are not doing research *on* Indigenous Peoples participating in environmental negotiations; we are doing research *with* Indigenous Peoples that are performing and shaping their politics through environmental negotiations to defend their place of living. Ethical research, in this context, requires recognition of and participation in Indigenous politics of conveying social, territorial and environmental problems as hindering and blocking their extended places of living (Mato 2000) – or, to say it differently, of their rights to life. This in turn means embracing a different way of conducting research, such that a ready-made research question brought to the negotiation site may have to be left behind, or at least opened up, to allow the research question to be shaped by the politics and the relations that the groups whose relations and work that you follow, and which are shaping you, are shaping the research you undertake. For me, this has meant that I have built my research through direct and practical engagement with the political participation of these groups during the negotiation, as well as before and after it, which informs the understanding of ethical research that I present in this chapter. This also serves as a reminder that climate change negotiations and the world-changing scenario of catastrophe and risk that it brings us to, is most of all an invitation to rethink research questions as questions about civilizational problems (Krenak 2019), and Indigenous Peoples have a role to be observed, not as observers, but as political subjects in these process-events.

Through my research I have been able to build strong and durable connections in a multisited manner: at the territories, at the negotiations and virtually. First, I will present the concept of territory and why it was important to understand relationality and reciprocity for building protocols, written or tacit, for developing the research. It is worth stressing that this kind of research involves action and taking responsibility in shaping research questions, as I discuss in Section 5.3 on relations. This involves observing Indigenous diplomacies (Beier 2005) and the politics of building worlds (cosmopolitics), but also engaging with and practicing this diplomacy. I will then move to specify the continuous activity of doing research with Indigenous Peoples and situate this continuity in the study of agreement-making as a way of understanding how Indigenous politics is built and its role in composing or contending order making. Finally, we go back to discuss and synthesize what are the ethical stakes for studying Indigenous cosmopolitics through agreement-making and why it could be important to decentralize the study of environmental negotiations to contribute toward a global environmental politics otherwise.

5.2 Starting from the Territory

The most important thing that I have done in my research is to engage in climate and biodiversity negotiations informed by territorial dynamics, and I did this by starting in the territories. I was already an international relations (IR) scholar when I first approached Indigenous groups. In my PhD, I was looking at Indigenous politics at Amazonian borders and the influence of such politics in shaping the political environment in these areas related to trespassing, limitations and control, but also to frictions and possibilities for becoming political. Indigenous politics and subjectivity within borders were permeated by a way of living and building possibilities of life that could go beyond state politics, although encompassed by and in contention with it. As such, the very territory that Indigenous groups are living in, whether at the borders or not, are "borderized." The strategies used in Indigenous territorial politics to go beyond these territorial borders (state and nonstate), and to experience and defend their territory as a much larger *place* for mobilizing bodies, politics and life was interesting and politically promising to me to observe. In Amazonian areas, this extensive and intensive politics of life at the borders – as well as the relations situated within territories assembled and reassembled politically by the movement of Indigenous groups through rivers and floodplains across different places – is a constitutive part of the environment and of the Rainforest. It makes the Rainforest a social place rather than an empty and pristine nature. By realizing this was part of Indigenous Peoples' lives, I was taught by them, at an early stage of my fieldwork, that borders cut across Indigenous lifeways and that the forest is a political and social place that goes beyond borders, and which entails a nonseparability between nature and society, peoples and forests.

Those perceptions were an important point of departure for the research practices that I started developing in 2009. From this point of perception, I understood that to negotiate Land Use, Land Use Change and Forestry (LULUCF), Reductions of Emissions from Deforestation and Degradation (REDD) or Access to Benefit Sharing (ABS) is also to negotiate the effects of and adaptation to climate change and biodiversity loss on Indigenous territories and beyond their territories. These are negotiations that are frequently without Indigenous participation, leading to consequences that cut across Indigenous lifeways. Thinking about lifeways in the Amazon as particular ways of organizing life, not as a lifestyle but as a cosmology or renewed tradition of being and becoming in place as a group, allowed me to think that there was more to borders than providing order and defining what the nation-state is as described in IR. This perception was also important for building the ethics of doing research and conceptualizing political and ethical relations across these borders – disciplinarily and ordinarily – with Indigenous Peoples. It became critical to and necessary for my research to situate the territory of politics according to the lifeways of the Peoples I was working with. This situational and territorial dialogue was important both to define this politics and the politics of the research, as departing from Indigenous territories and toward the territories of Indigenous Peoples' foreign relations, in other words, Indigenous diplomacies (Beier 2005; Vecchione-Gonçalves 2009).

This field research, and the concepts that derived from it described here, started in Kampa do Rio Amônia Ashaninka Indigenous Territory at the border between Peru and Brazil, in the state of Acre, Southwestern Amazon Rainforest. I came to the Indigenous territory to follow an activity organized by the Ashaninka people to discuss deforestation and agroforestry in a knowledge center that they had created. It was a very diplomatic process in the sense that, in order to recover and undertake forest restoration in their territories, they had to engage the other groups, such as Riverine communities and rubber tappers, that also used and relied on the forest for their living and as a lifeway. This was a form of diplomacy based on an understanding of the forest as an integrated social and biological space. Thus, in order to talk about and undertake the protection and recovery of their territory, which would be the recovery of their world, it would be necessary to talk to others surrounding it.

Ashaninka people have been navigating transborder politics and belonging in the Andean-Amazonian region since the seventeenth century. They have always been doing this diplomacy – it was only my first time to experience it, my first insertion into their world, and it really struck me and decentered my understanding. What was the space of the political? What was the space of environmental negotiation? What was the territory of this? I was in a territory at the border of Brazil and Peru and with people from both sides of the border, people speaking Portuguese, Spanish, Ashaninka, Hãtxa Kuĩ – it was a cosmopolitical space – where they were negotiating and talking about what to do about this integrated space of the forest so that they could survive. There was conflict, not everyone was agreeing, it was a negotiation. Observing this shifted my understanding of the place of politics and, later, my understanding of the place of environmental negotiations. It gave me the sense that I had to engage with this cosmopolitics – the diverse, purposeful interactions that I observed – seriously. This was not just an abstract, philosophical way of doing politics, but a practical politics being produced in the forest within the very national borders that theoretically defines and limits the political.

The meeting in the knowledge center was mediated by Benki Pyanko. Benki is part of the Ashaninka people and one of the leaders of the Kampa do Rio Amônea Ashaninka Indigenous Territory. At one point in the meeting he said to me "I am going to Copenhagen as part of the Coordinator of the Indigenous Organizations of the Amazon Basin [COICA] delegation and I am going to be presenting the experience of this there. Do you want to go with me and help me to translate this and put it in the appropriate language?" I said "Yes, I can do that." This invitation and my response was critical to building the connection: through engaging seriously with the politics in the territories, and informed by this, came the possibility to physically follow this event and its translation – if ever completely possible – at global climate negotiations.

From this fieldwork, and following Benki from the negotiation in the territory to recognized sites of global environmental negotiation, concepts emerged that brought to light different understandings of the purpose of global environmental agreement-making, and, if embraced, what this could produce and mean for global politics. What makes these concepts critical is that they are informed by the political practices of the Indigneous groups that I observed, rather than adopted from a theorist and applied to the research problem at the outset (see Chapter 4). Such concepts emerged and captured what I observed and the relations I built, and how these informed and shaped my research and understanding of these. Drawing from this, I realized there was another politics going on at and across territories that was performed both to mobilize territorial defense and to build a world in common with others even if in a situation of disagreement. That was cosmopolitics, and I will start with that before unpacking Indigenous diplomacies at the negotiations and how together these unsettle disciplinary notions of territory and politics.

5.2.1 Cosmopolitics

For Indigenous Peoples, and for people that have been working with Indigenous communities for the past fifteen years, debate and discussion has emerged around the term "cosmopolitics" (Blaser 2014; De la Cadena 2010). This has not been a political philosophical discussion of cosmopolitanism, although there has been an attempt to define cosmopolitanism in a more critical way than Kant and other philosophers have in the past, as we can see in the writings of Kwame Apiah (2006) and Seyla Benhabib (2006). This has been a discussion about the politics of practicing cosmopolitanism or *cosmopolitics*. For Indigenous Peoples and for anthropologists, philosophers and sociologists working with Indigenous communities, to talk about cosmopolitics is to talk about a politics of creating worlds, which means that you accept the idea that it is possible to craft and build a world that is different from the world that we have now, with all its problems – the exploitation of people and planet, the disparities and inequalities. It is possible to create other worlds, and when you accept this you become aware of other political subjects that are able to create worlds. Moreover, we acknowledge that these worlds are already in existence.

I came to understand this from observing how the Ashaninka people created a space to bring together other users of the forest for its preservation, and from observing Benki as he presented a window into this world at the climate negotiations. Benki went to Copenhagen as a climate champion, an entrepreneur of the forest, and through him people got to know about the violence associated with illegal logging in the Ashaninka territory, but also the approaches that the Ashaninka people took to navigate and negotiate this for their survival. There are many other examples of this too. Since 2015, COICA, as the Coordinator of the Indigenous Organizations of the Amazon Basin, has been presenting on side events and submitting proposals on activities and policy packages to the UNFCCC Secretariat for the Local Communities and Indigenous Peoples Platform (LCIPP), which was established through the Paris Agreement in 2015. These are proposals that would be effective in keeping territories in the region under good conservation, with social and biological diversity, and in balance with the climate.

In these submissions, Indigenous representatives are providing concrete experiences of their attempts to make survival possible under very difficult circumstances. These worlds do not exist as they used to, and they are subject to continuous encroachment, violence and dispossession. Despite this, by bringing their cosmopolitics, and representations of it, to sites of global environmental negotiations, Indigenous groups are making other worlds possible for climate and biodiversity balance – giving this concrete contribution to the negotiation as a whole for the formation of agreement and the realization of less destructive worlds. This is an example of Indigenous diplomacy and cosmopolitics in practice. Indigenous actors carry this diplomacy inside themselves, in their being, and to the negotiations – where it is observable on the outside, through their lifeways and the territorial practices they describe (even though these territories have altered), and where it shapes global environmental agreement-making.

So, ultimately, when we talk about cosmopolitics, we are talking about making worlds. And as researchers, we are studying these interactions, observing the different subjectivities, the negotiations between worlds and the creation of new worlds within the global environmental meeting or within the forest. Making the link with agreement-making, when we have this cosmopolitics at the table in negotiations, we're talking about negotiating practices, measures, activities that are not just related to amending the world that we have and the problems that the negotiations are directly attempting to tackle, but also the possibilities for bringing in these different worlds through the negotiation and, by bringing these different worlds to the negotiation, to creating a different kind of world, which would be a different kind of reality. This notion of agreement-making is part of the cosmopolitics as it recognizes the possibility of allowing different worlds in: worlds that are brought into the crafting of an agreement through Indigenous diplomacy. In this sense, agreement-making is a part of cosmopolitics.

5.2.2 Indigenous Diplomacies

When we consider cosmopolitics as not simply the product or expected result of agreement-making but as a fundamental part of the process, the possibility of having another world and politics can become embedded in the agreement. This form of diplomacy is not just a diplomacy that represents a specific group of people, but a diplomacy of the group (Vecchione-Gonçalves 2014).

When you study diplomacy and diplomatic practices, there is an idea that the diplomat is representing interests; these are not exactly the diplomat's interests per se, they are acting on behalf of a state. As such, the state delegate is expected to put their emotions and feelings for the object of negotiation to the side, to represent an interest and to act in the interest of the state. When you're talking about Indigenous diplomacies it's not a representative scheme, it's not an acting on behalf of; you're acting for a group because you are part of this group. This means that it is not a diplomacy *on behalf of*, but a diplomacy *for*, because you are part of the group and share its stakes. Because of this, when you are negotiating and making an agreement you are actually bringing in, to a certain extent, the interests and the lifeways that are practiced in the territories. There is a difference, and when you are researching, you have to take into consideration that you are talking about a diplomacy that is not just related to the negotiation event per se, but is bringing in a temporality and a spatiality that spills over the room because it comes prior to the negotiation room. This prior to, is not just in terms of procedures or diplomatic practice, but in terms of the politics of creating worlds – of living and lifeways in the territories that connect to making this politics of building worlds in the negotiation room. It is making a political space, which is also making a politics that is expanding the meaning of what it is to be political and who is the political.

5.2.3 Territory

Territory plays an important role, but perhaps not how an IR or politics reader expects, which are the expectations that I arrived at the Ashaninka territory with as an IR student. Of course, a student of IR knows that an international negotiation connects to territories in the sense of the national interest and nation-state. But, precisely because territory departs from a totally different ontological construction for Indigenous Peoples compared to what we see as territory in geopolitics, the way territorial interest is negotiated by Indigenous Peoples is going to be in dialogue with another way of defining what a political interest is, what the space of the political is and who the political subjects operating territorial politics are. To a great extent, putting territories at the center of negotiations is an attempt to save their worlds – and our world, which is in a state of climate and biodiversity emergency. Perhaps, because for Indigenous Peoples many times their worlds have already come to an end, there are different approaches to dealing with and to coexisting with emergencies. It is important to observe how they participate and play a role in agreement-making because they are already talking about worlds that came to an end, and yet they are showing very concrete possibilities of maintaining existence otherwise. They are living examples of it.

5.3 Studying Indigenous Agreement-Making Through Relations

Identifying the relations Indigenous groups I worked with have with territory and politics is important to show how I attempted to assemble a research methodology along the lines of producing a politics of relations with them. The fact that this politics of relations was built a few months after I arrived at the territory, which coincided with their preparation for the COP, made me realize in practice what relationality is. Relationality informs a manner of producing concepts and methods *with* the subjects in the research, immersed in their realities and considering what their own concepts about a subject matter are. Taking this conceptual production seriously, and making clear to the Indigenous groups how my process of meaning-making was nailed by their (Indigenous) politics, paved the way for me to produce knowledge in relation to their concepts. Producing knowledge (and concepts) is part of the ethical relation in relationality through which my research question was shaped through and by the political problems and issues mobilized in and for the territory.

When I got to the Kampa do Rio Amônia Indigenous Territory and to the Ashaninka extended living territory at the borders between Brazil and Peru, I was very much informed by the way Indigenous scholar Linda Tuhiwai Smith defines relationality. For her, relationality must be the basis for developing an Indigenous research methodology and for conducting research with Indigenous Peoples, because they have experienced so many extractions in their lives, including the extractive practices of research. Relationality, for her, implies more than identifying the research as a collaboration, when frequently the stages of shaping the research problem, interpreting data and deciding how the research is used are defined and controlled by non-Indigenous persons and scholars (Smith 1999, 43–45). Opposing this shallow basis of relating to the subject of research, Smith tells us that relationality implies reciprocity and reparation in the sense of searching for healing processes in research, which can contribute to coming to terms with appropriations, violence and hierarchization in the ways that research has been conducted. For Tuhiwai Smith, movements that produce inappropriate categorizations, or simply categorizations of the lives of others, which science and politics produce, lead to and enable control and colonization of everyday life aspects. Therefore, avoiding an approach that aims to control the participation and ways of engagement of Indigenous persons in research on negotiations

– negotiations that are shaping decisions about the future of the planet and that until now have impinged in a very extractivist manner on Indigenous Peoples' lives – is part of a relational process of bringing in reciprocity, for repairing, and for healing political control and scientific colonization.

This approach to research needs to be centered on equal relations and appreciation for Indigenous groups' approaches to organizing territory and politics (see Reflection Box 5.1), as well as their strategies for designing life projects based on territory during global environmental negotiations. Saying yes to Benki and following him to Copenhagen was critical to building a relational connection based on healing and reparation through agreements with the community and following a demand that was not mine but theirs. Thus, it was not a movement to conduct research to have a product such as a dissertation or an article; it was mostly an extended path to build the terms of relational research so that the kind of product emerging out of it could reflect other possible relations in research and contribute to building politics for the process of agreement-making. In the end, it was an attempt at reflecting other views about the future of the planet, and, even more so, about other politics for creating possibilities for other worlds of living as a plural project of equal permanence on Earth.

Following the meetings at the territory in preparation for Copenhagen, and after that for other COPs, I realized that serious engagement with the politics in the territories came first, and then came the possibility to physically follow this (cosmo)politics to the negotiations. This can be an expensive way to do research: it takes time and dedication, but it is also what is necessary to understand and see the international arena otherwise. From this starting point, I was able to see that within international negotiations there is more than representing a particular interest; there is a territorialized process that precedes this "international" and invades it. My research, unfolding as it did in this way, gave me a different departure point and provided me with a different kind of engagement with an Indigenous group. As a consequence of this, I was not observing political performances at one particular stage of negotiations, nor was I defining on which stage political actors – including Indigenous Peoples – should participate. I was following the articulation of a global, diverse, political subjectivity that was not mediated by statehood, but by relations beginning at the territory. Shaping such political subjectivity entailed relating and situating it to the past, present and future conditions and projects that have been designing Indigenous lifeways and diplomacies along space (territories, regions, borders and spaces of negotiations) and time (Indigenous stories and colonial histories, socio-ecological periods and the timeline of negotiations).

One of the things that came from this engagement was the different meanings of climate change and biodiversity loss, which are also revealing of the ethical stakes involved. These different understandings come from the different meanings given to life and the very immediate threats to its continuation, which take you in a different direction and give you a different knowledge of the issue than might be read in an Intergovernmental Panel on Climate Change (IPCC) report. This is particularly true for biodiversity and relevant to the design of the Intergovernmental Science-Policy Platform on Biodiversity and Ecosystem Services (IPBES). For many Indigenous groups, biodiversity is the diversity of life – not just the categorization of plant and animal species, but the diversity of all ways of living life relationally, which are lifeways. To take this perspective seriously is also to be part of this, to observe the diverse lifeways that we are a part of as a researcher and to recognize that there are other ways of ordering the world, even if it is just during a specific negotiation. If we are talking about agreement-making this is crucial, as different ways of ordering the world have been excluded, killed, exterminated because they were not seen and acknowledged as an order or as a "politics" to begin with. These are the stakes in Indigenous diplomacies, and in the research with Indigenous Peoples. Going back to relationality, the researcher and the research will be shaped by this politics, by these relations and by these ways of understanding. When seeing the ethical stakes as this, you (and your research) are affected and changed from inception, and the ethics of the method will never again be a simple procedure to check. Covalidation and credits in knowledge creation will be traded not only with the scientific community, but also with Indigenous groups understood as a People.

This perception – that as a researcher we are dealing with a People, and not a particular person or representative in negotiations – is fundamental to building relations and to conveying the dimension and character of Indigenous groups' participation in environmental negotiations, particularly if, as a researcher, we are only able to follow one or two specific meetings or to conduct virtual ethnography on meetings of a representational caucus. In this case, when analyzing positions and evaluating ways of approaching an Indigenous person representing a People or a regional Indigenous association, for example, in the Local Communities and Indigenous Peoples' Platform (LCIPP), it is vital to be aware of the nuance and variations of peoples, regions and, critically, relationalities of different colonial histories in the past and in the future. To illustrate, it was through political engagement with the representational politics of Ashaninka people as a People in regional and global politics that I built relations – to Benki and to others – through which I came to see biodiversity as the diversity of ways of living life (lifeways). Observing how their territorial issues were presented at negotiations as global problems, beyond the idea of Indigenous contributions to a previously set agenda, I was able to formulate that Indigenous diplomacy in agreement-making has the potential to create new worlds and other possibilities of environmental management. Engagement with Indigenous politics as a way of conducting research is key, and it is not easy to have this form of engagement from or at a single meeting.

The issue with doing research on Indigenous activism or participation in negotiations at a single event – turning up, documenting and conducting interviews – is that you end up with a partial view, analysis and evaluation of the politics described earlier. Nonetheless, if acknowledgment of Indigenous politics and history of participation in negotiations is made, instead of trying to engage Indigenous persons participating in negotiations through a presettled research agenda and questions, it could allow for conveying openly the partiality of research. By doing this, one can unveil and clarify limits of interpretation of the politics of how to develop and organize agreement-making by reflecting on the whole scenario for the participation of a complex and diverse political ensemble such as Indigenous Peoples that can reflect, perhaps, a limit on the very structure of the negotiations. Thus, even if not everyone has the opportunity to undertake extended engaged research beginning at the territories, it is important to consider the possibility of doing medium- or long-term research that is developed through this acknowledgment that allows you to accept and connect partial views over time.

Engaged research also needs to come with a cautionary note, in that in developing this engagement and the reciprocal relationships that it is dependent on, a researcher must not promise things to an Indigenous group that cannot be delivered. False promises begin from announcing things in an article and not delivering on these in the paper or from collaborating to write a project or translate a declaration during a negotiation meeting that you ultimately do not provide. Coming to terms with this is part of building the equal relations I talked about in the beginning of this section, and which is a fundamental constitutive element of reciprocity and reparation in research. This is also true when we are extracting information on site in dialogue or interviewing Indigenous persons. In this situation, when the relation was built on site and is not continuous, it is important to follow up and return to participants the systematization and analysis of the material, which is really a translation of a "voice" on a particular issue and not the researcher giving "voice" to Indigenous participants.

5.4 Methods of Relational Research

The methods used in research can facilitate building the relations that this type of research depends upon. Multisited ethnography, as a method, attuned me to the importance of engaging with the groups that I was working with in different places – I started from where they live and where they relate to each other. These are sites that are places of building life and territory for living, as well as sites where groups negotiate how they relate to each other and to specific representational spaces. It is often not enough to look at one specific place, because other sites and relations are informing the socialities within that place (Clifford 1997; Tsing 2005). Had I just turned up at a COP, I would not have understood that the negotiation had begun within the territory and between a different set of groups and actors to those they were making agreement with at sites of global climate or biodiversity negotiations. Acknowledging this multi-spatiality as a way of building a broad territory for Indigenous politics can help to come to terms with relationality even when it is not possible to be at multiple territories of political performance and actuation.

In many respects, I came to this research method without being consciously aware that I was doing it at the time. This was before my PhD, before I started to think about borders, when I was working with the Guarani People. When I first approached Indigenous Peoples' politics in 2007, it was through research that later I came to understand as activist research. At that time, I was working for an NGO in partnership with the Federal Public Attorneys in Brazil, also called the Public Ministry. The aim of the partnership was to identify possibilities for creating a transborder Guarani Citizenship through law and public policies for Guarani People living across the territories of Argentina, Bolivia, Brazil and Paraguay. Although Guarani Citizenship was already practiced in terms of transiting across borders at the southern end of Brazil, there was no legal recognition for this. Citizenship for the Guarani People would mean more than a document and access to rights, such as to health and education, within countries in the Southern Cone, as important as these are;

it would enable legal transit and to be in transit despite borders. They also wanted to be able to reside in places weaved by kinship according to tradition, but not limited to this, as land disputes and environmental degradation were confining and dispossessing territories. Mobility that has always been part of their lifeways, in many cases, turned into survival, making place through places (Vecchione-Gonçalves 2014) and expanding the space and possibilities of politics throughout the region.

The simplicity of turning the sources of our (research) questions to the problems the Guarani People were pointing out and, mainly, to let the research and its application to be guided by the issues they were classifying as problems, engendered a way of doing research and social work that was completely different from what most of us working on the project were used to. It was through this social cartography of the ecology of problems – going from accommodating tri-national Guarani children in regular schools to managing lands at borders, and environmentally thinking the territory in terms of policies beyond borders – that we realized the ethics of the research. Shaping politics for and with the Guarani People would be to recognize *their politics* of conveying social, land and environmental problems as hindering and blocking their extended places of living (Mato 2000).

In this project, Indigenous persons were not our objects of social work and public policy implementation, but political subjects crafting their politics in motion. The object was not to find the right answers, but to make an effort to build the appropriate questions. Information given and turned into data by the Guarani People was a way of designing the research problem and situating their world as an ontological political problem for those working with them. They were as involved as us in designing the social and the political fact as an international problem and as a problem of negotiating worlds. Their gift in sharing had to be combined with our debt (Strathern 1990), paid in doing research differently – reporting, citing and returning (giving back). For this project, ethics could not be theoretical, but forged in practice, taking the making of Indigenous Peoples' politics seriously and their concepts about mobility, land and lifeways even more seriously as a politics of making places (Escobar 2008) and worlds of living (cosmopolitics) through their own diplomacies.

Reflection Box 5.1 How do I conduct ethical research on Indigenous Knowledge?

Questions from Silvia Carolina Ruiz Rodriguez

Silvia: I read in the chapter that conducting research with Indigenous People and Local Communities (IPLCs) in their territories and international negotiations is a slow process (or slow research) that involves ethical challenges. Since many researchers lack the opportunity to research with IPLCs, I conduct research about IPLCs and their traditional knowledge in international negotiations. What would you identify as the ethical challenges faced by research about IPLCs and their traditional knowledge in international negotiations? What could be potential "solutions" to address these challenges?

In the chapter, we highlight the distinction between research "on" and research "with" Indigenous Peoples. We describe how Marcela's research with the Guarani People and Ashaninka People took shape, not at recognized "sites" of negotiation within global environmental governance but within their territory and as shaped by their stakes and concerns rather than a ready-made research question. Through the relations Marcela built, her participation and the practical support she provided, she gained an understanding that departed from the discipline because it was informed by Indigenous practices of diplomacy and the lifeways these bring to global environmental agreement-making.

From this work, Marcela doesn't give us solutions but highlights some of the ethical considerations that the researcher needs to become aware of and sensitive to in their research practice. In terms of forming these relationships and engaging in Indigenous politics, Marcela stresses that reciprocity is key to this research and for building the relationships that it rests upon, and that it is vital not to promise what you can't follow through with and provide.

Not all researchers have the opportunity to undertake the types of fieldwork that has enabled Marcela to form the relationships and perspectives described in this chapter. Thus, research "on" or "about" may appear to be the only available and practical option for conducting the research. From our perspective, this raises questions of whether the research risks interfering, hindering or, even worse, extracting from the purposes of Indigenous diplomacy at global environmental meeting sites. As the chapter describes, the stakes in preserving Indigenous lifeways are unfathomably high, and so the question is: does my research detract from that? There are also questions about who gains from the research, from the participant's time and the resulting outputs? Often as a researcher, our research is informed by our own purposes – a PhD, a funding proposal, a research grant, publications – which aren't necessarily of any benefit to research participants, unless their concerns and purposes are allowed to shape it. The same for conducting interviews: the researcher has questions of validity that indicate that a certain number of participants need to be approached, interviewed, recorded and transcribed to obtain the required data for analysis. The practices of research Marcela describes are not circumscribed by set disciplinary concerns – she allowed her fieldwork to unravel and reshape her research questions and, reciprocally, this provided insight for the research through the practical support she provided to her participants. Of course, there are individual consequences in terms of academic advancement, and even personally and emotionally, in conducting this type of research because it does not align with academic timelines and institutional requirements.

Silvia: How can researchers approach IPLCs at a COP? What could be considered "rules of thumb" in this regard? For example, what spaces, in a COP venue, are most appropriate for approaching IPLCs? Besides carefully listening, how else could researchers show respect to IPLCs when interacting with them?

Marcela doesn't offer a ready-made guide in this way. There may be specific guidelines for engagement prepared by the Indigenous groups that you intend to research, and many institutions also have guidelines for research involving Indigenous Peoples. Work has been undertaken by members of the Local Communities and Indigenous Peoples Platform (LCIPP) within the UNFCCC to facilitate the preparation of these guidelines and to create a shared repository. On the LCIPP website, there are resources available, such as the guide on "working towards ethical engagement in research involving the Sami" (Holmberg 2021), as well as a webinar designed to address similar questions: "What does ethical and equitable engagement of Indigenous Knowledge of climate change look like?" (UNFCCC 2021).

Silvia: My PhD focuses on the role of different knowledge systems in marine biodiversity negotiations. In my short experience on site, only representatives of IPLCs with a natural science background have consented to have an interview with me. Beyond the politics of knowledge, what other issues could spark interest in IPLCs to become research participants?

In many respects, this question goes to the heart of Marcela's discussions on the centrality of relationality and reciprocity in Indigenous research, which indicate that research interests need to be informed and shaped by Indigenous interests in and at the sites of study. More and more researchers are interested in Indigenous groups as political actors and Indigenous knowledge as informing global environmental governance. As this chapter makes clear, however, Indigenous leaders and representatives come to these events with their own political purposes, which may or may not include engaging researchers and participating in engaged research.

Increasingly, we wonder whether there is another way that Indigenous diplomacies can inform research: for example, by allowing what we learn from and through Indigenous political engagements and practices – windows into Indigenous lifeways – to interrogate our own relationship to and on the world. After all, it isn't Indigenous cultures that are destroying the world. The majority of research is conducted by researchers – like ourselves – embedded within and structured by a culture that is extractive and destructive of human and environmental worlds. What if we used these windows into Indigenous lifeworlds as openings to better understand our own so that we may learn how we have internalized and reproduce degrading relations and learn to remake ones that are healthier for ourselves, for our research interactions and for the planet?

Without realizing it, I started to do activist research (Hale 2006) and multisited ethnography (Marcus 1995), experimenting and collaborating in an emergency and an emergent Indigenous political mobilization that conjoined a situated problem with a structural world issue concerning Indigenous communities living within nation-state borders.

5.4 Conclusion

In this chapter, there was an attempt to show, through the stories of my research experiences, that research questions can be or may be shaped during the process of doing research in relation to the political subjects that are shaping the very space of observation. The agreement-making territory is not just the space of the official negotiations, it is a point of convergence that connects the past, present and future of the Indigenous groups that I have been working with. This perception was not something that I brought beforehand, when I planned the data collection. It came to me as a process, when I was following the politics of Indigenous groups to define what would be important to them to defend their territories and their lifeways at home. At the end of the day, for them to be at global environmental negotiations was to be shaping their endurance in the world and the continuation of their worlds. These movements were what shaped Indigenous diplomacies and cosmopolitics through and to sites of environmental agreement-making. This is not something that I realized by myself, but an understanding that I was able to come to through the process of doing research with Indigenous groups before, during and after environmental negotiations.

This chapter has been written in collaboration between Marcela and Hannah. In many ways our collaboration reveals that just as the approach to ethical research with Indigenous Peoples described by Marcela is dependent on building relations, so too is bringing this research to light.

Further Reading

1. de La Cadena, M. (2015) *Earth-Beings: Ecologies of Practice Across Andean Worlds*. Durham, NC: Morgan Lectures Series: Duke University Press.

In this book, Marisol de la Cadena tells us stories and strategies of Indigenous Peoples in the Andes on building relations with humans and nonhumans to achieve balance in contention to difference between many different lifeways and environments. Although it is not a book on the role of Indigenous Peoples or of a specific Indigenous group in negotiations, it addresses in a detailed and relational way how the Turpos, an extended family of Quechua people, have been building what she calls *political strategies* to keep their world alive in relation to the other political environments or worlds that make the Andean region. By telling this story, she also expands on her way of doing research with them and producing knowledge about politics there and elsewhere.

2. Brysk, A. (2000). *From Tribal Village to Global Village: Indian Rights and International Relations in Latin America*. Stanford: Stanford University Press.
3. Escobar, A. (2018). *Designs for the Pluriverse Radical Interdependence Autonomy and the Making of Worlds*. Durham, NC: Duke University Press.
4. Li, T. M. (2014). *Land's End Capitalist Relations on an Indigenous Frontier*. Durham, NC: Duke University Press.

References

Apiah, K. A. (2006). *Cosmopolitanism: Ethics in a World of Strangers*. London: Allen Lane Books.

Beier, J. M. (2005). *International Relations in Uncommon Places Indigeneity, Cosmology, and the Limits of International Theory*. London: Palgrave Macmillan.

Benhabib, S. (2006). *Another Cosmopolitanism*. Oxford: Oxford University Press.

Blaser, M. (2014) Is Another Cosmopolitics Possible? *Cultural Anthropology*, 13(4), 545–570.

Clifford. J. (1997). *Routes: Travel and Translation in the Late Twentieth Century*. Cambridge: Harvard University Press.

de la Cadena, M. (2010). Indigenous Cosmopolitics in the Andes: Conceptual Reflections beyond "Politics." *Cultural Anthropology*, 25(2), 334–370. https://doi.org/10.1111/j.1548-1360.2010.01061.x.

de la Cadena, M. with Blaser, M., eds. (2018). *A World of Many Worlds*. Durham: Duke University Press.

Escobar, A. (2008). *Territories of Difference Places, Movements, Life, Redes*. Durham, NC: Duke University Press.

Hale, C. (2006). Activist Research v. Cultural Critique: Indigenous Land Rights and the Contradictions of Politically Engaged Anthropology. *Cultural Anthropology*, 21(1), 96–120.

Holmberg, A. (2021). *Working Towards Ethical Guidelines for Research Involving the Sámi*. Sámiráđđi–Saami Council. Available at https://lcipp.unfccc.int/sites/default/files/2022-06/Working%20towards%20ethical%20guidelines%20for%20research%20involving%20the%20Sami_0.pdf (last accessed 11.08.2022).

Krenak, A. (2019). Ideias para adiar o Fim do Mundo. São Paulo: Companhia das Letras, *Revista ANTHROPOLÓGICAS*, 31(1), 317–326.

Marcus, G. (1995). Ethnography in/of the World System: The Emergence of Multi-Sited Ethnography, *Annual Review of Anthropology*, 24, 95–117.

Mato, D. (2000). Not "Studying the Subaltern," but Studying with "Subaltern": Social Groups, or, at Least, Studying the Hegemonic Articulations of Power. *Nepantla: Views from South*, 1(3).479–752.

Smith, L. T. (1999). *Decolonizing Methodologies: Research and Indigenous Peoples*. London: Zed Books.

Strathern, M. (1990). *The Gender of the Gift: Problems with Women and Problems with Society in Melanesia*,1st ed. Berkeley: University of California Press.

Tsing, A. L. (2005). *Friction: An Ethnography of Global Connections*. Princeton, NJ: Princeton University Press.

UNFCCC (2021): *LCIPP Webinar 2: What Does Ethical and Equitable Engagement of Indigenous Knowledge of Climate Change Look Like?* https://lcipp.unfccc.int/calendar-events/lcipp-webinar-2-what-does-ethical-and-equitable-engagement-Indigenous-knowledge-climate-change-look (last accessed 16.08.2022).

Vecchione-Gonçalves, M. (2009). Between the Leader of Virtù and the Good Savage Indigenous Struggles and Life Projects in the Amazon Basin. In J. M. Beier, ed., *Indigenous Diplomacies*. New York: Palgrave Macmillan, pp. 133–154.

Vecchione-Gonaçalves, M. (2014). *Managing Borders, Nurturing Life: Existences, Resistances and Political Becoming in the Amazon Forest*. Unpublished PhD dissertation, Hamilton: McMaster University. Available at https://macsphere.mcmaster.ca/handle/11375/1609.

Part II

Navigating Sites

6

Negotiations

Navigating Global Environmental Conferences

TRACY BACH AND BETH MARTIN

6.1 Introduction

Global environmental meetings provide a locale for understanding how multilateral environmental agreements (MEAs) become words on paper that shape international practices and norms. These meetings are central sites of global environmental agreement-making, because they provide diverse actors with a negotiation space and process for the development of treaty text. Some meetings occur in the early stages of treaty-making, where exploratory groups are convened to determine the need for a new international agreement and begin drafting its contours. For example, the United Nations has convened, since 2017, an intergovernmental conference to establish an international, legally binding instrument on the conservation and sustainable use of the marine biological diversity of areas beyond national jurisdiction under the United Nations Convention on the Law of Sea (commonly referred to as BBNJ) (UNGA 2017). Some meetings take place after MEA ratification, where conference of party (COP) decisions reflect parties' interpretation and refinement of their treaty obligations. Notable examples of these kinds of meetings are those held under the United Nations Framework Convention on Climate Change (UNFCCC) and the Convention on Biological Diversity (CBD). These decisions, and the treaty language they interpret, result from detailed drafting and extensive negotiations that seek to achieve consensus on party-driven agenda items.

Agreement-making processes before and after treaty formation can serve as different but equally relevant sites of research. Observing these global environmental negotiations – whether in large climate change COPs or smaller negotiations to form new agreements – provides meaningful opportunities for understanding the power relations that shape MEAs. But MEA negotiation sites can be large and complex, with an array of spaces, activities, participants, and objectives. First entering a site venue can be overwhelming: Who are all these people? Which room is the plenary? Where are the side-event rooms? Where do I find who to talk to? Wait, the negotiators are talking about which document?

Placing oneself and one's research at an MEA COP requires understanding the physical space and the governance mechanisms that shape it. All MEAs establish core governance structures, such as COP plenary decision-making, subsidiary body technical analysis and discussion, and a secretariat's administrative support. Likewise, all MEAs operate by rules and procedures developed for agenda setting and voting, and the kinds of documents under consideration (see Chapter 8). With this foundation, the researcher can put on-site activity in context, placing the actors on this stage – from state parties and their negotiation groups to observers and media – within the spaces they engage.

This chapter provides practical guidance to those who attend, observe, and collect data at MEA negotiation sites. It will help researchers design and implement their studies, and situate their academic work in the negotiation process. Scholars, students, and observers at all stages of their careers will find this chapter useful when preparing to attend an MEA supreme body meeting, navigating on-site, and working to understand and analyze their observations afterward. It can also help when choosing whether to attend in person or not, highlighting the digital resources now available that make that decision easier. In sum, by unpacking the multiple actors, sites, and processes through which environmental agreements are made and the new arrangements these create, this chapter helps the reader find the appropriate site for their research and navigate events more confidently.

6.2 MEA Governance and Structure

Large MEAs typically take the form of a framework convention. Within the conventions, countries agree to an environmental goal, common principles, commitments to collect and share pertinent information, and procedures for making collective decisions that help advance the MEA's aim. Framework conventions anticipate refinement, amendment, and additional collective obligations as problem-solving knowledge grows (Bodansky 2010). For example, the UNFCCC is the basis for the Kyoto Protocol and the Paris Agreement. The CBD has led to the Cartagena and Nagoya Protocols. The Montreal Protocol is now more well-known than its framework convention, the Vienna Convention for the Protection of the Ozone Layer (UNEP 2019).

Each MEA creates a governance structure through which parties deepen their knowledge of how to achieve collective goals and negotiate how to refine treaty obligations accordingly (Brunnée 2018). MEA governance relies on collective decisions taken by a supreme body that is composed of all parties at annual meetings called conferences of parties. To prepare COP decisions, supreme bodies rely on subsidiary bodies composed of experts from party delegations who research, negotiate, and recommend draft decisions. In addition to standing subsidiary bodies defined by individual MEAs, ad hoc bodies such as working groups and constituted bodies can be created by COP decision to focus on specific topics. Figure 6.1 illustrates these layers of governance as they have evolved under the climate regime.

In all levels of MEA governance structures, leadership is carefully composed by geographic region and development status to ensure inclusiveness and move decision-making toward consensus. Agenda setting is the subject of intense negotiation at each governance level, as all items placed on plenary, subsidiary body, and ad hoc body agendas result from a process of negotiation and compromise. A secretariat provides administrative support throughout the year. When conducting research at a COP, understanding an MEA's governance structure gives insight into the organization of the negotiation site and context for research observations.

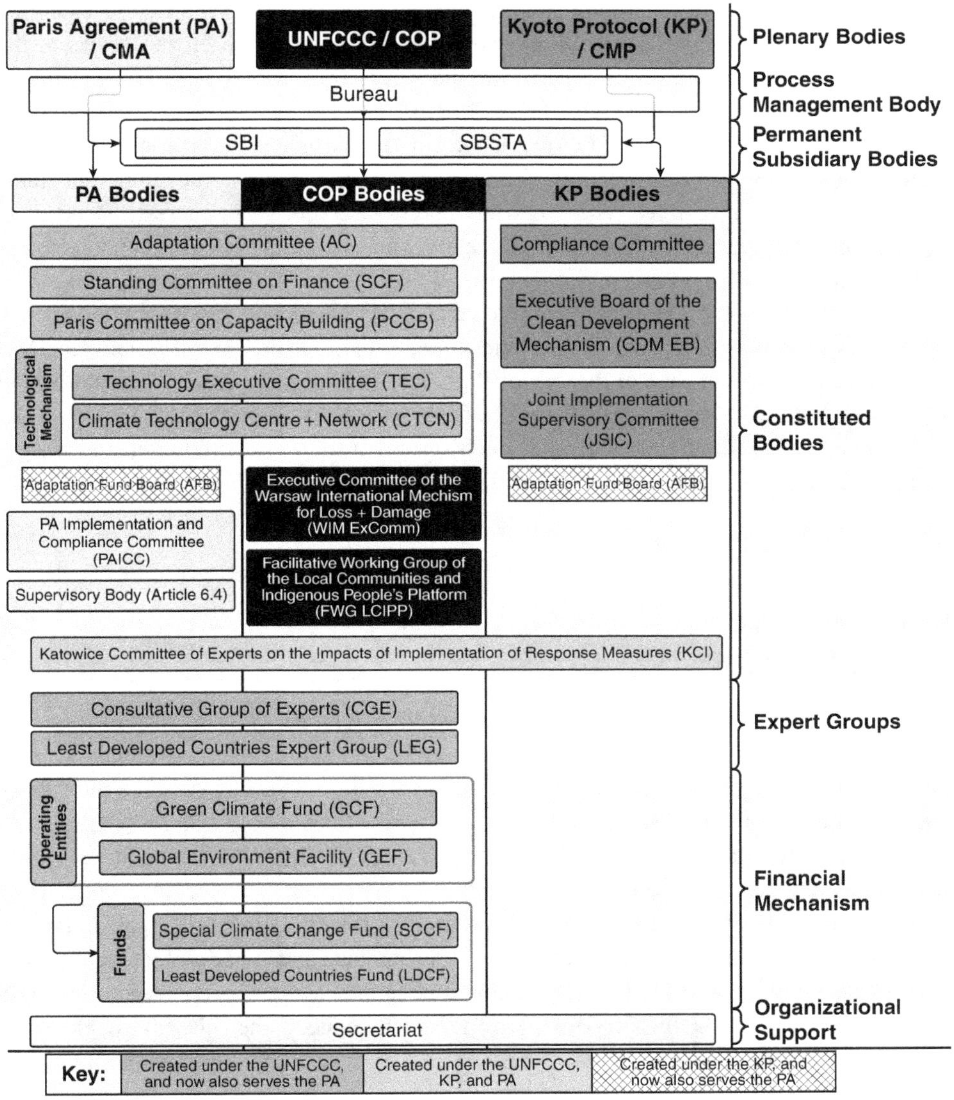

Figure 6.1 UNFCCC climate change governance structure.

6.2.1 Supreme Bodies

Supreme bodies of MEAs keep treaty implementation "under regular review" (UNFCCC 1992, art. 7.2; UN CBD 1992, art. 23.4). This plenary power manifests at periodic COPs, where parties take "the decisions necessary" for effective implementation (UNFCCC 1992, art. 7.2). Each COP is led by a country presidency selected from one of the five recognized UN regions – Africa, Asia, Latin America and the Caribbean, Central and Eastern Europe, and Western Europe and Others – in a regular rotation (UNFCCC 2002). COPs are numbered to delineate the number of times the supreme body has met. For example, the December 2021 climate negotiations were the 26th Conference of the Parties to the UNFCCC, the 16th meeting of the parties to the Kyoto Protocol, and the 3rd meeting of the parties to the Paris Agreement (COP26/CMP16/CMA3).

To support the success of a COP presidency, a Bureau is elected at each session. Its members are deliberately drawn from countries of diverse economic development status from all geographical regions. With this wide representation of party interests, the Bureau supports the COP president's leadership of the meeting, such as negotiations on key points of disagreement, and provides continuity throughout the year (UNFCCC 2002). For example, in the climate arena, the Bureau comprises the COP president, seven vice-presidents, the chairs of the two subsidiary bodies, and a rapporteur. Of these eleven members, two are selected to represent each of five regional groups, and one to represent the small island developing states (UNFCCC 1996, Rule 22). During the COVID pandemic of 2020–2021, the Bureau provided continuity and made decisions on the delay, rescheduling, and reorganizing of COP26 and SB52 (UNFCCC Press Office 2020).

6.2.2 Permanent Subsidiary Bodies

The next layer of governance within MEAs consists of permanent subsidiary bodies that report to the COP. These subsidiary bodies and their charges are established by the treaty language and are permanent, existing for the duration of the treaty. The number, mandate, and composition of permanent subsidiary bodies varies with each MEA.

In the climate regime, two subsidiary bodies were created in the text of the UNFCCC: the Subsidiary Body for Scientific and Technological Advice (SBSTA) and the Subsidiary Body for Implementation (SBI) (see Figure 6.1). These bodies now also serve the Kyoto Protocol and the Paris Agreement. Both advise the COP/CMP/CMA on matters within their mandates, drafting recommendations for COP decisions on specific agenda items (Kyoto Protocol 1997, art. 15). The SBSTA advises on scientific, technological, and methodological matters, including on technology development and transfer, technical guidelines for data collection (such as national communications and emission inventories), and methodological work (UNFCCC 1992, art. 9). It also connects the scientific work of the Intergovernmental Panel on Climate Change (IPCC) to the COP's policymaking needs, ensuring that continuously updated scientific knowledge feeds into the negotiating process. The SBI advises on implementation matters, including analyzing information submitted by the parties (such as national communications and emission inventories) to determine the Convention's, Protocol's, and Agreement's effectiveness (UNFCCC 1992, art. 10). The SBI also monitors budgetary and administrative matters. However, issues may cut across both SBSTA and SBI areas of expertise. For example, at SB51, agenda items on the Warsaw International Mechanism on Loss and Damage associated with Climate Change Impacts, the Koronivia joint work on agriculture, and the Adaptation Committee appeared on both the SBI51 and SBSTA51 agendas. Each subsidiary body is led by a chair, and has a vice-chair and rapporteur, who are chosen with geographic and development status diversity in mind. Party delegates participate in SBSTA and SBI sessions, drawing on their relevant expertise. The SBSTA and the SBI meet twice a year, at a mid-year meeting held in Bonn, Germany, at the UNFCCC secretariat and a year-end session held in conjunction with the annual COP/CMP/CMA.

Other MEAs have similar structures and practices related to subsidiary bodies. The CBD, for instance, established a Subsidiary Body on Scientific, Technical, and Technological Advice (SBSTTA) in 1994, which meets yearly with the aim to provide the COP with assessments on the state of biodiversity and responses to COP questions. In practice, the CBD SBSTTA has transformed into a "pre-COP" or "mini-COP," wherein state representatives (often the same ones that attend CBD COPs) prepare draft decisions in advance of upcoming CBD negotiations, which makes SBSTTA meetings interesting objects of research. In 2016, and similar to UNFCCC, CBD parties established an SBI to replace the nonpermanent Ad Hoc Open-ended Working Group on Review of Implementation of the Convention.

6.2.3 Ad Hoc Bodies

Layered within the work of the subsidiary bodies, a researcher can find ad hoc bodies such as working groups and constituted bodies. MEAs commonly give their supreme bodies the power to create additional subsidiary bodies via COP decision. Both ad hoc working groups and constituted bodies are used to complement, not duplicate, the work of permanent subsidiary bodies (MEA Handbook 2007).

Ad hoc working groups are used to address specific issues on an as-needed basis and typically have a defined timeline. In the climate regime, for example, when parties began negotiating the terms of what would become the Paris Agreement, the UNFCCC COP created the Ad Hoc Working Group on the Durban Platform for Enhanced Action (ADP) (UNFCCC 2022c). Once the Paris Agreement was negotiated, this COP established the Ad Hoc Working Group on the Paris Agreement (APA) to establish the guidelines needed to operationalize the agreement's entry into force (UNFCCC 2022a). Both the ADP and the APA concluded when their mandates were completed.

Constituted bodies, in contrast, are ad hoc subsidiary bodies with a defined membership and focus that have an open timeline. They provide "advice, technical input and expertise" to the supreme and subsidiary bodies within their prescribed mandates (UNFCCC 2017a, 15). The number of constituted bodies can grow and evolve as treaty implementation becomes increasingly technical. For example, in the climate regime, the COP/CMP/CMA have created fifteen constituted bodies to date (see Figure 6.1). Most of the constituted bodies originally created under the COP and CMP now help implement the Paris Agreement, including the Adaptation Committee, Adaptation Fund Board, Standing Committee on Finance, and Warsaw International Mechanism on Loss and Damage Executive Committee. The lone constituted body created by the Paris Agreement, developed through CMA decisions only, is the Committee to Facilitate Implementation and Promote Compliance referred to in Article 15, paragraph 2 of the Paris Agreement (PAICC) (UNFCCC 2022d).

It is important to note that while constituted and other ad hoc bodies may meet during the actual COP meeting, more often they occur during the intersessional period between meetings of the subsidiary bodies and the COP. This timing enables their work to feed into subsidiary body and COP decision-making.

6.2.4 Procedural Rules

MEAs give COPs the authority to establish procedural rules for the supreme, subsidiary, and ad hoc bodies. These operating rules can govern a wide range of logistical issues. For example, in the UNFCCC, they govern place and date of sessions, admission of observers and credentialing of parties and appointment of meeting officers (UNFCCC 1996). Procedural rules such as those governing agenda setting and the conduct of business, including voting, shape the negotiations in tangible ways.

6.2.4.1 The Importance of the Negotiation Agenda

Setting the negotiation agenda is a highly regulated part of MEA negotiations. Items placed on the agenda will receive the formal attention of all parties, as well as dedicated UNFCCC staff and consultant support. Items that are not placed on the agenda will not be discussed this way, even though side events, press conferences, protests, and other gatherings may keep them in the public eye. Given these stakes, plenary, subsidiary body, and ad hoc body agendas result from an intense process of negotiation and compromise.

In the climate regime, the draft rules of procedure that govern the COP/CMP/CMA negotiations lay out a two-step process for agenda setting. First, provisional agendas for the COP and SB meetings are drafted by the secretariat, agreed to in advance of the session by the COP president and SB chair(s), and sent to the parties in all six official UN languages at least six weeks before the session begins (UNFCCC 1996, Rules 9 and 11). Items make it on to this provisional agenda if they:

- arise under the COP's mandate set out in Article 7 of the UNFCCC,
- were mandated by previous COP decision,
- were forwarded under Rule 16 (UNFCCC 1996), or
- are "any item proposed by a Party and received by the secretariat before the provisional agenda is circulated" (UNFCCC 1996, Rule 10).

Second, the plenary or subsidiary body adopts the final agenda as the first order of business at its opening plenary. At this session, parties may ask to "add, delete, defer or amend items," although "only items which are considered by the Conference of the Parties to be urgent and important may be added to the agenda" (UNFCCC 1996, Rule 13).

Lack of agreement on the negotiation agenda happens regularly in the opening plenaries of both supreme and subsidiary bodies in the climate regime. One strategy commonly used to move the session forward is to hold contested items "in abeyance pending further consultations," which allows adoption of, and work on, the rest of the agenda while the presiding officer consults with parties on the disputed item (UNFCCC 2017a, 4–5). That officer will report on these consultations at a plenary meeting, and if no consensus has been reached by the final plenary meeting, the body may adopt the agenda without the item or choose to place it on the provisional agenda for the next session (UNFCCC 2017a, 5).

In the climate regime, a recent example of this kind of agenda negotiation occurred at COP22, when Turkey sought to add an item about granting access to the Green Climate Fund (GCF) and Climate Technology Centre and Network (CTCN) support for Paris Agreement parties like itself "whose special circumstances are recognized by the COP" (Chasek 2016a). Turkey is listed as an Annex 1 country under the UNFCCC and Kyoto Protocol, along with developed countries. Annex 1 countries are not eligible to receive financial and technology consulting support from the GCF and the CTCN, which are targeted to developing countries. Turkey had raised this same issue at the close of COP21. To achieve consensus on the Paris Agreement adoption, the French Presidency agreed to hold consultations on the issue before COP22. France reported at COP22's opening plenary that several negotiating groups opposed adding the agenda item. Turkey demanded a clear COP decision on the matter, and parties agreed to adopt the agenda with Turkey's request left pending under other matters (Chasek 2016a). At the close of the meeting, the COP22 president reported that no consensus had been reached and that consultations would continue on this item (Chasek 2016b). Further consultations took place at COP23 and, lacking consensus on Turkey's request, the COP "agreed to conclude its consideration of the matter" (UNFCCC 2017b). Because Turkey was unable to garner enough support from other parties, its agenda proposal was lost after several years of negotiations.

6.2.4.2 Conducting Business and Coming to Agreement

MEA procedural rules vary significantly on how COPs must agree when making decisions. Practices range from consensus on all substantive decisions (e.g., UNFCCC, CBD, BBNJ) to simple majority votes (e.g., amendments under CITES are adopted by a two-thirds majority of parties present and voting). The climate regime draft rules embody these diverse approaches and parties' conflicting opinions about them. Draft Rule 42 contains two alternative versions. Both assume that parties will "make every effort" to reach consensus on decisions but, when unable to, will resort to a voting scheme (UNFCCC 2018a, 11, art. 32). Alternative A defaults to requiring a two-thirds majority to pass all decisions, with some limited exceptions. Alternative B would require a two-thirds majority on substantive decisions and a simple majority on procedural decisions. Because the UNFCCC parties have not yet agreed on a voting rule, decisions taken by the COP, CMP, CMA, SBI, and SBSTA must be adopted by consensus.

Notably, consensus is not defined in MEA procedural rules. While many assume that consensus means unanimity, in fact it means that no party formally and explicitly objects to a decision. Instead, nonobjecting parties will typically note their specific concerns on the record via statements of position, reservations, and interpretive statements, usually captured in the report of the session. For example, in the climate regime, during the final plenary at COP21, when parties were poised to adopt the Paris Agreement, Nicaragua's attempt to take the floor to speak against it went unseen by the COP21 president as he gaveled the decision. Afterward, as parties gave their closing statements that were included in the COP21 report, Nicaragua recorded its objections (Chasek 2015).

MEA parties may also stop a burgeoning consensus by signaling that they will take the floor to disagree. For example, in the climate regime, a late night "Copenhagen Accords" at

COP15, negotiated by the world's major economies, was rejected by a group of developing countries at the closing plenary. The lack of consensus to "adopt" the Accords resulted in it merely being "taken note of," which lessened its impact on parties' behavior (Bodansky et al. 2017, p. 76). The perceived strength of consensus decision-making lies in including all countries to build a workable outcome that is accepted as legitimate (Brunnée 2002, 3). The weakness of seeking consensus can empower a small group that brings COP decision-making "toward the lowest common denominator." (Bodansky 2012). In the end, much of the Copenhagen Accords made its way into the consensus outcomes at COP16 and COP17, and led to the adoption of the Paris Agreement in 2015.

6.2.5 The Secretariat's Administrative Role

MEA secretariats provide organizational support and technical expertise for treaty negotiation and implementation. Their main functions are making practical arrangements for governance sessions; preparing official documents and reports; providing support to ongoing negotiation and implementation mandates; and coordinating with relevant international bodies, such as the Global Environmental Facility (GEF) and GCF, UN Development Programme (UNDP) and UN Environmental Program (UNEP), and related treaty bodies. Recent scholarship has noted the influence that these technical and administrative roles can give treaty secretariats over agreement-making (Bauer 2006; Biermann and Siebenhüner 2009; Depledge 2007; Jinnah 2014).

MEA secretariats vary in size, from the UNFCCC's staff of 450 in Bonn to the CBD's staff of 110 in Montreal (Secretariat of the Convention on Biological Diversity 2005). Each is institutionally linked to the United Nations via appointment of their Executive Secretaries, who report to the UN Secretary General and are accountable to their respective COPs. Given competing demands for their time and expertise, secretariats work with guidance from the COP Bureaux, which are consulted throughout the year.

The organizational structures of MEA secretariats vary with the work of each treaty. All typically have operations divisions focused on legal affairs, conference affairs, and administration services, like human resources and information technology. As of 2020, the UNFCCC secretariat's structure also reflects the current substantive work through program divisions on adaptation, mitigation, transparency, and means of implementation (finance, technology development and transfer, and capacity building), as shown in Figure 6.2.

6.3 Navigating a Supreme Body Meeting

The physical spaces of environmental negotiations, such as a COP, provide a stage for the myriad of activities that occur. Understanding how the physical space at an event is configured, the types of meetings that occur within it, and how construction and design are influenced by the governance structure is critical to a researcher. The following sections describe the physical setting encountered at a UNFCCC climate COP meeting. As a supreme body meeting, the UNFCCC COP has one of the more complex MEA governance

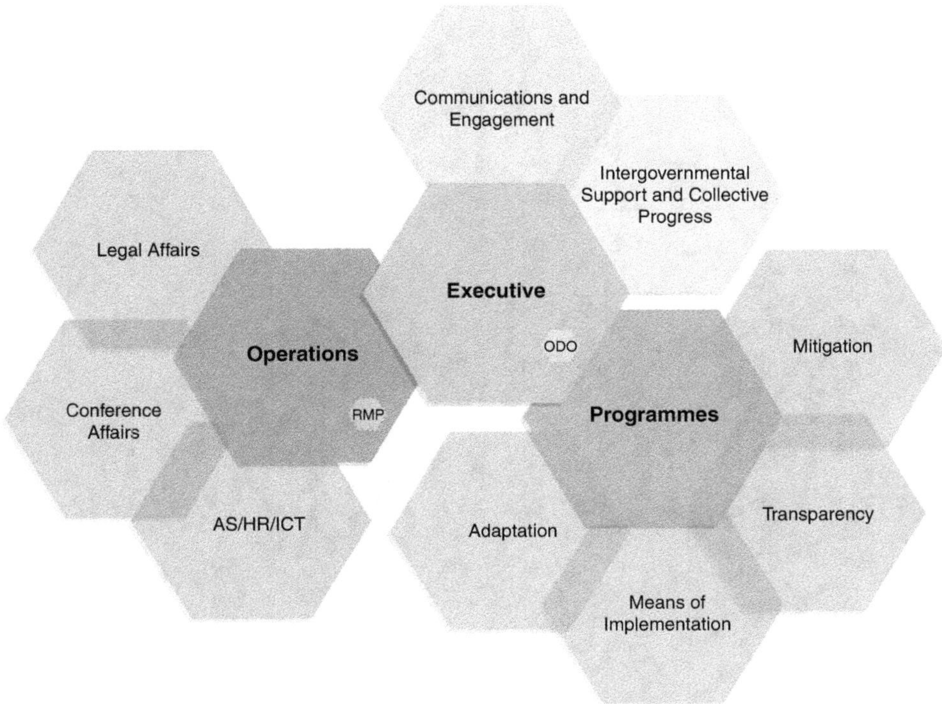

Figure 6.2 UNFCCC secretariat structure.
Source: UNFCCC 2022g.

structures which, combined with a large number of attendees, provides a comprehensive physical setting for examination.

6.3.1 The Venue

The venue at a COP is designed to enable a supreme body and subsidiary bodies to conduct the work put forth on their agendas. The venue will typically contain the following key spaces (see COP25 map in Figure 6.3):

- Negotiating spaces: plenary rooms (large enough for all parties), meeting rooms.
- Civil society spaces: side-event hall with meeting rooms, exhibit space, NGO pavilions, constituency offices.
- Party spaces: Party delegation offices, meeting rooms and pavilions.

Access to the venue requires a badge provided by a party or an official observer organization, as detailed in Chapter 2. Badges are colored according to role (i.e., party, observer, media) and are used to control access to certain spaces. For example, some negotiating sessions may be limited to party delegates only and UN security can ask to see a delegate's badge before the delegate is allowed to enter certain spaces (see Box 6.1).

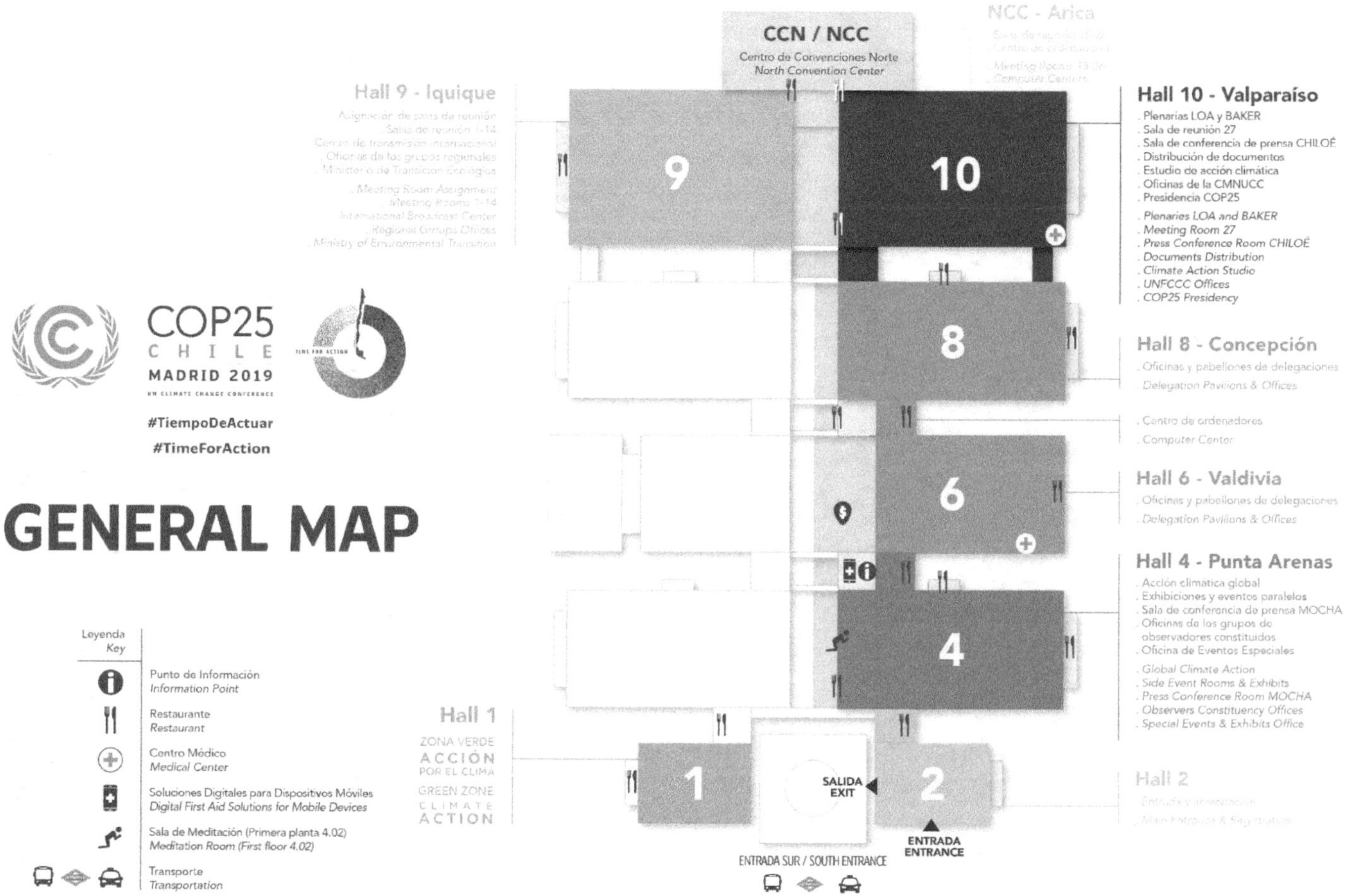

Figure 6.3 UNFCCC COP25 venue map, Madrid Spain, December 2019.
Source: UNFCCC 2019b.

6.3.2 Negotiating Spaces

Within the venue, different types of meetings are held in specific meeting spaces configured to facilitate discussion and negotiations (as listed in Table 6.1). As discussed in Section 6.7.2, an observer can find room location and open/closed status in each day's Daily Programme and in real time via CCTV and the UNFCCC negotiator app. Understanding the access to and purposes of these different spaces is important for locating your research (see Reflection Box 6.1).

The opening of the meeting of an MEA supreme body and subsidiary bodies will each begin with a plenary session held in a plenary room that is large enough to hold representatives from each party (as shown in Figure 6.4). A plenary room (see Figure 6.4) is arranged

Table 6.1 *Meeting types found at MEA COP and subsidiary body meetings*

Type of meeting	Task	Attendees/access	Format and location (2)
Contact group	"[T]o conduct negotiations on specific agenda items, with the aim of achieving an agreed outcome" (UNFCCC 2017a, par. 66)	Parties Observers	Plenary or large meeting room Typically theater style with long tables facing a front elevated dais
Informals	Facilitate open-ended consultations on designated agenda item. Outcomes are reported to the chair or presiding officer of the governing body, typically the contact group or subsidiary body (UNFCCC, 2017a, C)	Parties Observers – recommended that first and last sessions are open to observers. Parties retain right to request informal sessions be closed	Meeting room Rooms are typically arranged with tables in a square. Chairs often are lined behind the tables and available for additional party delegates and observers
Informal informals	A smaller group of parties working together on particular components of agenda items such as drafting a specific portion of language for an agenda item text (UNFCCC, 2017a, D)	Parties Rarely open to observers	Can be a room for delegates to meet informally or in a meeting facilitated by a delegate assigned by the presiding officer. (UNFCCC 2017a, par. 75)
Huddles and other informal gatherings	An impromptu meeting of negotiators that occurs during a session – often due to challenges in reaching agreement. Can be bilateral or multilateral	Parties Observers often gather on the outside of the huddle	Wherever negotiators happen to be. Can include party offices, conference rooms, hallways

Table 6.1 (*cont.*)

Type of meeting	Task	Attendees/access	Format and location (2)
Non-negotiating meeting (workshops, roundtables, dialogues)	Non-negotiating meetings in support of the negotiations. In the climate regime, these are created by a COP/CMP/CMA decision and can serve as ways for parties to gain deeper knowledge in a particular area, as ways to move past difficult points in the negotiations, and as a mechanism to operationalize or develop items requested by a COP (3)	Parties Observers These are typically open and are scheduled with agendas developed prior to the session beginning	These can be held in conjunction with larger meetings such as a COP or an SB or during an intersessional period between the COP and SBs
Coordinating meetings	Specific groups discuss, align interests and positions, and develop statements and talking points for various agenda items	Parties – Closed meetings accessible only to parties that are members of the group Observers – Closed to members of the constituency (some constituencies will have open meetings)	Assigned meeting rooms

Table 6.1 highlights the remaining types of negotiation meetings that can generally be found during a meeting of the COP or subsidiary bodies of an MEA. For details on side events see Chapter 7.

Notes:

(1) Agenda items referred to contact groups often have multiple and interrelated parts that require focused negotiation on each part. Focused negotiations often happen in informals where recommended decisions are then brought back to the contact group for balanced consideration of all components before being reported back to the plenary.

(2) All meetings other than plenary negotiations and associated documents are conducted in English.

(3) As an example, UNFCCC COP Decision 1/CP21 recognized the need and established a platform for local communities and Indigenous Peoples to strengthen knowledge, technologies, practices and efforts while exchanging experiences and sharing best practices on mitigation and adaptation (UNFCCC 2016, par. 135). While the platform was created, what it would actually contain and how it would work was undetermined. After a multistakeholder dialogue to gather views on the purpose, content, and structure, the COP through 2/CP.23 outlined the purpose and functions of the platform and decided that the first activity would be a multistakeholder workshop focused on implementing the articulated functions.

Reflection Box 6.1 The BBNJ negotiation sites

By Ina Tessnow-von Wysocki and Arne Langlet

After a decade of pre-negotiations – namely ad hoc working group and preparatory committee meetings (2006–2017) – the United Nations General Assembly decided to convene five **Intergovernmental Conferences (IGCs)** (2018–2022) to develop a new legally binding instrument for the conservation and sustainable use of Marine Biodiversity of Areas Beyond National Jurisdiction (BBNJ) under the United Nations Convention on the Law of the Sea (UNCLOS). During BBNJ IGCs governments negotiated the provisions of a new treaty, including the rules and procedures of its decision-making body (i.e., the future BBNJ COP).

Compared to large UNFCCC COPs, BBNJ IGCs were fairly small, with about 1,100 participants including state delegations, IGOs, and NGOs. Participation in the conference sessions was open to all stakeholder groups, but required prior registration to gain access to the **UN Headquarters in New York** and the conference rooms. The formal negotiations took place in the plenary room, with morning and evening sessions (three hours each morning and afternoon). **Plenary sessions and informal working group meetings** were accessible to all participants of the conference and were broadcast live on the **UN web-TV** (https://media.un.org/en). Prior to the conference, UNDOALOS prepared an agenda with topics to be covered. However, the president can decide to convene "**informal informals**," with limited space for NGOs.

Our research team, composed of three PhD students and one PI, combined **collaborative event ethnography (CEE)** and **digital ethnography** to collect data from all IGCs. Participation in plenary sessions and informal working group meetings helped us get a sense of the main positions and conflict lines, enabled systematic data collection (fieldnotes were taken on the basis of a matrix) and allowed us to identify and approach potential interviewees. **Side events** served a similar purpose: to approach interviewees, and to gain a deeper understanding of (a) aspects related to the contents of the treaty and (b) the purpose and effect of side events. Other venues, included **the Vienna Café**, **other lounges in the UN building**, **smaller conference rooms** where regional coordination and bilateral meetings took place, and **the corridors**. Although these are "sites" that play a crucial role in agreement-making (see Chapter 7), they are either difficult to study or closed to observers.

With its comparatively small size, a BBNJ IGC could be comprehensively studied with a small team of researchers. We could cover parallel sessions and conduct interviews during the meeting itself, which would be virtually impossible at a climate COP. Amongst such a small circle of participants, however, a researcher can be visible even within a seemingly crowded negotiation room.

theater style, with long tables facing a front elevated dais. Each party has a place at a table arranged alphabetically from front to back. Observers also have places at the tables behind parties. Plenary session are "open to participation by all Parties, observer States and organizations, the media and other participants registered for the climate change sessions" (UNFCCC 2017a, par. 64). While specific negotiations rarely take place in a plenary, the plenary provides space for agenda setting and statements by parties and observers on issues germane to the agenda as well as consideration and adoption of decisions put forward by

Figure 6.4 Informal stocktaking plenary held at COP26.
Source: Photo by IISD/ENB Mike Muzurakis (Muzurakis 2021b).

Figure 6.5 Informal negotiations on finance at COP26.
Source: Photo by IISD/ENB Mike Muzurakis (Muzurakis 2021a).

other fora. It is in other fora, such as contact groups, informals (Figure 6.5), informal informals, and unofficial huddles, that text negotiations and deliberations occur. The presiding officer of the plenary, during the agenda-setting item of the opening plenary, will send parties to work on specific agenda items in such fora, requesting that they report back to the supreme body (COP/CMP/CMA in the climate regime) at the conclusion of their work. Plenaries held at the end of sessions serve as the place at which fora report on their work and forward any recommended "decisions or conclusions for consideration or adoption" (UNFCCC 2017a, par. 64). Plenary is the only meeting space with simultaneous translation in the six official UN languages: Arabic, Chinese, English, French, Russian, and Spanish. Plenary documents are also issued in each of the six languages.

6.3.3 COP Actors and Their Spheres of Influence

Each COP venue is filled with a variety of actors, each with their own role and agenda. By definition, COPs are meetings of MEA parties, and so the main actors in the venue are country delegates. The second largest group are nonstate actors, who represent nongovernmental organizations (NGOs) and intergovernmental organizations (IGOs) working on international environmental issues. MEA COP attendance has grown significantly since 1992, when the UNFCCC and CBD were adopted. For example, the climate COPs before COP15 in 2009 averaged around 5,000 attendees, evenly distributed among parties, observers, and media (UNFCCC, 2022l). That changed dramatically in 2009, when more than 27,000 people came to Copenhagen for deliberations on the Kyoto Protocol's future. Climate COPs since COP21 have averaged more than 20,000 participants per year.

6.3.3.1 Parties and Their Groupings

MEAs typically have more than 100 parties who have ratified the treaty. For example, the UNFCCC currently has 197 parties, the Kyoto Protocol has 192 parties, and the Paris Agreement has 189 parties (United Nations Treaty Collection 2022b, 2022c, 2022d). The CBD has 196 parties, while the Montreal Protocol on Substances that Deplete the Ozone Layer has 198 parties (United Nations Treaty Collection 2022a, 2022e). Parties bring delegations to the supreme and subsidiary body meetings that are composed of a wide range of national actors, from government scientists and environmental ministry regulators to specialists in chemicals, biodiversity, and climate change. Higher-level ministers and heads of state and government may join their delegations when political compromises are needed. The size of party delegations varies widely, with typically a quarter numbering fewer than 30, host countries leading with more than 100, and the majority somewhere in between.

Within the broader UN system, countries with shared interests work within negotiating groups or blocs to gain leverage through alliances. Some negotiating groups, such as the G77, have become permanent actors in the system, including in MEA negotiations. The large number of MEA parties and time constraints at COPs can make working through negotiating groups a pragmatic choice: by agreeing on collective priorities, group positions can focus the negotiation agendas (MEA Handbook 2007). Being a member of a negotiating group can also build the capacity of smaller country delegations to track issues and improve the depth of their engagement in them. Of course, membership also means that internal bloc negotiations can lead to individual countries compromising on preferences in order to gain negotiating clout through the larger group.

In the climate regime, about 15 groups currently represent the collective interests of the almost 200 parties, as Figure 6.6 illustrates. (The climate regime is one of the most complex, in terms of the range of issues as well as the number of parties.) To operate effectively, group members coordinate intensively during supreme and subsidiary body meetings to agree on common positions. They hold preparatory sessions throughout the year and regular meetings during the COP, and choose a leader to speak for the group for a one- or two-year period. While individual countries may – and do – speak for themselves, the important role that negotiating groups play in managing the negotiations is recognized in opening and closing plenary practice: the four negotiation groups whose memberships do not overlap – the G77+China, the European Union, the Umbrella Group, and the Environmental Integrity Group – make interventions before the other groups, and only after individual countries have spoken (UNFCCC 2017a, 22).

Notably, most countries belong to more than one negotiation group, as the complexity of the graphic in Figure 6.6 depicts. For example, Senegal is simultaneously a member of the African Group, the Least Developing Countries (LDCs), and the G77 and China. Some large countries, like China, continue to speak individually while also affiliating with the group positions of the G77, BASIC, and LMDCs, depending on the issue at hand. Given the compromises inherent in negotiating as a group, it is critical to understand when a country speaks for itself or for a specific group. For example, if China speaks for G77, then its words represent the consensus position of a very diverse group of more than 130 countries. If speaking for BASIC, China speaks for only four members – Brazil, South Africa, India, and China – who are all emerging economies choosing to band together to advance common positions on access to climate finance, parity for adaptation and mitigation, and differentiated commitments. If speaking for the Like Minded Developing Countries (LMDC), China may take a position adverse to those of the G77 and BASIC, drawing a hard line on differentiation and finance as it emphasizes the importance of equity between developed and developing country commitments.

6.3.3.2 Observers and Their Constituencies

All MEAs have recognized the benefits of having nonstate observers attend and engage in the negotiations. In the climate regime, for example, the draft rules state that, "[a]ny body or agency, whether national or international, governmental or nongovernmental, which is qualified in matters covered by the Convention, and which has informed the secretariat of its wish to be represented at a session," may be admitted to attend (UNFCCC 1992, art. 7.6; UNFCCC 1996, Rule 7). Inherent in "qualified" are the knowledge, skills, and experience that NGOs, IGOs, and UN system bodies bring to the process. This can manifest in providing information on domestic implementation of MEA obligations, raising new issues not sufficiently addressed by an MEA, suggesting decision text and lobbying country delegations, and more generally holding information sessions on their activities and publicizing issues to the media (MEA Handbook 2007). As of 2017, 2,133 NGOs and 126 IGOs have been admitted as observer organizations in the climate regime. Two-thirds come from the Western Europe and Others regional group, 14% from Asia, 9% from Africa, 8.5% from Latin America and the Caribbean, and 1% from Eastern Europe (UNFCCC 2022j).

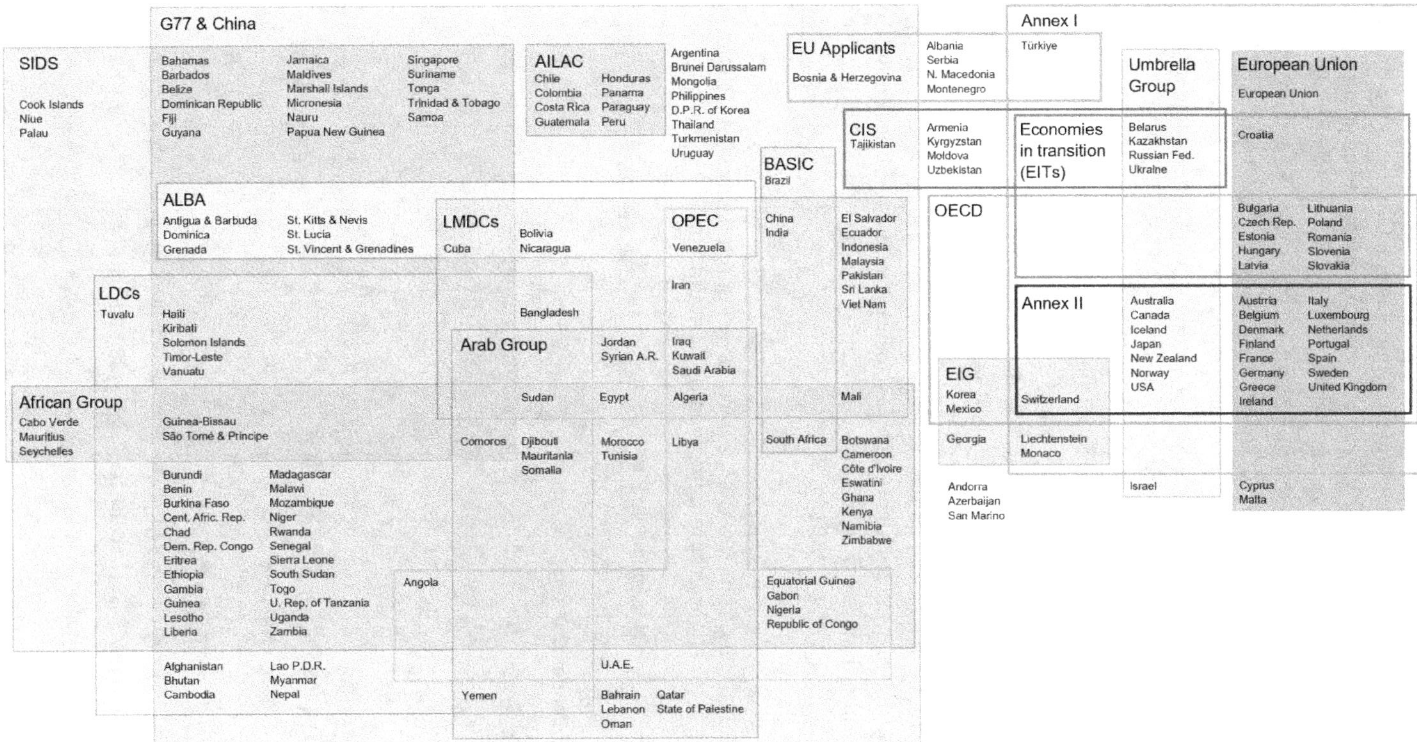

Figure 6.6 UNFCCC party negotiating groupings.
Source: Haller (2018).

Observers may attend open negotiation sessions, and representatives from each constituency may give statements at opening and closing plenaries. Observers are usually invited to briefings with the MEA's Executive Secretary and supreme and subsidiary body leaders at each COP. They may also organize and participate in side events, and file submissions per information requests by the parties. In the climate regime, NGO and IGO observers at COP22 organized 374 of the 473 side events offered, with ENGO and RINGO leading 243 of them (UNFCCC 2022i). Between 2015 and 2017, admitted NGO and IGO observers filed almost 60% of all nonparty stakeholder submissions, with the remainder submitted by UN system members and other nonparty stakeholders (UNFCCC 2022i).

Accredited NGO observers to the climate regime are organized within nine constituencies, affiliating with those that match its interests and activities. Many engagement opportunities, such as making plenary statements, attending limited-seating sessions, and nomination to constituted body meetings, require constituency affiliation (UNFCCC 2022b). ENGO and BINGO were the largest constituencies originally, but the growing number of NGOs participating in MEA COPs has led to the creation of new, smaller constituencies. RINGO is the lone constituency that is not advocacy oriented, instead serving as the platform for researchers and academics focused on evidence-based policymaking and fair procedure. Figure 6.7 highlights the relative distribution of NGO observers by constituency during COP26/CMP16/CMA3.

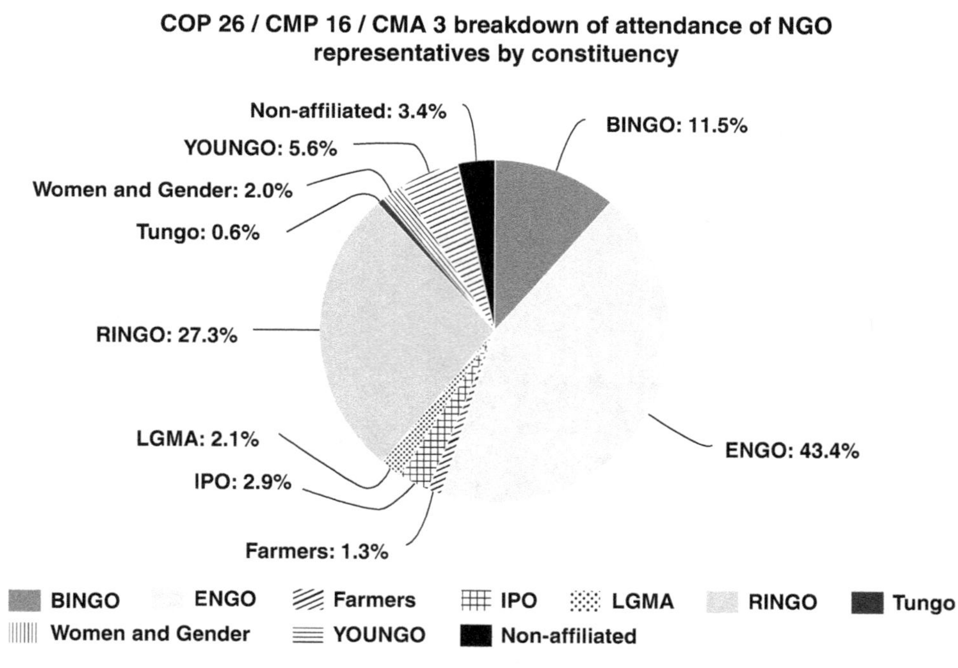

Figure 6.7 COP26/CMP16/CMA3 breakdown of attendance of NGO representatives by constituency.
Source: UNFCCC 2022e.

6.4 Tools for Navigating the Climate Negotiations

Preparing to engage in an MEA process is essential, whether attending in person or virtually. In addition to understanding the governance structure and physical space, successful COP engagement also has a temporal dimension. Learning what to expect at a COP takes place before departure; is adjusted daily, if not hourly, on-site; and is reflected upon and revisited when analyzing collected information. Arriving at an event with knowledge of the key issues a researcher is interested in as well as where to find related discussions (both in person, online, and in writing) is critical to efficient use of time. But how is that done?

6.4.1 Prior to the Event

Prior to an event occurring, it is important to become familiar with the evolution and content of a given topic area (see Chapter 2). As topics of interest in MEAs evolve, they are considered through ad hoc groups, constituted bodies, or placement on a meeting agenda. This evolution and current "location" of the topic of interest will be helpful for a researcher to understand before attending. Let's say, for example, that a researcher focusing on gender in the climate regime was attending the UNFCCC COP25 and wanted to observe discussions broadly around gender within the UNFCCC. First, it is important to understand the evolution of gender discussions in the negotiations. The UNFCCC Gender webpage provides a chronology of gender and the climate negotiations. This can help a researcher see how gender topics have originated from decisions and evolved through time. The webpage also includes links to key documents and other resources, such as a link to sign up for a gender newsletter. Next, a researcher would start with a visit to the UNFCCC website, specifically the home page for the session they are interested in – in this case, COP25 (UNFCCC 2022n). That page will provide a link to the provisional schedule and to a provisional agenda and an agenda for each body that is meeting at that session.

The provisional schedule provides a researcher with a high-level overview of events that will occur at the session (UNFCCC 2019d). It includes presessional meetings, preparatory as well as mandated events, and presidency initiatives and sessional meetings. The sessional meetings schedule includes negotiating meetings, mandated events and workshops, presidency events and other events. A review of the COP25 provisional schedule indicates, for example, that there is a presessional technical workshop on gender hosted by the presidency as well as a mandated event, "Gender Day."

Each body with negotiations during the event will have an agenda that is approved at the opening plenary. Agendas and their associated annotations are available in the weeks leading up to a session and are valuable starting points for a researcher. Reviewing the agendas for COP, CMA, CMP, SBSTA, and SBI at COP25 reveals that gender will be discussed in the negotiations under COP Agenda Item 13: "Gender and Climate Change," and SBI Agenda Item 17: "Gender and Climate Change." Reviewing the associated annotations provides details on the background of the topic, reports and decisions related to the topic, ongoing areas of work, and actions that are currently before the body (UNFCCC 2019a). Annotations will often also include key documents and document numbers and links to the topic website (if one exists). Also helpful are any information notes or reflection notes written by the chair or facilitators of the session. For gender at this session, there was not a note for the SBI session, but as an example a note was provided by the SBSTA chair for the SBSTA session (UNFCCC 2019c).

Reviewing submissions on a particular topic prior to attendance at an event is another way to gain insight into perspectives of parties, negotiating groups, and observers. Submissions are a way in which parties and organizations can provide input on a certain agenda item or topic under discussion. The governing body will issue a call for written submissions on topics under negotiation to provide parties an opportunity to weigh in on a written and deliberative manner. Calls for submissions can also be extended to NGOs where appropriate. The Submissions and Statement Portal is a public site that allows a visitor to search by keyword, document type, body, year, submitter, and language (UNFCCC 2022h). Continuing with our example, a query on the keyword "gender" pulls up five "Calls for Submissions, Elections and Statements for Consideration at Upcoming Session" and nine "Calls for Submissions, Elections and Statements considered at Past Sessions."

In addition to submissions are a wide variety of documents that serve to, among others, document decisions, provide draft negotiating texts, report on questions and requests that arise in decisions and through negotiations, and provide insight as to progress on work or detail ways forward for work. A variety of documents are associated with a conference and are explained in detail in Chapter 8. Reviewing key documents that are associated with your area of research can help with premeeting preparation.

While the aforementioned resources address the negotiating sessions, side events, pavilion events, exhibits, and other activities occurring in the venue will also address research topics. While negotiating schedules are published daily, side-event schedules and exhibit locations are published several weeks prior to the conference. Pavilion event schedules are also often published prior to the conference. Recently, the secretariat has been posting pavilion schedules on the conference webpage (UNFCCC 2022k). Reviewing the event schedules, calendaring relevant events, and identifying exhibits and pavilions of interest will make days at the event a bit less chaotic. Figure 6.8 depicts two days in an anticipated schedule (one prepared before they arrived) for a student who was following gender at COP25.

6.4.2 At the Event

Upon arriving at a COP, well prepared about the content of your interest area and what will be discussed, armed with your event schedules with interesting exhibits and pavilions identified, what now? How will you know what negotiation events are occurring and be able to place them into your calendar for the day?

In the climate arena, The Daily Programme is essential in shifting from the provisional schedule and the annotated agenda (UNFCCC 2022m) to day-to-day activities under agenda items and in the venue. The Daily Programme highlights the specific times and locations of meetings that are scheduled to move the agenda forward. It is produced daily by the secretariat and serves as a guide to meetings occurring each day.

Agenda Items:	Gender	LCIPP
	13 (COP 25)	8 (SBSTA 51)

UNFCCC event
Side event

Time	Tuesday, December 10 – Event	Tuesday, December 10 – Notes	Time	Wednesday, December 11 – Event	Wednesday, December 11 – Notes
08:00			08:00		
08:30			08:30		
09:00			09:00		
09:30			09:30		
10:00			10:00	Pre-2020	
10:30			10:30		
11:00			11:00		
11:30			11:30	Global South -Gender	Women for -Gender *There is a third
12:00			12:00		
12:30			12:30		
13:00	Towards ambitious and gender inclusive climate action	-Room 1 -Promoting Implementation	13:00	United Nations Secretary-General António Guterres briefing on the outcomes and follow-up of the 2019 Climate Action summit -Other Event	Gender-responsive urban climate policies and NDCs -Gender
13:30			13:30		
14:00			14:00		
14:30			14:30		
15:00	Gender Day		15:00	Gender equality	-Gender
15:30			15:30		
16:00			16:00		
16:30		Human rights in the -Room 5	16:30	Building resilience -Room 1	Loss and Damage -Room 2
17:00			17:00		
17:30			17:30		
18:00			18:00		
18:30	REDD+ and Market-Based Approaches: A REDD+ Registry and Trading Platform	-Room 2	18:30	Advancing climate action in agriculture and food	-Room 6
19:00			19:00		
19:30			19:30		
20:00			20:00		

Figure 6.8 Excerpt of a draft schedule prepared prior to attendance for an observer following gender at COP25.
Source: Gothi (2019).

The Daily Programme contains links to the live (CCTV) schedule for meetings associated with the Convention and Protocol Bodies. These are organized by body and by agenda item. This is the critical link to know what is being discussed, at what time, and in what location. The schedule designates whether a meeting is open to observers, and it is crucial to monitor the CCTV schedule because the open or closed status of a meeting can change. The CCTV schedule can be accessed online, on TVs throughout the venue (see Figure 6.9) and on mobile phones via the UNFCCC negotiator app. The Daily Programme also provides links to in-session documents and agenda item information. The Daily Programme will also contain announcements and other information, such as links to side-event and exhibit schedules, wireless instructions, and medical emergency information.

While the Daily Programme will help you organize the day ahead, the *ENB*, *ECO* Newsletter, and *TWN* blog can help you begin to make meaning of sessions you observe and those you miss (see Chapter 8). A visit to the RINGO constituency website will also reveal notes from other researchers on sessions they attended. A daily read of each of these for your topic area can be helpful in staying abreast of negotiations.

It is 9:00 AM: you have reviewed the daily schedule and program, and read the *ENB*, *ECO*, *TWN*, and other newsletters and notes that were produced overnight. Your next stop is a daily constituency meeting. Held in the hours before negotiations start for the day, these meetings afford observers the opportunity to meet in constituency groups. Agendas for these meetings vary, but they provide an opportunity for constituencies to update one another on the status of the negotiations. Advocacy constituencies will use this time to develop and hone strategies designed to influence negotiation outcomes. A researcher's

Figure 6.9 A delegate to the UNFCCC June 2019 Bonn Climate Change Conference watches the live schedule (CCTV).
Source: Photo by IISD/ENB | Kiara Worth (Worth 2019).

most likely constituency is the Research and Independent NGO (RINGO) constituency. The RINGO daily meeting is open to all COP attendees; however, some constituencies limit their daily meetings to members. At the RINGO daily meeting, researchers can expect to find information about negotiation status and are also able to connect with other researchers. RINGO leadership works to provide relevant and timely information on the negotiations by hosting speakers and experts both from within and outside the UNFCCC and facilitating conversations amongst attendees. If certain negotiation sessions are closed, or there is limited attendance based on constituency, then the constituency meetings are where you would find information about tickets and access. The RINGO website is also a useful designation for researchers for relevant session information, as well as a repository of notes that RINGO members have taken during sessions. These notes serve as a historical record, but also as an ongoing record for a session a researcher may not be able to attend during a COP/SB/ad hoc group meeting.

As the day progresses, while side-event, workshop, and dialogue schedules will be consistent, negotiation sessions can and do change. Sessions that were open may close at the request of a party. Sessions that were closed may open. Informals may be suspended to allow the parties time for informal informals. Keeping track of all of these can be difficult, if not impossible. That said, the CCTV is an invaluable resource as it provides as up-to-date information as is possible. It is also important to note that during plenaries and contact group meetings, the schedule for informal consultations for the week ahead may be announced. At the end of each informal session, the cofacilitators will often outline the dates, times, and expected content to be covered in the next meeting. There can also be an opportunity to sign up for updates on the agenda item by sending an email request to the secretariat.

Once the day or the event is over, a researcher will want to make meaning of and perhaps act upon their observation at the COP itself. For example, observation of events within a COP is an iterative and circular process. For a researcher of the process itself, activities observed or people interviewed may cause the researcher to question assumptions or redirect a line of inquiry. For a researcher trying to understand where their work might be best placed, observations might identify new people to speak with or opportunities for additional observation. All of this leads to activities after the event.

6.4.3 Attending Virtually

Observation at MEA meetings has traditionally been limited to in-person attendance. Yet, in the climate arena some constituted bodies developed the capacity and practices for virtual participation early on. For example, the Warsaw International Mechanism (WIM) ExComm and the Standing Committee on Finance (SCF) have used hybrid meetings to decrease participation barriers for developing country members and observers. Over time, both constituted bodies increased virtual engagement in break-out sessions and more informal Q&A sessions during agenda items.

The COVID pandemic challenged the UNFCCC secretariat to build on this limited virtual experience, finding and testing a variety of platforms and "learning by doing."

In 2020, when COP26 and SB52 were postponed, non-negotiating events such as the June Momentum (held during SB52's original time frame), regional dialogues on Action for Climate Empowerment (ACE) and Gender Action Programme (GAP), and Global Climate Action Climate Champions events took place virtually. Constituted bodies moved their meetings completely online. The May – June 2021 Climate Change Conference continued mandated SB work during the pandemic, although no decisions were taken. The experience at COP26 tested this trend: as conditions related to the COVID-19 pandemic evolve, the meeting landscape looks to be integrating virtual components with in-person meetings.

These virtual formats arguably provide more access for observer researchers. They lower impacts on carbon and research budgets. They can increase the opportunities for engagement: depending on the meeting, observers have been able to watch a remote stream (that is later archived for on-demand viewing) and participate via comment box, or participate on the meeting platform, including speaking opportunities. While the first option expanded public access, the last two require observer credentials and are subject to quotas, akin to in-person meetings. A recent study found that more than 80% of experienced UNFCCC participants support continued and expanded virtual work, seeing online meetings as best suited for thematic workshops and expert meetings (75%), technical review processes and informal consultations (64–65%), and constituted body and Bureau meetings (53–55%) (Klein et al. 2021). A range of concerns remain, from technical capacities to deep-seated issues related to trust and power. But in terms of enabling more access and engagement, one African civil society stakeholder noted that "if everything is done in a really meaningful, inclusive manner, I think the digital dimension is really potentially transformational" (Klein et al. 2021, 10).

6.4.4 After the Event

Background knowledge is essential not only when preparing for and attending an MEA COP, but also when making meaning of one's observations and drawing conclusions afterward. Once an MEA COP has ended, a vast amount of information is available about what happened, from news articles and blog posts to critical analyses of the conference documents (see Chapter 8 on analyzing conference texts). In order to begin to make sense of your observations and the meaning of meeting outcomes, there are several important steps. The first is to consult the report of the session as well as the final decisions of the supreme bodies, specifically the sections relevant to your research. Note the relevant decision text and any specific requests for further work contained within the decisions, which may lead to different types of activities and resultant outputs (see Method Box 6.2). Second, refer to other conference documents that were generated during the session, such as reports of workshops and dialogues. Finally, consult external analyses. The last issue of the *ENB* provides a summary and analysis of the conference as a whole. There will be a myriad of sources that provide analysis of the conference and its success or lack thereof, but the strongest sources for specific analysis will vary based on research area.

Method Box 6.1 Evaluating sessions and outcomes

MEA supreme and sub-body meetings will often host negotiations, meetings, workshops, or dialogues on similar topics during the same session. Understanding the origination and the goals of a session is important to a researcher's ability to properly assess and analyze their observations. For example, the UNFCCC COP, through Decision 2/CP.23, called for two specific and separate activities related to the Local Communities and Indigenous Peoples Platform. These activities occurred during the subsidiary body meetings (SB48) in June of 2018.

SBSTA undertook negotiations as requested in paragraph 10, on operationalization of the platform, including the establishment of a facilitative working group. Negotiations were conducted as informal consultations held over the course of the SB meetings and were cofacilitated by two party representatives. Through the informal consultations, draft decision text was developed, and the session concluded with SBSTA recommending text negotiations continue at SBSTA49 (UNFCCC 2018d). SBSTA also held the mandated multistakeholder workshop of the Local Communities and Indigenous Peoples Platform, which was comoderated by a party representative and a representative of local communities and Indigenous peoples' organizations (UNFCCC 2022f). The workshop was held on one day, with morning and afternoon sessions, and included sessions with presentations by the secretariat, parties, and Indigenous and NGO organizations, followed by facilitated dialogue of all attendees. The workshop concluded with a report summarizing activities and further views (UNFCCC 2018c).

These two different events occurred at the same SB session and originated from the same COP decision, yet have very different modes of work and resulting products, which highlights the need for a researcher to understand the differences in specific types of sessions, such as workshops and informal consultations and their resulting outputs. The context, work product, evolution, and future work of and for each of the sessions would be critical to making meaning of observations.

6.5 Conclusion

This chapter has sought to provide practical guidance to those who research MEAs, offering tools, sources, and insights for situating academic work in the negotiation process. We have organized it temporally – preparing to attend an MEA meeting, navigating the site, and working to understand and analyze observations afterward – based on our experiences during the last decade. We highlight the increasing availability of digital resources and virtual meetings, to help readers decide how to attend most meaningfully. We hope that by unpacking the multiple actors, sites, and processes through which environmental agreements are made and governed, this chapter will help the reader to find and navigate their research site with confidence, and to place their analysis of it in context.

Further Reading

1. Bodansky, D., Brunée, J. and Rajamani, L. (2017). *International Climate Change Law*. Oxford: Oxford University Press.

Essential primer on the UNFCCC, Kyoto Protocol, and Paris Agreement

2. Brunnée, J. (2002). COPing with Consent: Law-making under Multilateral Environmental Agreements. *Leiden Journal of International Law*, 15(1), 1–52

Thoughtful exploration of how MEA negotiations form international law.

3. Klein, R., Harris, K., Bakhtaoui, I. et al. (2021). *Building Climate Diplomacy Back Better: Imagining the UNFCCC Meetings of Tomorrow*. Stockholm Environment Institute. www.sei.org/publications/building-climate-diplomacy-back-better.

Recent analysis of COP participants' views on improving the UNFCCC negotiations.

References

Bauer, S. (2006). Does Bureaucracy Really Matter? The Authority of Intergovernmental Treaty Secretariats in Global Environmental Politics. *Global Environmental Politics*, 6(1),23–49.

Biermann, F. and Siebenhüner, B. (2009). *Managers of Global Change: The Influence of International Environmental Bureaucracies*. Cambridge, MA: MIT Press.

Bodansky, D. (2010). *The Art and Craft of International Environmental Law*. Cambridge, MA: Harvard University Press.

Bodansky, D. (2012). Legitimacy. In D. Bodansky, J. Brunée, and E. Hey, eds., *The Oxford Handbook of International Environmental Law*. Oxford: Oxford University Press.

Brunnée, J. (2018). The Sources of International Environmental Law: International Law, In S. Besson and J. d'Aspremont, eds., *The Oxford Handbook on the Sources of International Law*. Oxford: Oxford University Press, pp. 960–984.

Chasek, P., ed. (2015). Earth Negotiations Bulletin Summary of the Paris Climate Change Conference: 29 November–13 December 2015. Online report. New York: International Institute for Sustainable Development. https://enb.iisd.org/download/pdf/enb12663e.pdf.

Chasek, P., ed. (2016a). Earth Negotiations Bulletin Marrakech Highlights: Monday 7 November 2016. Online report. New York: International Institute for Sustainable Development. https://enb.iisd.org/download/pdf/enb12679e.pdf.

Chasek, P., ed. (2016b). Earth Negotiations Bulletin Summary of the Marrakech Climate Change Conference: 7–19 November 2016. Online report. New York: International Institute for Sustainable Development. https://enb.iisd.org/download/pdf/enb12689e.pdf.

Depledge, J. (2007). A Special Relationship: Chairpersons and the Secretariat in the Climate Change Negotiations. *Global Environmental Politics*, 7(1),45–68.

Gothi, S. (2019). COP 25 Draft Schedule, Coursework: Enst 357. Washington University in St. Louis.

Haller, J. (2018). UNFCCC Party Groupings. Figure. https://en.wikipedia.org/wiki/Environmental_Integrity_Group#/media/File:UNFCCC_Party_Groupings.svg.

Jinnah, S. (2014). *Post-Treaty Politics: Secretariat Influence in Global Environmental Governance*. Cambridge, MA: The MIT Press. http://dx.doi.org/10.7551/mitpress/9780262028042.001.0001.

Kyoto Protocol (1997). Resolution FCCC/CP/1997/L.7/Add.1, opened for signature 11 December 1997, entered into force 16 February 2005.

Multilateral Environmental Agreement Negotiator's Handbook (2007). [MEA Handbook]. https://unfccc.int/resource/docs/publications/negotiators_handbook.pdf

Muzurakis, M. (2021a). Informal Negotiations on Finance. International Institute for Sustainable Development. Photo. https://enb.iisd.org/Glasgow-Climate-Change-Conference-COP26-11Nov2021.

Muzurakis, M. (2021b). Room view During the Informal Stocktaking Plenary. International Institute for Sustainable Development. Photo. https://enb.iisd.org/Glasgow-Climate-Change-Conference-COP26-11Nov2021.

Secretariat of the Convention on Biological Diversity (2005). *Handbook of the Convention on Biological Diversity Including its Cartagena Protocol on Biosafety*, 3rd ed., Montreal, Canada. www.cbd.int/doc/handbook/cbd-hb-all-en.pdf.

UNEP (2019). *Handbook for the Vienna Convention for Protection of the Ozone Layer*, Ozone Secretariat, Nairobi: UNEP. https://ozone.unep.org/sites/default/files/2020-01/VC_Handbook_2019.pdf.

UNFCCC (1996). Adoption of the Rules of Procedure, FCCC/CP/1996/2. UNFCCC Report.

UNFCCC (2002). *A Guide to the Climate Change Convention Process*. UNFCCC Guide. https://unfccc.int/resource/process/guideprocess-p.pdf

UNFCCC (2016). Report of the Conference of the Parties on its twenty-first session, held in Paris from 30 November to 13 December 2015, Decision 1/CP.21, FCCC/CP/2015/10/Add.1. UNFCCC Report.

UNFCCC (2017a). Guide for Presiding Officers. UNFCCC Guide. https://unfccc.int/sites/default/files/20170919_guideforpresidingofficers_final.pdf.

UNFCCC (2017b). Report of the Conference of the Parties on its twenty-second session, held in Marrakech from 7 to 18 November 2016, FCCC/CP/2016/10. UNFCCC Report.

UNFCCC (2018a). Report of the Conference of the Parties on its twenty-third session, held in Bonn from 6 to 18 November 2017, FCCC/CP/2017/11. UNFCCC Report.

UNFCCC (2018b). Report of the Conference of the Parties on its twenty-third session, held in Bonn from 6 to 18 November 2017, FCCC/CP/2017/11/Add.1. UNFCCC Report.

UNFCCC (2018c). Report of the Multi-Stakeholder Workshop: Implementing the Functions of the Local Communities and Indigenous Peoples Platform. Workshop Report. https://unfccc.int/sites/default/files/resource/20190426_LCIPP%20Workshop%20Report_final%20version.pdf.

UNFCCC (2018d). Report of the Subsidiary Body for Scientific and Technological Advice on the first part of its forty-eighth session, held in Bonn from 30 April to 10 May 2018, FCCC/SBSTA/2018/4. UNFCCC Report.

UNFCCC (2019a). Chair's Reflections Note for SBSTA 51. UNFCCC Reflections Note. https://unfccc.int/sites/default/files/resource/SBSTA51%20reflections%20note.pdf.

UNFCCC (2019b). COP 25 Venue Map. https://unfccc.int/documents/202585.

UNFCCC (2019c). Overview Schedule – COP25. Conference Schedule. https://unfccc.int/sites/default/files/resource/Overview%20Schedule_COP25.pdf.

UNFCCC (2019d). Provisional Agenda and Annotations, FCCC/CP/2019/1. UNFCCC Agenda.

UNFCCC (2022a). Ad Hoc Working Group on the Paris Agreement (APA). Online article. https://unfccc.int/process/bodies/subsidiary-bodies/apa.

UNFCCC (2022b). Admitted NGOs. UNFCCC Online article. https://unfccc.int/process-and-meetings/conferences/side-events-and-exhibits/admitted-ngos#eq-1.

UNFCCC (2022c). ADP Bodies Page. Online article. https://unfccc.int/adp-bodies-page.

UNFCCC (2022d). Committee to Facilitate Implementation and Promote Compliance referred to in Article 15, paragraph 2 of the Paris Agreement (PAICC). Online article. https://unfccc.int/process-and-meetings/bodies/constituted-bodies/committee-to-facilitate-implementation-and-promote-compliance-referred-to-in-article-15-paragraph-2.

UNFCCC (2022e). COP22/CMP12/CMA breakdown of attendance of NGO representatives by constituency. Figure. https://unfccc.int/process-and-meetings/parties-non-party-stakeholders/non-party-stakeholders/statistics#eq-2.

UNFCCC (2022f). Multi-stakeholder Workshop of the Local Communities and Indigenous Peoples Platform. Website. https://unfccc.int/topics/local-communities-and-Indigenous-peoples-platform/events-meetings-and-workshops/multi-stakeholder-workshop-of-the-local-communities-and-Indigenous-peoples-platform.

UNFCCC (2022g). New Secretariat Structure. Chart. https://unfccc.int/about-us/what-is-the-unfccc-secretariat/secretariat-structure.

UNFCCC (2022h). Party Submissions and Statements. Online article. https://unfccc.int/submissions_and_statements.

UNFCCC (2022i). Pavilions at COP 26. Website. https://unfccc.int/cop26/pavilions.

UNFCCC (2022j). Statistics on Admission. UNFCCC Online article. https://unfccc.int/process-and-meetings/parties-non-party-stakeholders/non-party-stakeholders/statistics-on-non-party-stakeholders/statistics-on-admission.

UNFCCC (2022k). Statistics on Non Party Stakeholders. UNFCCC Online article. https://unfccc.int/process-and-meetings/parties-non-party-stakeholders/non-party-stakeholders/statistics-on-non-party-stakeholders#eq-2.

UNFCCC (2022l). Statistics on Participation and In-Session Engagement. UNFCCC Online article. https://unfccc.int/process-and-meetings/parties-non-party-stakeholders/non-party-stakeholders/statistics-on-non-party-stakeholders/statistics-on-participation-and-in-session-engagement.

UNFCCC (2022m). The Daily Programme. Website. https://unfccc.int/process-and-meetings/conferences/past-conferences/bonn-climate-change-conference-may-2017/events-and-programme/daily-programme.

UNFCCC (2022n). UN Climate Change Conference – December 2019. Website. https://unfccc.int/cop25.

UNFCCC Press Office (2020). COP Bureau Reschedules UNFCCC Subsidiary Body Meetings to 2021. UNFCCC Press release. https://unfccc.int/news/cop-bureau-reschedules-unfccc-subsidiary-body-meetings-to-2021

United Nations Convention on Biological Diversity [CBD] (1992). Resolution A/RES/64/203, opened for signature 5 June 1992, entered into force 29 December 1993.

United Nations Framework Convention on Climate Change [UNFCCC] (1992). Resolution FCCC/INFORMAL/84, opened for signature 4 June 1992, entered into force 21 March 1994.

United Nations General Assembly [UNGA] (2017). International Legally Binding Instrument Under the United Nations Convention on the Law of the Sea on the Conservation and Sustainable Use of Marine Biological Diversity of Areas Beyond National Jurisdiction, A/RES/72/249, UN Resolution.

United Nations Treaty Collection (2022a). Chapter XXVII: 2.a. Montreal Protocol on Substances that Deplete the Ozone Layer. Website. https://treaties.un.org/Pages/ViewDetails.aspx?src=IND&mtdsg_no=XXVII-2-a&chapter=27&clang=_en.

United Nations Treaty Collection (2022b). Chapter XXVII: 7. United Nations Framework Convention on Climate Change. Website. https://treaties.un.org/Pages/ViewDetailsIII.aspx?src=IND&mtdsg_no=XXVII-7&chapter=27&Temp=mtdsg3&clang=_en.

United Nations Treaty Collection (2022c). Chapter XXVII: 7.a. Kyoto Protocol to the United Nations Framework Convention on Climate Change. Website. https://treaties.un.org/Pages/ViewDetails.aspx?src=TREATY&mtdsg_no=XXVII-7-a&chapter=27&clang=_en.

United Nations Treaty Collection (2022d). Chapter XXVII: 7.d. Paris Agreement. Website. https://treaties.un.org/Pages/ViewDetails.aspx?src=TREATY&mtdsg_no=XXVII-7-d&chapter=27&clang=_en.

United Nations Treaty Collection (2022e). Chapter XXVII: 8. Convention on Biological Diversity. Website. https://treaties.un.org/pages/ViewDetails.aspx?src=TREATY&mtdsg_no=XXVII-8&chapter=27.

Worth, K. (2019). A Delegate Watches the Live Schedule to Keep Track of the Day's Events. International Institute for Sustainable Development. Photo. https://enb.iisd.org/events/bonn-climate-change-conference-june-2019/highlights-and-images-main-proceedings-26-june-2019.

7

Beyond Negotiations

Studying Side Events, Exhibition Booths, and Other Neglected Conference Spaces

JENNIFER BANSARD

7.1 Introduction

An apt image of an international environmental conference would be that of an ant's nest. Picture hordes of people scurrying through a labyrinth of busy corridors, tending to specific tasks in different corners of a grand, buzzing dome. Much like the ant queen, the negotiations are at the heart of this frenzy. Indeed, intergovernmental decision-making is the raison d'être of most of these conferences: be it to secure common principles and international commitment to environmental protection; to explore the need for a new environmental treaty; for the concrete outlining of such a treaty; or for advancing the work program of an existing multilateral environmental agreement (MEA).[1] Yet, as central as they are to such conferences, not everyone directly engages with the negotiations or engages with them in the same way. Some carry out various kinds of supporting tasks, and there is much going on at the negotiations' and even at the conferences' peripheries.

Finding your place in this labyrinth and knowing what to look out for is especially challenging if you are an ant caught in the middle of this frenzy, with only a rough idea of what the rest of the colony is up to. This is where this chapter ties in: it is intended as a practical guide for navigating these events, focusing on what there is to international environmental conferences beyond the negotiations (which are specifically addressed in Chapter 6). To this end, the first part of the chapter takes readers on a walk through a conference, first touching upon spaces within conference venues, such as side events and press briefings, before zooming out to consider how conferences manifest outside and beyond their dedicated venue. It sensitizes readers to the existence and specificities of conference spaces and practices which, despite having received scant attention in the literature, each affect conference dynamics in their own way. This scene-setting makes explicit much of the implicit knowledge that enables seasoned participants to smoothly navigate these events.

The second part of the chapter invites reflection on how to attend to these spaces from a scholarly perspective. It outlines the distinction between using the various conference

[1] Examples for these different types of conferences include the following: (1) the World Summit on Sustainable Development; (2) the meetings of the Ad Hoc Open-Ended Working Group towards a Global Pact for the Environment; (3) the sessions of the Intergovernmental Conference on the Conservation and Sustainable Use of Marine Biodiversity of Areas Beyond National Jurisdiction; and (4) the COP sessions of the United Nations Framework Convention on Climate Change. The last type constitutes the bulk of environmental conferences, given the sheer number of existing MEAs whose decision-making bodies meet at regular intervals, often annually.

spaces as *sites* for data collection and treating them as research *objects* in their own right, substantiating this distinction with examples from the literature and delineating key considerations for data collection. The chapter not only makes the case for further research into these neglected conference spaces, it also underscores the need for comparative research across MEAs by demonstrating that the United Nations Framework Convention on Climate Change (UNFCCC), which has received the most attention to date, is a significant outlier. As Hughes et al. (2021) emphasize by advancing the notion of agreement-making, international environmental conferences are, among others, sites of networking, learning, and agenda setting and give way to struggles over participation rights, peer recognition, and, ultimately, global order. This not only plays out in the negotiations, but also in more marginal conference spaces such as side events and civil society protests – which is the rationale for attending to these spaces to advance our understanding of global environmental governance.

7.2 Navigating the Conference

Let us start with the basics: international environmental conferences[2] take place in the headquarters of intergovernmental organizations or in (commercial) convention centers. If need be, the venue space is expanded using temporary, tent-like structures.

Tip: Print out the map and use it to check off the types of spaces you identify at a given conference and to structure your on-site observations

Although venues differ, there are recurrent features to them. Figure 7.1 provides a schematic overview of the functional spaces associated with international environmental conferences. The map distinguishes between the negotiations and the side events as the two main spaces in such conferences, with others including the security check, the corridors, restoration areas, and offices. It also highlights these conferences' embeddedness within the wider infrastructure of their host cities in terms of transportation and accommodation, and draws attention to interlinkages between the different spaces within and outside the venue, especially in terms of actors and issues.

Tip: Print out the map and use it to check off the types of spaces you identify at a given conference and to structure your on-site observations

The map in Figure 7.1 follows a maximalist approach, meaning that not all spaces depicted on the map will be found at each conference and some, such as pavilions in the side-event space, are specific to the UNFCCC. The actual layout of a given conference depends on a number of factors, including the size of the venue, the process at hand, and whether it is a high-profile meeting or more of a routine event. What is more, in practice the boundaries between the different spaces are less sharp than the map depicts. A given room might be used for regional coordination purposes at the start of the day, negotiations in the

[2] The term international environmental "conference" should not be equated with the specific notion of a "conference of the parties" and is used interchangeably with the terms "meetings" and "events" to avoid repetition. The chapter refers to a variety of conference types, as outlined in footnote 1. Many points are also relevant for plenary sessions of the Intergovernmental Panel on Climate Change and the Intergovernmental Science-Policy Platform on Biodiversity and Ecosystem Services. Smaller events, such as regional workshops or constituted body meetings, are very different in scale and beyond this chapter's scope.

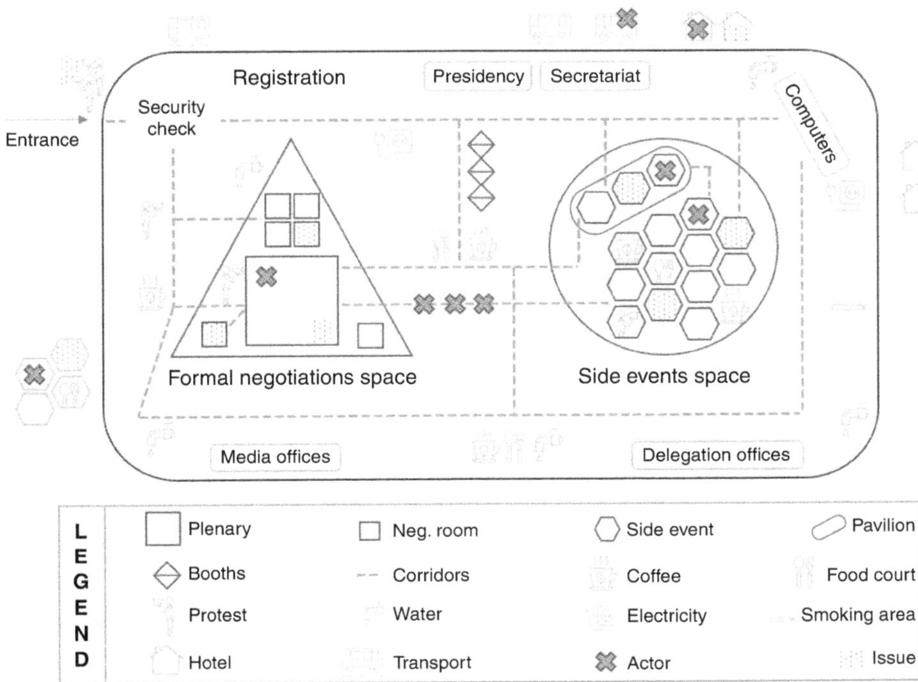

Figure 7.1 Schematic overview of a conference venue.

morning, and side events during lunch break. In such cases, the functional spaces identified in the map are not spatially distinct, but actually superimposed.

The remainder of this section delineates the specificities of these spaces in more detail. It first walks through spaces and practices *within* conference venues before further zooming out from this delimited perimeter.

7.2.1 Walking into a Conference Venue

The **security check** is the first distinct space one encounters in a conference venue. Much like at the airport, you have to take your coat off and put your laptop and other items in a tray to be scanned. You also have to walk through a scanner yourself and might get a pat down. You may see people taking a sip from their water bottles to demonstrate the innocuousness of the liquids they carry to the security staff. In some venues, there are separate security lines for secretariat staff, government representatives, and observers – a status differentiation that is perceptible throughout conferences. In most cases, the security check is a low-profile, routine practice. Activists carrying banners, stacks of flyers, or other larger items, however, might be faced with more intense scrutiny, and security staff can decide to confiscate certain items. People carrying large camera equipment might also be faced with entry barriers, as security staff sometimes insist that only participants with media accreditation can enter the venue with this equipment. In the (rare) event that you were thinking about bringing a tripod or similarly bulky equipment to conduct some form of videographic data collection at an environmental conference, you might want to check ahead of time whether you would be allowed to do so, being accredited as an observer.

In most cases, the first step after passing through the security check on your first conference day is to go to the **registration area** to get your badge. Unless you encounter problems with your badge, the registration area is a space you only visit once during a conference. Conference badges are typically color-coded by affiliation type, making it easy to distinguish between government delegates and other types of participants (see Figure 7.2). This color coding facilitates the enforcement of access restrictions in certain spaces, especially the negotiations.[3] It can also prove helpful in the event that you are seeking to engage with a specific actor type for your research.

The entrance area leads to a network of **corridors**, which are not the liminal space they might appear at first glance: they are the arteries of the conference, funneling participants toward their specific tasks, and monitoring them will help you get a sense for the pulse of the conference. At times, the corridors are bustling with delegates rushing between meetings. The corridors are then full of energy; they are vibrant. Other times, you may feel a tension in the air. The corridors will be flanked with pockets of delegates harboring grim or concentrated faces, perhaps going over their notes before entering their next meeting. Then there are the times when everything is in slow motion: it is late at night; there are only a few delegates around, napping in a corner or aimlessly wandering the corridors to stay awake, waiting for draft decision text to be released. If you wonder why you repeatedly see delegates sitting on the floor at a specific place in the corridors, it is likely because they spotted

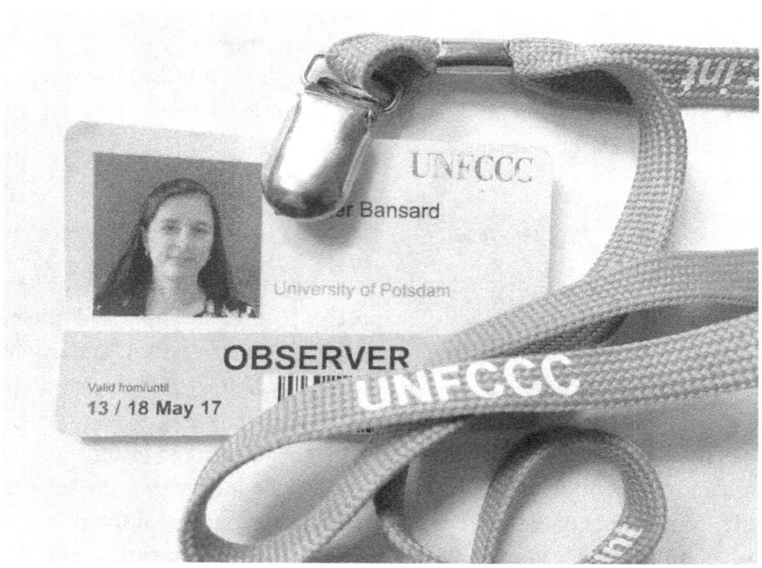

Figure 7.2 Author's "observer" badge for a UNFCCC conference.

[3] See Chapter 5 for details on access restrictions in the negotiations.

an **electrical outlet** to charge their laptops or phones – these can become coveted spaces. It could also be that the delegates are standing around a CCTV monitor, looking for the time and location of a session they need to attend.

Readers of the *Earth Negotiations Bulletin* (*ENB*)[4] will be familiar with the rich insights gained in the corridors: if you are attentive, you can pick up on the latest conference murmurs, the hot takes on contentious issues, and assessments of the latest bridging proposals on certain agenda items. You will notice delegates leaving plenary, commenting on countries' statements and debating the next steps in the negotiations, pondering which issues might be easiest to resolve and which ones will be hardest fought over. For example, referring to a late session of the contact group on access and benefit sharing at the Nagoya biodiversity conference, Marion Suiseeya (2014) noted that "delegates were overheard saying 'we failed,' and news of the failure circulated rapidly throughout the conference venue" (p. 102). The corridors are a space of impromptu encounters, something that was lost as environmental negotiations were held online during the COVID-19 pandemic.

7.2.2 Side Events

Side events are relatively short panel-discussions that provide a platform for experts from different organizations to discuss the latest developments in the field and showcase their work on a given issue (see Figure 7.3). Any type of organization[5] can apply for a side-event slot at a given conference, and doing so is free of charge, save for optional catering. With demand often exceeding capacity, not all applicants are granted slots by the secretariat responsible for organizing the conference. Within a given process, the spatial set-up of the side-event space can change from one conference to another depending on the layout of the venue. Side events can either take place in rooms dedicated to that purpose or in rooms that are used for negotiations at other times of the day. These rooms can in turn be sprinkled throughout the venue or form a contiguous area. This spatial set-up affects the visibility of the side-event space: dedicated side-event rooms are marked on floor plans, making them stand out next to the negotiations rooms, even more so when they form a contiguous area.

Surveying side-event participants at the UNFCCC's COPs 13 and 14, Hjerpe and Linnér (2010) indicate that these events perform a number of functions for their organizers and participants, but also for negotiating processes more generally. Key among them are sharing and accessing information, establishing contacts, gaining policy influence and support, and introducing potential negotiation items. They highlight that "[s]ide-events involve participants in a collective learning process, where they can access up-to-date knowledge about scientific results, best practices, policy initiatives and programmes, and NGO experiences" (p. 177), and that side events "may be seen as incubators for subjects that cannot

[4] The *ENB* is the de facto record of multilateral environmental negotiations since 1992. *Tip: If you have never read an ENB, take a break from this book to catch up on thirty years of reporting on environmental conferences!*

[5] Side events can be organized by a range of actors, including representatives of government agencies, intergovernmental organizations, universities, businesses, and nongovernmental organizations (NGOs); nonstate actors usually first have to obtain observer status with the given process before being able to get accreditation for specific conferences and apply for side-event slots.

Figure 7.3 Side event on low-carbon transport at the UNFCCC's COP20.
Source: Photo by IISD/ENB, Francis Dejon.

be discussed in the formal negotiations" (p. 177). Schroeder and Lovell (2012) echo their colleagues' findings and also note that the type of actor responsible for organizing the side event and the intended audience (international versus domestic) affect the extent to which its content relates to the negotiations.

With limited possibilities for observers to speak up in the formal negotiations, side events are a key space for nonstate actors to make their voice heard in international environmental conferences. Thew (2018), however, underscores an important impediment to side events' inclusiveness: since it takes significant forward planning to apply for and host a side event, it is easier for better-resourced actors to make use of this mode of engagement. She notes that youth organizations – as actors with (financial) capacity constraints – are more likely to gain speaking opportunities at events organized by others, rather than hosting their own side events. This opens up important questions for researchers interested in notions of participation and agenda setting.

To date, literature on side events is not only scarce, but is also centered on the UNFCCC. This is especially problematic insofar as the UNFCCC is an outlier case, as I demonstrate with regard to three key side-event characteristics: timing, spatial set-up, and number.

In most processes, side events take place during the negotiation breaks. The timing illustrates the intended complementarity between the side events and the negotiations. In contrast, at the UNFCCC, side events take place throughout the day, in parallel to the negotiations, and are more of a stand-alone act. This contributes to explaining Schroeder and Lovell (2012)'s finding that networking at side events is a key reason for many nonstate actors to attend UNFCCC meetings in the first place. However, the UNFCCC is not the only process featuring side events throughout the day. Conferences, such as the 2017 UN

Ocean Conference, with a strong focus on fostering exchanges among participants rather than intergovernmental decision-making, also display this feature.

Two features make the UNFCCC stand out in terms of spatial set-up. For one, while most processes host side events in close proximity to the negotiations, this distance tends to be wider at UNFCCC meetings, where side events have at times even taken place in an entirely different venue. Such distance makes it difficult for participants to move between the negotiations and the side-event space. Second, in addition to hosting side events in standard conference rooms, as is the case across processes, the UNFCCC also features so-called "pavilions" at its COP sessions.[6] Pavilions are spaces that can be rented by parties and observers on a commercial basis. They can be customized to delegations' liking and offer them space to host additional side events and other meetings. While some pavilions remain fairly simple, others are very ornate, and some even feature little cafés or bars (see Figure 7.4).

Finally, while the average number of daily side events varies greatly between processes (see Table 7.1),[7] the magnitude of the side-event phenomenon is especially large at the UNFCCC. Despite a strict rule of only one application per proponent (both for parties and observers), the UNFCCC's COP25 featured an average of 25.8 daily side events administered by the secretariat.[8] This number alone would put it at the high end of the spectrum

Figure 7.4 Café corner at the German pavilion at the UNFCCC's COP23.
Source: Photo by IISD/ENB, Hernán Aguilar.

[6] The UNFCCC, CBD, and UNCCD jointly hold a "Rio Conventions Pavilion" (RCP) at each other's COPs (and sometimes other events). However, despite its name, the RCP does not generally take the form of the pavilions described here; rather, it constitutes a series of side events curated by the secretariats of the three conventions and hosted in a dedicated, but standard conference room.

[7] Note that Table 7.1 does not constitute a comprehensive comparative or longitudinal analysis, but merely a first step toward a more robust understanding of the side-event phenomenon across MEAs. The overview focuses on governing-body meetings within a four-year time frame to provide some sense of comparability. Subsidiary body meetings and, even more so, meetings of intergovernmental negotiating committees, are smaller overall than COPs and feature comparatively fewer side events (see Reflection Box 7.1).

[8] https://seors.unfccc.int/applications/seors/reports/archive.html.

Table 7.1 *Average number of daily side events across different conferences/processes*

Meeting	Average no. of side events/day
Vienna Convention for the Protection of the Ozone Layer, COP11 (2017)	2.4
Convention on the Protection and Use of Transboundary Watercourses and International Lakes, MOP 8 (2018)	3.2
Basel, Rotterdam, and Stockholm Conventions, triple COP (2019)	3.6
International Treaty on Plant Genetic Resources for Food and Agriculture, 8th Session of the Governing Body (2019)	5
UN Convention to Combat Desertification, COP13 (2017)	10
Convention on International Trade in Endangered Species of Wild Fauna and Flora, COP18 (2019)	10.1
Ramsar Convention on Wetlands, COP13 (2018)	12.5
Convention on the Conservation of Migratory Species of Wild Animals, COP13 (2020)	13.75
UN Convention on Biological Diversity, COP13 (2016)	30.4

Source: Author's own analysis based on data extracted from MEA websites.

of MEA's COPs taking place around the same time, which spans in the range of 2.4–30.4 per day. Yet the actual number of side events at COP25 is much higher when also counting pavilion events. For reference: the German pavilion alone hosted 108 side events during this conference. As there were more than two dozen other pavilions, back-of-the-envelope calculations put the average number of daily side events for COP25 well above the 100 mark. This underscores the dire need for comparative research to gain a better understanding of side events' role within different processes. See Reflection Box 7.1 for a description of side events in the negotiations for a new high seas biodiversity treaty.

Reflection Box 7.1 Side events in the BBNJ context

By Ina Tessnow von Wysocki

Side events have been prevalent throughout the negotiations for a legally binding instrument for the conservation and sustainable use of marine biodiversity of areas beyond national jurisdiction (BBNJ), with 63 side events, organized by state and nonstate actors, in the intergovernmental conferences (IGCs) alone. As a comparatively small conference (approximately 800 participants), the side events are quite visible. They have operated as a site where specific topics are explored by invited experts and as a space for exchange between stakeholders.

BBNJ side events last around 1 hour and are generally attended by between 15 and 40 people, depending on location and interest. In contrast to climate conferences, the side events are often announced by the chairs and facilitators and take place in the same rooms as the plenary and informal informals. These events are scheduled during lunch time (up to 4 simultaneously) and sometimes overlap slightly with the negotiations. There are also workshops on the weekends, which provide more time for discussion and are hosted at different locations across New York City.

As well as formally recognized side events, there are roundtables and other evening events that aim to bring together different stakeholders on topics relevant to the BBNJ negotiations. These events may be advertised by flyers at the venue or via word of mouth and do not appear on the official conference agenda. There are also art exhibitions outside the conference rooms in the UN building and campus, which draw attention to ocean biodiversity issues.

In my research, I am interested in how science shapes the BBNJ negotiations, and side events are an important object of research. Side events provide a pathway for scientific input into the negotiations, where scientists present research findings and discuss scientific topics with other stakeholders in the process. By combining event ethnography with interviews and text analysis, we trace the mention of scientific concepts through side events, statements in plenary, and iterations of draft text.

As representatives from governments, academia, NGOs, and businesses attend side events, these sites can also be used to gather information about the topics of the conference, to identify relevant actors, and to make contact with potential interview participants, which also makes side events important sites of research. As the secretariat publishes the list of side events before the meeting, data collection can begin in advance of the session. As a research team we used this list to prepare and organize our participation. For example, I researched the backgrounds of panelists, speakers, and hosts and identified discussion topics and potential interview participants. This leaves more time once on site to focus on following the issues and to explore the connection and relationship between side-event settings and the overall conference and its outcomes.

7.2.3 Other Spaces Within Conference Venues

Many conferences feature another small but very tangible space that somewhat resembles the UNFCCC's pavilions: **exhibition booths**. Like side events, booths provide organizations with an opportunity to showcase their work and engage with conference participants. Any accredited organization can submit a request for a booth to the responsible secretariat. In most cases, these are rented on a commercial basis. In terms of surface area, they are much smaller than pavilions (see Figure 7.5): they often hold little more than a high table, stool, brochure stand, and possibly a flat screen pinned on the back wall to display more elaborate communication material. At times, booths can be larger and somewhat more elaborate, typically when corporate organizations use them to showcase their latest technical innovations. From a scholarly perspective, we know little about exhibition booths: What are their functions and how do these differ from those of side events?

Although not necessarily a stationary space, **civil society actions** represent another noteworthy element of international environmental conferences. Attention-grabbing actions are part of the toolkit of civil society engagement at these events. Often, specific spots in conference venues crystallize as recurrent spaces for civil society actions. These tend to be high-traffic spots, such as a stairway linking the entrance area to the conference rooms or the corridor area near plenary. Most actions consist in activists holding up banners, possibly accompanied by some chanting, but they can also take more creative forms, such as small theater plays. At the 2019 meeting of the conferences of the parties to the Basel, Rotterdam, and Stockholm Conventions, civil society representatives distributed egg salad

Figure 7.5 Exhibition booth at the Seventh Meeting of the Parties to the Cartagena Protocol. Source: Photo by IISD/ENB, Francis Dejon.

crackers to participants entering plenary to draw attention to the adverse effects of dioxin intake resulting from hens foraging on e-waste dumping grounds. At conferences of the Convention on Biological Diversity (CBD), artist/activist Leo Fidjeland carried around a stuffed pink chicken to raise awareness of the risks associated with gene drive technology. Thew (2018) indicates a mixed picture regarding the effectiveness of these civil society actions, with some being overlooked while others successfully resonated with negotiators.

In most processes, civil society action is limited, and in some cases there is none at all. In this regard again, the UNFCCC is a significant outlier: at climate conferences, not a day goes by without at least a handful of civil society actions – which surely ties in with the comparatively high civil society participation at UNFCCC meetings. While there too actions generally remain fairly mild, over the years the UNFCCC has seen more confrontational actions. At COP6, protesters interrupted informal consultations among parties and an activist threw a pie at the US lead negotiator during a press conference (IISD 2000). In

2017, civil society actors disrupted a US-led side event on "cleaner" fossil fuels, staging a mass audience walkout with chants of "What do we want? Climate justice!"[9] In 2019, several hundred participants engaged in a protest inside the venue, holding a demonstration outside plenary just before UN Secretary-General António Guterres was scheduled to speak. While most civil society actions are welcomed as part of the process, in this case UN security banned the protesters from the venue for the rest of the day and, for a time, floated the possibility of debadging them altogether for the remainder of the conference. As Hadden (2014) and others discuss, most NGOs generally comply with restrictions on protest forms within conference venues to avoid jeopardizing their participation in the process. This is a trade-off that activists weigh differently, and these calculations may change as environmental degradation further progresses.

Conference venues sometimes feature rooms for **press conferences** and other forms of **briefings**, which can be organized by governments, nonstate actors, or the conference leadership. The UNFCCC secretariat, for example, holds regular observer briefings throughout its conferences. Again, we know little about these practices from a scholarly standpoint. Anecdotal evidence suggests that they can have a noteworthy influence on the negotiation process: at the Copenhagen climate conference, Barack Obama, then President of the United States, created havoc by breaking news of an agreement reached between the United States, India, Brazil, South Africa, and China – an agreement that had, at the time, not been discussed with other countries in plenary. On a more positive note, at the Paris climate conference, the press conferences of the High Ambition Coalition instilled momentum and were especially useful for prominently showcasing additional countries that joined in. Betzold et al. (2016) – who provide the first groundwork on what motivates governments to organize press conferences at UNFCCC COPs – find that although the number of press conferences held per meeting has increased over time, until 2011 only 25 percent of UNFCCC parties had ever held such a briefing. Does this still hold true today? And how prevalent are such briefings across processes?

Finally, conference venues also typically feature (more or less numerous and elaborate) **restoration areas**, and sometimes other spaces such as **offices** for delegations to retreat to, **computer pools** with publicly usable printers, and designated on-site **smoking areas**.

7.2.4 Outside the Conference Venue

While conference venues are a clearly delimited perimeter, pinpointing the boundaries of the conference as a phenomenon is not as easy. Conference-related practices at times manifest in the immediate vicinity of a venue and, in many ways, conferences permeate their host cities and transcend their specific locality and timing. This section draws attention to the different elements through which conferences manifest *outside* and *beyond* the dedicated venue, which also contribute to shaping the conference experience and are hence worth reflecting upon.

[9] www.reuters.com/article/us-climatechange-accord-usa/protesters-disrupt-u-s-pro-coal-event-at-u-n-climate-talks-idUSKBN1DD29S.

Zooming out from the conference venue to its close vicinity, a first noteworthy element is the **(outside) civil society protests**. These can be much larger in magnitude than the actions held within the venue and these protests can also attract/be organized by actors that do not have access to the conference itself. Examples include protests against genetically modified organisms at CBD meetings or against deep-sea mining at meetings of the International Seabed Authority. Again, the magnitude of civil society actions outside conference venues is especially large at UNFCCC conferences. There, protesters holding up signs and distributing flyers typically flank the area surrounding the venue entrance on a daily basis. Civil society actions outside conference venues can also be larger in scale. Think of marches taking place throughout the host city or even coordinated transnational actions with decentralized marches all around the world: they might not take place within the conference, but they are certainly geared toward influencing the negotiations and political decision-making on the issue more broadly. Uldam (2013), for example, examined London-based protests during the UNFCCC's COP17 in Durban.

Policing is another practice you might encounter outside international environmental conferences. Unsurprisingly, UNFCCC conferences offer especially tangible examples of local authorities taking quite drastic policing measures. This policing can start with determining who is allowed into the country: for example, in 2018, Polish border officials blocked several activists from traveling to COP24 in Katowice. At times, special legislation is passed to expand police powers during conferences, which notably gave way to large-scale "pre-emptive" detention alongside COP15 in Copenhagen.[10] As Hadden (2014) notes, there is a remarkable history of arrests in conjunction with climate conferences, and the presence of riot police has become increasingly common. Although not a common feature of international environmental conferences, intense policing is neither limited to climate change conferences nor new. Media reports from the 1992 Earth Summit, for example, show that police forces cleared homeless people off the streets of Rio de Janeiro ahead of the conference and put the city's favelas under lockdown until it was over.[11] Yet, we currently lack robust insights into the phenomenon, especially from a comparative perspective across host countries and processes.

Further, the on-site conference program is sometimes complemented by **(unofficial) side events** taking place outside the conference venue. These events, which typically take place in consulates or research institutes, are not sanctioned by the secretariat that administers the on-site side events and they can take many forms. Some such events constitute longer workshops, taking place over the weekend break between conference weeks. Others resemble evening lectures and entail cocktail receptions. Not every conference will be accompanied by such events, but it usually is the case for meetings taking place in New York and Bonn, among others.

The reality of environmental conferences is that there is not much downtime: the conference is a full-on performance. You might think that you will clock out of "conference mode" once you get to your **accommodation**, but that might not always be the case. As there are a limited number of hotel rooms in a given city, you might very well spot

[10] www.theguardian.com/environment/2009/nov/26/denmark-police-powers-copenhagen.
[11] www.theguardian.com/environment/2012/jun/19/rio-20-earth-summit-1992-2012.

delegates at your breakfast buffet. You might witness their early morning briefing rounds or see them having a celebratory drink at the hotel bar in the evening. The same goes for **on-site transportation**. At peak hours the subways, trams, bike lanes, and taxis may be crowded with conference goers. Further, in many cases you will cross paths with conference participants before even entering the country of the conference. This is especially true for remote or small locations, where the planes and trains reaching that destination will be bustling with delegates days prior to the start of the conference. If you ostensibly carry conference-related material, such as provisional negotiation agendas or the latest issue of the *ENB*, you will likely wind up in conference-related discussions long before you reach the venue. This contributes to blurring the boundaries of the conference phenomenon.

In addition to physical manifestations in and beyond their host cities, conferences also materialize **virtually**. This materialization occurs in different ways, ahead, during, and after the actual conference takes place.[12] It starts with people accessing secretariat documentation, such as the provisional agenda or the conference's side-event schedule, or participating in preparatory briefings and reading up on news reports to learn about countries' and stakeholders' priorities for the conference. Further, there are many forms of virtual materialization that make it possible to "access" conferences in real time without physically being there. In some processes, conference segments such as plenaries or individual side events are webcast in real time – a practice likely to become more prevalent following the advent of digital conferencing amid the COVID-19 pandemic.

Actors also use social media, especially Twitter, both to provide real-time insights into the conference proceedings and to comment on these "from outside." Marion Suiseeya and Zanotti (2019), for example, highlight how "[o]rganizations such as Kebetkache, a women's environmental and development organization from Nigeria, used digital spaces to engage in COP21 because representatives could not attend" (p. 45). Meanwhile, Uldam (2013) underscores that online modes of action are better suited for activists with reformist rather than radical demands. Finally, for many conferences, the *ENB* not only publishes daily briefs on the negotiations, but also coverage of selected side events and photographic and videographic coverage of the conference more generally (see Chapter 8). This provides a sense of the conference to both on-site participants and those participating remotely. Conferences' virtual materialization opens up valuable opportunities for scholarly investigation, not only for those who cannot or do not want to physically attend these events (e.g., for financial reasons, to avoid travel-related greenhouse gas emissions, or to avoid contributing to "COP tourism"). It also opens up possibilities to dive into a conference on a post-hoc basis, as much of this data remains available long after the conference ends.

Zooming out one last step, there is merit in acknowledging that while we often treat individual conferences as discrete events, they are actually part of a **continuum**. International environmental conferences do not materialize out of thin air and vanish a few days later: it takes months of forward planning, both on the organizers' part and on that of conference participants,[13] and there is much follow-up activity in a conference's

[12] See also Chapters 5, 10, and 12.
[13] See Chapter 2 for details on how to prepare for one's conference participation.

wake – not least to implement newly adopted decisions. Further, conferences are rarely one-off events. MEAs' governing and subsidiary bodies' meetings take place at regular intervals, with each conference building on the last and advancing the MEA's work program. Many other conferences take place in irregular series or celebratory intervals, as was the case for the ten- and twenty-year anniversary conferences of the 1992 Rio Earth Summit. In any case, these conferences federate actors that meet elsewhere in various constellations, and they constitute only the temporary apex of longer-lasting governance processes. It is therefore important to keep in mind that what happens at an environmental conference is conditioned not only by the institutional specificities and the history of the process at hand, but also by the broader environmental governance landscape of its epoch.

7.3 Reflecting on Research Design

Equipped with this thorough understanding of the constitutive parts of international environmental conferences, let us now reflect on how to apprehend these spaces and practices from a scholarly perspective. The following sections illustrate two key points: the conference spaces presented in this chapter can play different roles in a research project, and there are many ways to go about data collection and analysis (see Table 7.2).

Table 7.2 *Illustrative overview of scholarship on non-negotiation spaces*

Research sites
Blum (2020)
▪ Combined participant observation during UNFCCC side events with semistructured interviews conducted remotely
▪ Examined the discursive legitimation of carbon markets
Buhr and Hjerpe (2012)
▪ Conducted a survey among participants of business-related side events at the UNFCCC's COP16
▪ Examined the expectation for corporate climate action in the absence of a new climate treaty post-Copenhagen failure
Corson et al. (2014)
▪ Conducted a collaborative event ethnography at side events held during the CBD's COP10
▪ Analyzed discursive struggles over the protected area concept
Gaventa (2010)
▪ Relied on event webcasts of parallel events held at the UNFCCC's COP13
▪ Performed a discourse analysis of business groups' and city coalitions' positioning at the conference
Lövbrand et al. (2017)
▪ Drew on observant participation, surveys administered at climate conferences and to side-event participants, and interviews conducted on-site
▪ Examined the purpose of UN climate summitry and the roles of different actors therein

Table 7.2 (*cont.*)

Nasiritousi et al. (2016)
- Conducted a survey among side-event participants and relied on submissions to the UNFCCC (available online)
- Examined the perceived governance roles of different nonstate actor constituencies, contrasting the survey results with the self-perceptions of these actors as identified in their official submissions

Nielsen (2016)
- Relied on negotiation documents, interviews, participant observation at side events, and secondary data (including press releases, blogs, and policy reports)
- Examined the "integrated landscape approach"-discourse at the UNFCCC
- Took a bird's-eye view of the UNFCCC, not differentiating between the different spaces/data sources

Site/object middle ground

Campbell et al. (2013)
- Conducted a collaborative event ethnography at side events held during the Rio+20 conference and examined the conference's outcome document of "The Future We Want"
- Analyzed the framing of ocean issues at the Rio+20 conference, contrasting side-event observations with the outcome document
- Provided insights on side events as research objects

Marion Suiseeya and Zanotti (2019)
- Combined a feminist collaborative event ethnography at the UNFCCC's COP21 with a digital ethnography of the conference
- Examined the Indigenous presence at the conference
- Provided insights on the virtual materialization of conferences

Thew (2018)
- Combined participant observation at UNFCCC conferences with interviews and a focus-group discussion
- Examined youth representatives' participation and agency in UNFCCC conferences
- Differentiated her analysis along the different conference spaces
- Provided insights on access to conferences, the effectiveness of civil society actions, and impediments to increased side-event pluralism

Research objects

Betzold et al. (2016)
- Used the UNFCCC secretariat's daily event program (and a range of other data sources for their independent and control variables)
- Examined the rationale behind press conferences at UNFCCC meetings

Hadden (2014)
- Relied on participant observation, interviews, media reports, and reporting by the *ENB*
- Examined changes in civil society protests at climate change conferences

Hjerpe and Linnér (2010)
- Combined a survey administered remotely to side-event organizers and on-site to both side-event and conference participants, with interviews conducted remotely

Table 7.2 (*cont.*)

- Examined the role of side events at UNFCCC COPs

Schroeder and Lovell (2012)

- Combined a survey administered on-site to side-event participants with interviews, informal discussions in the corridors, and participant observation
- Examined the role of side events (and nonstate actors) in UNFCCC conferences

Uldam (2013)

- Combined participant observation at outside and conference-remote protests, with interviews and data collected from activist movements' websites and social media presence
- Explored the relationship between activist demands (radical/reformist) and modes of action (London-based protests and online) during the UNFCCC's COP17

7.3.1 Research Site versus Research Object

Fundamentally, there are two ways to incorporate conference spaces in your research: either as *sites* or as *objects*. The first type of research typically centers on a given issue or actor and would lead you to collect data "at" side events or in the corridors, while the second type of research specifically addresses the nature of side events or press conferences and requires data "on" them. Table 7.2 provides examples of these types of research, also noting what data scholars used and to what end (see Section 7.3.2).

The vast majority of scholarship to date falls in the first category, treating conference spaces as *sites* of data collection (see top row in Table 7.2; also Reflection Box 7.1). Sometimes, this type of research directly addresses questions related to the process – for example, examining the influence of certain actors over specific negotiations. Often enough, scholars merely leverage the fact that conferences are prime sites of interactions between actors from different organizational backgrounds, geographical locations, and governance levels, making it easy to observe governance communities and gather respondents for interviews or surveys, among other forms of data collection. Scholars then use these settings as proxies to analyze broader debates and discourses within a given community (see Table 7.2). Corson et al. (2014), for example, conducted a collaborative event ethnography[14] to analyze discursive struggles over the protected area concept, as manifested in side events at the Nagoya biodiversity conference, and Buhr and Hjerpe (2012) conducted a survey among participants of business-related side events at the climate conference in Cancún to examine the expectation toward corporate climate action in the absence of a new climate treaty post-Copenhagen debacle.

As to the second category (Table 7.2, bottom row), while there is a lot of research on the negotiations (both in terms of process and output), surprisingly little scholarship focuses on other conference spaces and practices as *objects* of research. Although side events are often praised in passing for providing a space for nonstate actor engagement in multilateral processes, we know surprisingly little about them. Hjerpe and Linnér (2010) and Schroeder and Lovell (2012) – the seminal pieces on side events – both underlined the need for further

[14] See Chapter 11.

research, yet a decade later the research gap remains. We know even less about exhibition booths, local conference infrastructure in host cities, and other marginal spaces and practices. Not only is there a dearth of this type of research, with existing literature largely focusing on UNFCCC conferences, our understanding of phenomena such as side events is also skewed toward an outlier case.

Evidently, the *site* versus *object* distinction is not always clear cut (Table 7.2, middle row). Some scholarship primarily uses spaces such as side events for data collection purposes, but, in doing so, contributes to expanding our understanding of them. Hjerpe and Buhr (2014) notably examined longitudinal changes in the framing of climate change based on the synopses of UNFCCC side events available online, but also highlighted insights such as the lack of events addressing more critical issues (e.g., fossil fuel dependency). Similarly, Campbell et al. (2013) analyzed the framing of ocean issues at the Rio+20 conference, but also note in passing that with side events attended by those with similar interests, "different understandings of problems were seldom expressed in the same venue, much less debated" (p. 445).

7.3.2 Data Collection on and at Sites

As Table 7.2 illustrates, approaches to conducting research on/at international environmental conferences greatly vary and span the qualitative–quantitative spectrum. Participant observation often comes into play (to varying extents) in this type of research, with interviews, surveys, and official conference documents constituting other prominent data sources. Many scholars rely on data triangulation, combining different sources within one research project. Blum (2020), for example, combined participant observation during UNFCCC side events with semistructured interviews to examine the discursive legitimation of carbon markets. Some, such as Nasiritousi et al. (2016) and Marion Suiseeya and Zanotti (2019), use data collected both on-site and remotely. The methodological toolkit one could use to investigate conference-related questions is vast and, as always, approaches should be tailored to the specific research question.

To plan your data collection approach, it is key to reflect on which spaces are relevant for your object of study. A given actor can make a statement in plenary, participate in a side event, stop for a quick chat when running into a familiar face in the corridor, and tweet about their day on the way back to their hotel. You might not want or be able to follow your actor(s) of interest across all these spaces, but it is important to reflect on how your choice of observation setting and what you define as your research site influences your findings. Nonstate actor agency, for example, widely differs between spaces, and focusing on just one space could greatly skew your analysis. Similarly, a single issue might be discussed very differently between spaces and depending on the audience: analyzing the discourse on climate finance in the context of civil society actions in conference venues will yield different results than the same type of analysis based on data from the negotiations, side events, or Twitter.

A related question to ponder is whether to take a bird's-eye view of the conference or to contrast the different spaces and practices contained therein, highlighting their specificities. Nielsen (2016) opted for the first approach: his aim was to break down the main elements of the storyline around the integrated landscape approach, with differences relating to actors being either in support or critical of the approach's tenants rather than to the spaces in which the discourse materializes. Examining youth agency at UNFCCC conferences, Thew (2018), on the other hand, differentiated her analysis along the different spaces in which she observed youth participation, including side events and civil society actions. For her research, this differentiation was key and added much depth and nuance to her findings.

Something to keep in mind regarding research "on" conference spaces and practices: on-site data collection is not a precondition for every research question, and "on-site" does not necessarily mean collecting data within the space you are researching.[15] If you were to research exhibition booths, you could, among other things: observe this space directly, administer a survey in the corridors, or conduct phone-based interviews with booth holders after the conference.

A final point is acknowledging that some spaces are more conducive to data collection than others. While you can conduct observations in a range of spaces, data collection that relies on some form of interaction – and thus on peoples' inclination to respond to you – is easiest in spaces in which people are stationary and have time. As side events are thematically focused and geared toward networking, they constitute fertile ground for identifying stakeholders with specific thematic inclinations (see, e.g., Buhr and Hjerpe 2012). Civil society protests are, by their nature, intended to catch peoples' attention, which in return suggests activists' openness to engage with their audience (after their actions). The corridors are neither a quiet nor a private space, meaning they are not well-suited to conducting interviews in the classical sense. Negotiators, in particular, are unlikely to have time for a dedicated one-on-one talk if you catch them in the corridors – but they might tell you "walk with me" and give you the opportunity to conduct a blitz interview (see Chapter 9).

The coffee carts are a space where conference participants become temporarily stationary as they usually have to wait in line for some time. This is not downtime for everyone, as some will be preparing for their side-event presentation, checking the latest iteration of draft text on their phone, or coordinating with colleagues; but it is generally a more conversation-friendly setting than the corridors, since people have to wait there for a set period of time before they can rush to their next meeting. For their research into the purpose of UN climate summitry and the roles of different actors, Lövbrand et al. (2017) conducted interviews with "respondents [that] were randomly selected in the whirl of coffee drinkers outside the main plenary hall" (p. 585) at a climate conference in Bonn. Similar points can be made with regard to food courts or public transportation to the venue, except that in such cases delegates are more likely found in groups, contrary to the coffee carts where you are more likely to spot them individually. Further, while spaces such as side events and pavilions are fairly well-suited for targeting specific actors, coffee carts and smoking areas are more conducive to impromptu encounters. Regardless of the space, good timing is essential. Water dispensers, for example, are not ideal settings for catching people because delegates often do their water refills last minute before their next meeting. What can be considered good timing also depends on your interlocutors: some might be open for a chat at the hotel bar in the evening; others might be keen to wind down once they leave the venue.

[15] See Chapters 1 and 2.

7.4 Conclusions

This chapter constitutes a practical guide on the many spaces and practices that effectively mediate one's conference experience but are rarely explicitly addressed in the literature. As such, it contributes to leveling the playing field for first-time attendees who lack the implicit knowledge of more seasoned conference participants. It makes clear that although conferences often center on intergovernmental negotiations, they present a breadth of engagement forms, both on- and off-site, including side events, exhibition booths, and protests. It shows that the boundaries of the conference phenomenon are not clear cut, in space or time.

The chapter highlights research gaps, adds novel insights – especially on side events – and calls for an increased focus on neglected conference spaces and practices as *objects* of research in their own right, especially looking beyond the case of the UNFCCC. It underscores that much of the richness these conferences have to offer remains un- or underexplored. As Hughes et al. (2021) make the case by advancing the notion of agreement-making, we should broaden our scope toward increasingly examining notions of power, participation, and agenda setting beyond the negotiations.

Further Reading

1. Hjerpe, M. and Linnér, B-O. (2010). Functions of COP side-events in climate-change governance. *Climate Policy*, *10*(2), 167–180.

This article examines the functions of UNFCCC side events for participants, organizers, and the negotiation process more broadly. It constitutes an excellent primer on the side-event phenomenon.

2. Schroeder, H. and Lovell, H. (2012). The role of non-nation-state actors and side events in the international climate negotiations. *Climate Policy*, *12*(1), 23–37.

This article explores linkages between side events and the negotiations. It underscores the special relevance of side events for nonstate actors.

3. Thew, H. (2018). Youth participation and agency in the United Nations Framework Convention on Climate Change. *International Environmental Agreements: Politics, Law and Economics*, *18*(3), 369–389.

This article provides critical food for thought on a range of UNFCCC conference spaces, including side events and civil society actions.

References

Betzold, C., Bernauer, T., and Koubi, V. (2016). Press briefings in international climate change negotiations. *Environmental Communication*, *10*(5), 575–592.

Blum, M. (2020). The legitimation of contested carbon markets after Paris: Empirical insights from market stakeholders. *Journal of Environmental Policy & Planning*, *22*(2), 226–238.

Buhr, K. and Hjerpe, M. (2012). Expectations on corporate climate action under regulatory uncertainty. *International Journal of Climate Change Strategies and Management*, *4*(4), 403–419.

Campbell, L. M., Gray, N. J., Fairbanks, L. W., Silver, J. J., and Gruby, R. L. (2013). Oceans at Rio+ 20. *Conservation Letters*, *6*(6), 439–447.

Corson, C., Gruby, R., Witter, R. et al. (2014). Everyone's solution? Defining and redefining protected areas at the Convention on Biological Diversity. *Conservation and Society*, *12*(2), 190.

Gaventa, J. (2010). Environmental mega-conferences and climate governance beyond the nation-state: A Bali case study. *St Antony's International Review*, *5*(2), 29–45.

Hadden, J. (2014). Explaining variation in transnational climate change activism: The role of inter-movement spillover. *Global Environmental Politics*, *14*(2), 7–25.

Hjerpe, M. and Buhr, K. (2014). Frames of climate change in side events from Kyoto to Durban. *Global Environmental Politics*, *14*(2), 102–121.

Hughes, H., Vadrot, A. B, M., Allan, J. I., et al. (2021). Global environmental agreement-making: Upping the methodological and ethical stakes of studying negotiations. *Earth System Governance*, 10.

IISD. (2000). Summary of the Sixth Conference of the Parties to the Framework Convention on Climate Change. 13–25 November 2000. *Earth Negotiations Bulletin*, *12*(163): 1–19.

Lövbrand, E., Hjerpe, M., and Linnér, B.-O. (2017). Making climate governance global: How UN climate summitry comes to matter in a complex climate regime. *Environmental Politics*, *26*(4), 580–599.

Marion Suiseeya, K. R. (2014). Negotiating the Nagoya Protocol: Indigenous demands for justice. *Global Environmental Politics*, *14*(3), 102–124.

Marion Suiseeya, K. R., and Zanotti, L. (2019). Making influence visible: Innovating ethnography at the Paris Climate Summit. *Global Environmental Politics*, *19*(2), 38–60.

Nasiritousi, N., Hjerpe, M., and Linnér, B.-O. (2016). The roles of non-state actors in climate change governance: Understanding agency through governance profiles. *International Environmental Agreements: Politics, Law and Economics*, *16*(1), 109–126.

Nielsen, T. D. (2016). From REDD+ forests to green landscapes? Analyzing the emerging integrated landscape approach discourse in the UNFCCC. *Forest Policy and Economics*, *73*, 177–184.

Uldam, J. (2013). Activism and the online mediation opportunity structure: Attempts to impact global climate change policies? *Policy & Internet*, *5*(1), 56–75.

Part III

Collecting and Analysing Data

8

Texts

Collecting and Analyzing Event Documents

JENNIFER IRIS ALLAN AND PAMELA CHASEK

8.1 Introduction

There is nothing quite like walking into a multilateral environmental negotiating conference. As Chapter 6 on negotiation spaces and Chapter 7 on side-event spaces show, large multilateral meetings can resemble a giant trade show or carnival. You walk through all the various spaces, into one of the negotiating rooms, and see government delegates sitting around a table or in a large auditorium, often with a document projected on a screen. If this is your first time at these negotiations, you may be a bit confused. What is this document? Where did it come from? Why are all those square brackets in the text? Why are they arguing over the use of the words "should" or "shall"?

Or, you could walk into a plenary room, where government and nongovernmental stakeholders are speaking from their desks. There is a link to the meeting's internet portal on a screen in the front of the room, where statements and other documents can be found. But how do you navigate this portal, and how do you understand the different types of texts that can be found there?

One way to study agreement-making and its actors, processes, sites, and influence on global order is through texts produced along the way. In any given multilateral environmental negotiation, there are implementation reports, decisions, resolutions, statements, newsletters, and other technical reports that are often written in a language all of their own. They contain phrases that have a long history and may indicate more than is apparent at face value. Choices of words, phrases, and qualifying language often tell part of the story of how governments, and other delegates at conferences compromised and reached agreement. Language can also be coded so that those "in the know" understand the real intent behind the words. The use of jargon or "constructively ambiguous" phrases can signal one's insider status or exclude many from truly grasping a text's meaning. For these reasons, it is extremely important to understand the words as well as the context in which these words are used.

Treaties, resolutions, and decisions are often the most carefully scrutinized form of text, but they represent only some of the written communications at multilateral negotiations (see Table 8.1). As the agreement-making framework shows, a range of actors are involved in producing the final agreement. Government delegates, nongovernmental organizations (NGOs), international organizations, businesses, and academics communicate

Table 8.1 *Types of documents*

Category	Type	Actors involved	Description and what to look for	Where to find
Formal intergovernmental outcomes	Treaties, decisions, resolutions	Governments or parties to the MEA; sometimes NGOs	Official documents; look for agreed text describing actions going forward	Official website of the MEA or other UN process
Draft decisions and negotiation texts	Draft treaties, decisions, resolutions or action plans	Governments or parties to the MEA; sometimes NGOs	Unofficial documents still under negotiation; often contain square brackets around text lacking agreement. Check date (and time) at the top to understand the evolution over time	Not always publicly available on the official website; sometimes on the intranet at meetings; sometimes distributed by email
Secretariat background documents	Synthesis reports	Secretariat, by request of governments or parties	Background reports that synthesize submissions from governments aimed to inform the negotiations	Official website of the MEA or other UN process
	Summary reports on activities	Secretariat, by request of governments or parties	Documents that summarize the activities of the secretariat during the intersessional period	Official website of the MEA or other UN process
	Technical papers	Secretariat, by request of governments or parties	Technical report aimed to inform the negotiations	Official website of the MEA or other UN process
Statements	Opening statements	Governments, NGOs and IGOs	Statements given at the opening plenary. Sometimes only regional groups or coalitions speak. Provides an indication of a country or group's priorities.	Sometimes posted on the official website of the MEA or other UN process; sometimes they can be watched on a livestream that is recorded.

Category	Type	Actors involved	Description and what to look for	Where to find
	Ministerial or high-level statements	Governments (sometimes other invited guests or NGOs)	Statements given by ministers and other high-level officials during a ministerial or high-level segment; provides an indication of a country's priorities	Sometimes posted on the official website of the MEA or other UN process; sometimes they can be watched on a livestream that is recorded. Sometimes posted on the ministry's website
	Closing statements	Governments, NGOs and IGOs	Statements given at the closing plenary Sometimes only regional groups speak Provides an indication of how they think the meeting went and what was or was not adopted	Sometimes posted on the official website of the MEA or other UN process; sometimes they can be watched on a livestream that is recorded Summary provided in the *ENB*
Earth Negotiations Bulletin (*ENB*)	External publication	Produced at meetings by writers from the International Institute for Sustainable Development	Provides daily summaries of negotiations at COPs and other high-level meetings; provides a summary after meetings.	Available at https://enb.iisd.org/ Limited number of hard copies distributed at meetings
Observers' policy briefs, updates	Policy briefs	NGOs/IGOs/ governments	Unofficial documents written to influence the negotiations; can be used to identify positions	Available on the organization's website and limited number of hard copies distributed at meetings
	Blogs	NGOs and other groups	Unofficial commentary on negotiations	Available on private websites
	Social media posts	NGOs/IGOs/ governments	Unofficial commentary on negotiations; can be used to identify positions	Available on Facebook, Twitter, Instagram, and other social media sites
	Press releases	Secretariat/NGOs/ IGOs/governments	Official press releases	Available on secretariat/NGO/IGO or government websites

Table 8.1 (*cont.*)

Category	Type	Actors involved	Description and what to look for	Where to find
	Newsletters, e.g., *ECO* and *Third World Network*	Produced by NGOs	Unofficial commentary on negotiations; can give readers insights from the NGO perspective	Available online or by email distribution Limited number of hard copies distributed at meetings
	Exhibit materials	Secretariat/NGOs/IGOs/governments	At selected meetings, there are opportunities for governments and others to showcase success stories	Can be viewed at the meeting site
Submissions	From parties	Governments	Government submissions/reports are often required and can give insights as to government accomplishments or negotiation position	Official website of the MEA or other UN process
	Observers	NGOs, international organizations	Provides the NGO or international organization's view and suggestions on a specific issue	Official website of the MEA or other UN process

constantly, including through various types of documents. These documents are not created in a vacuum. As we hope to show in this chapter, the social and institutional context of negotiations can influence the communications encapsulated by these texts. In our contribution to the framework, we seek to show how the context within the negotiations and, at times, beyond the immediate talks can influence how actors communicate. These contextual factors shape actors' word choices individually and collectively, and, in turn, the final agreements that they make. We highlight three such factors: power relationships, social expectations, and history.

Throughout this chapter, we underscore the need to "triangulate" sources of information. Texts cannot be understood separately from their context, which would likely require gathering information from interviews (Chapter 9), participant observation (Chapters 10 and 11), and other methods explored throughout this book. The words used can sometimes reveal or conceal the power-laden relationships among actors. But to understand the intersecting forces and contexts that shaped the final documents, a core product of agreement-making, means looking beyond the texts themselves.

This chapter examines the importance of understanding documents at multilateral environmental negotiations in context, and what they can and cannot tell you. First, we explain why studying negotiations through the documentation is important. We then give a brief overview of the different types of documents you encounter at a COP or other negotiating session. We turn to the question of context and show how social norms and institutional settings can influence the creation of texts, which in turn could influence research that relies on those texts. Finally, we utilize a case study to show how to consider context when using documents for research.

8.2 Why and How to Study Texts?

Scholars using types of text analysis tend to view documents as a resource or as a topic worth scrutinizing: how the texts came to be and what dynamics shaped their production (Prior 2008). Using documents as resources lends itself to a focus on the document's content and how actors strategically employ that content. Texts can help trace the rise, fall, and semantic shifts of concepts, as expressed in NGO policy briefs or press releases, states' written statements, or secretariat technical papers (e.g. see Meadowcroft and Fiorino 2017). Texts can help us to understand how actors interpret key concepts, from fairness in the climate change regime (Tørstad and Sælen 2018) to sustainable development (Hadden and Seybert 2016). Or, as newer actors communicate their views in a negotiation setting, the texts they produce can elucidate their narratives and shared views (Blaxekjær and Nielsen 2015).

Treating documents as resources means considering the content's creation and influence on the wider context – in our case, environmental governance. Studies of treaties, specific provisions, resolutions, or COP decisions tend to fall into this category (e.g., Klein et al. 2019 on the Paris Agreement; Morgera and Tsioumani 2010 on the Convention on Biological Diversity). Texts can work in conjunction with one another; for example, using countries' "submissions" (written statements of their position on an issue), the draft negotiation text, and the final treaty can help a researcher trace which countries "won" or "lost" on particular issues, and identify which issues were controversial.

In the quest for an origin story, however, content analysis has limits. The human dimension, from the effects of all-night negotiations to interpersonal relationships, cannot be seen in documentation. Texts struggle to elucidate multicausal, complex relationships. Draft and final documents cannot tell the story of which issues were subject to last minute tradeoffs to achieve a compromise. NGOs may claim victories if their issues or draft language were taken up, but some countries may separately have supported similar wording. Comparing the positions expressed beforehand by NGOs with the final outcome cannot provide much insight into the true extent of NGO influence (Betsill and Corell 2008). Texts are an important source of information but, like all tools, they cannot decode everything.

Throughout this chapter, we draw on work that studies texts qualitatively, such as legal analyses of treaties, and quantitatively, as with computer-aided content analysis (e.g., with atlas.ti or MAXQDA), to show the utility of texts to elucidate the strategic speech acts captured in those texts. Studying how actors choose to communicate their views – their "communicative action" – can shed light on the broader "life world" those actors inhabit (Habermas 1987). The textual documents generated at, or feeding into, global environmental negotiations capture what Habermas would call "strategic speech acts." These are created within a particular institutional and social culture; therefore, it is necessary to look at the context of these strategic acts (who is the intended audience, what is the purpose of the communication), as well as the routines and norms that construct the communicative acts, and in turn, the texts.

8.3 Types of Texts

Thousands attend multilateral negotiations, many of whom arrive armed with written documents intended to help them achieve their aims. Some texts are intended for the actual negotiations and others are for side events or presentations. Here, we quickly outline the various texts that many researchers are likely to encounter. We discuss who tends to produce these documents, questions of accessibility, and other issues that may influence data collection.

8.3.1 Formal, Intergovernmental Outcomes

Generally, international agreements are captured in decisions, resolutions, or, occasionally, treaties. Most treaties constituting all or part of multilateral environmental agreements (MEAs) are legally binding, while COP decisions are not. These documents are the product of formal negotiations among governments. The text of a decision can be drafted by the secretariat or by parties. During the meeting, the secretariat will often issue a provisional version for parties' adoption, and, after the meeting, a final version of the text as adopted by states and including any amendments.

There are a range of documents generated through negotiations. Resolutions are formal expressions of the opinion or will of the treaty body or other UN organization. Decisions represent the view of parties concerning procedural matters, recording the adoption of a text, or setting out a work program. The first part of a resolution and a decision are the preambulatory clauses, which focus on the reasons the body is addressing the topic and highlight previous resolutions or decisions on the issue. The second part, the operative clauses, offer the solutions to the issue in question. It is primarily the operative clauses that are the most challenging to negotiate and are often the basis of scholarly research. Each word of these outcomes matters. Verbs need to be read carefully in negotiated outcomes, particularly the verbs beginning a paragraph in an operative clause. Paragraphs beginning with "shall" have the strongest legal obligations, while "should" or "encourage" provisions outline the expectations for parties' behavior.

Other words or phrases can speak volumes about negotiation dynamics. Hedging phrases – such as "to the extent possible," "as applicable," or "as appropriate" – can allow countries an out in the future, such as to say that they could not implement a provision due to national circumstances. Such phrases could indicate that not all countries envision themselves as able to fully implement the provision, or that some countries view this provision as a valuable activity that others should undertake (e.g., a developed country responsibility). The ubiquitous "inter alia" further allows for flexibility in interpretation. It usually precedes a list, and allows for countries to choose which actions or items in the list to implement or enact (see Biniaz 2016 for creative uses of grammar to achieve agreement). Such a list may indicate disagreement, or a lack of time to reach agreement on what exact items to specify.

8.3.2 Draft Decisions and Negotiation Text

Draft negotiation texts are works in progress. The starting points may differ. Indeed, parties sometimes have protracted debates about whose version of a text should serve as the starting point for negotiations. Countries may propose a starting point via a conference room paper (CRP) submitted before or during the meeting. The secretariat may propose a draft before the meeting, often in consultation with the Bureau. Occasionally, the chairs of a given body may be tasked by parties to develop a "zero draft" to serve as the basis for negotiations (for an excellent summary of the various types of negotiation texts, see Depledge 2005). Some decisions move quickly from starting point to finalization. Decision texts may take years to develop, or may never be adopted. Comparing successive drafts can help uncover the story of how a decision or treaty evolves.

There are procedures common across negotiations for countries to indicate levels of agreement or disagreement with text as it evolves. Square brackets around a word, phrase, paragraph, or even the entire document indicates that at least one party objects to its inclusion. For example, here is what Article 2 of the Paris Agreement looked like heading into the final round of negotiations in Paris:

> Parties [shall][agree to] to take urgent action and enhance [cooperation][support] so as to (a) Hold the increase in the global average temperature [below 2 °C][below 1.5 °C][well below 2 °C][below 2 °C or 1.5 °C] [below 1.5 °C or 2 °C][as far below 2 °C as possible] above pre-industrial levels by ensuring deep cuts in global greenhouse gas [net] emissions.

Each set of brackets indicates the preference of a country or, in this case, a coalition of countries. Reading a draft can show the range of options on the table. On occasion, these options are attributed to states; however, that practice has largely ended. Reading a draft text with brackets cannot in itself tell the reader which country holds which position, but it does give a sense of the option set.

Some notations are agreed on a case-by-case basis by those in the room, underscoring the need to be there. For example, #### was used in the negotiations for the Paris Agreement to denote whether countries would undertake commitments, contributions, actions, or plans (or some combination). For those on the outside, #### was a confusing notation with little meaning. For those directly involved in talks, it was a useful shorthand standing in place of the contentious issue of the nature of countries' obligations.

Drafts have no legal standing. They may be called nonpapers, CRPs, or simply drafts. Most MEAs have procedural rules stating that any progress in the negotiations, captured in a draft document, is lost. In the UN Framework Convention on Climate Change (UNFCCC), "Rule 16" is invoked when parties cannot agree to even a procedural conclusion; the issue is placed on the agenda for the next meeting, but draft documents are not forwarded. Other treaties have similar practices set out in their rules of procedure. Parties occasionally use these rules to their strategic advantage, to have unpalatable proposals removed from future consideration.

Drafts are not always publicly available. Some may be posted on the website. Most meeting convenors use an intranet only available to those on-site, or with a password. Drafts are often emailed to a list of delegates working on the issue (to avoid publicly posting drafts with sensitive proposals). Researchers generally have access to a first version (issued publicly before the meeting) and the final version, potentially leaving many twists and turns unseen (see the SDG case study in Section 8.6). Finally, draft documents tend to "disappear" on websites. They may be on one page during the meeting, and then when you go back to that document months or years later you may not find them. Thus, it is important to download and save documents when you find them.

8.3.3 Secretariat Background Documents

Parties may mandate the secretariat to produce preparatory documents. These include technical papers on a given issue, synthesis reports of parties' views, and reports on activities undertaken. They are usually produced under the secretariat's responsibility with little or no consultation with parties (while remaining within the mandate set by parties). Some secretariats may produce technical papers of their own volition, although likely with the blessing of the Bureau. For example, the Basel, Rotterdam, and Stockholm Conventions secretariat published technical papers on the illegal movement of chemicals and wastes, and on how the Rotterdam Convention could learn from the Stockholm Convention's review mechanism. These documents were considered by parties. Ultimately, parties agreed to further work on illegal activities, but rejected the proposed review procedure for the Rotterdam Convention.

These documents are available on the meeting website. Usually, the documents recall the mandate parties set out for their production. Sometimes, it is useful for the researcher to go back to that decision itself, as it may include terms of reference (e.g., for an external consultant to complete an independent assessment) or elaborated wording beyond what is included in the secretariat's report. The mandates are negotiated documents and can give insight into the balance that the secretariat had to strike when producing these reports.

8.3.4 Statements

Statements are an inevitable, inescapable fact of MEA meetings. There are opening statements delivered on the first day of each meeting. There are ministerial statements, other types of high-level statements (if there is a high-level segment), and closing statements on the last day. These statements highlight the important issues to the coalition, country, NGO, or international organization. Opening statements set out expectations for the meeting. These statements can also be used to provide implementation updates, such as emissions reductions, extension of protected areas, or protections for endangered species. High-level statements by world leaders or ministers often attempt to showcase their domestic record, and closing statements can reflect on the progress made at the meeting (vis-à-vis the priorities originally articulated) or set expectations for the next meeting.

These are verbal speech acts, but are nearly always read from a written document. For coalitions of countries and NGO constituencies, these texts are negotiated until all members of the collective agree on the content. Often, the Group of 77 and China (G-77/China) statement is an amalgamation of the often-conflicting priorities of its membership. Subsequent statements by developing countries will begin with "We support the statement made by [lead country] on behalf of the G-77/China." This does not indicate full support for all parts of the statement. A quantitative count of the co-occurrence of "support" and "G-77/China" may overestimate consensus among the group

There may be written versions posted online, or a crafty researcher could find a written copy in the venue. Failing that, a transcription from a webcast may be possible (for a few meetings only). Notes taken while sitting in the room are often the most reliable option.

8.3.5 Earth Negotiations Bulletin

The *ENB* has been a de facto record of multilateral environmental negotiations since 1992. Founded as a way to increase the transparency and accountability of environmental and sustainable development negotiations, the *Bulletin* summarizes the negotiations and is publicly available. The *Bulletin* is produced by a team of PhD candidates, academics, and other experts. It summarizes the discussions on a daily or summary basis. Each daily *Bulletin* summarizes the key issues discussed during that day and is published that night. Summary reports identify the key issues, positions, and outcomes for every agenda item and also include an analysis of the meeting. For this reason, the *ENB* can be used to follow the evolution of negotiations, such as shifts in issues and positions over time in the climate change regime (Baya-Laffite and Cointet 2016; Venturini et al. 2014).

ENB writers usually have access to informal negotiations and contact groups, as well as more formal sessions. However, *ENB* writers may not be able to attend the negotiations on the most contentious issues. As a result, using word counts or keyword searches may underestimate the prevalence of "hot button" issues. Rules around attribution vary in *ENB*s depending on the negotiation process. These rules are established by agreements between the *ENB* and the relevant secretariat. Generally speaking, the *ENB* will attribute statements in publicly open settings, such as plenaries or formal working groups. In informal negotiations or contact groups, the *ENB* usually does not attribute, if requested by the chair or secretariat.

Two of the *ENB*'s main value propositions are its neutrality and succinctness. Writers do not express an opinion or advocate for a given outcome. Words are carefully chosen. There is a list of verbs that writers use, with "lament" standing as the strongest verb in an *ENB* writer's arsenal. The strict style guide may seem dry to readers, but it helps avoid editorializing. However, it does require readers to read carefully for nuance. *ENB*s are produced to tight word counts. They are not transcriptions of the meeting, but are perhaps best seen as expertly curated accounts of the main issues negotiated (for a reflection on their strengths and limitations as research documents, see Reflection Boxes 8.1 and 8.2).

There are limits to using *ENB*s for cross-MEA comparisons. *ENB*s often use the lingo of the meeting, because writers are embedded in the negotiations and the audience is primarily negotiators. The *ENB* is written for the audience engaged or interested in a given process; it will rarely compare across processes. Also, the word count and the predominantly insider readership may limit the extent to which *ENB* writers explain certain terms. The summary reports usually provide more context.

Limited numbers of hard copies are available at the venue, but the Bulletins are available on the *ENB* website and are sent out to email lists each night. Summary reports and an analysis of the meeting are available on the *ENB* website (https://enb.iisd.org/) forty-eight hours after a meeting's completion.

Reflection Box 8.1 Using *ENB* reports in ethnographic research

by Harriet Thew

My research ethnographically explores youth participation in UNFCCC conferences over several years (Thew et al. 2020, 2021, 2022). I have regularly used *ENB* reports which are helpful for anyone looking to gain "inside information" into the negotiations and expert opinions on the significance of debates and decisions. I have also used the *Bulletin* for:

1. Identifying potential interviewees. *ENB* publishes many photographs of individuals and groups on its website, often with people's names and titles: e.g., Name, Minister of X, Country.
2. Checking names and job titles of speakers.
3. Looking at photographs of breakout groups to determine who was speaking to whom and to look at body language.
4. Catching up on side events and negotiations I could not attend. There are always simultaneous negotiations and events and it is impossible to conduct participant observation of the entire conference (unless working in a team, as discussed in Chapter 11), so reading daily *ENB* reports is a great way to catch up.

However, *ENB* reports are not a sufficient source of information on their own. Due to word count constraints and its primary focus on state actors, I have found that the detail is not always relevant to my deep qualitative study of young people's participation in UNFCCC conferences. The extent to which youth participants engage with the negotiations varies greatly, with some tracking and striving to influence particular policy areas whilst others avoid the negotiation rooms entirely, instead channeling their efforts into side events, actions, constituency meetings, and communication activities. During my PhD research, I was particularly interested in the power dynamics experienced by youth participants and these cannot be adequately studied through text analysis of *ENB* reports (or any other document that does not explicitly focus on these dynamics). To get a real sense of power relations, I need to be there to observe and document the following:

1. Which comments are met with enthusiastic nods and which are met with frowns, as well as whose comments are repeated by the session chairs and whose seem to fall on deaf ears: for example, at COP26 in Glasgow I saw, for the first time, the UK presidency repeating comments previously made by youth participants, suggesting recognition of young people's perspectives.
2. How side-event speakers were chosen and the extent to which their comments are representative of broader views.
3. Who is allowed into the room and who has to wait outside in a one-in/one-out queue due to "space limitations." In the UNFCCC's first Open Dialogue between parties and observers in 2018, for example, parties were given preferential access and observers were forced to queue, resulting in many youth participants feeling dissatisfied with the event, which was framed as a landmark moment for nonstate actor input.

8.3.6 Observers' Policy Briefs, Updates

NGOs, the private sector, local authorities, and international organizations also attend negotiations and advocate for their issues and promote their activities. This can take the form of blogs, social media posts, press releases, policy briefings, and even draft language for decisions or treaties.

Some NGOs in the climate regime produce regular accounts of the negotiations. The Climate Action Network (CAN) produces *Eco*, a daily publication that focuses on one or two issues under negotiation and provides an update on the negotiations through the lens of CAN's position on the issues. Third World Network produces updates during some meetings (mostly climate-related) that also focus on a given issue from a critical perspective and with the interests of developing countries at the center. As with any of these texts, knowing who produces them can be as important to understanding the content as the words and phrases.

8.3.7 Submissions

Submissions are formal documents containing a country's or observer's negotiation position. They can be submitted to the secretariat at any time. Usually, there is a call for submissions on a particular topic when states collectively want to learn more about one another's positions, or have input from observers. The mandate for the submissions is usually contained in a decision, and should be carefully read by the researcher before examining the submissions themselves. That mandate is the product of negotiations and could shape how countries position their views. For content analysis, the structure is helpful because the mandate often provides a common format and context for the submissions.

8.4 Behind the Words: The Context of Common Texts

Qualitative and quantitative research scholars need to understand the context in which the strategic communicative acts occur. We highlight three: power relationships, social expectations, and history. Each of these forms of context can shape the interactions among state diplomats, NGO representatives, and the secretariat. They are each difficult to "pin down" and may require ethnographic methods, as described in Reflection Box 8.1, but each of them influences actions, strategic calculations, and, in turn, text.

First, texts are products of power relationships. There are norm makers and takers; those trying to influence and those deferring to authority. Some states and NGOs simply have more sway than others. Their ideas may appear more often and even shape the nature and production of the document. For example, the US requirements regarding ratification strongly shaped the provisions of the Paris Agreement (Kemp 2016). Powerful countries may be able to realize their preferences more often in global negotiations, but researchers should not underestimate the moral authority of smaller states that often are on the frontlines of environmental change.

Second, social expectations around diplomatic norms and the structure of multilateral events also shape interactions, discourse, and, as a result, texts. MEAs are institutional environments, but also social ones. Understanding social norms of behavior and other structured patterns of interactions is an important step toward reading past the words and exploring what a text means.

Practices may influence the data as it appears in text (see Pouliot and Thérien 2018 on practices at COPs). For example, some countries always speak on behalf of their coalition (e.g., Australia for the Umbrella Group in the UNFCCC). The quantitative approach employed by Baya-Laffite et al. (2014) found stability in the relative visibility of countries in the UNFCCC negotiations. The data was based on *ENB* mentions of a country. What perhaps they picked up (at least in part) is the stability of practices.

Third, historical context matters. Texts are produced at a given point in time and reflect not only the power and the social environment in which they are produced, but also the state of the regime at that time. Many scholars, for example, are already using the treasure trove of climate pledges made in countries' nationally determined contributions (NDCs). To name a few studies, scholars have used NDCs to identify salient issues (e.g., Barkemeyer 2017; Hein et al. 2018), discursive positioning (Mills-Novoa and Liverman 2019), common narrative threads (Jernnäs and Linnér 2019), and ideas of fairness (Tørstad and Sælen 2018).

NDCs are a popular and public source of data and the analyses have produced valuable insights. Yet, much of the scholarship using NDCs has thus far underestimated the multiple ways that the negotiations may have influenced what countries submitted, and how those dynamics could, in turn, influence the analysis. Disagreements over the scope of NDCs influenced the extent to which adaptation and finance were included by developed countries (the 2018 Paris Agreement rule book was not yet adopted). Normative pressure to submit an NDC meant many were prepared by consultants or captured current rather than planned, future, climate policies. Overall uncertainties in the negotiations could also influence the content and the form of NDCs. The round of NDCs submitted in 2015 could be ephemeral glimpses at climate change pledges developed and submitted under a unique set of circumstances.

Reflection Box 8.2 Combining texts with other methods to study science–policy interfaces for ocean protection

By Ina Tessnow-von Wysocki

Text analysis constitutes an integral part of my research and includes different types of documents that I analyze for different purposes, including academic literature, policy briefs, *ENB* reports, and formal treaty documents. To identify at what point scientific concepts have emerged in the literature, I review scientific papers, as well as policy and technical briefs. Then I look at the draft treaty texts to see whether these concepts appear in one form or another in the final agreement.

Through a comparison of different draft texts over time, the emergence and disappearance of legal text can be analyzed. In this way, I trace newly introduced concepts, their authors, and their communicators, and can make predictions about how they found their way into the international negotiations. *ENB* reports can provide a valuable addition here, identifying which actors were active within the negotiations and might have contributed to changes in the treaty text, although none of these documents provide evidence for why certain scientific concepts were included or excluded from discussions and negotiation texts. These sources are also unable to provide clarity on the treaty drafting process, or the variety of actors, their interests and expectations, their differing individual interpretations of scientific concepts, or which external events and policy entrepreneurs have contributed to shaping the formulations. To capture these dynamics, I have used text analysis in conjunction with event ethnography.

Event ethnography enables me to draw a clearer picture of which actors are present and active in the discussions and shape the debates, as well as the final wording. This helps reveal the influential actors that shape the agreement, such as government representatives and inter- and non-governmental organizations, as well as facilitators and the president of the conference. Observing in person has also enabled me to "be part" of the negotiations, to experience the science–policy interfaces on-site, including formalized UN processes but also formal and informal interaction between scientists and policy-makers, and to conduct interviews. Qualitative interviews can help one to understand dynamics throughout the negotiation process which cannot be studied by analyzing written documents. A combination of these additional methods with text analysis was useful to identify and explain pathways by which science influences policy-making.

8.5 Context and Power in MEA Texts: Key Questions to Ask When You Begin

There are many contextual factors and power relationships that can shape several types of texts and how we study and read them. Here, we offer some general questions for researchers to ask about their chosen texts, then explore the implications of these questions for the study of specific types of texts.

8.5.1 How Was This Text Produced?

The first, most fundamental consideration is the processes that generated the text. Is it the result of bargaining among states or within a coalition of NGOs? Or is the text a report of proceedings as curated by official rapporteurs, the *ENB*, or another NGO, and how did those curators summarize hundreds of hours of discussions into a relatively short document? What types of documents did the secretariat base its technical report on?

Also, conventions and traditions can shape a text or speech. A notable tradition is diplomatic language: the tradition and practice of speaking carefully, adhering to convention and procedure. Diplomatic language precludes emotive statements (save, perhaps, for small island states and other vulnerable countries in climate negotiations). In turn, this shapes how official reports and the *ENB* relay parties' statements.

Such language also limits the extent to which parties will point the finger at others. Texts, from position statements to press releases, will infer divisions with others without calling out another country or countries explicitly. During UNFCCC COP21 in Paris, US Climate Envoy Todd Stern told the media: "This is our moment, and we need to make it count … There are some countries here who are not in the [High Ambition] coalition and, indeed, would seek a more minimal outcome" (Clark and Stothard 2015). Here, he specifically meant India, Saudi Arabia, and, to a lesser extent, China – countries that were (at the time) blocking the inclusion of language related to the 1.5°C climate target in the Paris Agreement. Similarly, Tuvalu suggested that the United States could be complicit in human rights abuses related to loss and damage in the closing plenary of UNFCCC COP25 in 2019, by referencing "a party that will soon not be a party to the Paris Agreement" in conjunction with denying the effect of climate change "could be interpreted by some to be a crime against humanity." Understanding such gaps and nuance in text and statements can only be filled in with knowledge of the context of the limits and nuances of diplomatic language.

The institutional environment can affect the texts. Most of the hands-on discussions and crafting of text takes place in English. This can disadvantage delegates working in their second or third language. Native English speakers have an advantage in crafting negotiation texts on the fly, dictating them to the secretariat staff member who types them out so they can be displayed on a screen in the room.

There are also likely to be multiple negotiations happening at the same time. Smaller delegations may not be able to send a representative to all the relevant negotiations and events happening concurrently. Who is in the room, and who isn't but should be? Smaller delegations may not be present when key phrases and compromises that directly affect them are made. This may mean that the text does not represent all views, or help explain why a draft text had to be subsequently changed.

8.5.2 Who Produced the Text and What Is Their Motivation?

There are pushes and pulls – strategic motivations – that influence actors and, in turn, the texts they produce. The result is that a "direction of bias" may influence the content and the origins of the texts. A common example of direction of bias is that NGOs have incentives to overstate their influence in a negotiation, while states are likely to understate NGO influence, to avoid the optics of being swayed by an unelected lobby group (Betsill and Corell 2008).

This is fundamental to the strategic act of producing documentation. Word choice, framing, information selection, and other decisions are influenced by an actor's direction of bias. For some, there may be an incentive to overstate success, whereas others will be more inclined to identify weaknesses and failings. The final text may very likely be the result of these motivations rather than an attempt at a factual documentation of events.

For press releases, blogs, and other (perhaps less formal or technical) texts, the direction of bias may be particularly salient. The secretariat and parties may exaggerate the extent of agreement or the achievements of a meeting. Secretariats are charged with safeguarding the legitimacy of the MEA. Press releases may laud the meeting's accomplishments while understating ongoing tensions or multilateral failures.

For different reasons, NGOs may also spin the nature of an agreement; for example, a coalition of NGOs described the 2019 plastics decision by the Basel Convention COP as a "ban" in an online campaign.[1] This helped them gain support for their campaign and show that they made an impact. In fact, the decision only made the international trade of some types of single-use plastics subject to the prior informed consent procedure.

8.5.3 Who Is the Audience?

Documents written for negotiators will use different language than texts written for a public or "lay" audience. The text may be a tool to motivate new supporters to a movement, educate youth, or try to influence other delegations. The language in the text can reveal much about how the authors wish to position themselves with the audience. It can also provide clues about what the author believes the audience needs or wants to hear. These aspirations and assumptions may shape common words or phrases used and the overall framing of the issue explored in the document.

One example is jargon. It is powerful – it differentiates those "in the know" from those new to a subject; it is a shorthand that can marginalize some outside of the circle of those governing an issue. Heavy reliance on jargon, whether it is a technical term or a reference to a previous decision (e.g., recalling decision 1/CP.16, para 70), often means that the

[1] The Avaaz campaign is here: https://secure.avaaz.org/campaign/en/plastic_in_paradise_rts/.

text is inward facing, addressed to those directly engaged in the negotiations. Jargon can therefore be a signaling device for some organizations on the edges of power, a claim to authority and belonging in the regime (Allan 2018). The BBC has its own climate change glossary, brought about in part by the deliberate use of jargon to obfuscate what is happening.[2] The use of jargon is not always strategic; it can also be a case of scientists using shorthand to efficiently communicate with one another. Context matters: depending on whether the text is produced for experts or for a wider audience, the use of jargon could have very different implications.

8.5.4 Is the Topic Particularly Salient or Sensitive?

Political sensitivities can influence transparency and, in turn, the availability of texts. The more politically sensitive an issue is, the fewer textual accounts may exist. When issues are particularly sensitive, *ENB* writers and other observers may not be permitted into the room. The relative absence of particular words from the *ENB*s may be a better indicator of political salience or divisive negotiations than the presence of the issue (although this has yet to be tested empirically). Absence from the room limits direct knowledge, thus, other than firsthand accounts by the few delegates in the room, the details of last-minute compromises are largely lost, unless recounted in memoirs years afterward (see, for a few examples, Benedick 1998; Brun 2016; Engfeldt 2009; Kamau et al. 2018; McConnell 1996).

Political sensitivities can shape the words themselves. For deeply divisive issues, actors create "constructive ambiguity," using grammar to create sentences that can be read multiple ways, thereby allowing various countries, or other actors, to have their own interpretation (Biniaz 2016). The final wording in a treaty or a COP decision reflects agreements reached through power-laden bargaining to find wording that all parties can accept. For example, the Biosafety Protocol refers to "living modified organisms" rather than genetically modified organisms. The United Nations Convention to Combat Desertification shifted from references to "zero net land degradation" in 2012 to "land degradation neutrality" by 2015. These seemingly odd phrases only make sense in the context of negotiations and the need to realize a consensus among parties with widely varying interests.

NGOs similarly work to achieve consensus on their statements, leading to carefully crafted phrases with significant underlying meaning that could be overlooked. For example, in the early years of the global climate justice movement, activists were divided on whether to focus their work solely on reducing emissions from deforestation and forest degradation (REDD+) or on all market mechanisms. As a compromise, the group agreed to the principle that "Climate Justice Now! is against market-based mechanisms, such as REDD+" (Allan 2020, 110).

This constructive ambiguity makes a researcher's life more difficult. It requires paying attention to words and phrases, but also to the various ways actors may interpret their meaning. COP decisions commonly refer to previous agreements and decisions to avoid reopening previous compromises or re-negotiating foundational issues captured in that

[2] See www.bbc.co.uk/news/magazine-34858199.

previous decision. Analysts may need to attend to not only the words, but also their various possible interpretations.

8.6 Case Study: The Sustainable Development Goals

The negotiation of the Sustainable Development Goals (SDGs) provides an excellent example of how researchers can gain a better understanding of the development of the goals by studying official documents and statements.

The negotiations took place over thirteen sessions from 2013 to 2014 in what was called the Open Working Group (OWG) on SDGs. To maintain a high level of transparency, the secretariat posted all statements and documents on their webpage throughout the process. This makes it fairly easy to compare the drafts of the different iterations of the SDGs to see how they evolved. While the documents themselves do not tell the researcher what the dynamics were in the room or who said what during the negotiations, a close look at these documents can provide important clues.

For the first year, over eight sessions, the OWG delayed negotiations until completing a period of mutual learning and discussion. This "course" in sustainable development involved formal discussion of more than fifty-eight issues, enhanced by presentations from eighty experts (Kamau et al. 2018). In March 2014, at OWG-9, delegates shifted gears and began the process of developing the goals. The co-chairs distributed a "focus areas" document, which was prepared based on the exchange of views during the eight stocktaking sessions and other communications from OWG members and observers, and *ENB* reports. This February 24, 2014 document contained nineteen focus areas. After OWG-9, the co-chairs released an amended focus areas document on March 19, 2014, which mapped out how different focus areas could come together through interlinkages. Following OWG-10, the co-chairs issued a revised focus areas document containing draft goals dated April 17, 2014, which contained sixteen areas and possible goal text. The zero draft contained seventeen goals and indicative targets and was released on June 2, 2014. After OWG-12, a revised zero draft was released. Following the negotiations at OWG-13, the SDGs were adopted and forwarded to the UN General Assembly with 17 goals and 169 targets.

Just looking at the iterations of the goals, as presented in Table 8.2, can give researchers an idea of how the goals developed. But other documentation is necessary to understand country positions and potential "red lines," including statements that were also posted on the website. That said, not every statement was uploaded, and there are no written records of multiple statements during the negotiations. However, the OWG created a unique document that can help researchers. After the March 19 focus areas document was released, many participants and observers submitted amendments, proposals, and comments both during and following OWG-10. In advance of OWG-11, the co-chairs asked the secretariat to compile all the proposals submitted by governments, civil society, and stakeholders into a single, organized document to serve as a reference tool. This 182-page list of proposals became the "Encyclopedia Groupinica: A Compilation of Goals and Targets Suggestions from OWG-10 in Response to the Co-Chairs' Focus Areas Document Dated

Table 8.2 *Evolution of the Sustainable Development Goals*

March 2014 Focus Areas1	**April 2014 Focus Areas2**	**June 2014 Zero Draft3**	**July 2014 Zero draft (revised)4**	**July 2014 Final5**
Focus area 1. Poverty Eradication	Focus area 1. Poverty eradication, building shared prosperity and promoting equality	Proposed goal 1. End poverty in all its forms everywhere	Proposed goal 1. End poverty everywhere	Goal 1. End poverty in all its forms everywhere
Focus area 2. Sustainable agriculture, food security, and nutrition	Focus area 2. End hunger and improve nutrition for all through sustainable agriculture and improved food systems	Proposed goal 2. End hunger, achieve food security and adequate nutrition for all, and promote sustainable agriculture	Proposed goal 2. End hunger, improve nutrition, and promote sustainable agriculture	Goal 2. End hunger, achieve food security and improved nutrition, and promote sustainable agriculture
Focus area 3. Health and population dynamics	Focus area 3. Healthy life at all ages for all	Proposed goal 3. Attain healthy life at all ages for all	Proposed goal 3. Attain healthy lives for all	Goal 3. Ensure healthy lives and promote well-being for all at all ages
Focus area 4. Education	Focus area 4. Provide quality education and life-long learning for all	Proposed goal 4. Provide equitable and inclusive quality education and life-long learning opportunities for all	Proposed goal 4. Provide quality education and life-long learning opportunities for all	Goal 4. Ensure inclusive and equitable quality education and promote life-long learning opportunities for all
Focus area 5. Gender equality and women's empowerment	Focus area 5. Attain gender equality and women's empowerment everywhere	Proposed goal 5. Attain gender equality, empower women and girls everywhere	Proposed goal 5. Attain gender equality, empower women and girls everywhere	Goal 5. Achieve gender equality and empower all women and girls
Focus area 6. Water and sanitation	Focus area 6. Water and sanitation for a sustainable world	Proposed goal 6. Secure water and sanitation for all for a sustainable world	Proposed goal 6. Ensure availability and sustainable use of water and sanitation for all	Goal 6. Ensure availability and sustainable management of water and sanitation for all

March 2014 Focus Areas1	April 2014 Focus Areas2	June 2014 Zero Draft3	July 2014 Zero draft (revised)4	July 2014 Final5
Focus area 7. Energy	Focus area 7. Ensure access to affordable, sustainable and reliable modern energy for all	Proposed goal 7. Ensure access to affordable, sustainable and reliable modern energy services for all	Proposed goal 7. Ensure sustainable energy for all	Goal 7. Ensure access to affordable, reliable, sustainable and modern energy for all
Focus area 8. Economic growth	Focus area 8. Promote sustainable, inclusive, and sustained economic growth and decent jobs for all	Proposed goal 8. Promote strong, inclusive, and sustained economic growth and decent work for all	Proposed goal 8. Promote sustained, inclusive and sustainable economic growth, full and productive employment and decent work for all	Goal 8. Promote sustained, inclusive and sustainable economic growth, full and productive employment and decent work for all
Focus area 9. Industrialization	Focus area 9. Promote sustainable industrialization and equality among nations	Proposed goal 9. Promote sustainable industrialization	Proposed goal 9. Promote sustainable infrastructure and industrialization and foster innovation	Goal 9. Build resilient infrastructure, promote inclusive and sustainable industrialization and foster innovation
Focus area 10. Infrastructure	Focus area 10. Build inclusive, safe and sustainable cities and human settlements	Proposed goal 10. Reduce inequality within and among nations	Proposed goal 10. Reduce inequality within and between countries	Goal 10. Reduce inequality within and among countries
Focus area 11. Employment and decent work for all	Focus area 11. Promote sustainable consumption and production patterns	Proposed goal 11. Build inclusive, safe and sustainable cities and human settlements	Proposed goal 11. Make cities and human settlements inclusive, safe and sustainable	Goal 11. Make cities and human settlements inclusive, safe, resilient and sustainable

Table 8.2 (*cont.*)

March 2014 Focus Areas1	April 2014 Focus Areas2	June 2014 Zero Draft3	July 2014 Zero draft (revised)4	July 2014 Final5
Focus area 12. Promoting equality	Focus area 12. Take urgent and significant action to mitigate and adapt to climate change	Proposed goal 12. Promote sustainable consumption and production patterns	Proposed goal 12. Promote sustainable consumption and production patterns	Goal 12. Ensure sustainable consumption and production patterns
Focus area 13. Sustainable cities and human settlements	Focus area 13. Take urgent and significant actions for the conservation and sustainable use of marine resources, oceans and seas	Proposed goal 13. Promote actions at all levels to address climate change	Proposed goal 13. Tackle climate change and its impacts	Goal 13. Take urgent action to combat climate change and its impacts
Focus area 14. Sustainable consumption and production	Focus area 14. Protect and restore terrestrial ecosystems and halt all biodiversity loss	Proposed goal 14. Attain conservation and sustainable use of marine resources, oceans and seas	Proposed goal 14. Conserve and promote sustainable use of oceans, seas and marine resources	Goal 14. Conserve and sustainably use the oceans, seas and marine resources for sustainable development
Focus area 15. Climate	Focus area 15. Strengthen global partnership for sustainable development	Proposed goal 15. Protect and restore terrestrial ecosystems and halt all biodiversity loss	Proposed goal 15. Protect and promote sustainable use of terrestrial ecosystems, halt desertification, land degradation and biodiversity loss	Goal 15. Protect, restore and promote sustainable use of terrestrial ecosystems, sustainably manage forests, combat desertification, and halt and reverse land degradation and halt biodiversity loss

March 2014 Focus Areas[1]	April 2014 Focus Areas[2]	June 2014 Zero Draft[3]	July 2014 Zero draft (revised)[4]	July 2014 Final[5]
Focus area 16. Marine resources, oceans, and seas	Focus area 16. Peaceful and inclusive societies, rule of law and capable institutions	Proposed goal 16. Achieve peaceful and inclusive societies, rule of law, effective and capable institutions	Proposed goal 16. Achieve peaceful and inclusive societies, access to justice for all, and effective and capable institutions	Goal 16. Promote peaceful and inclusive societies for sustainable development, provide access to justice for all and build effective, accountable and inclusive institutions at all levels
Focus area 17. Ecosystems and biodiversity		Proposed goal 17. Strengthen and enhance the means of implementation and global partnership for sustainable development	Proposed goal 17. Strengthen the means of implementation and the global partnership for sustainable development	Goal 17. Strengthen the means of implementation and revitalize the global partnership for sustainable development
Focus area 18. Means of implementation Focus area 19. Peaceful and non-violent societies, capable institutions				

1 The complete document is available at https://sustainabledevelopment.un.org/content/documents/3276focusareas.pdf.

2 The complete document is available at https://sustainabledevelopment.un.org/content/documents/3686WorkingDoc_0205_additionalsupporters.pdf.

3 The complete document is available at https://sustainabledevelopment.un.org/content/documents/4528zerodraft12OWG.pdf.

4 The complete document is available at https://sustainabledevelopment.un.org/content/documents/4523zerodraft.pdf.

5 The complete document is available at https://sdgs.un.org/documents/a68970-open-working-group-general-assem-20396.

19 March 2014."[3] This document is instrumental in understanding different countries' positions at that point in the negotiations and identifies some of the potential red lines. It also shows which issues were eventually incorporated into the 17 SDGs and 169 targets and which ones were not – and which governments or other stakeholders may have won or lost on particular issues. Unfortunately, most processes don't have this type of document. And, it must be remembered, this document marked a moment of time and many positions changed between March and July 2014.

The availability of these documents can aid researchers in understanding how the negotiations evolved. Encyclopedia Groupinica and the statements posted on the OWG's webpage can enable researchers to determine which country had which priorities and how these were later incorporated into the text. The *ENB* can also be used to identify which countries spoke on which issue; the researcher can then go back and see if the relevant statement is posted or if there is an appropriate entry in Encyclopedia Groupinca. For example, if you were to look at SDG 13 on climate change, without understanding the negotiations you would think it is a very weak goal. But by reading the different drafts, the *ENB*, and Encyclopedia Groupinica, you would find that many countries did not want to prejudge or prejudice the parallel negotiations on the Paris Agreement and put in a footnote acknowledging that the UNFCCC is the primary international, intergovernmental forum for negotiating the global response to climate change (Kamau et al. 2018, 194).

By combining these different types of text, the researcher can better understand the use of jargon, negotiating priorities of the key governments and groupings, and the flow of the negotiations. However, if the researcher was unable to attend the negotiations, just looking at the statements, the *ENB*, the drafts, or Encyclopedia Groupinca would give an incomplete understanding of the nuances of the process. Even with these documents, the final endgame of many negotiations, including the SDGs, often takes place behind closed doors. Making an accurate assessment of how negotiators got from point A to point B requires interviews with multiple participants who were in those contact groups or consultations (see Chapter 9).

8.7 Conclusions

There are many reasons (and temptations) to accept a final text as a "fact" of global environmental governance. Texts represent rules and norms of global governance, as agreed to by states or espoused by NGOs and others. They are clearly vital touchstones for understanding how a global community of actors seek to improve our natural environment (or, more cynically, to obfuscate their responsibility). But textual analysis can be much more. Analyzing texts can help elucidate the trajectory of the negotiations and could shed light on the power relationships among a wide range of actors by showing the tradeoffs made in arriving at a final agreement. This makes texts a critical resource and an essential method in studying the underlying dynamics elucidated by the agreement-making framework.

[3] This document is available at https://sustainabledevelopment.un.org/content/documents/3698EncyclopediaGroupinica.pdf.

Understanding the power dynamics often requires more than the text itself, however. Triangulation through attending a conference, interviewing attendees, and piecing together multiple documents is often necessary to truly "read" a text, as illustrated by the SDG case study. Reading a draft text without knowing which countries proposed which options in bracketed text shows the various options, but not which countries ultimately prevailed in the final compromise version that was adopted by states. Reading an *ENB* without an understanding of diplomatic language that may be gained through observation can lead a researcher to mistake a very pointed comment for a muted observation.

Text analysis therefore must be combined with other information sources. Nothing can replace "being there" to gain a sense of the institutional and social context. However, for reasons of carbon and financial budgets, "being there" may not be possible. These constraints make texts valuable sources of data. Still, reading the final product is not enough. Scholars need to view texts as products of their power-laden environment. Actors, and their communications, are embedded in particular power dynamics, routines, and incentive structures that can influence how they choose to convey their thoughts in writing.

Further Reading

1. Paltridge, B. (2012). *Discourse analysis: An introduction.* London: Bloomsbury Publishing.

A useful practical guide that provides overview of various types of discourse analysis.

2. Johnstone, B. (2017). *Discourse analysis.* Hoboken, NJ: John Wiley & Sons.

This book includes theoretical and practical advice on how to locate context, roles, and power in text.

3. Kuckartz, U. (2014). *Qualitative text analysis: A guide to methods, practice and using software.* Sage.

This book provides a wide-ranging look at qualitative text analysis, including hermeneutics, various qualitative text analysis methods, and computer assistance. It provides practical advice throughout.

4. Grimmer, J., and Stewart, B. M. (2013). Text as data: The promise and pitfalls of automatic content analysis methods for political texts. *Political Analysis*, 21(3),267–297.

For those considering using computer models to identify commonalities or patterns in large amounts of text, this is a helpful resource on the use of such techniques.

References

Allan, J. I. (2018). Seeking entry: Discursive hooks and NGOs in global climate politics. *Global Policy*, 9(4),560–569.

Allan, J. I. (2020). *The new climate activism: NGO authority and participation in global climate governance.* Toronto: University of Toronto Press.

Barkemeyer, R. (2017). Climate policy: Uncovering ocean-related priorities. *Nature Climate Change*, 7(11),761–762.

Baya-Laffite, J., Gray, I., De Pryck, K, et al. (2014). Absolute and relative visibility of countries in the UNFCCC negotiations, 1995–2013. http://climaps.eu/#!/map/absolute-and-relative-visibility-of-countries-in-the-unfccc-negotiations-1995-2013.

Baya-Laffite, N., and Cointet, J. P. (2016). Mapping topics in international climate negotiations: A computer-assisted semantic network approach. In A. Kaun and S. Kubitschko, eds., *Innovative methods in media and communication research*. London: Palgrave-Macmillan, pp. 273–291.

Benedick, R. (1998). *Ozone diplomacy*. Cambridge, MA: Harvard University Press

Betsill, M. M., and Corell, E., eds. (2008). *NGO diplomacy: The influence of nongovernmental organizations in international environmental negotiations*. Cambridge, MA: MIT Press.

Biniaz, S. (2016). Comma but differentiated responsibilities: Punctuation and 30 other ways negotiators have resolved issues in the international climate change regime. *Michigan Journal of Environmental & Administrative Law*, 6(1),37.

Blaxekjær, L. Ø., and Nielsen, T. D. (2015). Mapping the narrative positions of new political groups under the UNFCCC. *Climate Policy*, 15(6),751–766.

Brun, A. (2016). Conference diplomacy: The making of the Paris Agreement. *Politics and Governance*, 4(3),115–123.

Clark, P., and Stothard, M. (2015). "COP21: US adds weight to group pushing for strong climate deal." *Financial Times*. www.ft.com/content/d690ddea-9ec2-11e5-b45d-4812f209f861.

Depledge, J. (2005). *The organization of international negotiations: Constructing the climate change regime*. London: Routledge/Taylor and Francis.

Engfeldt, L-G. (2009). *From Stockholm to Johannesburg and beyond*. Swedish Ministry for Foreign Affairs.

Habermas, J. (1987). *The theory of communicative action*, Vol. 2. Cambridge: Polity Press.

Hadden, J., and Seybert, L. A. (2016). What's in a norm: Mapping the norm definition process in the debate on sustainable development. *Global Governance*, 22(2),249–268.

Hein, J., Guarin, A., Frommé, E., and Pauw, P. (2018). Deforestation and the Paris climate agreement: An assessment of REDD+ in the national climate action plans. *Forest Policy and Economics*, 90,7–11.

Jernnäs, M., and Linnér, B. O. (2019). A discursive cartography of nationally determined contributions to the Paris climate agreement. *Global Environmental Change*, 55,73–83.

Kamau, M., Chasek, P., and O'Connor, D. (2018). *Transforming multilateral diplomacy: The inside story of the sustainable development goals*. London: Routledge.

Kemp, L. (2016). Bypassing the 'ratification straitjacket': Reviewing US legal participation in a climate agreement. *Climate Policy*, 16(8),1011–1028.

Klein, D., Carazo, M. P., Doelle, M. Bulmer, J. and Higham, A., eds. (2019). *The Paris Agreement on Climate Change: Analysis and commentary*. Oxford: Oxford University Press.

McConnell, F. (1996). *The Biodiversity Convention: A negotiating history*. London: Kluwer Law International.

Meadowcroft, J., and Fiorino, D., eds. (2017). *Conceptual innovation in global environmental governance*. Cambridge, MA: MIT Press.

Mills-Novoa, M., and Liverman, D. M. (2019). Nationally determined contributions: Material climate commitments and discursive positioning in the NDCs. *Wiley Interdisciplinary Reviews: Climate Change*, 10(5),e589.

Morgera, E., and Tsioumani, E. (2010). Yesterday, today, and tomorrow: Looking afresh at the Convention on Biological Diversity. *Yearbook of International Environmental Law*, 21(1),3–40.

Pouliot, V., and Thérien, J. P. (2018). Global governance in practice. *Global Policy*, 9(2), 163–172.

Prior, L. (2008). Repositioning documents in social research. *Sociology*, 42(5),821–836.

Thew, H., Middlemiss, L., and Paavola, J. (2020). “Youth is not a political position”: Exploring justice claims-making in the UN Climate Change Negotiations. *Global Environmental Change*, *61*,102036.

Thew, H., Middlemiss, L., and Paavola, J. (2021). Does youth participation increase the democratic legitimacy of UNFCCC-orchestrated global climate change governance? *Environmental Politics*, *30*(6),873–894.

Thew, H., Middlemiss, L., and Paavola, J. (2022). “You need a month’s holiday just to get over it!” Exploring young people’s lived experiences of the UN Climate Change Negotiations. *Sustainability*, *14* (7),4259.

Tørstad, V., and Sælen, H. (2018). Fairness in the climate negotiations: What explains variation in parties’ expressed conceptions? *Climate Policy*, 18(5),642–654.

Venturini T., Baya-Laffite, N., Cointet J.-P. et al. (2014). Three maps and three misunderstandings: A digital mapping of climate diplomacy. *Big Data & Society* 1(2),1–19.

9

Interviews

Conducting and Using Interviews on and at Negotiations

YULIA YAMINEVA

> Frankly 'getting the interview' is more art than science.
>
> *(Goldstein 2002, 669)*
>
> [Interviews] take a lot of persistence, time, and whatever passes these days for shoe leather, but they are immense fun … If you like both politics and political science, it's one terrific way to spend your time.
>
> *(Aberbach and Rockman 2002, 676)*

9.1 Introduction

For scholars interested in the empirical study of agreement-making, interviewing can be the best – and often the only – method by which to learn about the inner workings of global environmental negotiations. Interviewing on negotiations, however, is beset with perils and pitfalls that can ensnare the unsuspecting researcher new to the setting. This chapter provides guidance on how to conduct interviews for researchers with no previous experience of UN environmental meetings.

There is a rich literature on interviewing for social science research[1] and I do not plan to provide a complete account of it in this chapter. The aim is rather to explore interviewing in the context of global environmental negotiations: how it differs from other contexts, what challenges you can expect, and how to overcome them. This chapter should be read together with Chapter 2 on getting started with your fieldwork.

The advice given in the chapter applies not only to interviewing on-site at global environmental conferences, but also to a variety of settings around negotiations, as discussed in Chapter 7. Although the formal negotiation process has a central place in global environmental agreement-making, the global ordering takes place through multiple actors, sites, and processes. This expands the universe of relevant contexts and actors for interviewing.

In the first part of the chapter, I discuss the choice of interviews as a method and the purposes they can serve in research on global environmental negotiations. I also explain the specifics of interviewing *at* and *on* negotiation sites, and discuss what to do before,

[1] See Recommended Reading section. You can also search for literature on elite interviewing or expert interviewing. The differences between the terms lie in highlighting different qualities of respondents (whether they belong to a political elite or have an expert knowledge about some subject), but otherwise the approaches to interviewing are similar. The latter term is adopted in this chapter.

during, and after interviewing. In the second part, I recount my own experiences of interviewing for my PhD research on the IPCC in 2006–9. This account is complemented by two reflection boxes by Alice Vadrot on Oral History interviews and narrative interviews, as alternative approaches in the study of global environmental agreement-making.

9.2 Why Conduct Interviews?

Using interviews as a method of data collection is by no means compulsory in research on global environmental negotiations. Its relevance depends on whether interview data will help in answering research questions. If this is the case, it does not automatically mean conducting interviews *at* negotiation sites during UN meetings. There may be good reasons for arranging interviews at other sites or remotely, as discussed in Section 9.3.

That said, for many academics, interviews in general and interviews 'on-site' are important means of gaining understanding of global environmental affairs. Interviews, especially combined with participant observation and ethnography of the process (see Chapters 10 and 11), can give insights on the subtleties of international decision-making, negotiating positions and strategies, and the choices made by actors on-site and the motivations behind these. They can also help deconstruct an event or a series of events. Interviews, especially for a new researcher, can be used for exploratory purposes – to become acquainted with key topics, actors, and negotiation settings – and may accordingly be helpful in terms of developing an analytical framework for a project. In other words, interviews can be used for various research purposes, including orientation in a new field at the beginning of a research project (exploratory interview); information-gathering (systematizing an interview); and/or for analytical purposes, for example, testing a hypothesis or reconstructing social patterns and actions (theory-generating interview) (Bogner et al. 2009). Interviews often form part of a multi-method research strategy alongside, for instance, documentary research (Chapter 8), participant observations and ethnography (Chapters 10 and 11), legal doctrinal analysis, historical analysis, and/or statistical analysis. The approach adopted for interviewing will depend on the research question and the types of information or data that need to be collected through this method (see Reflection Box 9.1 on oral history interviews for illustration).

Reflection Box 9.1 Oral history interviews

By Alice B.M. Vadrot

Oral history is a method traditionally used in historical research based on interviews conducted between an interviewee who participated in or observed a historically significant event and a well-informed interviewer. In the context of agreement-making, oral history interviews could, for instance, be used to study past events – the sites, actors, and processes that have shaped order-making – or to collect the memories of those that have participated in global environmental conferences for decades. An oral history interview can be understood as both an archival document adding information to a historical record and as a narrative construction of an event based on the interviewee's selective memory, subjectivity, and identity (Shopes 2014).

I have used oral history interviews in the context of my ERC project MARIPOLDATA to complement ethnographic and bibliographic data collected to trace the emergence of the BBNJ process. MARIPOLDATA aims to study science–policy interrelations in marine biodiversity politics by studying how science shapes the BBNJ negotiations and to identify the science that gains influence during the process. To this end, I conducted oral history of science interviews with fifteen key scientists in marine biodiversity research active in the negotiations, whose experiences encapsulate a unique part of the evolution and shifts of both the scientific field and the site of agreement-making. Interviewees were selected based on various criteria, including scientific publications, disciplinary background, and participation in global environmental negotiations and assessments related to marine biodiversity. Hence, oral history interviews allow us to gain insights not easily found in printed and published sources and provide a clearer understanding of the subjective interpretation of facts and record events and trends in science and policy interactions (Weiner 1988; Doel 2003).

Oral history interviews require considerable preparation and preliminary research. For the MARIPOLDATA project, we prepared a dossier for each interviewee, including a detailed CV and a compilation of sources, including scientific publications, media, press articles, videos, and other information available on the interviewee and their work. We arranged three interview sessions, each lasting two hours on (1) their childhood, education, and scientific career, (2) their experiences and perspectives on the development of marine biodiversity research, and (3) their involvement in agreement-making, assessments, and science advice, with specific emphasis on the BBNJ process and the CBD. In some cases, we approached interviewees on-site (during BBNJ IGCs). However, we did not conduct the oral history interviews on-site, as the dynamic and sometimes chaotic context of negotiations is not ideal for this form of interview.

Oral history interviews are often conducted at the workplace or home of the interviewee. We conducted them via Zoom, which gave us some flexibility and reflected the context of the interviews, which were almost exclusively conducted during the COVID-19 pandemic. Oral history interviews are very personal and can be highly emotional, especially if interviewees talk about difficult moments in their lives or career or if the event itself had traumatizing elements. Because of these aspects, oral history interviews tend not to be analysed or compared: they are documents that stand alone.

It is helpful to look briefly at accounts of how interviews can support the study of agreement-making. In the three examples that follow, interviews are conducted for different analytical purposes, but in each case they are used to gain insight on a specific aspect of the research problem.

For Allan (2020), for instance, the central research question was why NGOs and social movements decide to get involved in the UNFCCC, and the challenges they face (and their solutions) in achieving recognition for the issues they espouse. In this project, interviews were used as part of a multi-method approach, along with social network analysis and participant observation. Interviews were useful for identifying the motivations and perceptions of NGO representatives as well as internal debates in their organizations and causal mechanisms, which could not be uncovered using the other two methods.

In the second example, Toussaint (2021) used interviews to complement his legal analysis of the relationship between climate litigation and UNFCCC negotiations on loss and damage. He first conducted legal doctrinal research and a literature review to describe how court cases relate to the UN negotiations. After that, he conducted interviews with key stakeholders engaged in policy discussions on loss and damage with the goal of assisting in the interpretation of the main narratives on linkages between climate litigation and UNFCCC policymaking.

For Hughes and Vadrot (2019), the main aim was 'to provide an account of the controversy over biocultural diversity and use it as a site for illuminating the social and political struggles that characterize the approval of intergovernmental texts' in the IPBES. The researchers adopted an iterative and collaborative approach to data collection and analysis. They started with a review of documents and several exploratory phone interviews to identify the main sites of political struggle and the issues at stake. This was followed by participant observation at an IPBES plenary meeting and further on-site interviews. Another round of virtual interviews was conducted after analysing the data from the meeting.

The following sections guide you through the various steps involved in research interviewing on negotiations, including preparation (before interviewing), the interview itself (during interviewing), and data management and analysis (after interviewing); a checklist is provided for each stage (see Tables 9.1, 9.2, and 9.3).

9.3 Before Interviewing

Various stages are involved in planning fieldwork on global environmental negotiations, including developing an analytical framework (Chapters 3 and 4), meeting research ethics requirements (Chapter 2), and ensuring access to international meetings (Chapter 2).

One of the first questions to confront a new researcher is *whom to interview*. Selecting respondents, or sampling, is important in the context of international negotiations, as interviewees are not of equal weight for research purposes. Various criteria for selection can be applied: for instance, the prospective interviewee's level of engagement with a particular topic, their decision-making power, their geographical representation, and the constituency they represent (civil society, private sector, Indigenous Peoples, etc.).

How does one create a list of potential interviewees? One way is to consult the *Earth Negotiations Bulletin* (*ENB*) for coverage of negotiations and side events, as it often contains specific names and affiliations. Another is to check participant lists, though these do not in themselves provide sufficient information and should be combined with other information sources. Observing the meetings either in person or via webcast can also be a helpful way to identify who makes interventions in the plenary and who chairs informal working groups. If you are on site, you could approach that individual to make the first personal contact by introducing yourself and exchanging business cards, and ask if it is possible to follow up with them later. This of course requires quite a bit of self-confidence, but it can be very effective. Side events (Chapter 7) draw a smaller group of people and the atmosphere is more relaxed. Consequently, they are very useful for networking and finding potential respondents, especially among various stakeholders such as academics and members of NGOs. Finally, social media can be helpful in identifying relevant people to talk to: Twitter, in particular, appears to be an active space for sharing day-to-day developments during UN climate meetings.

Once you have several interviewees lined up, you can use a 'snowball technique' and ask each participant to suggest other relevant respondents. At the same time, it is never good to rely on one technique alone: with the snowball method, people tend to suggest those with similar views or profiles. Use several sampling approaches and keep in mind the need for diversity of views.

Research ethics, including personal data protection and prior informed consent, should be considered before interviewing (Chapter 2). It should be noted that although there are common principles, the specific requirements set by your jurisdiction, institution, or funder may vary, for instance as to how consent to an interview should be obtained or how personal data should be processed. Consequently, you should always check relevant norms and guidelines before outlining your approach to research ethics. As a rule, before the interview all respondents should be familiarized with the research project, their rights (including the fact that participation is voluntary) and the relevant rules governing personal data processing. It is good practice – and may even be required – to prepare a written project description. Some funding agencies require the participant's written consent; if not, other ways to give active consent are possible – for instance, in verbal form.

Should a researcher attend a global environmental meeting for the purpose of interviewing? Can interviews be conducted elsewhere or arranged remotely via video platforms? There are no set answers to these questions.

A large global environmental meeting like the COP may be a good setting because you have the possibility to talk to a diverse crowd that converges for a limited period of time on one spot from quite literally all over the world. It may also be more cost- and emissions-effective to travel to one major meeting than to several sites. Furthermore, witnessing environmental meetings in person – whether to carry out interviews or to observe – gives an indefinable, yet invaluable, sense of the collective mood and dynamics of the meeting and the process in general. This benefits research in multiple ways, including in terms of how you conduct and analyse interviews (see Chapters 2 and 6). However, large UN summits are also hectic. Key negotiators tend to be very busy during these meetings and are often unable to allocate time for a research interview. It can be difficult to gain formal access to the meetings and expensive to travel to them, or simply too difficult (if not impossible) in the context of a pandemic (see Chapter 2).

What are the alternatives, then? One possibility is to consider other sites for interviewing. Smaller settings, such as meetings of UNFCCC-constituted bodies (for instance, the Adaptation Committee) have a more informal character, which can facilitate the process of approaching your research participants. That said, such meetings can also be more difficult to gain access to and be attended by a less representative group of people. Perhaps one question to ponder is whether there is another site where you can meet relevant respondents. For instance, I was able to talk to several IPCC authors at a major scientific conference in which I myself participated. Another possibility is to travel to respondents' workplaces, which may offer a more relaxed setting for an in-depth discussion and enable you to experience the research participant's working environment. In any case, each option calls for careful consideration in the context of the often-limited time, resources, and carbon budget of most research projects.

Virtual and phone interviews are also an option and can be combined with interviews conducted on site (see Hughes and Vadrot 2019). In general, political scientists tend to favour face-to-face over virtual interviews (Mosley 2013, 7), although there are advantages and disadvantages to both. As compared with face-to-face interviews, virtual interviews are often considered to lack the same degree of contextual information important for interpreting interview data, to make it more difficult to establish a trusting relationship within, and to potentially give rise to ethical risks around anonymity through the use of technologies (Mosley 2013, 7). Of course, there are also clear advantages as virtual interviews afford both interviewer and interviewee greater flexibility in terms of time and lack of need to travel, eliminate the challenge of access to international meetings, and are cost effective to organize.

Personally, I have not found virtual interviews to be less effective; however, many were arranged following face-to-face contact or a reference from a mutual contact. What I did experience was that the response rate when contacting respondents by email for a virtual interview without prior contact was lower. This was often the case for some countries – typically non-Western – where respondents may not have the same familiarity with the concept of research interviews or may not find it relevant to participate in them. Respondents from some countries may also experience practical difficulties in the form of unstable internet connections or lack of access to the same video platforms as the interviewer.

Taking these perspectives into account, a hybrid, iterative approach to interviewing may be the most effective. This may include some exploratory interviews in advance of the event, with interviewing on site focused on respondents that are less likely to be reachable afterwards, and on making first contact with those who would agree to being interviewed virtually later on.

Table 9.1 *Before interviews checklist*

Before interviews: Key questions and actions
Questions 1. Could interviews help me to gather information and gain knowledge of my research problem? 2. Who holds the knowledge and information I am looking to collect? 3. How does my analytical framework shape/inform my interviews? 4. What questions do I need to ask to gain knowledge and understanding of my research problem? 5. Do I need to conduct interviews in person?
Actions • Check research ethics requirements. • Prepare project information sheet and prior consent forms. • Arrange access to international meetings, if these are interview sites. • Check country visa requirements and allow time for visa application. • Identify respondents. • Make first contact and arrange interviews and/or identify where in the venue you might 'bump' into them.

9.4 During Interviewing

The next – and often the biggest – challenge for a new researcher is gaining access to respondents. There are several practical tips that can help.

After selecting potential respondents, it is good to make first contact by email, briefly introducing yourself and providing an overview of the research project. This can include a short list of topics or questions for discussion. When explaining the nature of a research project, it is best to use simple language and avoid academic jargon, such as naming the concepts or theoretical approaches used (Leech 2002, 666). It is also important to briefly list the ground rules for interviews relating to anonymity and personal data processing, in line with the relevant research ethics rules. A positive response is more likely if the topic is relevant or otherwise interesting to a respondent. It can be useful to use connections – supervisor, colleagues, other respondents – for introductory emails to potential interviewees.

If you are interested in speaking to a representative of a particular country or constituency, then plenary meetings are good venues at which to identify those actors. One practical tip here is to note the location of a delegation in the room, as this saves time when you try to catch them at the end of the meeting. Finally, it is worth highlighting that the negotiation setting, with its long (sometimes overnight) sessions, numerous side events, and coffee and lunch breaks, creates a unique community. Being part of that community not only helps one to gain insight into the process, but also to gain access to negotiators and other participants. It might sound odd, but simply wandering around – and preferably in the main corridor – can be a surprisingly productive strategy with a view to bumping into someone who might be useful for your research.

Specific time arrangements made by email do not always work as planned at UN summits. This is due to the intensive and somewhat unpredictable day-to-day dynamics in play. Being online on various messaging apps is important as it makes you reachable at any time, and one should keep in mind that different apps are popular in different parts of the world.

It goes without saying that when you approach someone for an interview you should respect their time. Being politely persistent is important (Aberbach and Rockman 2002, 673), but, as mentioned earlier, it is also possible to use an opportunity to make the first contact and arrange an interview later. Another point to consider is that in some countries government employees are required to obtain official permission to give interviews, including for research purposes. They may be more willing to talk if a research interview appears to be less formal, more like a conversation, without the use of a voice recorder and the need to sign forms. Whether such conversations can be used as interview data or only as contextual information depends on the research ethics requirements applicable to your project.

Exchanging business cards at the start of the interviewing process helps establish an atmosphere of mutual trust, shows the professionalism of the researcher, and helps smooth the flow of the conversation. This ritual is especially important in some Asian cultural contexts.

There are lengthy discussions in the literature on whether to use a voice recorder or to take notes in expert interviewing (Burnham et al. 2008, 239). In addition to other considerations, the choice is dependent on your research design and epistemological approach. Furthermore, although note-taking facilitates a more informal atmosphere, it can be challenging for a new researcher to take notes and manage the interview at the same time. In any case, if you take notes it is useful to find a quiet corner afterwards and to check them immediately after the interview to ensure the accuracy of the data.

Expert interviews typically follow a semi-structured format, where some questions are defined and others remain open ended. Open-ended questions allow respondents to 'articulate their views, explaining why they think what they think' (Aberbach and Rockman 2002, 674). It is indeed important to let a respondent talk as it may give a broader view and lead to disclosure of information beyond the scope of the questions posed as well as opening up perspectives the researcher had not considered (Dexter 1970, 19). In view of this, it is good to adopt a trusting and informal style to make the interview resemble a conversation: 'excellent interviewers are excellent conversationalists' (Berry 2002, 679). This is particularly important for oral history interviews, as discussed in Reflection Box 9.1. Some textbooks even advise having a list of topics to be covered instead of a predefined questionnaire (Burnham et al. 2008, 213).

Expert interviewing can be challenging as it requires both good communication skills in general and sufficient preparation and knowledge of the field to establish rapport with a respondent and gain his/her trust (Korkea-Aho and Leino 2019, 33). Sometimes interviews in the context of global negotiations have to be conducted with 'people who exercise disproportionally high influence on the outcome of events or policies in your research area' (Pierce 2008, 119). Conducting a semi-structured interview also requires confident moderating, as respondents sometimes draw the conversation away from the topic. This can pose a challenge for a new researcher, especially when confronted by a renowned scientist or a high-level diplomat (see also Stephens 2007).

A good command of English is necessary and usually sufficient for interviewing on negotiations, and it is helpful to be accustomed to various accents. It is also good to remember that for most respondents in this context English is a second or third language. It can also be beneficial to speak other UN languages.

Last but not least, interviewing in the UN negotiations' context involves interacting with people from different countries and cultures. Basic cultural literacy and good intercultural communication skills are essential. However, it is not the same as going to another country and interviewing people on the ground: UN summits draw people who are themselves used to communicating in global circles.

If you attend a UN meeting to conduct an interview, then it is obviously good to understand the meeting sites well. Still, life is full of surprises. At the very start of my PhD, I once missed an interview arranged on the first floor because I had been waiting on the ground floor, completely forgetting that in English the 'first floor' means the second floor, unlike in Russian (which is my mother tongue).

At UN meetings, one also has to be flexible as to time and place. Many interviews are conducted at the back of negotiation rooms or in cafes, during a coffee break or even over lunch. It is interesting that political science methodology textbooks strongly advise against lunch interviews for a variety of reasons (Burnham et al. 2008, 237). However, at negotiation sites, a lunch break is often the only available opportunity to get an interview done. This speaks to the need for flexibility and adaptiveness, reflecting a central principle of real-world research: 'sometimes one does something that is not the ideal because the less than ideal approach is better than the alternative' (Aberbach and Rockman 2002, 674).

How long should the interview be? Political science textbooks suggest that an interview typically lasts for 45–60 minutes or more, depending on the respondent's availability (Burnham et al. 2008). However, in a busy UN meeting setting, the respondent may have little time to spare and a realistic expectation is about 30 minutes or so.[2] This requires us to prioritize interview questions, for instance, according to the role the respondent plays in the process. Prioritizing questions is an acquired skill which you develop as you acquire interviewing experience and a better understanding of the research object and context. UN summits also offer opportunities for very short interactions on specific issues. These may be useful to clarify a specific issue, for instance for triangulation purposes, or gain insights into a negotiation item. In other words, such 'blitz interviews' do have research value, but they also raise questions as to how to treat these interactions and the resulting data. The answer possibly depends on whether ethical requirements are fulfilled or not. Such interviews may also be viewed as providing contextual knowledge rather than interview data.

Expert interviewing is demanding in terms of both time and energy so one should be realistic as to how many interviews are possible in a day.[3] The literature suggests no more than two interviews a day (Burnham et al. 2008, 237). However, in my experience, this is not something you have control over if interviewing at a UN meeting. It may well be that a day of unproductive wandering in the corridor is followed by a day filled with several interviews in a row.

So much for the process of interviewing and interviewees. What about the interviewer? How does his/her persona influence the conversation and responses? Depending on one's epistemological orientation, this effect can be viewed as the 'interviewer effect', which may influence the answers given and needs to be recognized for the analysis and interpretation of data (Mosley 2013, 12). Or it can be viewed in the interpretivist tradition as 'positionality', which is unavoidable, should be accepted, and leads to interview data being 'somewhat subjective and contextual' (Mosley 2013, 12).

Regardless of one's epistemological starting point, it is important to recognize and reflect on similarities and differences between interviewer and interviewees, and how

[2] This speaks in favour of offsite or remote interviews: see Section 9.3.

[3] Time demands also include time spent arranging interviews and transcribing and analysing data. Burnham, for instance, estimates that at least twelve hours of a researcher's time is needed per interview (Burnham et al. 2008, 234), but the figure may even be higher for interviewing in the context of global environmental negotiations due to travel and related logistics.

these influence the process of interviewing and the responses received. The interviewer's individual characteristics may impact their prospects of securing access to interviewees. For instance, it may be easier for you to speak to the members of your national delegation than those of other delegations, or more difficult, or the issue of nationality may have no effect at all. Gender dynamics is also something to bear in mind: it may be easier for a young female PhD student to obtain agreement from a male respondent to be interviewed but, in the interview process, some respondents may not take that young female interviewer seriously. It goes without saying that safety is an important consideration here and interviews should be organized only in public places (see Chapter 2). Other factors, such as age, experience, and disciplinary background, can also play a role. At the same time, if you compare UN meetings to other contexts, there are likely to be important similarities between researcher and respondent, for instance concerning the level of education and expectations from a research process. Another point to remember is that even if there are differences between the interviewer and interviewees, these are not necessarily impediments to the interview process. It has been suggested in the literature – and confirmed by my experience – that outsider status can in fact facilitate access to respondents and the process of interviewing itself (Mosley 2013, 14).

How many interviews are sufficient is a difficult question to answer. The literature suggests 20–30 interviews for a project where expert interviewing is a key method (Burnham et al. 2008, 234), but ultimately it depends on the research question and research design. Sometimes it is possible to interview the whole 'population' of respondents if the total number is small (Burnham et al. 2008, 233). I would say that for expert interviewing the quality of the interviews is more important than their quantity. You may find at some point that additional interviews do not generate new insights and responses become repetitive, suggesting that you have reached 'saturation point' (Burnham et al. 2008, 234).

Table 9.2 *During interviews checklist*

During interviews: Actions
• Make first contact and arrange interviews and/or identify where in the venue you might 'bump' into them.
• Make sure that the interview location is public and that you feel secure.
• Introduce yourself and exchange business cards.
• Provide overview of the project and how you will use the data.
• Gain interview respondent's consent.
• If recording, request permission (remember to press record and check it's working!).
• Prioritize questions depending on time available.
• Conduct interview.
• At the end of the interview, ask respondent if there's anyone else you should speak to?
• Safely and securely store interview data.

9.5 After Interviewing

Data management and analysis for research on global environmental negotiations are perhaps not very different from other settings. Still, I would like to highlight several issues, one of which concerns the need to revisit interview notes or recordings immediately after the interview, in a quiet corner at a meeting site or in the evening. This is especially critical if interviews are conducted during UN summits, as important details and context can fade quickly with time. This exercise can help revise your approach to interviewing for the next day, for instance in terms of questions and respondents. You may also have to work on your fieldnotes (see Chapters 2 and 10), and it is advisable to maintain a table with general information about interviews, including, for instance, date, duration, place, and the respondent's details.

Another important consideration is the management of interview data. Depending on the applicable rules, you might have to anonymize data and store it separately from identifiers on a password protected laptop or server. There may also be specific requirements concerning the retention and destruction of data.

In analysing data, their validity and reliability are obviously important matters to consider, and it is good to remember that 'it is not the obligation of a subject to be objective and tell us the truth' (Berry 2002, 680). George and Bennett suggest asking four questions to critically evaluate interview data: Who is speaking? Who are they speaking to? For what purpose are they speaking? Under what circumstances? (George and Bennett 2005, 99). If you translate these questions into negotiation settings, you would reflect on such issues as the interviewee's background, the official position of the country or negotiating group of which they are part, and the agendas of the institutions or constituencies they represent.

The risk of finding a particularly knowledgeable or assertive interviewee, or one with similar political views to oneself, more persuasive than others is a related issue (Berry 2002, 680). It can be difficult to maintain objectivity in such situations, especially with increased immersion at the site and/or a personal relationship with interview respondents. It is important to reflect on how this shapes your ability to analyse the data alongside any normative assumptions. The principle of triangulation is obviously useful, whereby new and sensitive interview data are crosschecked across several interviews and other types of data, such as participant observations and documents.

Some researchers use specialized software such as Atlas.ti or MAXQDA for data analysis. However, I am not sure this would be my general recommendation. I think the approach depends on the number of interviews, the research goals, how you treat text data, and the data management requirements. One important consideration is that learning to use a specialized software package can take a lot of effort and time. I have seen good research outputs where the number of interviews was small and the qualitative analysis was conducted manually.

Finally, sharing benefits from research with research participants is an important dimension of research ethics. Many participants in negotiations do appreciate it if a researcher who has interviewed them follows up with publication (drafts) or other research updates.

Table 9.3 *After interviews checklist*

After interviews: Key questions and actions
Questions 1. After the interview, reflect on the interview and information gathered: are your approach and your questions helping you to address your research problem? 2. Have you got all the information you require or do you need to identify new respondents and conduct further interviews? Actions • Revisit, reflect, and elaborate interview notes. • Update information on interviews and respondents. • Safely and securely store interview and analysis data according to your ethics and data management plan. • Evaluate the limitations of interview data: the perspectives gathered, the authority of the respondent, your relationship and positionality. • Code and analyse data. • Email respondents to share research findings and publications with interviewees.

9.6 Interview-Based Research on the IPCC

This section describes my interviewing experiences as part of my PhD fieldwork in 2006–9. Although a considerable period of time has passed and I have conducted many research interviews at UN meetings and in other settings since then, recounting those early experiences may be especially beneficial for those at the start of their research journey.

I became interested in the global governance of climate change thanks to my PhD supervisor, Dr Joanna Depledge. As I was reading about it, I was particularly intrigued by the role of science and this inevitably led me to the IPCC, which is a UN institution that provides regular assessments of scientific literature on climate change. Although the panel is governed by member states, its assessments are prepared by selected scientists and experts. To date, the IPCC has published six assessment reports, the latest of which was finalized in 2021–3.

As I started reading about the IPCC, I came across an academic reflection describing the panel in terms of post-normal science, which aroused my curiosity. The post-normal science perspective suggests that, in situations characterized by high decision stakes and a high level of uncertainty, science–policy interfaces should be based on extended participation, a plurality of views, incorporation of uncertainties, interdisciplinarity, reflexivity, and mutual learning (Funtowicz and Ravetz 1996). However, at the time there was no literature describing and explaining how the ideas of post-normal science translate into international science–policy institutions (or any type of institution, in fact). In my PhD project I therefore focused on exploring the IPCC, specifically its fourth assessment process (2002–7), through the lens of post-normal science.[4]

To examine the extent to which and how the panel follows a post-normal science approach in its scientific assessments, I identified five relevant areas of the assessment process: participation, the literature basis for the assessment, treatment of uncertainties, interdisciplinarity, and institutional learning. Background research revealed that there was

[4] See Yamineva (2017).

only limited documentation and literature[5] available to analyse these elements of the panel's work. This and the project's focus on the panel's internal institutional practices and processes led me to the conclusion that interviews and participant observations would be the best means of obtaining research data.

After clarifying the analytical framework, I developed several interview questions broadly corresponding to the above-mentioned five areas of the assessment process – for instance: 'how do you assess the current geographical representation of experts on the panel?' and 'in your opinion, is there sufficient dialogue among different disciplines during the assessment process?' The questions provided a framework for each interview. However, I sometimes changed the exact questions or their emphases, depending on an interviewee's role in the IPCC. Some questions also evolved over time as my research progressed.

In my experience, research design is an iterative process whereby the analytical framework guides and shapes data collection (interviews in this case), but insights from data can also influence the development of the theoretical and conceptual approach (see Chapter 4). We can also see this reflected in Alice's box on the concept of narratives and the approach to interviews that she adopted to study and analyse these (see Reflection Box 9.2).

The post-normal science lens, with its focus on extended participation and plurality of views, shaped my approach to selecting interview participants: it was important to secure diverse representation of institutional roles, geographical areas, and scientific disciplines. The first list of people to talk to was compiled based on literature review, participant lists, and the contacts of Dr Depledge, who was familiar with UNFCCC negotiations. Later, as I gained more confidence, I frequently relied on the 'snowball technique' and used my own observations at the meetings to identify potential interviewees.

I conducted my interviews during UN meetings, at other sites or virtually. The other sites included, for instance, two technical support units, one in the United Kingdom and the other in the Netherlands, as well as a major scientific conference in Beijing that I attended as a participant. I would say that visiting technical support units resulted in considerably longer interviews in a more relaxed atmosphere compared to conversations at UN meetings. At the same time, I was able to visit only two sites in Europe, relatively close to my university base. Visiting interviewees' workplaces can be a useful strategy for fieldwork, but there are of course implications in terms of financial costs, travelling, emissions, and interviewees' geographical diversity.

Most of my interviews were therefore conducted at UN meetings: three IPCC sessions and one UNFCCC Subsidiary Bodies' meeting. Prior to the actual interviewing, I attended an UNFCCC Subsidiary Bodies' meeting in 2006 in Bonn, Germany, to familiarize myself with the UN meeting environment. In retrospect, I am glad I started with a smaller meeting as climate COPs are much bigger and could perhaps be overwhelming as a first experience of a UN meeting. I did most of my interviews while attending the meetings as an academic researcher. However, several interviews towards the end of the fieldwork were conducted when attending the meetings as a writer for *ENB*. Working for *ENB* undoubtedly helped me to gain access to both negotiation sessions and interviewees. At the same time, being part

[5] This has changed in the last decade and there is now diverse social science scholarship on the IPCC.

of the process is not always an advantage for a researcher as it brings its own challenges, such as maintaining a certain distance for the purposes of research. When you don't simply observe but actively participate in the daily life of an institution, you inevitably become entangled with its institutional identity and with the people involved, and this may impact upon your criticality towards the research object.

The fact that I then held a Russian passport presented a considerable challenge when arranging fieldwork as it was necessary to arrange a visa for every meeting. This added substantial paperwork and expense to fieldwork and required logistical planning as it often took two to three months to arrange a visa for a single meeting. Passport privileges and their impact on non-Western scholars are rarely, if ever, acknowledged in research methodology textbooks.[6] Arranging visas takes time and involves paperwork and additional expenses, giving rise to uncertainty that should be factored into your interview planning.

After selecting potential respondents, I made the first contact by email or, if at a UN meeting, simply by approaching them directly. In total, I conducted forty-five interviews. The saturation point mentioned earlier clearly manifested itself as, after a number of interviews, additional conversations did not add new insights to the data. It also became clear that some respondents were only superficially involved with the IPCC and did not have specific reflections or experiences to share that would be useful for my research project.

I personally did not find it challenging to use a voice recorder for interviewing, as participants usually did not mind this.[7] Most interviews were conducted in English although several were done in Russian. Using Russian was beneficial as it opened access to perspectives which would otherwise remain outside the focus of my attention: several Russian-speaking respondents were less fluent in English and, in any case, speaking their native language helped to create a more trusting atmosphere.

Concerning the process of interviewing, I would especially like to reflect on interviewing different groups of respondents, comprising scientists, governmental representatives, and international bureaucrats. Scientists were in general easier to talk to and could devote more time to interviews. One of the reasons for this was that the IPCC had been the subject of public criticism, which, many scientists felt, was unfair and based on a poor understanding of IPCC procedures. They were therefore keen to explain the assessment process to a researcher. Most scientists I interviewed had a background in natural sciences but, despite that, many expressed a great interest in and support for social science approaches. The main observation I drew from interviewing scientists was that they provided longer answers than other respondents, often using highly technical language, but at the same time they also had fewer insights and reflections to offer on institutional and decision-making practices.

Governmental delegates at UN meetings are experienced professionals and often high-level officials at their respective national ministries or agencies. It was generally more challenging to obtain their agreement to be interviewed than it was to obtain such agreement in respect to other categories of interviewees. Those participating in IPCC meetings mostly had a scientific background and some scientific advisory role so interviewing them

[6] On this topic, see https://blogs.lse.ac.uk/highereducation/2020/02/20/the-hidden-costs-of-being-a-scholar-from-the-global-south/.

[7] Post-PhD, however, I switched to note-taking as an easier and more informal approach.

was similar to interviewing scientists, although they were more attuned to the institutional side of the IPCC. Negotiators in the UNFCCC tended to be more careful with their words. It was rarely productive to interview heads of delegations as they were mostly less open and less available. Here, there are interesting parallels to the point raised by George and Bennett that lower-level officials are often better interview sources given their day-to-day involvement with political processes (George and Bennett 2005, 103). I would say that interviewing mid-level members of negotiating teams was indeed more useful.

I found senior officials at international organizations quite approachable and willing to talk, but mostly outside of UN meetings due to availability. At the same time, one challenge I encountered with high-level officials who give numerous interviews to the media is that their responses tended to be carefully phrased and composed of ready-made lines (see also Burnham et al. 2008, 237). One lesson from this experience is that you have to adjust your expectations for interview responses and reflect on your goals before and after. This may lead you to adapt your approach, for example by asking more specific or unexpected questions.

Reflecting on the interviewer effect, I would say that in my case there were factors both facilitating and hindering the process. For instance, affiliation with the University of Cambridge and the *ENB* was certainly helpful in accessing negotiation sites and obtaining respondents' agreement to be interviewed. At the same time, differences in age, gender, status, and experience carried challenges and even risks in some situations but were probably beneficial in others. One of the challenges that may arise is when a respondent does not consider an interviewer to be of equal status to them. This can hinder access or result in situations resembling a student supervised by a senior academic (see also Stephens 2007, 207–8). A certain degree of confidence is required to present oneself as a researcher and interviewer.

All my interviews were carried out under conditions of anonymity. I developed a coding system for respondents which only contained information on their role in the IPCC and developed or developing country origins. I recorded nearly all the interviews and then transcribed them manually. The transcription process was both arduous (and long!) and useful (I was able to identify major topics during that process). The analysis was conducted using Atlas.ti software available through the university. In my case, I felt that using this software was largely a waste of time and I would have probably obtained the same results without using it for data analysis, although, as Alice reflects in her box, it can be useful for particular purposes, such as for identifying shared narratives (see Reflection Box 9.2).

Reflection Box 9.2 How concepts can guide interviewing: Narrative analysis

By Alice B. M. Vadrot

The sites, processes, and actors of agreement-making can also be studied with a focus on narratives and narrative interviews. Through narratives, actors give meaning to the (negotiation) context in which they act, but at the same time, '"the agent" itself is narratively constituted' (Suganami 1999, 379). Narratives underlie habitual actions (recognizable by all participants) within the negotiation room and are open to change, contestation, and strategic action. Narrative interviews can be used to examine these processes and identify regularities in the stories of different actors on specific aspects of the negotiations, including decision-making and text, the purpose of a negotiation item, and emerging issues, concepts, and terminology. This interview method allows people to tell their stories and enables the researcher to identify regularities and patterns across actor groups and cohorts and to analyze how these different stories create meaning and collective identity.

For my PhD and book, *The Politics of Knowledge and Global Biodiversity* (Vadrot 2014), I conducted sixty-one narrative interviews with state and non-state actors to study the emergence of IPBES. I conducted interviews at six different biodiversity-related agreement-making sites within four years (2008 to 2012). In 2012, and shortly before the formal negotiations ended, I reached saturation. I heard the same types of stories repeatedly, which meant that I could start to describe, delineate, and unpack the different narratives. I transcribed interviews and entered these and other text-based sources into MAXQDA – a computer-based software for qualitative analysis – and inductively coded the material.

My data identified six narratives in the making of IPBES. The analysis of the narratives helped me to understand why some actors' expectations and perceptions changed over time. I came to the conclusion that in order to increase the chances of their interests being heard by others in the room, actors aligned their statements to the selectively structured discursive and institutional context. Actors using dominant narratives as part of their negotiation strategies were more likely to succeed even in cases when their interests were not in line with the majority and overall direction of the negotiation process.

9.7 Conclusion

Interviewing is an exciting method for doing research on global environmental negotiations. It can be used for exploratory, information-gathering, or theory-building purposes. It can help explain negotiating positions and strategies, uncover an actor's motivations, experiences and interpretations, unveil decision-making processes, and deconstruct the dynamics of events.

It is often assumed that being present during negotiations is a prerequisite for conducting research interviews. Attending global environmental meetings is indeed beneficial for research in many ways. However, gaining access may be a problem for new researchers. It is possible to arrange interviews offsite and there are even advantages to this approach in terms of, for instance, respondents' availability. Furthermore, in line with the agreement-making framework discussed in the introduction, you can adopt a broader perspective on relevant sites and actors: this allows one to step outside the boundaries of a specific institution or process and consider other sites as relevant for interviewing.

Interviewing at global meetings is also a horizon-expanding experience as you get to converse with a diverse, truly global crowd of people that you would probably not come across in your everyday academic life. For a new researcher, interviewing in this setting can also be intimidating. Remember that research fieldwork is a learning-by-doing process. Both successes and mistakes are unavoidable parts of it, and your skills as a researcher and interviewer will improve over time. I hope the advice given in this chapter is helpful in identifying potential challenges and practical ways to overcome them.

Further Reading

1. Burnham, P., Gilland Lutz, K., Grant, W. and Layton-Henry, Z. (2008). Elite Interviewing. In P. Burnham, K. Gilland Lutz, W. Grant, and Z. Layton-Henry (eds.), *Research Methods in Politics*. 1st ed. Basingstoke: Red Globe Press, pp. 231–46.

The chapter is an accessible and relatively short introduction to the technique and various steps of elite interviewing for political science research.

2. Korkea-Aho, E. and Leino, P. (2019). Interviewing Lawyers: A Critical Self-Reflection on Expert Interviews as a Method of EU Legal Research. *European Journal of Legal Studies* 12, 17–47.

This paper discusses the personal experiences of the authors – who are legal researchers – in respect of expert interviews.

3. Mosley, L., ed. (2013). *Interview Research in Political Science*. Ithaca, NY: Cornell University Press.

The book aims to provide a comprehensive guide to graduate students and faculty on interview-based research in political science.

References

Aberbach, J. D. and Rockman, B. A. (2002). Conducting and Coding Elite Interviews. *PS: Political Science and Politics* 35(4), 673–6.

Allan, J. I. (2020). *The New Climate Activism: NGO Authority and Participation in Climate Change Governance*. Toronto: Toronto University Press.

Berry, J. M. (2002). Validity and Reliability Issues In Elite Interviewing. *PS: Political Science & Politics* 35(4),679–82.

Bogner, A., Littig, B. and Menz, W., eds. (2009). *Interviewing Experts*. London: Palgrave Macmillan.

Burnham, P., Gilland, K. Grant, W. and Layton-Henry, Z. (2008). *Research Methods in Politics*. 1st ed. Basingstoke: Red Globe Press.

Dexter, L. A. (1970). *Elite and Specialized Interviewing*. Evanston, IL: Northwestern University Press.

Doel, R. E. (2003). Oral History of American Science: A Forty-Year Review. *History of Science* 41(4),349–78.

Funtowicz, S. and Ravetz, J. (1996). Global Risk, Uncertainty, and Ignorance. In J. Kasperson and R. Kasperson, eds., *Global Environmental Risk*. Tokyo: United Nations University Press, pp. 173–94.

George, A. L. and Bennett, A. (2005). *Case Studies and Theory Development in the Social Sciences*. Cambridge, MA: MIT Press.

Goldstein, K. (2002). Getting in the Door: Sampling and Completing Elite Interviews. *PS: Political Science and Politics* 35(4),669–72.

Hughes, H. and Vadrot, A. (2019). Weighting the World: IPBES and the Struggle over Biocultural Diversity. *Global Environmental Politics* 19(2),14–37.

Korkea-Aho, E. and Leino, P. (2019). Interviewing Lawyers: A Critical Self-Reflection on Expert Interviews as a Method of EU Legal Research. *European Journal of Legal Studies* 12,17–47.

Leech, B. L. (2002). Asking Questions: Techniques for Semistructured Interviews. *Political Science and Politics* 35(4),665–8.

Pierce, R. (2008). *Research Methods in Politics: A Practical Guide*. Thousand Oaks, CA: Sage Publications.

Shopes, L. (2014). 'Insights and Oversights': Reflections on the Documentary Tradition and the Theoretical Turn in Oral History. *The Oral History Review* 41(2),257–68.

Stephens, N. (2007). Collecting Data from Elites and Ultra Elites: Telephone and Face-to-Face Interviews with Macroeconomists. *Qualitative Research* 7(2),203–6.

Suganami, H. (1999). Agents, Structures, Narratives. *European Journal of International Relations* 5(3),365–86.

Toussaint, P. (2021). Loss and Damage and Climate Litigation: The Case for Greater Interlinkage. *Review of European, Comparative & International Environmental Law* 30(1),16–33.

Vadrot, A. B. M. (2014). *The Politics of Knowledge and Global Biodiversity*. London & New York: Routledge.

Weiner, C. (1988). Oral History of Science: A Mushrooming Cloud? *The Journal of American History* 75(2), 548–59.

Yamineva, Y. (2017). Lessons from the Intergovernmental Panel on Climate Change on Inclusiveness across Geographies and Stakeholders. *Environmental Science & Policy* 77,244–51.

10

Ethnography

From Method to Methodology at Plural Sites of Agreement-Making

KIMBERLY R. MARION SUISEEYA AND LAURA ZANOTTI

10.1 Introduction

Global environmental agreement-making sites pulse with energy. Upon arrival, you will become quickly overwhelmed by the space, its size, and the thousands of people creating this ephemeral community. Take note of these seemingly mundane or quotidian moments as they can help you understand what it means to be part of global agreement-making: standing in long security lines, reading the shaming Post-it note on the paper towel dispenser in the bathroom (see Figure 10.1), deciphering the meanings behind the rainbow array of badges and lanyards hanging around peoples' necks, feeling what it's like *not* to have a badge, and taking a second look at the crowd before joining them to crane your neck and see Al Gore walking by. These moments can help you understand both context and processual aspects of producing global environmental governance and how different forms of power imbue experiences of it. The security lines invite questions about accessibility, authority, and gatekeeping. The Post-it note calls into question the moral compass of fellow participants: shouldn't we all be environmentalists if we are at an international environmental treaty negotiation? Badge politics reveal the ordering of access granted to different individuals and groups that can make them more or less present in different spaces. The reaction to Al Gore is reflective of the role of celebrity politicians and actors at such sites, where Julia Roberts is the voice of Mother Earth and Harrison Ford is the Ocean.[1]

By experiencing what participants say at an event while also attending to the moments, relationships, values, discourses, and structures in place, ethnographers can reveal how sites of environmental agreement-making inform how global environmental governance

We would like to recognize the Indigenous Peoples upon whose land our universities are built, as well as the histories of dispossession that have allowed for the growth of these institutions. These include the peoples of the Council of Three Fires – the Ojibwe, Potawatomi, and Odawa, Menominee, Miami, Ho-Chunk, Peoria, Kaskaskia, Peankashaw, Wea, Mascoutin, Sauk, Mesquaki, Kickapoo, and Chickasaw nations, as well as Northwestern University's historical relationship with the Cheyenne and Arapaho. We acknowledge Purdue University is located on the traditional homelands of the Woodland People. We honor and appreciate these Indigenous caretakers which include the Bodéwadmik (Potawatomi), Lenape (Delaware), Myaamia (Miami), and Shawnee People. We would also like to thank Hannah Hughes, Alice Vadrot, and the authors in this volume for their valuable feedback in developing this chapter. Research assistance provided by Alexandra Anderson. Funding for our research has been provided by: Purdue University Center for the Environment, Climate Change Research Center, College of Liberal Arts, Department of Political Science; Northwestern University Center for Native American and Indigenous Research, Department of Political Science Farrell Undergraduate Research Fellowships, and the Undergraduate Research Assistance Program. This paper reflects the efforts of the larger team working on site in Paris, Honolulu, and Belém, which includes researchers Scott Benzing, Emily Colón, Michelle David, Sarah Huang, Kate Haapala, Moriah Lavey, Savannah Schulze, Bailey Smith-Hellman, Fernando Tormos, Suraya Williams, and Elizabeth Wulbrecht.

[1] See www.conservation.org/nature-is-speaking.

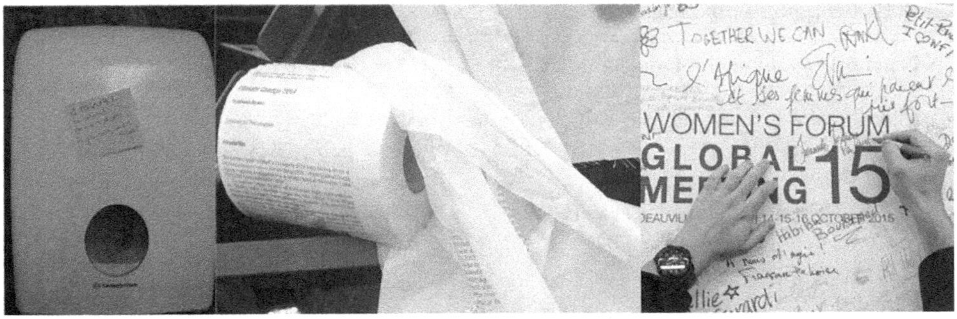

Figure 10.1 Micropolitics at sites of global environmental agreement-making.

is produced. An emphasis on the range of participant experiences and associated event artifacts – not only state actors and final agreement texts, but also brochures, swag such as pins, posters and bags, and more – often provides alternative and sometimes disruptive notions of agreement-making (see Table 10.1 for more examples). In doing so, ethnography captures phenomena that may be less visible through other methods more common in international relations (IR) scholarship, including content and discourse analysis, process tracing, institutional analysis, and agent-based modeling (MacKay and Levin 2015; Schatz 2009; Wedeen 2010). Specifically, ethnography draws attention to *power-in-place*, where *power* is something that emerges from multiple sources and *place* represents multiscalar notions of diverse physical and digital worlds that constitute the spaces in which we relate to others (Marion Suiseeya and Zanotti 2019; Zanotti and Marion Suiseeya 2020). It is the ethnographer's attention to lived experience that reveals insights into *power-in-place* at sites of environmental agreement-making that can help us get to questions of *how* and *why* governance is produced (see Barnett and Duvall 2005; Griffin 2012).

While this chapter cannot substitute for the extensive and rich literature on ethnography as a methodology in disciplines such as anthropology, sociology, and political science, among others, it does suggest multiple potential ways for engaging ethnographically at agreement-making sites.[2] We focus on ethnography, not solely ethnographic methods. The distinction here is significant: **ethnographic methods** are research techniques that focus primarily on the data *collection* phases of research. In contrast, **ethnography** extends across the research life cycle, entailing epistemological and ontological commitments that pulse throughout the entire research design from conceptualization to output. Ethnography as a methodology guides design, data collection, analysis, management, interpretation, *and* writing. We hope this chapter benefits researchers reaching "outside" of their disciplines to contemplate ethnography as a methodology for examining global environmental politics. We begin by exploring ethnography, especially at sites of global environmental governance, and then move toward more practical concerns. By elaborating the what, why, and how of ethnography, this chapter aims to help cultivate a foundation for researchers to

[2] A vast body of literature contemplates ethnography as method, methodology, and sensibility. This work spans multiple disciplines – anthropology, sociology, human geography, political science – each of which has its own perspectives and debates on the role of ethnography for understanding diverse social and political phenomena. We won't recount these here but have included references in. the Further Reading section.

Table 10.1 *Examples of ethnographies of global environmental agreement-making*

UN Framework Convention on Climate Change	UN Sustainable Development Goals
◦ Calliari, Serdeczny, and Vanhala 2020	◦ Ali et al. 2021
◦ Eastwood 2021, 2018	◦ Chakrabarti, Tiwaria, and Banerji 2021
◦ Marion Suiseeya and Zanotti 2019	**International Treaty on Plant Genetic Resources for Food and Agriculture**
◦ Marion Suiseeya, Zanotti, and Haapala 2021	◦ Jankowski et al. 2020
◦ Thew, Middlemiss and Paavola 2020	**World Conversation Congress**
Convention on Biological Diversity	◦ Adeyeye, Hagerman, and Pelai 2019
◦ Campbell et al. 2014 (special issue that includes multiple articles)	◦ Brosius and Campbell 2010
◦ Corson et al. 2014	◦ Corson et al. 2020
◦ Gruby and Campbell 2013	◦ Fletcher 2014
◦ Hagerman et al. 2012	◦ Gray 2010
◦ Jankowski et al. 2020	◦ MacDonald 2010
◦ Lövbrand, Hjerpe, and Linnér 2017	◦ Monfreda 2010
◦ Witter et al. 2015	◦ Peña 2010
Rio Summit	**Intergovernmental Panel on Climate Change**
◦ Beyers and Heinrichs 2020	◦ de Pryck 2020
◦ Corson et al. 2015	**Intergovernmental Science-Policy Platform on Biodiversity and Ecosystem Services**
◦ Little 1995	◦ Vadrot et al. 2020b
Biodiversity Beyond National Jurisdiction	**Basel Convention**
◦ Vadrot, Langlet, and Tessnow-von Wysocki 2021	◦ Kirby and Lora-Wainwright 2015
◦ Vadrot 2020a	**Multiple Sites**
UNESCO World Heritage Convention	◦ Brosius 2006
◦ Brumann 2021	◦ Milne et al. 2019
◦ Larsen and Buckley 2018	◦ Zanotti and Marion Suiseeya 2020
UN Forum on Forests	
◦ Eastwood 2013	

become more literate in and comfortable with responsibly engaging ethnography and its possibilities. We include resources at the end of this chapter to help you develop and realize an ethical research practice.

10.2 What Is Ethnography?

There is no simple answer to the question "what is ethnography?" Ethnography can be a researcher's only methodology or can be part of a broader suite of approaches; some researchers may use ethnographic methods for data collection but rely on other analytical techniques. Kim's first article from a collaborative event ethnography at the 2010

Convention on Biological Diversity (COP10), for example, used discourse and content analysis, which provoked an essential critique that this work was not ethnography.[3] In her analysis, Kim focused on identifying broad discursive trends by analyzing data collected through ethnographic methods (Marion Suiseeya 2014). While this work generated insights into *what* struggles for justice at COP10 looked like, in presenting the data without its broader context, the work sacrificed the more profound exploration into the immersive context of COP10 that could generate insights into *how* the various actors, sites, processes, and order-making produce the landscapes of possibilities for justice in global environmental governance.

Amongst the diversity and complexity that characterizes ethnography, however, much ethnographic work retains several core commitments: attentiveness to the politics of knowledge production, taking serious members' meanings, and attention to thick description or "accounts of behavior that provide rich context" (Boellstorff et al. 2012, 16). As Boellstorff et al. elaborate:

> For ethnographers, the outsider (etic) analyses of researchers are valid and informative – we do not expect that those we study will interpret their own lives exactly as we might in a scholarly context. However, ethnographers take insider (emic) analyses very seriously. We conduct research not just to mine data from informants, but to learn about their theoretical and pragmatic insights. (2012, 16)

In this way, doing ethnography is often born out of nonrandom sampling strategies, which prioritizes deep routes to knowing that emerge from researchers conducting interviews and actively engaging in immersive, multimodal, and multisensorial practices at different sites (see Bernard 2017 on sampling techniques). Researcher engagement can include active participation in an identifiable role or more observational experiences (see Johnson et al. 2006). Such sustained immersive participant observation and often (repeated) interviewing over set periods of time is meant to build relationships and thereby cultivate trust and rapport to reduce respondent bias and obtrusive effects. In short-term ethnographic work, attention should be paid to the intensity of the research encounter and the time needed for *postevent reflection* to develop the thick description required for ethnographic practice (Pink and Morgan 2013). Finally, although not a linear process, ethnographic research design involves concrete considerations about how we go about seeing and doing (see Box 10.1). First and foremost, this means grappling with your core ethical commitments, which in turn inform research design. Only after these initial two steps have been completed should you turn to some of the more practical elements of ethnographic practice (see also Chapter 2). Beyond these core elements, however, and although many scholars might passionately argue otherwise, there is no unified understanding of what ethnography is or is not. Its practice certainly shifts and changes across different disciplines.

[3] Collaborative event ethnography relies on collaboration in coordinating fieldwork, collecting and analyzing data, and thinking through meaning. The CBD COP10 CEE team is J. Peter Brosius, Lisa M. Campbell, Noella J. Gray, Kenneth I. MacDonald, Maggie Bourque, Catherine Corson, Juan Luis Dammert B., Eial Dujovny, Shannon M. Hagerman, Sarah Hitchner, Shannon Greenberg, Rebecca Gruby, Edward M. Maclin, Kimberly R. Marion Suiseeya, Deborah Scott, Daniel Suarez, and Rebecca Witter.

Box 10.1 Considerations in ethnographic research design

Designing ethnographic research requires consideration and decisions about *how*, *why*, and *with what commitments* we engage with communities and sites. Specifically, your design should reflect your logic and decisions around:

(1) the ethics of ethnographic practice;
(2) which epistemologies (decolonial, interpretivist, transdisciplinary, feminist) should guide ethnographic inquiries (Bernard 2017; Rinehart and Earl 2016);
(3) what forms of ethnography are appropriate (sole, auto, duo, team);[4]
(4) where (multisited, digital, physical), when (rapid, short-term, longitudinal), and at what scale (local, national, transnational, international, global) ethnography should take place;
(5) how ethnography should be practiced (mixed, visual, sensory, engaged);
(6) to whom or what ethnographers should direct attention to (people, objects, ideas, processes, situations, nonhumans, actants, relations, and so on);
(7) motivations for conducting ethnography (applied, advocacy, activism); and,
(8) modes of ethnographic inquiry (experimental, performance, visual, arts-based).

10.2.1 Ethnography in Global Environmental Politics Research

Distinct from other methodologies in global environmental politics, ethnography facilitates deep understandings of power as plural, sometimes conflicting, phenomena that flow through and emerge in *relations* and *processes* rather than *outcomes* of agreement-making (Barnett and Duvall 2005; Betsill and Corell 2008). Ethnographers have moved beyond agenda-setting and issue linkage as explanations, for example, of how particular topics or issues become focal points in agreement-making processes and instead ask how meaning around a specific topic or issue is made, contested, negotiated, and eventually traded off at these sites. How and why, for example, have human rights become a dominant theme for addressing Indigenous Peoples' concerns in international environmental regimes (Marion Suiseeya et al. 2021)? What conceptualizations of rights, justice, and equity crystallize through agreement-making processes (Corson et al. 2014; Doolittle 2010; Marion Suiseeya 2014)? Whose meanings gain and lose traction at these sites, how, and with what effects for global environmental governance (Hughes and Vadrot 2019; Scott et al. 2014; Vadrot et al. 2021a)?

Ethnographers have established a growing body of literature generating insights into how different actors use scalar politics to reconfigure conceptualizations of nation-state sovereignty at global agreement-making sites (Gruby and Campbell 2013). Others challenge conventional empirical claims of influence as observed primarily through outcomes by demonstrating how so-called marginalized groups of actors leverage the politics of performance to create "moments of influence" in spaces where they otherwise may have limited ability to activate other sources of power (Witter et al. 2015). Researchers

[4] Auto ethnography is where the researchers themselves are the subject of research, whereas sole, duo, and team ethnographers are conducting work with other subjects/participants.

have employed ethnography at sites of agreement-making as solo researchers (e.g., de Moor 2018; Pickering 2019), cooperatively (e.g., Widick and Foran 2016), and collaboratively (e.g., Brosius and Campbell 2010; Campbell et al. 2014; Corson et al. 2014; Gray et al. 2020; Marion Suiseeya and Zanotti 2019; see also Chapter 11 this volume). The sites in these studies have included Conferences of Parties and preparatory meetings for agreement-making processes, including the Convention on Biological Diversity (CBD), the UN Framework Convention on Climate Change, the Minamata Convention (UNFCCC), the Vienna Convention (Montreal Protocol), the UN Biodiversity Beyond National Jurisdiction processes (BBNJ), and the UN Forum on Forests; they also include the knowledge bodies that inform them, such as the IPBES and the IPCC, among others (see Table 10.1). Through systematic, direct experiences, whether in virtual or physical spaces of agreement-making, ethnography provides opportunities to see *power-in-place* at work (Barnett and Duvall 2005; Griffin 2012).

10.3 Becoming an Ethnographer

There is no one defined pathway to becoming an ethnographer. We have come to learn and practice ethnography from different starting points. Kim learned ethnography by doing: diving in head first, making mistakes, sometimes not knowing that what she was doing was called ethnography, struggling to articulate what she found so confusing, doubting her interpretations, and ultimately viewing ethnography as a particularly compelling approach for studying power at sites of global environmental governance. Trained as an anthropologist and ethnographer, Laura continues to hone her practice through ongoing, reflexive engagement with ethnography and theoretical commitments to feminist and decolonial scholarship. Here we share our own experiences because, like most researchers, our paths in research and practice have been ones of continuous growth. As non-Indigenous, white women faculty at research universities in the United States, our own institutional locations, power, and privilege as settler scholars need to be at the foreground, not the background, of our work. In sharing these experiences, we hope to inspire established and early career researchers. Ethnography demands embracing discomfort; simultaneously, it offers opportunities to see the inner workings of power-in-place in the most unexpected ways.

10.3.1 Ethical Commitments in Ethnographic Research

Your first decisions as an ethnographer should be around *whether* to engage ethnography and *how* to do so in ways that embody core ethical commitments (see Chapter 5). Ethnographers are accountable to a range of different ethical commitments and responsibilities, ranging from Institutional Review Boards and professional associations (American Anthropological Association Code of Ethics) to protocols and legal processes (international, national, Tribal, or community-based protocols).[5] Ethics are not just a checkbox

[5] The CARE Principles for Indigenous Data Governance are one example: www.gida-global.org/care.

but encompass all aspects of research design, from project conceptualization to project management (see Chapter 2). Such responsibilities include recognizing and addressing legacies of colonial and racialized institutional (e.g., higher education) and (inter) disciplinary practices and contemporary manifestations of settler colonialism that shape research. Considering the professional, relational, situational, and culturally specific ethics of the research process improves the rigor, credibility, and coherence of research; the resulting research collaborations also make practical contributions that have the potential to impact and disrupt institutional norms that extend within and beyond the academy (Balazs and Morello-Frosch 2013; Tracy 2010). Research outputs or data management practices, for example, that go beyond traditional approaches and which are designed and enacted in partnership (e.g., open-access, community-led, or Indigenous designed outputs or data sovereignty protocols) can help amplify the voices of individuals or diverse communities in international policy processes (e.g., Kukutai and Taylor 2016; Chapter 5).[6]

Essential ways ethnographers can build or expand upon ethical practices and principles include interweaving, bridging, or braiding ethnography with other approaches (see Tengö et al. 2017), such as feminist research methodologies (Zanotti and Marion Suiseeya 2020), community-based research, transdisciplinary research principles (Wilmer et al. 2021), and decolonizing and indigenizing research methodologies (Tuck and Yang 2012; Simpson 2014; Tuhiwai Smith 2021; Vine Deloria 1997; Zanotti and Palomino-Schalscha 2016), amongst many others. To move toward equitable research partnerships, for example, Wilmer et al. (2021) propose researchers consider integrating principles including representation, self-determination, reciprocity, and deference, "cross-cutting themes" of human and nonhuman, as well as expanding skill sets into their research. Particularly relevant for those interested in more effective and just global environmental governance – an endeavor that relies on improved modes of multistakeholder engagement – these strategies provide important opportunities to consider how and in what way IR scholarship can contribute to engaged work (Benjamin 2016; Low and Merry, 2010). Once you have actively considered and engaged your core ethical commitments, you can begin the process of designing your research, including defining your "field," exploring potential questions, and attending to the considerations outlined in Box 10.1 (see also Chapter 5).

10.4 Defining the "Field" as Sites of Agreement-Making

Although scholars of IR, and especially global environmental politics, have always considered international treaty negotiations worthy of study, until recently ethnography was largely absent from their methodological toolkits. Conceptualizing sites of agreement-making as *ethnographic* spaces responds to ethnography's commitment to relational and multisites of research (Marcus 2008) and also reflects the contributions advanced by the early pioneers of collaborative event ethnography (CEE) (e.g., Campbell et al. 2014; see also Chapter 11). Corson et al. (2014, 28–29), for example, characterize mega-events as "critical historical junctures," "bundles of social relationships and power dynamics," and "provid[e] the

[6] E.g., see the Exit Zero Project's work with the Southeast Chicago Archive and Storytelling Project: www.sechicagohistory.org/.

institutional context to … become field-configuring events." More recently, the rise of the digital as a site of ethnography and the need for short- and long-term work to be responsive to acute (e.g., disasters, conflict zones) change or short-term mega-events provide essential revisions to ethnography (Boellstorff et al. 2012). In the wake of the COVID-19 pandemic, for example, negotiation sites like those for Marine Biodiversity of Areas Beyond National Jurisdiction moved fully online, prompting researchers to shift toward digital ethnography (Vadrot et al. 2021a). **Environmental agreement-making sites thus include multiple, digital, visual, organizational, and ephemeral spaces** (Boellstorff et al. 2012; Campbell et al. 2014; Marcus 1995, 2008; Pink 2009; Pryzbylski 2020).

To demonstrate how we put ethnography into practice at sites of global environmental governance, we draw from our work at the International Society of Biology (ISE) meetings that took place in 2018 at the Hangar Convention Center in Belém, Brazil.[7] This event celebrated the 30th Anniversary of the Declaration of Belém that recognized the inextricable link between Indigenous Peoples and biodiversity conservation. At ISE, we were interested not only in the *what* of the event, but also the *where.* Part of the tourism and business industry in Belém, the Hangar Convention Center reflects the global industry of convention and trade centers that have surged since the 1980s due to the rise in the conference industry and their possibilities for city renewal (Sanders 2014). Because the history of conference-center design arguably has its roots in empire, colonialism, and subsequent state-based efforts at shoring up national patrimony and advances in technology, industry, and various forms of innovation, we were interested to see how the politics of Indigenous representation unfolded at an event like ISE (e.g., see Griffiths 2002). Although distinct from agreement-making sites such as treaty negotiations, the Declaration of Belém that emerged from ISE generated the foundations for Article 8(j) of the CBD; ISE and its interplay with other agreement-making sites is thus integral for understanding how Indigenous Peoples' *power-in-place* moves and shifts through multiple sites, including the UNFCCC and CBD.

Ultimately, what constitutes the "field" in your research will depend partly on your questions; for example, if you ask questions about the digital lives of agreement-making sites, your field could include both physical and digital spaces. Access restrictions may also scope the field for you (e.g., if you cannot secure credentials to attend specific meetings; see Chapter 6 this volume). It is essential not to allow access restrictions to scope your research question; instead, these are part of the political culture of agreement-making sites and therefore part of the story. But if you ask questions that are bound to specific locations within a site that require special access privileges, such as caucus rooms, then you may be limiting your research by allowing your questions to define your field. Chapter 2 provides some guidance on preparing yourself for navigating and understanding these types of spaces.

[7] Our ISE research was supported by Northwestern University's Department of Political Science, Center for Native American and Indigenous Research, and Undergraduate Research Assistant Program, as well as a Purdue University College of Liberal Arts Global Synergy Faculty Research Grant. CEE relies on collaboration, in coordinating field work, collecting and analyzing data, and thinking through meaning, and this report reflects the efforts of the larger team working on site in Belém in consultation with the organizers of Belém +30. The ISE-CEE team comprises project leaders Kimberly R. Marion Suiseeya and Laura Zanotti, with Emily Colón, Michelle David, Moriah Lavey, and Bailey Smith-Helman.

10.5 Doing Ethnography

10.5.1 Asking Questions

Ethnography begins with a series of broad questions that help develop and design research and relational practice. Key to posing questions is to accept that your specific research questions will transform through iterative, immersive, and reflexive practice. You should also consider whom your questions serve, how power and positionality shape relationships with participants, and how to practice reciprocity in your research (Przybylski 2020; see also Chapter 5).

In our ongoing collaboration, we are broadly interested in how the politics of representation shape the possibilities for justice in global environmental governance. We are specifically interested in how historically marginalized groups, such as Indigenous Peoples and women, access, engage, and influence global environmental governance. Most researchers approach such questions from an interpretive-constructivist lens and focus on human relational dynamics (Schaffer 2015). In our case, we also considered the performative and dramaturgical aspects of conferencing as "symbolic … and exemplary dimensions of summitry," rather than dismissing them as mere spectacle (Death 2011, 7). Often set-up and constructed in large conference centers, sites of global environmental governance are created, produced, curated, and made in different infrastructural and architectural spaces in cityscapes. Their site location, interior designs, and spatial layouts are far from simply backdrops of the conference. Instead, they contain hegemonic and alternative semiotic cues, discourses, and lived experiences that uphold dominant epistemes of technoscientific knowledge and good governance while simultaneously disrupting those very same practices that shape whose, how, and what representations are possible.

Since launching our project in 2015, our research questions have expanded to include investigations into these spatial dynamics of sites of agreement-making: how, for example, does the built environment impact the interactions of peoples, ideas, imagery, and diverse communicative forms and shape their contributions? As registered event participants and ethnographers inserted at these sites, credentials afforded us the following: freedom of social movement, access to event information, entrance assurance, and autonomy within our given roles across the events (Johnson et al. 2006, 118). We engaged in immersive participant observation to explore the built environment, visual cues, and other sensory aspects of the event and capture the "rituals of diplomacy" that can structure, restrict, and confine how actors shape and experience events (Death 2011, 7). Embracing inquisitive evolution enriches our understanding of *power-in-place* to include the materiality of agreement-making, therewith enhancing the significance of our work for understanding the production of global environmental governance.

10.5.2 Multimodal Data Collection Techniques

Deep routes to knowing are achieved from immersive, multimodal, and multisensorial approaches to systematic research that privilege actor perspectives and meaning-making around particular issues, themes, problems, situations, or concepts (Bernard 2017; Collins et al. 2021; Pink 2009; Schatz 2009). Whether a singular researcher or working within teams, most ethnographers recognize ethnography as a relational process constituted through interactions with the built environment, material artifacts, expressive forms, semiotic cues, and research interlocutors and participants. Because ethnographers themselves are one of their key research "instruments," attention to sensory subjectivity and sensory intersubjectivity is critical and necessary to its practice. Sensory subjectivity refers to "the ways individuals use sensory knowledge and practice … a way of understanding the world that is at once culturally specific but that is also shaped through other influences," such as the positionalities of actors in relation to each other, social institutions, and "experiences and ideologies originating beyond the local" (Pink 2009, 53). Sensory *inter*subjectivity helps researchers conceptualize how identities and social relations "are fully embodied and multisensory events" that are formed and reformed through engagement beyond physical, verbal, and visual encounters to also include material/sensory encounters (Pink 2009, 53). Reflection Box 10.1 highlights how multisensorial experiences shaped one researcher's practice.

Reflection Box 10.1 Multisensorial experiences in ethnography
By Kate Haapala[8]

The first year of my graduate program was designed to assimilate new students into the profession of political science. What does it mean to be a political scientist? How do you know good or bad work when you see it? The methodological training and coursework to socialize new students into the profession were steeped in positivism, causality, measurement and instrumentation, statistical inference, and bi/multivariate analysis. There was little room for dialogue let alone formal training on qualitative methodologies such as ethnography.

However, at the close of my first year of graduate school, I was a member of a CEE team studying the 2016 World Conservation Congress (WCC). Contrasting with the often literally muted or detached approach of quantitative methods, being trained in engaging ethnography was a sensory explosion. For example, the WCC's Opening Ceremony was held at the Neal S. Blaisdell Arena. Thousands of people poured into the arena, where the ceremony itself was a cacophony of dramaturgical performance; traditional dancers performed Hula, and song and speeches filled the air in equal measure to handheld devices.

My experiences at the WCC and the study of it through ethnography proved to be a pivotal moment in my graduate training. Listening, observing, moving across Honolulu, building relationships with other participants and team members, and even spontaneously being given badge credentials to vote on behalf of a conservation organization produced an epistemological rupture that remade how I understood myself as a political scientist. CEE opened new methodological possibilities for me to make sense of political phenomena. In Honolulu, and on returning home, I began to reimagine the types of research questions I wanted to ask and how to answer them as a political scientist. For me, CEE made political science a discipline that uses rigorous qualitative approaches to provide answers for how different ideas and forms of power move in governance settings by stuttering, stopping, and lurching forward, to impact political and legal outcomes.

[8] Kate Haapala is currently a fishery analyst at the North Pacific Fishery Management Council in Anchorage, Alaska. She trained as a political scientist at Purdue University and specializes in environmental governance and justice, with particular emphasis on the socio-cultural aspects of policy-making processes across Alaska's marine environment.

Once you are ready to turn toward data collection, consider how you might leverage triangulation. Ethnography can focus on the situatedness of microlevel, intimate, and affective dynamics of megaconferences' lived experiences, while also attending to the multiplicity of semiotic landscapes present at such events.[9] In activating a critical reflexive practice, ethnography facilitates capturing diverse "fragments" of the event, which researchers then weave together across similarly situated immersive, collective settings (Jaworski and Thurlow 2010, 7; see also Corson et al. 2014). To support this practice, ethnographers gather diverse types of information from immersive engagement and directed conversations or interviews, including different types of notes (descriptive, analytical, reflective), audio recordings, sketches, photographs, video recordings, social media data, and material artifacts (see Figure 10.2; Table 10.2; on interviews, see Chapter 8). Combined, these techniques provide the saturation necessary to triangulate research findings and provide the work's necessary rigor, credibility, dependability, transferability, and embodied and experiential immersion (Tracy 2010).

Figure 10.2 Multimodal data collection.

Table 10.2 *Examples of data types collected at ISE*

Method	Examples
Research notebooks (analog or electronic)	Analytical, descriptive, reflective, team meeting participant observation notes
Notes (from participant observation, interviews)* **Includes descriptive, reflective, analytical notes; team and individual notes*	Shifts in discourse and language; naming and/or shaming different actors/groups; police patrols (e.g., drawing attention to violations or neglect of duties, obligations, rights, etc.); fire alarms (e.g., drawing attention to urgent concerns); shifts in behavior, tone, discourse, alliances, identities, and language; enlisting the experiences of others; storytelling of one's own experience; aligning or distancing self/others in relation to others/self; use of dress, accessories, gestures to "speak" or be made visible without engaging verbally; use of scripts, rituals, and other forms of performance to signal indigeneity or Indigenous identities
Photos	Images of event spaces, signs, displays, participants, presentation materials (e.g., PowerPoint slides), team members, activities, protests, climate-related media, and materials around Paris (e.g., ISE Congress advertisements on bus stops), technology and other communicative devices

9 Semiotic landscapes refer to the "interplay between language, visual discourse, and the spatial practices and dimensions of culture, especially the textual mediation or discursive construction of place and the use of space as a semiotic resource in its own right" (Jaworksi and Thurlow 2010, 1).

Table 10.2 (*cont.*)

Method	Examples
Materials	Daily draft declaration text, stickers, buttons, promotional materials, books, flyers, pamphlets, swag (tote bags, pens, t-shirts), reports, maps, printed agendas
Audio recordings	Event sessions, protests, press conferences, interviews, team meetings, individual debriefs
Video	Navigating through the zones at the Hangar, commuting in Belém
Spatial biographies	Sketches and descriptions of different spaces at the Hangar, flows people/idea/object/communicative acts
Web materials	Preparatory reports, official documents from ISE, press releases and official documents from relevant organizations, Campaign material from different social movements, news reports
Social media	Twitter scrapes for selected hashtags, daily screenshots and material downloads of selected organizations social media engagement, team blog posts and team Twitter account
Data logs	Team member time logs, photo logs, material logs, field note logs

To integrate **multimodal data collection techniques** within our ethnography at ISE, we crafted several different practices meant to draw attention to and assist with documenting and reflecting upon the articulation of the semiotic landscape in which we were working. First, we formulated research questions, refined our analytical framework, reflexively considered our role in the research and knowledge production process, and regarded diverse participant observation and interview approaches. Because of our team-based approach to research, we dedicated time in our daily schedule for collaborative analysis and reflection (see Box 10.2). We then created a plan and guidelines for multiple different forms of field noting and interviewing.

Box 10.2 The inner workings of "doing" ethnography

5:30 am: Wake up, check event websites for updates/session and location changes, check social media for tips or other insights.

6:00 am: Morning meeting: revisit field notes, jot down or audio record new questions, insights, thoughts. Decide which sessions to attend, what data to collect, and when to take breaks and organize your data; check ethnography kit has all equipment and back-up batteries.

7:00 am: Travel to site, taking note of how you feel getting there, what the experience is like, and jotting down/recording thoughts and ideas that emerge during travel and waiting in security lines.

8:00 am–end of day on site: Collect data, jot reflections, attend to quotidian experiences. Be sure to include a break or two to download and organize data. Log data and materials.

End of day: Travel back to lodging.

Evening: Take time to sit quietly and write about the day: descriptive, analytical, and reflective field notes

Evening meeting: Organize and back up data; revisit experiences, jot down or audio record new questions, insights, and thoughts; look ahead to the next day's schedule; plug in all devices to recharge.

Our team ethnography kits include: notebook, multiple pens, pencils, labels for organizing material artifacts, digital camera, digital recorder, Go-Pro camera, extra memory cards for camera and recorder, back-up camera and recorder batteries, power bank and charging cords, laptop, headphone splitter, noise-reduction microphone attachment for recorder, safety information cards, project information cards (including IRB [Institutional Review Board] contact information), maps, external hard drive, and a brief on local safety, communication, and travel resources prepared by our team before departure.

Second, we reviewed our interview protocol and considered how we might want to expand or reword additional questions. Drawing from best practices for open-ended interviews, we reviewed how our questions were phrased, considered the need for translations into different languages, and discussed the questions between ourselves and others who were invested in the research process. Through this process of iterative consultation and review, we developed a set of queries. We recommend pretesting your questions to make sure they align with methodological norms, are culturally appropriate, and are flexible.

Next, to capture our experiences of these semiotic landscapes we explored visual protocols and ethical considerations for working with visual imagery at the conference (Haraway 1988, 581, 587). We expanded our field notes to make clear and explicit ways in which notes should capture the varied modalities of discursive visibilities of the conference, including visual and sensory elements.

Finally, we drew from ethnographic research on built environments to integrate spatial biographies into our practice to describe the space's flows of peoples, ideas, imagery, and diverse communicative forms. We applied these approaches to the various sites where the megaconference unfolded: fairs, forums, off- and on-site performances, and panels (see Reflection Box 10.2 for an example).

10.5.3 Forms of Writing as Data Collection

Writing ethnography does not begin at the conclusion of data collection, but rather is part of the ethnographic process. Literature reviews, memoing, fieldnotes, and other forms of writing during research all build toward writing up ethnography. During the data collection phase, ethnographic practices demand iterative and multiple forms of recording experiences and events. For example, three phases of **notetaking** may occur: (1) jottings, headnotes, scratch notes, photographs, sketches, or videos while engaging in participant observation; (2) summary, descriptive notes at the end of an event or day; and (3) analytical and reflective notes that occur systematically at the end of each day and/or regularly scheduled times during the research process so that you can review, assess, iterate, and update notes systemically (see Emerson et al. 2011; Wolfinger 2002). Notetaking can focus on several aspects of a site, ranging from identifying salient elements of specific events to comprehensively and holistically taking in entire scenes (Wolfinger 2002). Sensory aspects of sites, such as smells, sounds, haptics, kinesthetics/movements, and other sensations (interplay of light, temperature, and different affective dimensions) can be essential to understanding how processes and diverse forms and manifestations of power unfold, and how participants experience the everyday lived reality of the often intensive, short-term sites of global agreement-making.

In previous ethnographic work, we found that we tended to prioritize verbal expressions (in the form of talks/speeches) and were not as comprehensive or analytically attuned to the semiotic landscapes of mega-events. Semiotic reflections, instead, often came up as challenges of doing ethnography rather than sites of analyses of the event itself – for example, in feeling sensory overload at the end of the day, noting the visual impact of seeing the sheer number of mobile phones as attendees recorded opening ceremonies, or weariness from walking within and across the vast landscapes of conference ventures. To overcome these tendencies, we decided upon three kinds of notes for our ISE project.

First, we had note templates for singular events, moments, and processes that prompted us to consider whether to document that event visually or through a combination of text/photographs. We were aware of the trade-offs involved in our choices to actively listen, take notes, take photographs, or take another role. We provided prompts for documenting semiotic landscapes and instructions for how and in what ways to take photographs of events. For example, we approached photographing the event as a series of individual photos and used photographic essays to represent or evoke different moments and capture semiotic representations of discursive modalities. We took two types of photos: singular events, and pictures that captured the general, public spaces at the conference site (e.g., meeting rooms, common areas, exhibition spaces, press areas, transportation routes, signage, maps of event layout). We also took photos of print materials at events, including banners, signage, posters, and other materials that may need to stay at the event site after the event closes. We collected materials that were freely distributed for our project archive (e.g., reports, postcards, pamphlets, and other print materials; see Figure 10.3). We generated metadata and field notes for each image to provide context and explain what prompted us to capture the image and reflections.

Second, we prioritized daily written reflective and analytical field notes to capture thoughts and feelings as they were happening. These types of notes were especially important because of the intensity of such events.

Figure 10.3 Materials artifacts as data.

Finally, we created spatial biographies. Because of the critical role played by the conference venues, fairs, poster sessions, and other public-facing aspects of the event, the documentation of the "material semiotics" was essential to understanding the politics of representation (Dicks et al. 2006, 85). We developed a spatial biography technique to take temporally bounded moments of comprehensive visual and textual notes of the diverse spaces and modalities of the event. As Wolfinger (2002, 91) describes, comprehensive notes can not only assist with the sequence of what did take place but also document omissions or "non-happenings." To engage a holistic ethnographic practice, we integrated qualitative sketch mapping with visual ethnographic methods (Kuschnir 2016).

Reflecting normative elements of summitry, ISE was organized into large auditoriums and small meeting rooms, some with built-in AV equipment and neat rows of seating that presupposed a particular form of primarily orderly discourse, rhetoric, and presentation style. Each day, we chose one of many different sites of the conference (panels, fairs, book openings, etc.) or in-between spaces (e.g., hallways), which we would observe for an hour or two. We took note of the space and its location, layout, and structures; materials and objects; aesthetic and atmosphere; sensory aspects; movements and changes over time; inclusivity and exclusivity practices such as perceived or physical lack of accessibility; and bounded or unbounded (usually by walls) features (see Figure 10.4 and Reflection Box 10.2).

Through our multimodal approach to data collection, our work illuminated how, in a multilingual conference, audience reaction and spaces of the event were just as important as the featured speakers and performers at ISE. By flexibly alternating between modes to collect multiple forms of data simultaneously, we could focus on multisensorial aspects of the environment and move beyond relying solely on documentation of speeches and talks. Prioritizing the visual, spatial, and sensory generated analytical and theoretical reflections to consider how the politics of representation unfolded in scripted and unscripted spaces of the conference. Along with our interviews and participant observation, we could uncover tensions among and between public and private, designated and nondesignated areas, and "in-between" moments that engaged audience members, participants, and speakers alike.

Doing ethnography will generate a large and unique set of data documenting global governance processes in real time from which ethnographers can derive diverse insights.[10] Practical concerns, such as how ethnographers record such moments – for example, through jottings on a notepad, sketching a scene, or recording videos on a cellphone – should be considered carefully in terms of data ethics, management, security, and storage (see Chapter 2). Ethnographers should develop a system for how they log and manage their data prior to beginning their work to provide both secure ways to store information and to consider critical approaches to data management and stewardship (see also Table 10.2).[11] Importantly, storage and security should not reproduce extractive forms of research practice.

[10] Novice ethnographers often wonder whether the data they collect will be "enough" to develop insights into the particular phenomena or community they are exploring. A focus on quality over quantity is critical here: systematic, detailed, and iterative field notes that capture the researcher's experiences and observations provide the necessary and robust foundation for drawing out insights. Additionally, through ongoing and reflective reflexivity, researchers provide context for readers to understand *how* the researcher approached their work.

[11] See chapter 4 in Przybylski (2020) for a detailed discussion of data logging and management; Clemons et al. (2018) for a list of equipment in ethnographer's field bags; and Thatcher et al. (2016) on data colonialism.

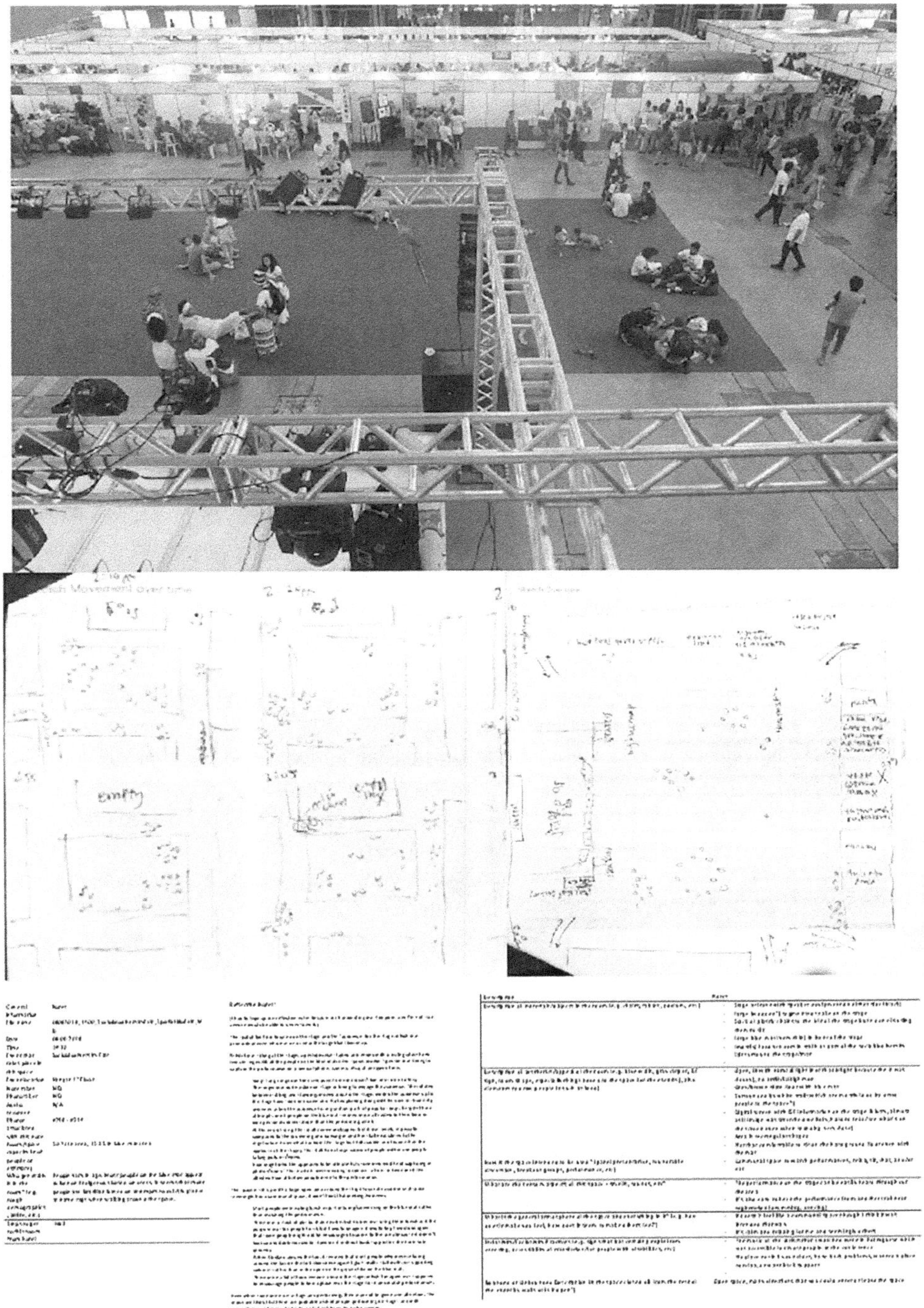

Figure 10.4 Examples of sketch maps from ISE.
Source: Photo by Michelle David (P2I Team).

Reflection Box 10.2 Spatial biographies

By Michelle David[12]

One of the largest sociobiodiversity fairs to date, the ISE's Sociobiodiversity Fair, showcased art, food, and culture from more than seventy vendors, organizations, Indigenous Peoples, and Traditional Peoples across a dense network of stalls organized via four themes: socio-biodiverse products and goods, intercultural festival, cultures of food and gastronomy, and ethnicity. As a member of Laura and Kim's ISE team, I passed the fair countless times, my attention usually drawn to the most eye-catching parts – an exciting performance or colorfully decorated stall. Through producing spatial biographies, however, I began to pay attention to more nuanced aspects of the spaces, exploring both the striking and less obvious facets of the fair to discern material and semiotic cues. Our team sought to capture how "this material organization (as opposed to other possible ones) contributes to the production of ethnographic meaning in the research setting" (Dicks et al. 2006, 83).

For example, one day at the fair I sat at the foot of the only formal stage to watch a string of performances, taking note of the performers, audience, aesthetics, and space layout. One performance included a lively singer and guitarist actively trying to engage the audience: they moved around the stage, invited audience members up to the stage, and even asked them to sing parts of popular songs. Despite these attempts, the audience was largely unengaged, except for the occasional mobile phone snapshot or film. The performers wore no specific costumes; one wore a simple dress, the other wore jeans. After each song, the small audience clapped quietly. Simultaneously, at the other end of the fair, another performance was underway in a vendor stall – its drumming and applause drowning out the music where I sat. Later, I found a crowd of people jostling outside the stall to take in the performance. Women in brightly colored traditional clothing danced as men beat drums.

After several hours at the fair, a clear pattern emerged: performers wearing traditional clothing attracted the largest audiences, the most cameras, and the loudest applause. The varying levels of engagement we observed at different performances raises questions about what work such performances, dress, and adornment are doing. Conklin (1997), for example, has argued that superficial associations of Indigenous Peoples and local communities with cultural manifestations such as dress, jewelry, or body paint mask the political identity of Indigenous Peoples and Indigenous ways of being. That the performers with highly visible cultural markers attracted large audiences could reflect such superficial associations, but could also reflect unique forms of political agency and identity. Was ISE reproducing the same kind of symbolic politics critiqued by scholars, or was it creating space for new politics of representation? How were Indigenous attendees and allies creating new forms of symbolic politics? If I had only explored the fair, I likely would have been drawn to the excitement of the packed stall without noticing the stage. Through spatial biography, however, I could see both performances in relation to one another and consider what role these sessions play in global environmental governance: who makes up the communities at these sessions, who do they engage, and how do they shape experiences, opportunities, and impacts at such events?

Because it forced careful observation of movements, objects, and environments, spatial biography was a potent tool for generating the critical contextual information often overshadowed in research privileging verbal documentation.

[12] Michelle David is a law student at the University of Chicago Law School, pursuing a career as a public interest attorney in environmental law with a focus on environmental justice. She studied political science and environmental policy as an undergraduate at Northwestern, where she was first trained in ethnography.

10.5.4 Analyzing and Writing Up

Typically, "measurement" in ethnography happens when the data set reaches saturation; salient themes and patterns emerge that identify frequently represented behaviors/attitudes/etcetera, less frequent but influential cases, and outlier examples. Often approaching data analysis through grounded theory, ethnographers conduct successive rounds of in vivo coding, identifying and refining themes or codes until reaching theoretical saturation (Charmaz 2006).[13] Ethnographers develop thematic narratives that "incorporate several analytic themes or concepts linked by a common topic" to organize field experiences, contextual information, participant voices, and analytic commentary into a coherent story or research product (Emerson et al. 2011, 201–202). Often, theme building can take place in a dialogical fashion with research participants to cross-check code or theme categories. Preliminary analysis and dialogical practices help ethnographers develop a standardized coding protocol for data analysis. Qualitative software, such as MAXQDA, Atlas.ti, or QSR NVivo, can assist with coding, triangulation, and analysis. Additionally, descriptive statistics can generate insights into agreement-making, especially related to event and participant demographics or attributes, keywords, and descriptive representation of terms, practices, or acts (frequency, mean, etc.). Through this triangulation, ethnographers interpret and represent findings; highlight meanings, experiences, and conceptualizations of the world; identify exemplary experiences, extended passages, and quotes from interviews; and ascertain other multivocal strategies that prioritize everyday experiences and ontologies. After re/reading, transcribing, reviewing, and coding these experiences, the ethnographer's task is to combine and refine analytical memos, interpretations, key quotes, and events. Stylistic choices on narrative forms and decisions about representing participants are all important decisions to make in developing thematic narratives. Finally, ethnographers should approach writing as relational: "writing is a form of accountability and ethical practice. We write to share scholarly findings, to tell stories that matter, and to share new insights about the human world that might change it for the better" (McGranahan 2020, 3).

10.6 Conclusion

In this chapter, we have provided a guide to ethnography that emphasizes many of the practical considerations researchers must attend to. This includes discussion on how to scope the "field," the diverse forms and roles of notetaking, and the opportunities afforded through a greater emphasis on the spatial and performative dynamics of agreement-making sites. Throughout, we have highlighted the nonlinear nature of ethnography; instead of moving from design to data collection to analysis, ethnography demands constant iteration and reflexivity.

We conclude this chapter by returning to ethnography as a relational practice – one that bears out not only at our research sites, but also in the relationships we shape within our disciplines, the academy, and with diverse communities that are directly or indirectly

[13] See Bernard (2017), Corbin and Strauss (1990), and Saldaña (2014) for important discussions on generating codes/themes and how these decisions interplay with your research question, approach, and design.

impacted by our research or the phenomena we study. Each decision an ethnographer makes throughout the research process, from ethical commitments and posing questions through to storing and stewarding data, reflects how we understand and engage power in our relationships. As researchers, we have the power and agency to determine our motivations and resist how disciplines silo and discipline our thinking – something that we both have been cultivating. We can reject tendencies of the academy to reproduce power hierarchies and idealize individualism, and instead embrace collaboration in various forms. Despite the scholarly and practical challenges of shifting toward such feminist, transdisciplinary work, approaching knowledge production as a collective, relational endeavor has the potential to broaden the reach of research and collaborations beyond the constraints of the academy, which can further deepen and strengthen what we "know" about the phenomena of global agreement-making.

As scholars and researchers, we have access to specific conditions of power and assumed authority that we must carefully attend to as we engage relationally with the communities and individuals, rightsholders, stakeholders, and other diverse groups at sites of global environmental governance and within our broader academic work. As we have articulated here, this reflexivity should not only be circumscribed to those moments at the beginning of research but should pulse throughout the entire research process so that the researcher continually engages with questions of power. Moreover, we have highlighted a range of ethical considerations that emerge when conducting ethnography, from questions about consent to relationships with other researchers and scholars, interactions with communities, and the purpose of research. These are essential questions to address and should not be taken lightly: before beginning any work, both veteran and first-time ethnographers should consider the ethics of their research and the associated commitments that accompany different forms of practice.

By way of closing, we end with some tips for ethnographic practice. We can't emphasize enough the importance of the preparatory time before fieldwork to gain the training and mentorship needed for such work and to do the deep work of ethics and reflexivity required for the methodology. Ethnography is immersive and intense, and in the middle of either shorter- or longer-term research projects it is critical to build in time for diverse forms of reflection as well as to find the time needed for careful and detailed note taking so that you do not disrespect the individuals you are working with by not correctly documenting or storing that information. As an immersive technique and one that can blend research cycles with daily life, recognizing the self-care that is needed and how to address ways in which research may become or is unsafe is essential.

Further Reading

1. Campbell, L. M., Corson, C., Gray, N. J., MacDonald, K. I., and Brosius, J. P. (2014) Studying global environmental meetings to understand global environmental governance: Collaborative event ethnography at the tenth conference of the parties to the convention on biological diversity. *Global Environmental Politics*, *14*(3), 1–20.

This special issue includes a collection of articles that emerged from a collaborative event ethnography at one site: the Tenth Conference of Parties to the Convention on Biological

Diversity. It provides an introduction into the diverse ways in which scholars have used ethnography at a global agreement-making site.

2. Emerson, R. M., Fretz, R. I., and Shaw, L. L. (2011). *Writing Ethnographic Fieldnotes*. Chicago, IL: University of Chicago Press.

This volume is a must-have practical guide for researchers engaging ethnography. It covers the entire ethnographic process from research development to data collection, analysis, and write-up.

3. Lightfoot, S. (2016). *Global Indigenous Politics: A Subtle Revolution*. London: Routledge.
4. Pachirat, T. (2017). *Among Wolves: Ethnography and the Immersive Study of Power*. New York: Routledge.

This book presents ethnography in a six-act play, drawing the reader deeply into the various ethical, epistemological, and practical considerations that ethnographers confront. It helps students understand what it means to cultivate an ethnographic sensibility.

5. Tuhiwai Smith, L. (2021). *Decolonizing Methodologies: Research and Indigenous Peoples*. London: Zed Books Ltd.

This volume is essential for all researchers, especially those who study power and politics. By engaging researchers in questions of how, why, and with/for whom we do research, Tuhiwai Smith demonstrates how researchers can and should practice iterative reflexivity throughout their work.

References

Adeyeye, Y., Hagerman, S., and Pelai, R. (2019). Seeking procedural equity in global environmental governance: Indigenous participation and knowledge politics in forest and landscape restoration debates at the 2016 World Conservation Congress. *Forest Policy and Economics*, 109, 102006.

Ali, T., Paton, D., Buergelt, P. T. et al. (2021). Integrating indigenous perspectives and community-based disaster risk reduction: A pathway for sustainable indigenous development in Northern Pakistan. *International Journal of Disaster Risk Reduction*, 59. https://doi.org/10.1016/j.ijdrr.2021.102263.

Balazs, C. L., and Morello-Frosch, R. (2013). The three Rs: How community-based participatory research strengthens the rigor, relevance, and reach of science. *Environmental Justice*, *6*(1), 9–16.

Barnett, M., and Duvall, R. (2005). Power in international politics. *International Organization*, *59*(1), 39–75.

Behar, R. (1996). *The Vulnerable Observer: Anthropology that Breaks Your Heart*. Boston, MA: Beacon Press.

Benjamin, R. (2016). Informed refusal: Toward a justice-based bioethics. *Science, Technology, & Human Values*, *41*(6), 967–990.

Bernard, H. R. (2017). *Research Methods in Anthropology: Qualitative and Quantitative Approaches*, 5th ed. Lanham, MD: AltaMira Press.

Betsill, M., and E. Correll, eds. (2008). *NGO Diplomacy: The Influence of Nongovernmental Organizations in International Environmental Negotiations*. Cambridge, MA: MIT Press.

Beyers, F., and Heinrichs, H. (2020). Global partnerships for a textile transformation? A systematic literature review on inter-and transnational collaborative governance of the textile and clothing industry. *Journal of Cleaner Production*, 261, 12113.

Boellstorff, T., Nardi, B., Pearce, C., and Taylor, T. L. (2012). *Ethnography and Virtual Worlds*. Princeton, NJ: Princeton University Press.

Brosius, J. P. (2006). What counts as local knowledge in global environmental assessments and conventions. *Bridging scales and knowledge systems: concepts and applications in ecosystem assessment*, 129–144.

Brosius, J. P., and Campbell, L. M. (2010). Collaborative event ethnography: Conservation and development trade-offs at the fourth world conservation congress. *Conservation and Society*, *8*(4), 245–255.

Brumann, C. (2021). *The Best We Share: Nation, Culture and World-making in the UNESCO World Heritage Arena*. Oxford: Berghahn Books.

Calliari, E., Serdeczny, O., and Vanhala, L. (2020). Making sense of the politics in the climate change loss and damage debate. *Global Environmental Change*, 64, 102133.

Chakrabarti, A., Tiwari, R., and Banerji, H. (2021). Migrants' narratives on urban governance: A case from Kolkata, a city of the global south. *Sustainability (Switzerland)*, *13*(2), 1–16. https://doi.org/10.3390/su13021009.

Charmaz, K. (2006). *Constructing Grounded Theory: A Practical Guide Through Qualitative Analysis*. London: Sage.

Clemons, T., Faas, A. J., Genovese, T. R. et al. (2018). What's in your bag, anthropologists? *Anthropology News*, *59*(4), e208–e220.

Collins, S. G., Durington, M., and Gill, H. (2021). Multimodal anthropologies. *American Anthropologist*, *123*(1), 142–146.

Conklin, B. A. (1997). Body paint, feathers, and VCRs: Aesthetics and authenticity in Amazonian activism. *American Ethnologist*, *24*(4), 711–737.

Corbin, J. M., and Strauss, A. (1990). Grounded theory research: Procedures, canons, and evaluative criteria. *Qualitative Sociology*, *13*(1), 3–21.

Corson, C., Brady, B., Zuber, A., Lord, J., and Kim, A. (2015). The right to resist: Disciplining civil society at Rio+ 20. *Journal of Peasant Studies*, *42*(3–4), 859–878.

Corson, C., Campbell, L. M., and MacDonald, K. I. (2014). Capturing the personal in politics: Ethnographies of global environmental governance. *Global Environmental Politics*, *14*(3), 21–40.

Corson, C., Worcester, J., Rogers, S., and Flores-Ganley, I. (2020). From paper to practice? Assembling a rights-based conservation approach. *Journal of Political Ecology*, *27*(1), 1128–1147.

De Moor, J. (2018). The "efficacy dilemma" of transnational climate activism: The case of COP21. *Environmental Politics*, *27*(6), 1079–1100.

De Pryck, K. (2020). Intergovernmental expert consensus in the making: The case of the summary for policy makers of the IPCC 2014 synthesis report. *Global Environmental Politics*, *21*(1), 108–129. https://doi.org/10.1162/glep_a_00574.

Death, C. (2011). Summit theatre: Exemplary governmentality and environmental diplomacy in Johannesburg and Copenhagen. *Environmental Politics*, *20*(1), 1–19.

Dicks, B., Soyinka, B., and Coffey, A. (2006). Multimodal ethnography. *Qualitative Research*, *6*(1), 77–96.

Doolittle, A. A. (2010). The politics of indigeneity: Indigenous strategies for inclusion in climate change negotiations. *Conservation and Society* *8*(4), 286–291.

Eastwood, L. E. (2013). *The Social Organization of Policy: An Institutional Ethnography of UN Forest Deliberations*. London: Routledge.

Eastwood, L. E. (2018). *Negotiating the Environment: Civil Society, Globalisation and the UN*. London: Routledge.
Eastwood, L. E. (2021). Using institutional ethnography to investigate intergovernmental environmental policy-making. In P. C. Luken and S. Vaughan, eds., *The Palgrave Handbook of Institutional Ethnography*. Cham: Palgrave Macmillan, pp. 193–211.
Fletcher, R. (2014). Orchestrating consent: Post-politics and intensification of Nature™ Inc. at the 2012 World Conservation Congress. *Conservation and Society*, *12*(3), 329–342.
Gray, N. J. (2010). Sea change: Exploring the international effort to promote marine protected areas. *Conservation and Society*, *8*(4), 331–338.
Gray, N. J., Corson, C., Campbell, L. M. et al. (2020). Doing strong collaborative fieldwork in human geography. *Geographical Review*, *110*(1–2), 117–132.
Griffin, L. (2012). Where is power in governance? Why geography matters in the theory of governance. *Political Studies Review*, *10*(2), 208–220.
Griffiths, A. (2002). *Wondrous Difference: Cinema, Anthropology, and Turn-Of-The-Century Visual Culture*. New York: Columbia University Press.
Gruby, R. L., and Campbell, L. M. (2013). Scalar politics and the region: Strategies for transcending Pacific Island smallness on a global environmental governance stage. *Environment and Planning A*, *45*(9), 2046–2063.
Hagerman, S., Witter, R., Corson, L. et al. (2012). On the coattails of climate? Opportunities and threats of a warming Earth for biodiversity conservation. *Global Environmental Change*, *22*(3), 724–735.
Haraway, D. (1988). Situated knowledges: The science question in feminism and the privilege of partial perspective. *Feminist Studies*, *14*(3), 575–599.
Haraway, D. (1992). The promises of monsters: A regenerative politics for inappropriate/d others. In Grossberg, L., Nelson, C., & Treichler, P., eds., *Cultural Studies*. London: Routledge, pp. 295–337.
Hughes, H., and Vadrot, A. B. (2019). Weighting the world: IPBES and the struggle over biocultural diversity. *Global Environmental Politics*, *19*(2), 14–37.
Jankowski, F., Louafi, S., Kane, N. A. et al. (2020). From texts to enacting practices: Defining fair and equitable research principles for plant genetic resources in West Africa. *Agriculture and Human Values*, *37*(4), 1083–1094. https://doi.org/10.1007/s10460-020-10039-3.
Jaworski, A., and Thurlow, C., eds. (2010). *Semiotic Landscapes: Language, Image, Space*. London: Continuum.
Johnson, J. C., Avenarius, C., and Weatherford, J. (2006). The active participant-observer: Applying social role analysis to participant observation. *Field Methods*, *18*(2), 111–134.
Kirby, P. W., and Lora-Wainwright, A. (2015). Exporting harm, scavenging value: Transnational circuits of e-waste between Japan, China and beyond. *Area*, *47*(1), 40–47.
Kukutai, T., and Taylor, J. (2016). *Indigenous Data Sovereignty: Toward an Agenda*, Canberra: Australia National University Press.
Kuschnir, K. (2016). Ethnographic drawing: Eleven benefits of using a scketchbox for fieldwork. *Visual Ethnography*, *5*(1), 103–134.
Larsen, P. B., and Buckley, K. (2018). *Approaching human rights at the World Heritage Committee: Capturing situated conversations, complexity, and dynamism in global heritage processes*. *International Journal of Cultural Property*, *25*(1), 85–110.
Little, P. E. (1995). Ritual, power and ethnography at the Rio Earth Summit. *Critique of Anthropology*, *15*(3), 265–288.

Lövbrand, E., Hjerpe, M., and Linnér, B. O. (2017). Making climate governance global: How UN Climate Summitry comes to matter in a complex climate regime. *Environmental Politics*, *26*(4), 580–599.

Low, S. M., and Merry, S. E. (2010). Engaged anthropology: Diversity and dilemmas: An introduction to supplement 2. *Current Anthropology*, *51*(S2), S203–S226.

MacKay, J., and Levin, J. (2015). Hanging out in international politics: Two kinds of explanatory political ethnography for IR. *International Studies Review*, *17*(2), 163–188.

McGranahan, C., ed. (2020). *Writing Anthropology: Essays on Craft and Commitment*. Durham, NC: Duke University Press.

MacDonald, K. I. (2010). Business, biodiversity and new "fields" of conservation: The world conservation congress and the renegotiation of organisational order. *Conservation and Society*, *8*(4), 256–275.

Marcus, G. E. (1995). Ethnography in/of the world system: The emergence of multi-sited ethnography. *Annual Review of Anthropology*, *24*(1), 95–117.

Marcus, G. E. (2008). The end(s) of ethnography: Social/cultural anthropology's signature form of producing knowledge in transition. *Cultural Anthropology*, *23*(1), 1–14.

Marion Suiseeya, K. R. (2014). Negotiating the Nagoya Protocol: Indigenous demands for justice. *Global Environmental Politics*, *14*(3), 102–124.

Marion Suiseeya, K. R., and Zanotti, L. (2019). Making influence visible: Innovating ethnography at the Paris climate summit. *Global Environmental Politics*, *19*(2), 38–60.

Marion Suiseeya, K. R., Zanotti, L., and Haapala, K. (2021). Navigating the spaces between human rights and justice: Cultivating Indigenous representation in global environmental governance. *The Journal of Peasant Studies*, *49*(3), 604–628. https://doi.org/10.1080/03066150.2020.1835869.

Milne, S., Mahanty, S., To, P. et al. (2019). Learning from "actually existing" REDD+ A synthesis of ethnographic findings. *Conservation and Society*, *17*(1), 84–95.

Monfreda, C. (2010). Setting the stage for new global knowledge: science, economics, and indigenous knowledge in "The Economics of Ecosystems and Biodiversity" at the Fourth World Conservation Congress. *Conservation and Society*, *8*(4), 276–285.

Peña, P. (2010). NTFP and REDD at the fourth world conservation congress: What is in and what is not. *Conservation and Society*, *8*(4), 292–297.

Pickering, J. (2019). Deliberative ecologies: Complexity and social–ecological dynamics in international environmental negotiations. *Global Environmental Politics*, *19*(2), 61–80.

Pink, S. (2009). *Doing Sensory Ethnography*. New York: Sage Publications.

Pink, S., and Morgan, J. (2013). Short-term ethnography: Intense routes to knowing. *Symbolic Interaction*, *36*(3), 351–361.

Przybylski, L. (2020). *Hybrid Ethnography: Online, Offline, and In Between*, New York: SAGE Publications.

Rinehart, R. E., and Earl, K. (2016). Auto-, duo-and collaborative-ethnographies: "Caring" in an audit culture climate. *Qualitative Research Journal*, *16*(16), 210–224.

Saldaña, J. (2014). Coding and analysis strategies. In P. Leavy, ed., *The Oxford Handbook of Qualitative Research*, Oxford: Oxford University Press.

Sanders, H. T., ed. (2014). *Convention Center Follies*. Philadelphia, PA: University of Pennsylvania Press.

Schaffer, F. C. (2015). *Elucidating Social Science Concepts: An Interpretivist Guide*, vol. 4. London: Routledge.

Schatz, E., ed. (2009). *Political Ethnography: What Immersion Contributes to the Study of Power*. Chicago, IL: University of Chicago Press.

Scott, D., Hitchner, S., Maclin, E. M., and Dammert B, J. L. (2014). Fuel for the fire: Biofuels and the problem of translation at the Tenth Conference of the Parties to the Convention on Biological Diversity. *Global Environmental Politics*, *14*(3), 84–101.

Simpson, A. (2014). *Mohawk Interruptus*, Durham, NC: Duke University Press.

Tengö, M., Hill, R., Malmer, P. et al. (2017). Weaving knowledge systems in IPBES, CBD and beyond – lessons learned for sustainability. *Current Opinion in Environmental Sustainability*, *26*, 17–25.

Thatcher, J., O'Sullivan, D., and Mahmoudi, D. (2016). Data colonialism through accumulation by dispossession: New metaphors for daily data. *Environment and Planning D: Society and Space*, *34*(6), 990–1006.

Thew, H., Middlemiss, L., and Paavola, J. (2020). "Youth is not a political position": Exploring justice claims-making in the UN Climate Change Negotiations. *Global Environmental Change 61*, 102036.

Tracy, S. J. (2010). Qualitative quality: Eight "big-tent" criteria for excellent qualitative research. *Qualitative Inquiry*, *16*(10), 837–851.

Tuck, E. and Yang, K. W. (2012). Decolonization is not a metaphor. *Decolonization: Indigeneity, Education & Society*, *1*(1), 1–40.

Vadrot, A. B. M. (2020a). Multilateralism as a "site" of struggle over environmental knowledge: The north-south divide. *Critical Policy Studies*, *14*(2), 233–245. https://doi.org/10.1080/19460171.2020.1768131.

Vadrot, A. B. M. (2020b). Building authority and relevance in the early history of IPBES. *Environmental Science and Policy*, 113, 14–20.

Vadrot, A., Langlet, A., and Tessnow-von Wysocki, I. (2021a). Who owns marine biodiversity? Contesting the world order through the "common heritage of humankind" principle. *Environmental Politics*, *31*(2), 226–250.

Vadrot, A., Langlet, A., Tessnow-von Wysocki, I. et al. (2021b). Marine biodiversity negotiations during COVID-19: A new role for digital diplomacy? *Global Environmental Politics*, 1–18.

Vine Deloria, J. R. (1997). Anthros, Indians, and planetary reality. In T. Biolsi and L. J. Zimmerman, eds., *Indians and Anthropologists: Vine Deloria, Jr., and the Critique of Anthropology*, Tucson, AZ: The University of Arizona Press, pp. 209–222.

Wedeen, L. (2010). Reflections on ethnographic work in political science. *Annual Review of Political Science*, *13*, 255–272.

Widick, R., and Foran, J. (2016). Whose utopia? Our utopia! Competing visions of the future at the UN climate talks. *Nature and Culture*, *11*(3), 296–321.

Wilmer, H., Meadow, A. M., Brymer, A. B. et al. (2021). Expanded ethical principles for research partnership and transdisciplinary natural resource management science. *Environmental Management*, 68(4), 453–467. https://doi.org/10.1007/s00267-021-01508-4.

Witter, R., Marion Suiseeya, K. R., Gruby, R. L. et al. (2015). Moments of influence in global environmental governance. *Environmental Politics*, *24*(6), 894–912.

Wolfinger, N. H. (2002). On writing fieldnotes: Collection strategies and background expectancies. *Qualitative Research*, *2*(1), 85–93.

Zanotti, L. and Marion Suiseeya, K. R. (2020). Doing feminist collaborative event ethnography. *Journal of Political Ecology*, *27*(1), 961–987.

Zanotti, L. and Palomino-Schalscha, M. (2016). Taking different ways of knowing seriously: Cross-cultural work as translations and multiplicity. *Sustainability Science*, *11*(1), 139–152.

11

Collaboration

Working Together Across Time and Space

NOELLA J. GRAY, CATHERINE CORSON, LISA M. CAMPBELL, PETER R. WILSHUSEN, REBECCA L. GRUBY, AND SHANNON HAGERMAN

11.1 Introduction

In 2008, our multidisciplinary team of researchers arrived at the World Conservation Congress in Barcelona to experiment with a new methodology: collaborative event ethnography (CEE). While relying on traditional ethnographic methods (participant observation and interviews), the methodology was novel in two respects. First, we approached the large international meeting as a field site – a place where ideas about biodiversity conservation are circulated, performed, and negotiated (Campbell et al. 2014). For a team of anthropologists and geographers accustomed to conducting research in rural communities and local-level field sites, "studying up" (Nader 1972) at an international event was a new experience. Second, in order to better manage the complex multitude of topics and events that comprise a single international meeting, we coordinated our research efforts as a group (Brosius and Campbell 2010). The result was a long-term endeavor to develop and continually refine a collaborative ethnographic methodology for the study of global environmental governance.

Global environmental governance (GEG) is "a field that includes the institutions, processes, initiatives, actors, and organizations that shape environmental actions and outcomes in the global realm" (O'Neill et al. 2013, 443). While many GEG scholars are grounded in political science, particularly international relations and global environmental politics, we approach the study of GEG from geography and anthropology traditions. This has informed our analytical focus (e.g., on scale, performance; see Campbell et al. 2014) as well as our emphasis on the logics, discourses, and social technologies that constitute GEG, rather than the institutions and structures (Corson et al. 2019). This approach to GEG is consistent with the concept of "agreement-making," as both assert the need to extend analysis beyond "the interplay among state actors in a negotiation room" (O'Neill et al. 2013, 450).

In this chapter, we reflect on our experiences with collaboration. While we have written about the CEE methodology elsewhere, describing its use at particular events (Brosius and Campbell 2010; Campbell et al. 2014) and exploring its utility for understanding GEG (Corson et al. 2014a; Corson et al. 2019), the purpose of this chapter is to offer an introduction to the methodology and to consider approaches to and benefits of collaboration in the context of GEG research more generally.[1] We recognize that not everyone is in a position to organize or join a CEE team. Regardless, our lessons regarding collaboration are more widely applicable to collaborative research. Further, less structured forms of collaboration for studying large international meetings are also possible, as we discuss later (and see Reflection Box 11.1).

Reflection Box 11.1 Reflections from a "lone" ethnographer
By Harriet Thew

Similar to the CEE approach, I used participant observation, interviews, and document analysis in my PhD. I also share an interest in power-laden interactions between participants within global environmental agreement-making spaces –in my case, the UN Framework Convention on Climate Change (UNFCCC). Building trust with participants to shed light on the invisible power dynamics shaping lived experiences of agreement-making was a critical component of my ethnographic research.

In my PhD, I studied youth participants' perceptions and articulations of justice in the UNFCCC, and I found that trust was crucial to determining whether their private perceptions matched their public articulations of justice claims. This led to a deeper understanding of justice claims making as a power-laden process (Thew et al. 2020). Although I was not able to interpret data with other researchers, as within a CEE team, having established trust with the youth participants I was studying, I was invited to their private meetings within which they engaged in similar processes of meaning-making to those described within a CEE team. Participants would regularly reflect on activities and events, comparing their individual interpretations and challenging each other's ideas, which helped me to incorporate a wider range of perspectives than just my own.

It is possible that working within a team could enable new researchers to benefit from trust already developed by more experienced team members, rather than "starting from scratch" in building relationships with key stakeholders. This would be particularly valuable if introductions could be made ahead of large conferences to alleviate the time pressures experienced researching these sites. As is encouraged in this chapter, this would depend upon a collaborative rather than competitive approach to sharing professional contacts with new researchers, challenging neoliberal tendencies in the academy and ultimately resulting in better working environments and better quality research.

Another issue with analyzing data alone is that it is more difficult to achieve "productive tension" – a key element of CEE – though if you are unable to join a CEE team this is still possible to incorporate in other ways. For example, I engaged my participants in "communicative validation" (Gaskell and Bauer 2000), checking my interpretation of previous interviews and observations with my participants during subsequent periods of data collection. Participants seemed to enjoy this process, and on several occasions offered alternative perspectives which helped to shape my thinking. Alternatively, it may be possible to discuss your observations with other researchers at the conference site – for example, the UNFCCC has an active young

[1] This chapter reprints and builds on material from Corson et al. (2019) and Gray et al. (2020). Corson, C., L. M. Campbell, P. Wilshusen and N. J. Gray (2019). Assembling global conservation governance. *Geoforum* 103: 56–65, with permission from Elsevier. Gray, N. J., C. Corson, L. M. Campbell, P. Wilshusen, R. L. Gruby and S. Hagerman (2020). Doing Strong Collaborative Fieldwork in Human Geography. *Geographical Review* 110(1–2): 117–132. Reprinted by permission of Taylor & Francis Ltd, www.tandfonline.com on behalf of © 2020 by the American Geographical Society of New York https://americangeo.org/.

researcher network – though ethical processes regarding anonymity and confidentiality would have to be adhered to.

As an ethnographer in this field, I have faced several challenges from more quantitatively minded reviewers who have questioned the rigor of my findings given the relatively small number of participants, which is common and often necessary in deep qualitative work. Although recognition of the value of deep qualitative approaches is growing, the collaborative nature of CEE could support students to overcome this hurdle to publishing their work by offering students a larger dataset to draw upon.

Finally, it is impossible to overstate the psychological benefits of attending global environmental conferences as part of a team. The experience is often physically and emotionally draining and having others to share it with is necessary for your wellbeing. If it is not possible to attend as part of a formal CEE team, I would strongly recommend creating an informal delegation with other attendees from your institution, case study organization, or country or joining the *ENB* team. I traveled with my research participants, stayed in the same accommodation or close-by, and met almost every evening for debriefs. The camaraderie of sharing stories, emotions, and challenges motivated me and is something I will treasure forever.

As authors, we have each participated in multiple versions of CEE, and are still working together to develop and apply the methodology. Some of us have participated in different capacities (e.g., Gray, Gruby, and Hagerman began the collaboration as graduate students), while others have always played a leadership role (e.g., Campbell was a co-principal investigator in the initial iteration of CEE in 2008). More than fifty researchers have contributed to our CEE efforts over time. We acknowledge their contributions to our work – including our experiences with and reflections on collaboration – but we do not claim to speak for all CEE participants.

The chapter proceeds in six parts. We begin by documenting the development of CEE across five events, focusing specifically on how we have organized our collaborative efforts, how this has changed over time, and how this enables a focus on agreement-making. Next, we consider the benefits of collaboration for GEG research in general, before moving to a discussion of the specific benefits of "strong" collaboration as practiced in CEE. We then reflect on the theoretical insights we have generated using CEE, noting how these relate to an understanding of environmental agreement-making and reflecting on how these were enabled by (and arose iteratively through) our collaborative methodology, which has directed our attention to transformations in meaning across time and space. Building on these theoretical and methodological reflections, we then discuss the more practical elements of CEE: how to do it, and lessons we have learned along the way. We conclude with a brief discussion of collaboration in the context of the broader scholarly landscape.

11.2 The Development of Collaborative Event Ethnography

We developed CEE to examine how actors who are normally dispersed in time and space come together at large international meetings to facilitate, structure, and disseminate shifting approaches to GEG. We have focused specifically on biodiversity conservation, though other scholars have adapted and applied our methodology to other fields (e.g., illegal wildlife trade: see Massé et al. 2020; climate change: see Marion Suiseeya and Zanotti 2019). CEE assembles teams of ethnographers, building on and adapting a variety of ethnographic approaches such as multisited ethnography (Marcus 1995), institutional ethnography (Smith 1987, 2006; Billo and Mountz 2015), multisited institutional ethnography (Lewis et al. 2003; Bebbington and Kothari 2006), collaborative multisited ethnography (Choy et al. 2009a, 2009b), and team ethnography (Erickson and Stull 1998). (For those new to ethnography as a methodology for studying GEG, Chapter 10 provides an introduction).

We have conducted CEE at five international environmental meetings, plus additional preceding events in some cases: the IUCN World Conservation Congress in Barcelona in 2008 (2008 WCC); the 10th Conference of the Parties of the Convention on Biological Diversity, held in Nagoya, Japan in 2010 (CBD-COP10); the United Nations Conference on Sustainable Development held in Rio de Janeiro, Brazil in 2012 ("Rio+20"); the IUCN World Parks Congress held in Sydney, Australia in 2014 (2014 WPC); and the IUCN World Conservation Congress in Honolulu, USA in 2016 (2016 WCC). These include both official meetings associated with multilateral agreements (e.g., the CBD COP) as well as meetings associated with international organizations (e.g., IUCN). This reflects our interest in environmental agreement-making more broadly (Hughes et al. 2021; see also Chapter 1), recognizing that formal environmental agreements are both informed by, and inform, myriad related international conservation policies and practices. At these meetings, we observe the multiple actors that constitute contemporary GEG; in addition to states, we observe nongovernmental organizations (NGOs), scientists, private sector representatives, Indigenous Peoples and organizations, and others. We also follow the multiple sites that constitute these events; in addition to official negotiations, we attend side events, press releases, protests outside of venues, and other related activities.

Our approach has evolved over time (see Table 11.1 for a summary). Large international meetings provide opportunities for researchers to observe "agreement-making" – the dynamic processes of governance that unfold in time-condensed settings – and to interview actors who are otherwise difficult to access (see Chapter 9). However, meetings typically occur over one to two weeks, with multiple parallel events (plenary sessions, contact groups, side events, press releases, informal sessions, etc.; see Chapters 6 and 7), making it difficult for an individual researcher to capture the scope and scale of the numerous processes and events that comprise a single meeting. To tackle this challenge, our initial experience at the 2008 WCC was modeled after conservation organizations and (some) national delegations who send large teams to events (Brosius and Campbell 2010).[2] Our collaborative approach enabled us to better make sense of this large, complex, fragmentary meeting – it gave us "more eyes and ears" across the event. However, although we shared an overarching focus on trade-offs between conservation and development and met daily to share insights and perspectives during a debriefing session, our approach to collaboration

[2] The initial idea for CEE emerged during a workshop hosted by Pete Brosius as part of the Advancing Conservation in a Social Context project. Brosius and participants Ken MacDonald and Lisa Campbell developed the CEE idea, and recruited interested graduate students and researchers to join the inaugural CEE. Pete Brosius credits Adam Henne with the original idea for CEE; Henne was unable to participate in our 2008 CEE, but sent a graduate student to join us.

Table 11.1 *Collaborative event ethnography sites*

Date/meeting	Location	Number of researchers	Group organization
2008 IUCN 4th World Conservation Congress (2008 WCC)	Barcelona, Spain	16 core researchers, 6 affiliated researchers*	Researchers pursued individual interests while addressing shared questions focused on conservation and development trade-offs
2010 CBD 10th Conference of the Parties (CBD COP10)	Nagoya, Japan	17 core researchers	Researchers organized into subteams, via a matrix of topics and themes, within larger theoretical frames. National Science Foundation–funding supported pre-event training and postevent analysis and writing retreat.
2012 United Nations (UN) Conference on Sustainable Development (Rio+20)	Rio de Jaineiro, Brazil	12 core researchers	Two main teams tracking the Green and Blue Economies. Two subteams within the Green Economy, tracking "business" and "civil society" engagement
2014 IUCN 6th World Parks Congress (2014 WPC)	Sydney, Australia	11 core researchers, 4 affiliated researchers	Three subteams, one tracking "business and biodiversity," one tracking "oceans," and one tracking both "rights and justice" and "conservation finance"
2016 IUCN 6th World Conservation Congress (2016 WCC)	Honolulu, Hawaii	13 core researchers	Four subteams, tracking "business and biodiversity," "rights," "oceans," and "forests." NSF funding supported pre-event training, postevent analysis and writing retreat, and a "cascade mentoring" model

* *Affiliated researchers are those who were also attending the conference, knew of or found out about our work, and joined in some parts of the collaboration on site or in later writing projects.*

was underdeveloped at this initial stage; we still worked primarily as individuals, followed distinct topics and interests, collected and analyzed data individually, and wrote most of the resulting papers individually.

Reflecting afterward, we realized that we had underestimated the potential for stronger collaboration. Very few of the collaborative insights generated during our collective debriefs – such as the impacts of the orchestration of the event or cross-topic thematic linkages – appeared in the final publications by individual authors. We wanted to push the methodology to ensure our collective interpretive efforts translated into research outputs. With this motivation, core members of the 2008 team decided to work together again, adopting a more structured approach to collaboration for our next CEE at CBD COP10 (Campbell et al. 2014). We have continued to adapt the CEE methodology over time, purposefully moving toward stronger forms of collaboration at all stages of the research, while also working within logistical constraints. In the following sections, we review the benefits and challenges that we have experienced as we have developed this methodology. We begin with the practical benefits and challenges, which apply to collaborative work more broadly. We then discuss the theoretical and methodological benefits and challenges of "strong" collaboration, as practiced in CEE.

11.3 Practical Benefits and Challenges of Collaboration

Whether they are engaged in CEE or not, researchers may benefit from collaboration. One pragmatic benefit is the intellectual and social support that individuals get from working in a team. Conducting research collaboratively provides researchers the opportunity to share concerns, challenges, and uncertainties, ranging from making sense of an observation to navigating public transportation. In CEE, we share accommodations, discuss observations over meals as well as during formal debriefing sessions, lament the absence of Wi-Fi or electrical outlets, share stories of over- or underheated rooms, vent after stressful encounters, send texts and instant messages to stay in contact and update one another on relevant items or agenda changes, bounce around ideas during subway and bus rides, and share a knowing smile when an "a-ha" research moment happens. At several iterations of CEE (2008 and 2014; see Table 11.1) we engaged less formally in "loose" collaborations with affiliated researchers who were also present at the events, but who were not core members of our CEE teams. For researchers working alone at large international meetings, there are always opportunities to connect with, learn from, and support other researchers.

In addition to benefits, there are a variety of challenges for conducting collaborative research (Erickson and Stull 1998). Team dynamics have affected our experiences with CEE. For example, we have previously acknowledged a gender imbalance in our work (Campbell et al. 2014) (see Chapters 2 and 5 for further discussions of gender and GEG research). Women have tended to share more, and richer, data; women have been more willing to perform team tasks vs. individual tasks (e.g., collect data for collective projects vs. individual projects); and women have performed more tedious, logistical tasks associated with conducting fieldwork (completing ethical applications, arranging access, booking tickets, finding accommodations, coordinating fieldwork activities). While there have been notable exceptions to this imbalance, it is necessary to consider and address any inequities that arise in and affect collaborative research.

On the other hand, we have had many women team members who have been pregnant, breastfeeding, dealing with teenage children in crisis from a distance, and otherwise navigating the challenges of combining motherhood and fieldwork. Having other women on the team was a valuable support mechanism. Support for women has also extended beyond fieldwork, as senior team members have mentored junior team members across institutions in the tenure process, grant writing, and networking. The fact that five of the authors of this chapter are women suggests that appreciation for the benefits of CEE, including personal support and professional mentorship, has outweighed the challenges related to gender inequality. We have also worked collectively to address our concerns regarding the gendered division of labor over time, both by recognizing it within the group and through more explicit communication regarding expectations and team commitments.

Another challenge relates to authorship. The time and effort required for collaborative research and writing is no less than for individual fieldwork and single authorship – in fact, often the collaborative negotiation takes more time. However, the accounting system of the neoliberal academy does not consistently reward this effort, attuned as it is to individual accomplishments (Choy et al. 2009a). What this accounting system fails to recognize is that strong collaborative work is also strong individual work – each author on a CEE paper has participated in all aspects of the research, and the collective interpretation reached would not be possible without the contribution of each individual involved (see Section 11.5). We have described this work carefully in tenure and promotion packages, for example, in order to ensure it is evaluated appropriately.

In addition to the challenge of effectively communicating the value of our efforts to external audiences, we have struggled to negotiate appropriate authorship strategies internally (see Section 11.3). In more than one instance, one of us or one of our collaborators has felt insufficiently recognized by their position in a list of authors; being the eighth of nine authors suggests a minor effort that is inconsistent with the work of CEE. However, we have maintained the practice of listing authors as individuals, in order based on their relative contribution to the text of any given paper, to meet institutional demands (and per our authorship protocol). In some instances, we have included footnotes to document equal contributions of authors. We have sometimes used collectively agreed language to acknowledge all members of a given CEE team, even where they are not authors, and we use this language to document our work for our institutions. Other strategies are possible, including explaining coauthors' contributions in methods sections and using unconventional author naming, such as collective names or merged names (Creamer 2005). Our goal of challenging traditional, individualist modes of knowledge production is difficult to reconcile with institutional demands and academic conventions.

For graduate students who wish to participate in CEE (or other collaborative research), we recommend discussing this with your advisor as soon as possible, including strategies for conducting collaborative research as part of, or in addition to, your thesis. One of us (Gruby) included a paper using CEE as one chapter in her dissertation (with Campbell as co-author). We have also advised other students who have included chapters in their thesis that use CEE, where they are the lead author; in other cases, students have led or participated in papers using CEE as side projects while completing dissertation research on related topics. While individual dissertation research has been the norm in most social science research, both norms and institutional rules are changing; be sure to know what these are in your specific context. Overall, we think the benefits for graduate students who engage in CEE far outweigh the challenges, so long as attention is paid to the recommendations and challenges we outline in this chapter.

11.4 Benefits and Challenges of "Strong" Collaboration

While the practical benefits of collaborating discussed here are important, the benefits of CEE specifically go beyond this, arising from our "strong" collaborative approach (Choy et al. 2009a, 2009b; Gray et al. 2020). In contrast with forms of collaboration characterized by a division of labor among researchers, where the aim is the production of outputs that represent the sum of this labor, strong collaboration focuses on productive tensions and requires an openness to rethinking questions, assumptions, and disciplinary perspectives. In addition to the logistical strength of more researchers (more "eyes and ears" at an event), CEE is characterized by an intensive, rigorous, reflexive, and synergistic approach to collaboration throughout the research process, from research design to data collection to analysis and writing. This distinguishes CEE from simply sharing data and ideas among a group of researchers.

Yet a core challenge is to transform our "dispersed consciousness" – created as each of us observes different events and speaks to different people – into a "collective," albeit dynamic, consciousness (Corson et al. 2019). Ethnography is an inherently individual endeavor, in which the data collected are embedded in an individual's situated knowledge and observations, informed by the individual's theoretical training and obtained by pursuing ideas that emerge in the process of research. In CEE, each of us comes with different theoretical training, background knowledge, and field experience that shape how we approach fieldwork and how we analyze, theorize, and write-up results. The tension between the process of ethnographic research as an individual experience and the benefits of the collaborative venture creates our greatest challenge: how to realize the benefits of collaboration – theoretically, practically, and substantively – without sacrificing the importance of individual flexibility and interest (Campbell et al. 2014; Corson et al. 2014a, 2014b).

However, this challenge is also the greatest benefit of CEE. Through strong collaboration, CEE has allowed us to develop a more comprehensive and nuanced understanding that would not have been possible working alone. For example, our efforts to understand the dominance of protected areas as conservation tools were strengthened by our different perspectives on how protected areas were invoked, by whom, and for what purposes at the 10th Conference of the Parties to the Convention on Biological Diversity (Corson et al. 2014b; Gray et al. 2014). Our initial discussions in relation to the Corson et al. (2014b) paper focused on trying to reconcile differences among our various individual observations and perspectives; some team members observed a dominance of market-based approaches and economic logic, while others emphasized the framing of protected areas in relation to Indigenous rights or science-based planning. Some of these differences arose because we observed different events (e.g., those featuring Indigenous actors vs. private sector actors vs. international NGOs), while others resulted from distinct theoretical orientations (e.g., drawing on Marxist political economy or science and technology studies). Working through our differences led us to a negotiated, collective understanding of protected areas as a hegemonic conservation tool. This collective understanding allows for a conceptualization of the role of protected areas in global conservation governance that would not have been possible otherwise – it is a whole that is different than the sum of its parts.

Collective interpretation of data is further supported through our continual learning from one another. Through collective debriefings at the events themselves as well as ongoing collaboration before and after the event, we learn about other team members' observations as well as how they interpret these observations. For example, our blue economy subteam at Rio+20 benefited from learning from other team members' analyses, as they interpreted their observations in relation to theoretical frameworks of "grabbing green" (Corson et al. 2013) and economistic approaches to environmental governance (Wilshusen and MacDonald 2017). By working alongside each other at the event and discussing our observations during debriefing sessions, we can compare how we apply a theoretical framework to observations, enabling continual reflection on how our theoretical framework shapes what we see at events and how we interpret these data. Later, when writing up our results, the subteam returned to these shared fieldwork experiences regularly, discussing both our observations and previous debrief conversations. Our large-group debriefs helped us to understand how framings of oceans as natural capital aligned with a dominant discourse of "green economy," while our subteam's shared observations of competing discourses related to the rights of small-scale fishers and the interests of small island developing states helped us to contextualize the blue economy as contested (Silver et al. 2015; Corson et al. 2019). While our collaborative efforts extend beyond the fieldwork phase of research, they are always and necessarily grounded in our shared experiences at the events themselves.

The main strength of strong collaborative ethnographic methodologies is thus the insight generated through negotiating the interpretation of data (Gerstl-Pepin and Gunzenhauser 2002; Creese and Blackledge 2012). Strong collaboration allows researchers to account for divergences in observations and to negotiate multiple understandings or disagreements over the meaning of data, while also building on one another's insights. Such efforts do not get closer to a definitive interpretation of "the truth"; rather, they incorporate multiple interpretations of and perspectives on the data. Although it is challenging to create the time and space to work through differences, it is the collective engagement in this interpretive zone that allows knowledge to be constructed.

11.5 From Methodology to Theory and Back Again

While the initial emphasis in CEE was on the study of a particular, bounded event, it subsequently expanded to look across and beyond individual events – both from international meetings to local research sites and across multiple international meetings. Now, as we investigate the historical context of particular issues, track intersessional activities, and relate observations at international meetings to place-based field sites, our data collection extends before and after specific conferences and across sites dispersed in both time and space (Campbell et al. 2014). In CEE, we take as the ethnographic object not the negotiations themselves, but the transformation in meaning and governance processes that they represent (Corson et al. 2014a, 2019); put differently, we are interested in *agreement-making* (including processes of meaning-making) rather than agreements themselves. Through the development of CEE as a methodology, we have tracked these changes in meaning over time (Corson et al. 2019).

As we explore in Corson et al. (2019), we have observed how even as advocates did not always reach their ultimate goals, they used these events to institutionalize narratives and logics that paved the way for future progress. For example, in contrast to the lack of interest by many parties at the CBD-COP10 in extending the CBD's work to areas beyond national jurisdiction (the high seas) (Gray et al. 2014), oceans advocates at Rio+20 pushed for the outcome document to include a commitment to negotiate an agreement under the UN Convention on the Law of the Sea that would pave the way for high seas marine protected areas (MPAs) (Campbell et al. 2013). Although this language was not ultimately included, deliberations at Rio+20 nonetheless served to build further support for the concept of high seas MPAs. Subsequent circulation of technological advances in visualizing and monitoring ecological conditions and threats on the high seas at the 2014 World Parks Congress further solidified the idea of introducing high seas MPAs as a governance approach. This example demonstrates how each meeting further solidified the logic of high seas MPAs as possible objects of global conservation governance and aligned diverse actors around this logic, even as advocates failed to realize their goals at any particular meeting (Gray 2018).

By treating transformation in meaning and governance processes as the object of study, CEE directs attention to differences across spaces within a single event, changes over time within a single body (e.g., the CBD-COP), and transformations across both time and events. For example, given the rise of goals-based environmental governance more broadly (Kanie and Biermann 2017), we have been interested in the increasing influence of targets in global biodiversity governance (Campbell et al. 2014). Targets are a key element for formal agreements (e.g., the CBD) and other major UN-sponsored meetings (e.g., Rio+20, which led to the Sustainable Development Goals), as well as featuring within the nonbinding outcomes of other major events. In contrast with CBD-COP10 and Rio+20, where negotiations of decision text were largely visible, the 2014 World Parks Congress did not feature formal negotiations or voting, and the production of its nonbinding outcome document, "The Promise of Sydney," was mostly hidden, with component parts drafted in technically open, but poorly advertised, groups of mostly IUCN staff and affiliates. This more informal deliberative process reflected the perspectives of a small subset of participants, such that when the document was revealed at the closing plenary, critics of the marine section argued that the recommendation that 30 percent of oceans have no extractive use permitted did not represent the views of the broader marine constituency, specifically those interested in small-scale fisheries (Charles et al. 2016; Campbell and Gray 2019).

Despite this, The Promise of Sydney would perform important political work at the subsequent 2016 World Conservation Congress. During negotiations on a resolution related to MPAs (WCC-2016-Res-050), representatives of nongovernmental organizations (NGOs) invoked The Promise of Sydney's recommendation that 30% of the oceans have no extractive activities as a pre-existing commitment, in spite of the protest at the WPC 2014 that it was not representative and objections to it voiced again during WCC deliberations. Ultimately, the preambular text of Res-050 repeated the WPC 2014 recommendation verbatim and the resolution called for 30% of oceans in highly protected MPAs with no extractive use. This 30% target then appeared again in the "zero draft" of the CBD's post-2020 global biodiversity framework (CBD 2020), making its way back to negotiations related to a formal international agreement. MPA proponents have thus perpetuated the logic of conservation enclosures, particularly "no take" MPAs, using the 30% target as a social device. Following discussions of biodiversity targets across multiple venues has allowed us to observe how various actors aligned around this device and how the GEG assemblage shifted in relation to this device over time.

Our continual refinement of the CEE methodology has coincided with an evolution in our understanding(s) of GEG – they have been mutually constituted. Elsewhere, we argue that the concept of "assemblage" is useful for examining the constantly shifting, indeterminate relations among diverse elements that constitutes GEG (Corson et al. 2019). Like others who have used strong collaborative ethnographic approaches (Choy et al. 2009a, 2009b), our CEE teams mimic the assemblages we study. However, in contrast with Choy et al., we did not begin with assemblage; rather, we arrived at assemblage as a useful theoretical approach through reflecting on our evolving methodology as part of our collective interpretive process (see Section 11.4). Throughout the fifteen years that we have been doing CEE, the research team has come together in different configurations at different moments in time, drawing on diverse and shifting experiences, theoretical interests, and topical expertise. Reflecting on our methodology as dynamic and relational has helped us to also understand how our research subjects adapt to an interplay between individual circumstances and organizational context and underscores GEG as continually produced (Corson et al. 2019).

11.6 Doing CEE: Guidelines and Lessons Learned

As we have developed and adapted CEE over time, our theoretical and methodological insights have been complemented by more practical "lessons learned" about how to conduct CEE. We review these here, offering a combination of guidance on how to conduct CEE specifically, as well as a set of considerations and advice for anyone interested in engaging in collaborative research on GEG, using CEE or another approach. Suggestive rather than prescriptive, these guidelines should be adapted to suit the particular team and project.

11.6.1 Prior to the Meeting

1. *Identify the meeting you will attend and the purpose of the research.* We have reflected elsewhere on our own approach to identifying meetings and research objectives through various iterations of CEE (Corson et al. 2019). The rationale for choosing particular meetings to study will vary across researchers, depending upon research questions and interests, meeting agendas, and practical considerations (timing, funding, etc.). Collaboratively developing specific research questions and a shared theoretical approach proceeds iteratively throughout the premeeting stage.
2. *Find funding.* For some events we have been successful in securing grants that support all aspects of the work (at CBD-COP10 and 2016 WCC); the core team applied for funding, then assembled the rest of the team (including recruiting students) once funding was in place. For other events individuals have found internal university grants to

support their participation. For those CEEs where we had core funding, we were better able to support the processes necessary to facilitate successful collaboration. However, we have worked together successfully under tighter budgets, so lack of a large grant should not deter collaborations.

3. *Assemble a team of good collaborators.* For graduate students interested in initiating collaboration, this could begin with conversations with your advisor or other graduate students in your program or network, or perhaps with other students/colleagues you meet at the first meeting you attend. What makes a "good" collaborator? First and foremost, they should have shared research interests and be interested in collaborating and in doing the work that this entails (see points 4–11). But the team is more than the sum of individuals; diversity within a team can enhance scientific insights as well as contribute to overcoming systemic barriers in the academy. We have included women at diverse career stages and students from equity-seeking groups, for example, although our teams have had few members from the Global South.
4. *Plan and conduct pre-event training and team building.* Identify the training that is required prior to the event (e.g., orientation to the event itself, the organizations involved, specific methods to be used, etc.). Plan a schedule of pre-event workshops (in-person or online) that address the team's training needs and identify individuals to lead each workshop. We held webinars on participant observation and note-taking, history and politics of the focal agreement or organization, and other topics. When organized into a syllabus, these may be eligible for course credit for students. This training stage should include collaborative refinement of research questions and research instruments (see point 9), informed by a shared theoretical framework (see Campbell et al. (2014) for one example). The theoretical framework may be developed by the PI(s), codeveloped by the larger team, or developed by subteams. Team building is also essential, especially if collaborators do not already know one another, and should include reviewing and/or negotiating and being transparent about responsibilities.
5. *Plan logistics.* Your team may need to register and be accredited (individually or as a group) to attend the meeting. Documents are required, sometimes with high-level university signatures. Some team members may need travel visas. Flights need to be purchased. Ground transportation and accommodations are needed on site. Coordinating this among team members requires time (and often patience). Refer to Chapter 2 for advice on logistical matters.
6. *Obtain ethical approval for the research.* Be sure to know and follow the ethical guidelines for research at your institution and in your country (see Chapter 2). When coordinating team members across multiple institutions/countries, make sure to coordinate ethical approval.
7. *Organize the team.* Clear organization is essential for on-site coordination. Discuss your options, including working together as one big team, in smaller teams focused on particular topics, or as intersecting smaller teams (i.e., with researchers participating in more than one small team). We have used various strategies at different events (see Table 11.1), depending on the size and structure of the meeting, team composition and interests, and other variables.

8. *Develop a data collection plan.* Depending on how you organize your team, discuss how this organization maps onto the event itself. Identify who will be responsible for collecting data at different event venues (e.g., plenary sessions, contact groups, side events, etc.) and how you will disperse individuals across the various event venues. At some meetings we maximized "coverage," dispersing team members across as many venues at an event as possible. At other meetings we experimented with sending multiple team members to the same venue, in order to focus on different aspects and facilitate collaborative interpretation of observations. And at still others, individuals prioritized venues that aligned with their own theoretical or topical interests. The size and focus of an event will be an important factor to consider in relation to team size, expertise, and organization.
9. *Develop shared data collection protocols.* In CEE, our data are drawn from a combination of documents, participant observation, and interviews. For documents, we systematically collect all formal documents associated with an event (e.g., draft and final decisions), as well as opportunistically collect other documentation (e.g., pamphlets, reports, etc., that are distributed at side events) (see Chapter 8). For participant observation, we have developed note-taking templates informed by our theoretical approach and specific research questions. These include file-naming protocols, lists of details to be observed and included, and guidelines for things to watch for and what to record (in notes, photos, audio recordings, etc.). For interviews, we have developed shared interview guides that can be adapted as needed (see Chapter 9). See Chapter 10 for further discussion of using ethnographic methods in GEG research.
10. *Develop a data storage plan and data sharing agreement.* A data storage plan will need to be developed consistent with ethical guidelines (see point 5). We have developed a secure data storage system at one of our institutions, where we have saved all CEE data so they are accessible for all team members. We have also developed data sharing protocols, noting who will have access to the data, the expectations of each team member for collecting and sharing data, and guidelines regarding who can use data for what purposes. Since our second CEE at CBD COP10, we have always committed to sharing our data collectively; our data sharing protocol has required ongoing negotiation and communication. We have defaulted to sharing certain kinds of data (e.g., recordings/transcripts, descriptive and sometimes verbatim fieldnotes), while limiting our sharing of interpretive fieldnotes to subteams working on publications together. CEE requires humility regarding the individual ownership of both data and ideas, alongside processes that aim to properly recognize and value individual contributions. We continue to grapple with how to define and bound collective vs. individual ownership of ideas and data generated through collaborative fieldwork, given the constructed, embodied nature of ethnographic data (see Section 11.4). It has been essential to set clear and transparent expectations and to agree on processes for addressing any conflicts or misunderstandings that arise.
11. *Develop shared authorship guidelines.* In addition to a data sharing protocol, authorship protocols are similarly critical. Authorship is one of the most contentious issues in academia, including questions such as who counts as an author and on what basis, who

is included/invited into collaborative publications, and in which order to list authors (alphabetical, amount of work, seniority). It is essential that a team discuss these issues well before data collection begins and agree on a set of principles and guidelines, as well as a process for reviewing guidelines as necessary. In CEE, we have agreed that each author on a paper must have participated in all aspects of the research (including the writing of the paper), given that the collective interpretation reached would not be possible without the contribution of each author listed (see Section 11.5). Our authorship guidelines have evolved over time, inspired most recently by the example provided by Liboiron et al. (2017). We recognize that graduate students and early-career researchers face particular challenges and pressures related to publishing, as discussed in Section 11.3.

11.6.2 At the Meeting

11. *Conduct daily debriefings*. Our insights often emerge initially through our daily debriefings. At some meetings, the schedule allowed us to debrief at a regular time when everyone can participate (best scenario). At other events, the logistics of the event (schedule, transportation logistics, etc.) required us to supplement ad hoc large group debriefings with smaller group meetings – sometimes on the bus or subway on the way to or from the event. Be attentive to power dynamics within group discussions (who speaks, who decides who speaks) and how discussions will be captured (who will take notes, whether or not to record).
12. *Coordinate daily activities*. Each day, adjust the team's data collection plan (who is going where, when) to suit the evolving event schedule (e.g., as contact groups are scheduled in relation to particular decisions, often on a day-by-day basis). Ensure that relevant data are collected related to the team's research questions and priorities. Schedule time for writing/cleaning up notes at the end of each day.
13. *Facilitate regular communication and adapt*. Event schedules change. Demonstrations occur spontaneously. High-profile politicians make surprise appearances. Be attentive to how the event is unfolding and share relevant details with other team members. We have used a variety of tools to keep in touch in real time – figure out what works best for your group and establish expectations for communication, schedule changes, and information sharing.
14. *Ensure all data are backed up and uploaded/shared per the data storage plan*. In our experience, the ideal time to ensure that fieldnotes are complete and that data are organized and appropriately stored is while you are still at the event.

11.6.3 After the Meeting

15. *Develop an analysis and writing plan*. After the event has concluded, develop a plan for analyzing data and writing up the research. While you likely had some idea going into the meeting of outputs that could be produced, discussions and observations at the event may have prompted new ideas. Develop a plan that clearly identifies paper

ideas, relevant data, plans for data analysis (e.g., use of software such as NVivo, who will analyze data and how), authorship (see item 10), and timelines.

16. *Organize a writing retreat.* Collaborators need time to engage in the "interpretive zone" to analyze data and write up results (see Section 11.5). We have found meeting in person to be critical for advancing collective interpretive analysis and writing. Funding to support postevent writing retreats helps (and has enabled this chapter!) If there is a lack of funding or other constraints, then dedicated time to work together remotely – a virtual writing retreat – can substitute.

11.7 Conclusion

Collaboration offers significant benefits for researchers that should not be underappreciated. Amidst changing working conditions for many academics within neoliberal institutions, including an increase in competition, working hours, record-keeping, and productivity expectations, collaborative research is one way to invoke the ideals of slow scholarship (Mountz et al. 2015) and to cultivate joy within our academic labor (Kern et al. 2014). We have developed our collective approach in order to support good scholarship and intellectual growth while cultivating an ethic of care toward one another. If slow scholarship is about "cultivating caring academic cultures and processes" (Mountz et al. 2015, 4), then strong approaches to collaborative research deserve greater attention as a means of fostering slow scholarship.

CEE is not a rigid methodology to be implemented consistently across field sites and research teams. Instead, its strength, and that of strong collaborative approaches more generally, is in its dynamism and flexibility. While CEE supports robust, collective interpretation and facilitates slow scholarship, it also accommodates and fosters individual research interests. For example, Gruby first participated in a CEE at CBD-COP10, while still a graduate student. She contributed to multiple subteams and collective writing projects (e.g., Corson et al. 2014b; Gray et al. 2014), while also pursuing her own individual research interests (Gruby and Campbell 2013). She later co-led a "marine team" at the 2014 World Parks Congress. Similarly, Corson adapted the methodology to lead a team of students in tracking UN negotiations of the Rio+20 "zero draft" over eighteen months in order to better understand what happens prior to as well as at meetings (Corson et al. 2015). CEE can be modified to suit different field sites, research questions, interests, areas of expertise, and capacities of individuals as well as teams.

While GEG research is diverse in its theoretical and methodological approaches, there is an increasing focus on multiscalar relations, networks, and assemblages – in short, on *agreement-making*. And while scholars have developed and adapted a range of innovative methodological approaches for studying GEG (O'Neill et al. 2013), there are limitations to what an individual researcher can do. Following Choy et al. (2009b), we highlight the benefits of strong forms of collaboration.

Collaboration presents many benefits to researchers at all career stages, along with challenges. However, we suggest that if the scholarly potential of collaboration is to be achieved, then it must go beyond team-based work premised on a division of labor, adopting reflexive research practices consistent with strong collaboration. In such efforts, more hands do *not* make light work. Collaborative fieldwork is difficult, time-consuming, and often fraught; we have also found it deeply rewarding, both personally and intellectually.

Further Reading

1. Choy, T. K., Faier, L., Hathaway, M. J. et al. (2009a). Strong Collaboration as a Method for Multi-Sited Ethnography: On Mycorrhizal Relations. In M.-A. Falzon (Ed.), *Multi-Sited Ethnography: Theory, Praxis and Locality in Contemporary Research.* New York: Routledge, pp. 197–214.

For those readers interested in strong collaboration, and how it differs from more common models of collaboration, this chapter elaborates on the relevant methodological and theoretical considerations.

2. Corson, C., Campbell, L. M., Wilshusen, P., and Gray, N. J. (2019). Assembling Global Conservation Governance. *Geoforum* 103, 56–65.

In this paper, we elaborate on how the concept of "assemblage" can be used to understand GEG. We also consider the iterative development of theory and methodology in CEE in more detail.

3. Erickson, K., and Stull, D. (1998). *Doing Team Ethnography: Warnings and Advice.* Thousand Oaks, CA: Sage.

For those interested in conducting CEE, this book provides more extensive and detailed advice regarding how to conduct ethnography collaboratively.

4. Sword, H. (2017). *Air & Light & Time & Space: How Successful Academics Write.* Cambridge, MA: Harvard University Press.

See, in particular, chapter 8 (pp. 123–134), which reflects on the collaborative writing process, including challenges, positive aspects, approaches, and resources for further reflection and learning. Chapter 9 (pp. 135–146) explores the benefits of writing retreats.

References

Bebbington, A., and Kothari, U. (2006). Transnational Development Networks. *Environment and Planning A: Economy and Space*, 38(5), 849–886.

Billo, E., and Mountz, A. (2015). For Institutional Ethnography: Geographical Approaches to Institutions and the Everyday. *Progress in Human Geography*, 40(2), 199–220.

Brosius, J., and Campbell, L. (2010). Collaborative Event Ethnography: Conservation and development trade-offs at the fourth world conservation congress. *Conservation and Society*, 8(4), 245–255.

Campbell, L. M., Corson, C., Gray, N. J. et al. (2014). Studying Global Environmental Meetings to Understand Global Environmental Governance: Collaborative Event Ethnography of the 10th Conference of the Parties to the Convention on Biological Diversity. *Global Environmental Politics*, 14(3), 1–20.

Campbell, L. M., and Gray, N. J. (2019). Area Expansion Versus Effective and Equitable Management in International Marine Protected Areas Goals and Targets. *Marine Policy*, 100, 192–199.

Campbell, L. M., Gray, N. J., Fairbanks, L. W., Silver, J. J., and Gruby, R. L. 2013. Oceans at Rio+20. *Conservation Letters*, 6(6), 439–447.

CBD (2020). Zero Draft of the Post-2020 Global Biodiversity Framework. (CBD/WG2020/2/3). www.cbd.int/doc/c/efb0/1f84/a892b98d2982a829962b6371/wg2020-02-03-en.pdf.

Charles, A., Westlund, L., Bartley, D. M. et al. (2016). Fishing Livelihoods as Key to Marine Protected Areas: Insights from the World Parks Congress. *Aquatic Conservation: Marine and Freshwater Ecosystems*, 26(S2), 165–184.

Choy, T. K., Faier, L., Hathaway, M. J. et al. (2009b). A New Form of Collaboration in Cultural Anthropology: Matsutake Worlds. *American Ethnologist*, 36(2), 380–403.

Corson, C., Brady, B., Zuber, A., Lord, J., and Kim, A. (2015). The Right to Resist: Disciplining Civil Society at Rio+20. *The Journal of Peasant Studies*, 42(3–4), 859–878.

Corson, C., Campbell, L., and MacDonald, K. I. (2014a). Capturing the Personal in Politics: Ethnographies of Global Environmental Governance. *Global Environmental Politics*, 14(3), 21–40.

Corson, C., Gruby, R. L., Witter, R. et al. (2014b). Everyone's Solution? Defining and Re-defining Protected Areas in the Convention on Biological Diversity. *Conservation and Society*, 12(2), 71–83.

Corson, C., MacDonald, K. I., and Neimark, B. (2013). Grabbing "Green": Markets, Environmental Governance and the Materialization of Natural Capital. *Human Geography*, 6(1), 1–15.

Creamer, E. G. (2005). Promoting the Effective Evaluation of Collaboratively Produced Scholarship: A Call to Action. *New Directions for Teaching and Learning*, 102, 85–98. https://doi.org/10.1002/tl.198.

Creese, A., and Blackledge, A. (2012). Voice and Meaning-Making in Team Ethnography. *Anthropology & Education Quarterly*, 43(3), 306–324.

Gaskell, G., and Bauer, M. W. (2000). Towards Public Accountability: Beyond Sampling, Reliability and Validity. In G. Gaskell and M. W. Bauer (Eds.), *Qualitative Researching with Text, Image and Sound: A Practical Handbook for Social Research*. London: Sage. pp. 336–350.

Gerstl-Pepin, C. I., and Gunzenhauser, M. G. (2002). Collaborative Team Ethnography and the Paradoxes of Interpretation. *International Journal of Qualitative Studies in Education*, 15(2), 137–154.

Gray, N. J. (2018). Charted Waters? Tracking the Production of Conservation Territories on the High Seas. *International Social Science Journal*, 68(229–230), 257–272.

Gray, N. J., Corson, C., Campbell, L. M. et al. (2020). Doing Strong Collaborative Fieldwork in Human Geography. *Geographical Review*, 110(1–2), 117–132.

Gray, N. J., Gruby, R., and Campbell, L. M. (2014). Boundary Objects and Global Consensus: Scalar Narratives of Marine Conservation in the Convention on Biological Diversity. *Global Environmental Politics*, 14(3), 64–83.

Gruby, R. L., and Campbell, L. M. (2013). Scalar Politics and the Region: Strategies for Transcending Pacific Island Smallness on a Global Environmental Governance Stage. *Environment and Planning A: Economy and Space*, 45(9), 2046–2063.

Hughes, H., Vadrot, A., Allan, J. I. et al. (2021). Global Environmental Agreement-Making: Upping the Methodological and Ethical Stakes of Studying Negotiations. *Earth System Governance* 10, 100121.

Kanie, N., and Biermann, F. (2017). *Governing through Goals: Sustainable Development Goals as Governance Innovation*. Cambridge, MA: MIT Press.

Kern, L. R., Hawkins, R., Al-Hindi, K. F., and Moss, P. (2014). A Collective Biography of Joy in Academic Practice. *Social & Cultural Geography*, 15(7), 834–851.

Lewis, D., Bebbington, A., Batterbury, S. et al. (2003). Practice, Power and Meaning: Frameworks for Studying Organizational Culture in Multi-Agency Rural Development Projects. *Journal of International Development*, 15(5), 541–557.

Liboiron, M., Ammendolia, J., Winsor, K. et al. (2017). Equity in Author Order: A Feminist Laboratory's Approach. *Catalyst: Feminism, Theory, Technoscience*, 3(2), 1–17.

Marcus, G. E. (1995). Ethnography in/of the World System: The Emergence of Multi-Sited Ethnography. *Annual Review of Anthropology*, 24, 95–117.

Marion Suiseeya, K. R., and Zanotti, L. (2019). Making Influence Visible: Innovating Ethnography at the Paris Climate Summit. *Global Environmental Politics*, 19(2), 38–60.

Massé, F., Dickinson, H., Margulies, J., Joanny, L., Lappe-Osthege, T., and Duffy, R. (2020). Conservation and Crime Convergence? Situating the 2018 London Illegal Wildlife Trade Conference. *Journal of Political Ecology*, 27 (1), 23–42.

Mountz, A., Bonds, A., Mansfield, B. et al. (2015). For Slow Scholarship: A Feminist Politics of Resistance through Collective Action in the Neoliberal University. *ACME: An International Journal for Critical Geographies*, 14(4), 1235–1259.

Nader, L. (1972). Up the Anthropologist: Perspectives Gained from Studying Up. In D. H. Hymes (Ed.), *Reinventing Anthropology*. New York: Pantheon Books, pp. 284–311.

O'Neill, K., Weinthal, E., Marion Suiseeya, K. R. et al. (2013). Methods and Global Environmental Governance. *Annual Review of Environment and Resources*, 38, 441–471.

Silver, J. J., Gray, N. J., Campbell, L. M., Fairbanks, L. W., and Gruby, R. L. (2015). Blue Economy and Competing Discourses in International Oceans Governance. *The Journal of Environment & Development*, 24(2), 135–160.

Smith, D. (1987). *The Everyday World As Problematic: A Feminist Sociology*. Boston, MA: Northeastern University Press.

Smith, D., ed. (2006). *Institutional Ethnography as Practice*. Lanham, MD: Rowman and Littlefield Publishers.

Thew, H., Middlemiss, L., and Paavola, J. (2020). "Youth Is Not a Political Position": Exploring Justice Claims-Making in the UN Climate Change Negotiations. *Global Environmental Change*, 61, 102036.

Wilshusen, P., and MacDonald, K. I. (2017). Fields of Green: Corporate Sustainability and the Production of Economistic Environmental Governance. *Environment and Planning A: Economy and Space*, 49, 1824–1845.

12

Networks

Collecting Data for Social Network Analysis

MATTHEW PATERSON

12.1 Introduction

If you've been to a negotiation site already, or even perhaps if you've just seen snippets on videos shared by NGOs, you'll have been struck by the busyness, with people constantly moving around, huddling in small groups over some document, pulling people aside to get their attention, flicking between their phones or tablets, the people they are with, and perhaps what is going on formally within the negotiating room. Outside, there may be NGOs mobilizing in ways that don't have any obvious central direction. If you haven't been to such a negotiation, but are planning to do so, then get ready for the bustle and hubbub, the quick shifts of attention, the pressing of business cards into palms, the oddness of how intense it is even when nothing actually seems to be happening. If this was a site in climate change politics, it will have been particularly intense and busy, but these dynamics are pervasive throughout environmental agreement-making.

All of these experiences attest to the centrality of networking as an activity within agreement-making processes. Negotiating sites are sites of networking: of making connections with others for a variety of reasons. The act of networking is a key practice for the negotiators, policymakers, lobbyists, campaigners, and experts involved in the negotiating process: key to how they seek to mobilize ideas, build coalitions, and gain support for their proposals.

And these processes of network building may extend way beyond the specific site of negotiations. Actors need to develop ongoing relations with others to generate the effects they seek and may have background networks (educational and/or professional, e.g.,) on which they can draw to build their specific networks in environmental negotiations. I got interested in networks when working on the politics of emissions trading, noticing how many of those involved moved across different identities in their careers (from think tanks or NGOs, to carbon trading firms, to national governments) and it was the sustaining of broad networks that enabled them both to navigate these careers and also mobilize to achieve specific goals by marshalling the diverse connections they had developed. Among other things, this led me to think about realizing the limits of focusing on agreement-making as a process between states, and, in talking in particular to Matthew Hoffmann, I realized the possibilities of using network analysis to unpack these processes more carefully. I also noticed, of course, how many of these people looked structurally like me – white, male,

English-speaking – with all the questions that raises both about the political sociology of global governance and about the positionality of researchers in studying it. My ability to carry out this research effectively may be aided by my own positionality, which privileges me in relation to other researchers, given my social-structural similarity and shared habitus to most of those I am studying.

Beyond the focus on interpersonal relations, networks are also key to understanding the context for any specific negotiating site. That site is part of an overall institution, which in GEP contexts, at least, is increasingly often part of a governance complex – a web of institutions, interstate and transnational, connected to each other in various ways.

Research methods for formally analyzing these networks, be they interorganizational, communicational, interpersonal, or even discursive, exist to enable us to understand the social processes that constitute agreement-making. The methodological tool we can use to do this is called social network analysis (SNA). This method is increasingly used within studies of environmental negotiations to help us understand a number of issues of interest, such as which actors are best placed to mobilize ideas or support for particular proposals; how those actors come to have such authority within a negotiation; how ideas, information, or norms flow and become popular over time within a negotiating process or across a governance complex; and how trust builds within a negotiation.

In this chapter, I hope therefore to show that SNA can make important contributions to understanding agreement-making processes. Recalling the elements of this concept developed in the book's introductory chapter, SNA can help us understand actors by emphasizing their relational ties and how this structures their agency. Regarding sites, it enables a structured analysis of the connectedness of sites across an agreement-making process, as well as of a specific site of agreement-making to the various other sites and contexts that enable it. Regarding processes, it helps us understand in particular relations of authority among actors within processes, as well as flows of information across a process, and hence to how learning might occur in agreement-making. Finally, regarding order-making, it can sharpen our focus on how background social-relational structures – of class, gender, race, education, and geopolitics, most notably – structure participation in agreement-making processes.

12.2 Social Network Analysis

The premise underpinning SNA is that the patterns of relationships within a social system are important determinants of social dynamics and outcomes. The basic unit of analysis is therefore these relations, not the entities to which such relations connect. SNA has become widely used across the social sciences (for introductions, see, e.g., Borgatti et al. 2018; Robins 2015; Scott 2012) and more recently in political science (Hoffmann 2017; Ward et al. 2011).

While many of the examples given in the introduction give a sense of networks as involving a high degree of informality, SNA analyzes networks in formal terms. A number of key concepts are worth describing briefly, as identified in Table 12.1.

Table 12.1 *Key concepts in Social Network Analysis*

Concept	Description
Network	A network in SNA is defined formally as a set of *nodes* and *ties* (the latter sometimes called *edges*). Nodes are the entities that make up the network (e.g., individuals, organizations, treaties, concepts) and ties are the ways in which they are connected (e.g., friendship, employment, parent–child, copresence at a meeting).
Whole network	A *whole network* is composed when we are able to identify all the nodes in the network (e.g., every country in a treaty system). For analyzing a whole network, a really important question is to be able to set the boundaries of the network effectively.
Ego network	An *ego network* is a network starting out from individuals and tracing their connections and relations.
Egos and alters	Nodes are the entities that make up the network. They can be referred to as *egos* or *alters*. This is mostly of importance for data entry, referring to a particular node as the ego and then all the other nodes it is connected to as its alters.
Ties, directionality, and weighting	Ties are the ways in which nodes are connected to each other in a network. Ties may be *directed* if the tie implies a one-way relationship (parent–child, employer–employee) or *undirected* if not (copresence at a meeting). Ties may also be *weighted* if the relationship might have levels of intensity (e.g., financial flows between countries) or *unweighted* if the relationship is simply binary yes/no (e.g., two people work together for the Worldwide Fund for Nature or they do not).
Path	A *path* refers to the sequence of ties that connect any two given nodes. The average path length in a network can be useful to understand the movement of information or the possibility of coordination across a network.
Network density	*Network density* is usually measured via the proportion of ties that exist relative to the total number of ties the network could logically have given its number of nodes. It can tell us about the intensity of relations across the network.
Components	*Components* refer to elements in a network that are unconnected to each other. This may help us understand fragmentation in the system we are analyzing.
Clustering	*Clustering* refers to ways that parts of a network may be more closely connected to each other than to the rest of the network. Clusters can be identified through exploring the degree to which the density of relations varies across the network and, for example, whether there may be *cliques* that merit exploration. A *clique* in network analysis refers to a group of nodes in the network that are completely connected to each other.
Core–periphery relations	This refers to structured patterns of hierarchy across the network where some collection of nodes dominates the network overall and others are relatively marginal. Core nodes in a network have dense connections among themselves while peripheral nodes have most of their connections with the core but not with other peripheral nodes.

Table 12.1 (*cont.*)

Concept	**Description**
Node centrality	At the node level, we are often interested in questions of their *centrality* in the network. There are a number of ways of working out the centrality of nodes within a network. The most commonly used in studies of GEP is the *betweenness* measure, which measures the proportion of the total paths across the network that must flow through any given node, and thus is a measure of that nodes' structural ability to coordinate the network by acting as a gatekeeper, a measure often referred to as *brokerage*.
Node attributes	These are not themselves network measures but, for example, sociological characteristics of nodes that we may be interested in (e.g., in environmental negotiations, we may want to know where NGOs, corporate actors, or state negotiators are in a network, or we may also be interested in the gender, nationality, or educational background of network members).

There are various issues to consider for research design. The most important, perhaps, is to adequately conceptualize the ties and nodes: what can you legitimately infer from these? Identifying the nodes is the easier of the two aspects of this question. But the nature of the ties is crucial and harder. For example, the contributors to this book are connected in a range of ways: friends, coauthors, former or current PhD supervisors or examiners, members of the International Studies Association or Earth Systems Governance Project, or participants in expert processes like the IPCC. A network analysis based on any of these ties would have a different structure, but we can infer very different things from each of these varied types of tie. In practice, there is often a lot more messiness to deciding how to construct these network ties, and to how the complexity of the world and its social relations that we observe then gets transformed into these "ties" between "nodes."

Note also here that some of these connect individuals directly (Hannah and I have written a couple of articles together), while others do so only indirectly (both Hannah and I have been to the ISA conference). These latter ties are called *affiliation* ties and less can be inferred about the strength of the "Hughes–Paterson" tie from them than from the coauthor tie.

The question of ethics also requires consideration. In particular, in network studies, especially of elite networks that are the case for most studies of environmental negotiation sites, we have powerful reasons not to anonymize our data, but this will often encounter difficulties with ethics review boards and, in the European context, GDPR regulations, as discussed in Reflection Box 12.2 and Chapter 2. In general, this is defensible on the grounds that we are studying public policy processes and thus participants in those processes cannot reasonably regard their inclusion as a question of privacy, but those rules do in particular limit us to only connecting data for which we have a legitimate research purpose.

A final consideration regards data availability. In research focused on whole networks, we need more or less complete data (see Reflection Box 12.1). Some types of data are

Reflection Box 12.1 The "analytical problem"

By Arne Langlet

The problem of incomplete data is something I faced in my research, which is often an issue when examining networks of actors involved in agreement-making processes. In my research project, I analyzed networks based on ethnographic data collected during intergovernmental conferences and identified *relations* between actors referencing each other in their statements and interventions. Due to the multitude of actors and the complexity of their interactions within and beyond the negotiation room, errors can occur at different stages of data collection and analysis. For example, typos in ethnographic field notes or confusion over the actors (e.g., when we mistakenly type that a state referred to the "USA" instead of the "ISA") could lead to wrong ties being coded in the computational data analysis.

I also found it difficult to accept that my data was complete and that I had recorded every node and tie that exists in the network. I always felt the need to expand and revisit my data to be sure I had captured all relevant relations and actors. Incomplete data has serious consequences in SNA, as any single missing link (or wrongly existing link) between two nodes can radically change the characteristics of the whole network (Borgatti et al. 2018; Marsden 1990; Paterson 2019).

Incomplete data brought substantial challenges during the analysis. In international negotiation settings, each observed tie brings a wealth of analytical nuances and varying qualities of interaction that may be lost when applying a strict statistical analysis. If we just analyze each reference as one connection, we fail to understand that some are very positive references (e.g., "we agree with the EU") or negative (e.g., "we disagree with the EU"). I had to bear in mind that there were potential gaps or inconsistencies, and I often asked myself "How can this data be analyzed given the possibility of incomplete data and acknowledging the qualitative nuances it contains?"

While many studies applying network analysis use ERGMs to statistically test tie creation (see Section 12.4) or explain the behavior of actors based on their network centrality (Frank 1999), these approaches normally assume the existence of a large and complete dataset. When researching networks in international negotiations, however, it is difficult to obtain a dataset large and complete enough to conduct such sophisticated statistical tests. This is particularly true when analyzing the agreement-making as a process that develops over time, which means that the researcher is required to hold complete datasets for a number of different moments in the process. The analytical approach that I applied instead draws its power from a combination of quantitative network plotting and qualitative observations from within the negotiations.

For example, I regularly looked at the qualitative dimension of the data when I coded a link between two actors. This qualitative analysis of my ethnographic observations confirmed that the relationship I coded did indeed "exist," and I explored the qualitative dimension of it to give meaning to the whole network. In this way, I used the graphical description from the quantitatively coded network analysis as an entry point to further qualitatively explore the data underlying this analysis. Hence, the focus lay on the qualitative dimension of the network data guided by a quantitative description of the network. The amount and the nature of relational data collected within international negotiations favors a more nuanced analysis in this way, which relies on a combination of ethnographic observations with quantitative network mapping.

more readily available than others. For example, Twitter makes automated data collection very easy. Most international organizations and many nonstate governance initiatives have readily accessible basic data – for example, regarding the bureaux or governing boards in their organizations – as well as participants' lists from meetings (although, of course, for many environmental agreement-making sites these latter may be enormous and provide relatively "thin" data). Expert processes are often fairly transparent, and their participants can be readily traced given they work in universities or research institutes. For the most part, these data sources give us data about affiliation ties. Getting data regarding direct tie connections can be much more laborious and difficult, as it will often involve interviews and surveys. But measuring a tie directly can enable richer inferences about node connections than simply measuring, for example, copresence at a meeting.

12.3 Data Collection and Entry

Data collection is centered on identifying and documenting ties between nodes. The first task, therefore, is to translate your answer to the question of defining the network into a clear sense of what the data sources are. Do you get them from documents, direct observation, interviews, surveys, social media, etcetera? The second is to work out what data you want to collect. Do you just want the names for each node, or do you want additional data? For example, if your nodes are individuals, you may want to record various attributes (see Table 12.1) of these individuals. What follows is a step-by-step account. However, in practice there will be a lot more messiness at these various steps: deciding what types of ties you are interested in; working out how to observe and record these ties; decoding various ambiguities in your documents, observations, or interviews; dealing with the various sorts of clunkiness in them (misspellings of names, individuals having more than one "hat") and meticulously cleaning up these issues. This is an inherently messy process, both in practical and analytical terms.

The precise form that data entry will take depends on the SNA software you will be using, as each has its own form. The account here is based on what you would use for UCINET (Borgatti et al. 2002), which is often the software people starting out in SNA use. Here, data entry is typically done in a spreadsheet, although it may be done directly in the spreadsheet within SNA software itself.

Data is most commonly organized either as a matrix or as a "nodelist." In a matrix, the names of the nodes are listed in row one and column one, and then each cell has a number indicating whether the two nodes are connected or not (see Figure 12.2). If the network ties are not weighted, then this will simply be a zero or a one. In a nodelist, column one contains the "ego" (the principal node whose relationships the row describes) and then the cells moving across contain all the other nodes ("alters") to which that node has a tie.

Figure 12.1 shows a screenshot of part of the nodelist that formed the basis of some of the analyses in Hughes and Paterson (2017). This is a coauthoring network (nodes are connected to each other if they had coauthored papers with each other), which we used to understand who is central to the large research teams within the IPCC. In this nodelist, therefore, the first column is a list of all the authors in the IPCC writing team we were

A. Bigio						
A. Bruvoll	B. Larsen	S. Magne	H. Vennemo			
A. DeLaVegaNavarro						
A. Faaij	M. Ahmed	H. Aiking	R. Akanda	F. AliMohamed	D. Arent	A. Awan
A. Gadgil	P. Craig	J. Koomey				
A. Gamez-Vazquez						
A. Garg	S. Ashina	I. Bashmakov	M. Bramley	K. Calvin	J. Christensen	S. Dhar
A. Grubler	X. Bai	F. Bodda	T. Buettner	V. Chirkov	F. Dentener	S. Dhakal
A. Inaba	M. Cohen	E. Hertwich	P. Hofstetter	S. Lorek	E. Sto	A. Tukker
A. Jaffe	R. Newell	K. Palmer	D. Popp	R. Stavins		
A. Kansal						
A. Lanza						
A. Loschel	V. Alexeeva-Talebi	C. Bohringer	A. Dannenberg	G. Kallis	A. Lange	T. Mennel
A. McKinnon	S. Cullinane	J. Edwards	A. Kreie	M. Piecyk		
A. Michaelowa	R. Betz	J. Buen	S. Butzengeiger	P. Castro	S. Feige	F. Flues
A. Muvundika						
A. Patt	A. Aaheim	K. Asante	L. Barras	A. Battaglini	F. Berkhout	G. Brundrit
A. Ramaswami	A. Amekudzi	M. Bernard	S. Carney	E. Chan	A. Chavez	M. Chertow
A. Romanovskaya	H. Ahammad	G. Berndes	H. Bottcher	M. Bustamante	H. Clark	H. Dong
A. Sagar	C. Bremner	M. Grubb	G. Habib	J. Holdren	N. Lam	K. Smith
A. Venables	P. Collier	M. Fujita	P. Krugman			
A. Verbruggen	M. AlMarchohi	M. Fischedick	W. Moomaw	A. Nadai	L. Nilsson	J. Nyboer
A. ZainAhmed						
B. Fungtammasan						
B. Knopf	T. Barker	N. Bauer	L. Baumstark	E. Bellevrat	B. Chateau	Y.-H. Chen
B. Lefevre	M. Yalçin					
B. VanderZwaan	T. Aboumahboub	N. Bauer	J. Bollen	C. Brink	M. Bunn	K. Calvin
C. Carraro	F. Bosello	V. Bosetti	B. Buchner	P. Buonanno	E. DeCian	R. Duval
C. DiazMorejon						
C. Gollier	K. Arrow	M. Cropper	B. Groom	G. Heal	B. Jullien	R. Newell
C. Kolstad	O. Deschenes	J. Freeman	C. Grainger	G. Johnson	D. Kelly	G. Mitchell

Figure 12.1 A screenshot of the nodelist that formed the basis of some of the analysis in Hughes and Paterson (2017).

studying, and the remaining columns are the names of each of their coauthors from all the papers they published that were cited in the bibliography to the IPCC report itself. In the language of network analysis, the authors in column one are each egos and, across their row, each name is one of their alters.

A matrix can be of two types: adjacency or affiliation. In the first of these, the nodes are the same across rows as in columns, and thus the 1 in a cell indicates a direct connection between the nodes (e.g., if you had asked people who their friends are, you could directly generate this sort of matrix). In an affiliation matrix, the nodes across row one and those down column one are different. For example, one common model, which has many analogies in GEP, is in thinking about connections between corporate boards of directors (e.g., Carroll 2010). Here, you would generate an affiliation matrix, with column one containing

Top 44	In institution-centered network?									
	IIASA	UFRJ	UNAM	UoTsinghua	LBNL	UoCalifornia_ Berkeley	UoHarvard	MIT	UoStanford	UoTokyo
Price	Y	Y	Y	Y	Y	Y		Y	Y	Y
Nakicenovic	Y	Y			Y	Y	Y	Y	Y	Y
Clarke	Y	Y		Y		Y	Y	Y	Y	
Grübler	Y				Y	Y		Y	Y	Y
Krey	Y	Y	Y		Y	Y			Y	
Michaelowa	Y		Y			Y	Y		Y	Y
Riahi	Y	Y			Y	Y		Y	Y	
Rogner	Y	Y		Y	Y			Y		Y
Sathaye	Y	Y	Y		Y	Y			Y	
Schaeffer	Y	Y	Y		Y	Y			Y	
Shukla	Y	Y			Y		Y	Y	Y	
Smith	Y	Y	Y	Y	Y	Y				
Van-Vuuren	Y	Y			Y	Y	Y	Y		
Weyant	Y				Y	Y	Y	Y	Y	
Edenhofer	Y	Y				Y	Y	Y		
Höhne	Y	Y					Y	Y	Y	
Ürge-Vorsatz	Y	Y		Y	Y	Y				
Bosetti	Y						Y	Y	Y	
Carraro				Y			Y	Y	Y	
Edmonds	Y					Y		Y	Y	
Faaij	Y	Y	Y			Y				
Gupta, Joyeeta	Y		Y				Y	Y		
Haberl	Y		Y			Y				Y
Hourcade	Y				Y			Y	Y	
Paltsev	Y						Y	Y	Y	
Stavins						Y	Y	Y	Y	
Tavoni	Y						Y	Y	Y	
Victor	Y				Y			Y	Y	
Den-Elzen	Y						Y	Y		
Guan				Y			Y		Y	
Hertwich	Y			Y		Y				
Kriegler	Y								Y	Y
Kunreuther	Y						Y	Y		
Patt	Y					Y	Y			
Sterner						Y	Y		Y	
Weber	Y						Y	Y		
Dhakal	Y									Y
Finus							Y	Y		
Rose	Y						Y			
Winkler		Y			Y					
Cervero						Y				
Creutzig						Y				
Allwood										
Geng										

Figure 12.2 Affiliation matrix of key authors and connected institutions. Note: It would be more normal to have a 1 instead of a Y in the cell, and when I put this into UCINET I must have transformed it in that way.

all the names of the directors you have been able to identify via lists of corporate board members, and row one containing all the names of the companies in your dataset. Each cell then contains a one or a zero, depending on whether a specific individual is on the board of a specific corporation.

Figure 12.2 shows what an affiliation matrix looks like. It is also a screenshot of part of the data used in Hughes and Paterson (2017) and is a matrix of some of the key IPCC authors we identified from the coauthoring network described earlier, combined with whether or not they are connected to some key institutions we identified as central to constituting IPCC research networks.

Affiliation matrices then generate "two-mode" networks: networks involving two different types of nodes. We are often more interested in "one-mode" networks involving only one type of node. For example, in the IPCC example in Section 12.2, we were interested both in the central authors in the network and these central institutions. SNA software allows us to transform these affiliation networks into adjacency networks to do this. Nevertheless, if the data source we have is something like a membership list of corporate boards or a participants' list at a negotiation, it is normally easier to enter the data via an affiliation matrix.

If you are recording attributes of your nodes (gender, nationality, etc.), you will need columns for these also. You will then need a clear means of separating them out from the network data so you can use them in the analysis without them getting in the way.

12.4 Data Analysis

Analysis of network data takes two forms. The first, most commonly identifiable with network research, is via visualizing the networks. Figure 12.3 shows the network of key institutions arising out of the matrix in Figure 12.2. You can see that the matrix has been transformed from its two-mode character (individuals and institutions) to a one-mode network of institutions. You can also see that the visualization shows that these are *weighted* ties: each number linking two nodes in this instance tells us how many authors connect the two institutions, and the thickness of the lines indicates the strongest inter-institutional connections. The visualization can also be aided in various ways – for example, changing the colors or shapes of the nodes to show different attributes of each node, and altering the size of the node to reflect their centrality within the network. Visualizing networks can be useful in a number of ways, in part for communicating effectively the character of networks, as well as for generating hypotheses about the network's character and effects to stimulate additional research. There is of course danger in the visualizations as well, in that they can generate powerful images which are then overinterpreted or fetishized. One dimension of this issue that is worth picking out from Figure 12.3 is that if our nodes are institutions rather than individuals, then there are a lot of assumptions that need to be interrogated regarding the coherence of that node as an "actor." In this case, these are either research institutes or universities, so even here there can be assumptions – for example, about whether, say, Harvard is a sufficiently coherent "actor" such that it can be regarded as

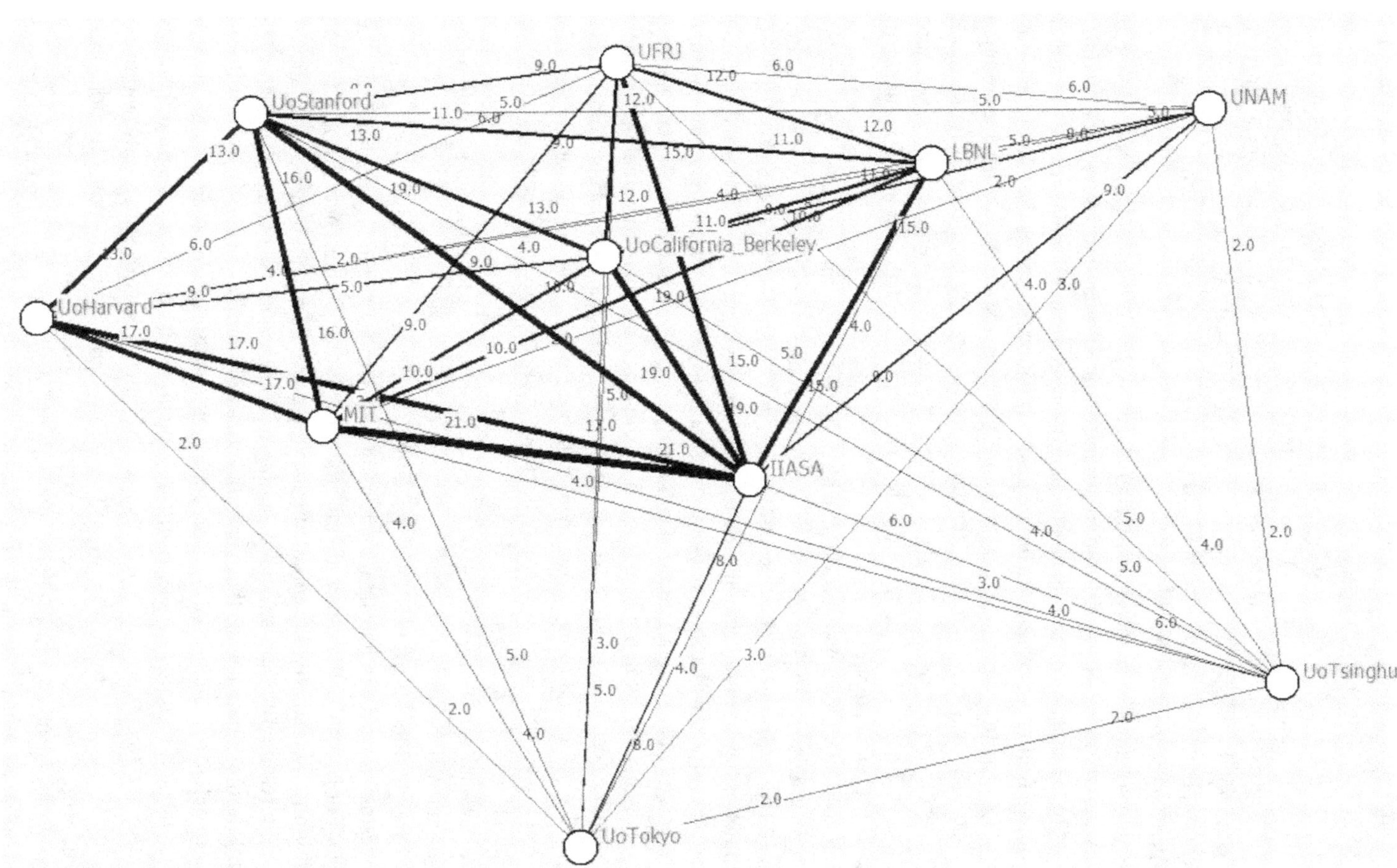

Figure 12.3 Network of key institutions behind the IPCC AR5 WGIII author team.
Source: Hughes and Paterson (2017, 755).

"coordinating" all the authors associated with it. If the node says "China," then even more care needs to be taken in this regard.

The second form of analysis is to analyze various statistical properties of the networks. Some of this is straightforward, entailing reporting the various measures outlined in Table 12.1. For example, with Figure 12.3 we can visually see a core–periphery structure, and we confirmed this statistically within the UCINET software. This is effectively the equivalent of presenting descriptive statistics in other sorts of research and can be a useful complement to the visualizations.

This can also entail advanced statistical analysis of the networks. This can be done by using network statistics as variables in more conventional quantitative research. Jennifer Hadden's (2015) analysis of the development of more confrontational tactics by members of the Climate Action Network and climate justice organizations uses the SNA to establish the centrality of particular organizations within the networks of NGOs in climate negotiations. She then uses the centrality measures (betweenness, specifically) as a key independent variable in a regression model to explain changes in movement tactics over time, showing that the closer an organization is to Friends of the Earth within the network, the more likely it was to adopt contentious actions over time.

Statistical analysis can also be done within the network analysis itself. A common approach is known as exponential random graph models (ERGMs: see Hollway and Koskinen 2016; Morin et al. 2017; Stadfeld et al. 2017), although a range of other statistical techniques has been developed. The simplest way to think of ERGMs is as analogues of regression analyses with more conventional quantitative methods. In conventional quantitative research, we are often interested in identifying the important correlations between variables, but an underlying premise to enable us to do this is that individual observations are not related to each other. In network research, this assumption does not hold; indeed, we are precisely focused on how relational dynamics shape actor behavior. ERGMs are thus models developed to try to examine the statistical properties of a network given this underlying shift in the nature of the data we examine. They can be used to analyze, for example, how and why ties get created among actors, or to explain the behavior of actors given their network centrality.

A final way to think of using SNA, especially in studies of environmental negotiations, is in mixed-methods research design, combining it with other methods (see also Reflection Box 12.1). For example, if we can identify the structure of a given network and the key nodes within it, then an obvious complementary piece of research would be qualitative or ethnographic research to gain an understanding of these actors (see Chapters 10 and 11), identifying in more detail what that centrality means in terms of their actions, and why other actors defer to them or go through them to achieve things. For example, the SNA on its own cannot tell us much about the different positionality or cultural capital that individuals have and thus their ability to make use of where they are structurally within the network to achieve specific goals. An individual may figure in a formal network but in practice be largely excluded from the discussions that go on within a network. If we see across the network diverse discourses being mobilized, then we could combine network analysis with critical discourse analysis to understand why certain discourses prevail and others get marginalized (see Chapter 8). Or, we can simply use interview responses, direct observations, and our reading of documents as means of triangulating with the network analysis itself – confirming the centrality of particular actors, or the flow of information, for example, that we might infer from the network structure but need to confirm in other ways (see also Reflection Box 12.1). Many of the other methods discussed in this volume can be creatively combined with SNA to enhance the overall power of the analysis of environmental negotiation dynamics.

12.5 SNA in Studies of Environmental Governance

How, then, have some of these techniques within SNA been used within studies of GEP in general and negotiation sites more specifically? Three aspects of this are worth bringing out.

The first concerns the sorts of analytical purposes to which SNA has been put. The key questions that SNA studies have been used for include those regarding fragmentation and coherence in governance complexes (Cao and Ward 2017; Green 2013; Widerberg 2016), including the debate about orchestration in such complexes; forms of power and authority in environmental governance, notably of expert authority (Corbera et al. 2016; Henriksen and Ponte 2018; Hughes and Paterson 2017; Morin et al. 2017; Paterson et al. 2014); the power of transnational corporate actors (Sapinski 2015); movement mobilization to shape environmental negotiations (Böhmelt et al. 2014; Hadden 2014, 2015); and processes of discursive framing and contestation to shape the ideas that inform such negotiations (Fisher et al. 2013; Venturini et al. 2014).

The second is to draw attention to the diverse ways that networks have been conceptualized and thus data collected which might be useful for thinking about how you might go

Table 12.2 *Nodes and tie types in SNA research in environmental governance*

Nodes	Type of tie	Examples
Members of international or transnational governance organizations	Joint membership in the governance organization	Kim 2013; Widerberg 2016; Hollway and Koskinen 2016
Individuals participating in these governance organizations	Joint participation in a governance process	Paterson et al. 2014; Fransen et al. 2016; Thistlethwaite and Paterson 2016; Henriksen and Ponte 2018
NGOs	Joint participation in particular campaigns or actions	Hadden 2014
Concepts or discursive terms	Copresence in the same document	Fisher et al. 2013; Venturini et al. 2014
Individuals	Shared participation in Twitter conversations	Pearce et al. 2014;

Table 12.2 (*cont.*)

Nodes	Type of tie	Examples
Individuals	Shared background, e.g., nationality, employer, educational institution	Thistlethwaite and Paterson 2016; Corbera et al. 2016; Morin et al. 2017
Individuals	Measure of collaboration, e.g., coauthoring (especially relevant for expert networks)	Corbera et al. 2016; Hughes and Paterson 2017

about such exercises. Table 12.2 represents the main ways this has been done in existing research.

Third, a few examples are worth drawing out to illustrate creative ways that SNA has been used, in particular highlighting those that enable strong inferences because of the ways the ties have been conceptualized. Green (2013) uses mutual recognition between carbon standard-setting organizations as a means of constituting network ties. Here we can infer a good deal regarding how each governance organization views the reputation and utility of others within the overall field. Corbera et al. (2016) and Hughes and Paterson (2017) analyze coauthorship networks among IPCC lead authors, implying much stronger ties between individuals than simply say a shared educational background. Finally, Henriksen and Ponte (2018) carry out an iterated survey of members of the policy network on aviation and climate change to establish the character of the network as subjectively experienced. This last approach is particularly promising, although it is labor intensive, as we will see in Section 12.6.

12.6 Agreement-Making and Network Research

It is perhaps worth thinking about the value of collecting and analyzing network data in relation to agreement-making processes in two different ways.

First, it could be done as a preparatory task for planning research at specific negotiating sites. This work can also be useful for studying those negotiating sites even if you are unable to do fieldwork at the sites themselves. Many of the studies highlighted earlier have not involved direct research at negotiating sites. Indeed, given the way that you may be conceptualizing the network you are studying, and that the concept of agreement-making is focused broadly, comprising the sites themselves and the various processes that make them possible, it may not be necessary to physically attend the negotiating site itself at all (see Chapter 2).

Let's say, for example, you are interested in the transnational corporate networks involved in your agreement-making process. You could devise a strategy for collecting data on these networks, prior to or independent of any fieldwork, based on existing documentary evidence. There will normally be documents from previous meetings on which you can draw. The key one will be a list of participants. These usually indicate the organizational affiliation of individuals, and some will be organized by broad groupings of types of organizations or constituencies (governments, NGOs, etc.; see also Chapter 6). It is possible to automate the extraction of data from these documents, although there is arguably some value to doing this manually (if the lists are not too huge) as you familiarize yourself with names as you enter the data and generate hunches about potential patterns. But there will be other documents you could use to generate this sort of data: the *Earth Negotiations Bulletin*, media sources, briefing documents, and so on (see Chapter 8).

Analyzing this sort of data prior to research at a site would help you prepare in a number of ways (see Chapter 2). It would tell you which sorts of corporate actors seem to have been central to corporate activity within the negotiations. It would give you a sense of key interviewees to approach. But it would also give you useful hunches about what to explore in interviews or other aspects of fieldwork: Why does, say, the steel sector seem to be so central? Is it really a clique of only four people driving forward corporate lobbying on this issue? What attributes of these individuals should I explore more systematically?

To give one example, in Thistlethwaite and Paterson (2016), we were interested in tracing the interpersonal connections across the key sites in the development of ways of incorporating sustainability principles into corporate accounts. This entailed identifying the key governance institutions in that field, working out how to identify those involved in "governing" each institution, mostly involving boards of governors, leadership teams, and sometimes expert advisory boards, and then collecting data regarding the members of those boards. This produced a fairly straightforward affiliation matrix structurally like the one in Figure 12.2. We also were interested in the sociological characteristics of these actors, so we collected attribute data regarding their gender, nationality, educational background, and employers, and coded them according to profession, such as lawyer, economist, or accountant (this last involving more researcher judgment). This sort of demographic data is often fairly readily accessible for these sorts of actors, as they mostly have publicly accessible biographical data via LinkedIn or short biographies on organizational websites.

Second, you can use the negotiating site itself as a site of network data collection. Here are two ideas about how this might be carried out.

One is to use the negotiating site as part of research designed to analyze networks in environmental governance that generate direct measures of network ties. This involves carrying out an iterated survey using a "name generator" method (Robins 2015, 96–99): you identify a number of participants to survey, where the core survey question is to ask them to name other people they have worked with in the context of this negotiation or governance process. The specific ways you phrase this question will need to be designed to reflect the conceptual underpinnings of the tie you seek to establish; for example, "who have you learned most from in these negotiations?" will give you a different sort of network than "who have you collaborated with in these negotiations?" or "who have your principal opponents been in these negotiations?," should all give you rather different networks to analyze, and improve the inferences that you can thus make. You then iterate the survey by sending it to the people mentioned in the initial round, and in principle you keep going until you cease to get new names, by which time you consider your network "saturated" – that is, you have something approximating a "whole network," even though you have not been able to bound it initially as such a network (Marsden

2005, 9; Robins 2015 115). This is the approach adopted by Henriksen and Ponte (2018) focused on the network around aviation and climate change. This survey can be carried out both at a negotiation site, by short interviews, and outside the negotiations, via an online survey system such as SurveyMonkey.

A key issue with this research design is the selection of the initial seeds for the survey. There are significant effects that can be generated by poorly considering this: for example, if your network has a component (i.e., a part unconnected to the rest) that has no person in your initial sample, you will miss that component completely. The most important consideration is to maximize the diversity of initial "seeds" for the survey (see Robins 2015, 114–116, for useful additional discussion).

Analytically, the advantage of this method is that it would enable a direct set of inferences about networks in environmental negotiations as they are experienced by participants themselves. Specifically, it would mean that if we wanted to know how a particular issue diffused across an agreement-making process, we would have data showing that actors themselves report how their network connections facilitated the flow of ideas, how resource flows between them generated diffusion of activity, or which actors are deferred to as authoritative. This survey data is "directed" (A may mention B but B not mention A), thus enabling additional inferences about flows and authority. Similarly, if we are interested in the centrality of different actors across a network, the inferences are different. With affiliation data it would be possible for an actor to emerge as central because they went to all the key meetings, even if they sat at the back of the room and never said anything. Such a person would be absent from the networks based on self-reported connections and relationships.

A second approach is to directly observe the interaction within formal and informal meetings at negotiation sites (Robins 2015, 127–128). This would entail noting down who

Reflection Box 12.2 The "sensitivity problem" of collecting network data in negotiating rooms

By Arne Langlet

As networks consist of nodes and ties, I had to find information on both variables in the negotiation context: in my case, the BBNJ intergovernmental conferences, where I conducted CEE "on site" (see Chapter 10). The first challenge I faced was to define what my set of nodes and ties would be. Once on site, I could observe a myriad of different actors that could be nodes, such as individual people, NGOs, IGOs, bureaucratic staff, researchers, and state delegations. I could have classified every recorded interaction – such as private conversations, references made to each other in statements and interventions, common negotiation positions, commonly organized side events, common research projects, etcetera – as possible ties.

Given the wealth of potential nodes and ties at international environmental negotiations, I decided that it made the most sense to use groups of actors such as organizations or states as nodes, and references made between them in statements and interventions as ties. The issue with this, however, is that within agreement-making processes, some people regularly speak on behalf of more than one organization – they have "different hats on." For example, some scientific actors may also act as consultants for an international organization and/or state delegation, which makes it difficult to clearly attribute their interaction to one institution.

Gaining relational information can be difficult as this data is often personal, intimate, and hard to measure. Nevertheless, it is important to gain comprehensive knowledge about the actors in order to draw inferences from their interactions. While relational data can also be collected on a large scale digitally through automatized web-scraping methods, such sources can only complement live data sampling at the agreement-making sites. Here, the researcher can also employ qualitative interviews to help make sense of the relational data. To do this while respecting ethical and data-protective considerations may require the researcher to participate in international negotiations. In my case, participating in the negotiations enabled me to inform actors about my research interests.

When collecting relational data, the researcher should at all times take into account ethical principles relating to the privacy of individuals. While the chapter provides compelling reasons not to anonymize data, in our team we decided to conduct detailed data on the impersonal level only – for example, referring to the organization that the individual represents rather than to the individual. We did so because, firstly, research based on personalized data risks encountering difficulties with ethical review boards, particularly in light of new data protection legislation. Secondly, it may be strategically important for the researcher to protect the identities of participants in order to gain access to the negotiation process and the trust of participants.

In terms of ties, I had to be a bit creative when operationalizing the ties that link actors. One avenue that I pursued was to use references that delegations make to other delegations or organizations in their statements. I figured that states refer to organizations to strengthen or weaken them in relation to the policy issue at hand and used these references as an entry point for data collection. I subsequently analyzed the evolving networks in the light of authority distribution as states tend to refer to institutions to which they wish to attribute authority (Alter and Meunier 2009; Raustiala and Victor 2004). For this research, I scanned the transcripts of delegation statements that our team had observed for references to international organizations or to other states. These references occurred in relation to a number of different treaty provisions, and hence could also be coded as ties from the organization to the treaty provision in relation to which it was mentioned.

speaks, in what order, who refers to whom, the substance of what they say, and how these interactions are managed by meeting chairs (see Reflection Box 12.2 regarding these sorts of strategies). This method of data collection may need to be carried out collaboratively, either to make sure to capture all the interactions adequately or to ensure (via intercoder reliability tests) that the observations of interactions are reliable enough to use in analysis (Marsden 2005, 25). This could be a way of formalizing the sort of work people are currently carrying out at sites like a COP under the framework of collaborative event ethnography (see Chapter 10), and using these multi-researcher observations to build formal accounts of network interactions inside a negotiation site, again to address questions about the learning, diffusion, and authority within and between negotiation processes. This approach, like that of the name-generator survey, can be approached both within formal spaces of negotiations and in the informal spaces – side events, NGO or corporate venues, protest sites (see also Chapter 7) – and designed, if you are interested in questions connected to "governance complexes," between negotiations in different institutions within a particular field of governance.

12.7 Conclusions

SNA has considerable potential to contribute to and enhance our understanding of environmental agreement-making. It can do so by providing formal analyses of the social structures that lie behind these sites and thus the background aspects of "order-making," understood in terms of how interpersonal and interorganizational networks structure who gets to participate in negotiations and whose participation in those negotiations carries weight and enables them to affect the outcomes of negotiations and the character of the environmental governance that results. And, given that many fields of environmental governance entail multiple institutions and therefore multiple sites of negotiations, it is a method well-suited to tracing the linkages across those varied institutions and sites, and the patterns of authority, learning, and diffusion that work between them. In other words, it enables us to understand the various contexts within which actors and sites in agreement-making processes are constituted.

Further Reading

1. Borgatti, S., Everett, M., and Freeman, L. (2002). *Ucinet for Windows: Software for Social Network Analysis*. Harvard, MA: Analytic Technologies.

This is the "entry level" software for carrying out SNA. It is simple to use and generates both statistical analysis and network visualizations. It can be downloaded here: https://sites.google.com/site/ucinetsoftware/home.

2. Borgatti, S., Everett, M., and Johnson, J. (2018). *Analyzing Social Networks*. London: Sage.

This is specifically designed to introduce you to the ucinet software.

3. Hadden, J. (2015). *Networks in Contention*. Cambridge: Cambridge University Press.

This is a particularly fine use of SNA in relation to environmental negotiations. It tracks NGO and social movement activism at UNFCCC COPs, and it shows how the spread of more confrontational tactics amongst movement actors in the run-up to the Copenhagen COP in 2009 was shaped by the structure of the networks of NGOs.

4. Scott, J. (2012). *Social Network Analysis*. Los Angeles, CA: Sage.

This is a readable, clear textbook on SNA, describing its underlying assumptions, key concepts and terms, and basic procedures regarding data collection analysis extremely effectively.

References

Alter, K., and Meunier, S. (2009). The Politics of International Regime Complexity. *Perspectives on Politics*, 7(1),13–24.

Böhmelt, T., Koubi, V., and Bernauer, T. (2014). Civil Society Participation in Global Governance: Insights from Climate Politics. *European Journal of Political Research* 53(1),18–36.

Cao, X., and Ward, H. (2017). Transnational Climate Governance Networks and Domestic Regulatory Action. *International Interactions*, 43(1),76–102.

Carroll, W. (2010). *The Making of a Transnational Capitalist Class*. London: Zed Books.

Corbera, E., Calvet-Mir, L., Hughes, H., and Paterson, M. (2016). Patterns of Authorship in the IPCC Working Group III Report. *Nature Climate Change*, 6(1),94–99.

Fisher, D. R., Leifeld, P., and Iwaki, Y. (2013). Mapping the Ideological Networks of American Climate Politics. *Climatic Change*, 116(3–4),523–545.

Frank, D. (1999). The Social Bases of Environmental Treaty Ratification, 1900–1990. *Sociological Inquiry*, 69(4),523–550.

Fransen, L., Schalk, J., and Auld, G. (2016). Work Ties Beget Community? Assessing Interactions among Transnational Private Governance Organizations in Sustainable Agriculture. *Global Networks*, 16(1),45–67.

Green, J. F. (2013). Order out of Chaos: Public and Private Rules for Managing Carbon. *Global Environmental Politics*, 13(2),1–25.

Hadden, J. (2014). Explaining Variation in Transnational Climate Change Activism: The Role of Inter-Movement Spillover. *Global Environmental Politics*, 14(2),7–25.

Henriksen, L. F., and Ponte, S. (2018). Public Orchestration, Social Networks, and Transnational Environmental Governance: Lessons from the Aviation Industry. *Regulation & Governance*, 12(1),23–45.

Hoffmann, M. (2017). Exploring Constitution and Social Construction Through Network Analysis. In J. S. Barkin and L. Sjoberg, eds., *Interpretive Quantification: Methodological Explorations for Critical and Constructivist IR*. Ann Arbor, MI: University of Michigan Press, pp. 72–95.

Hollway, J., and Koskinen, J. (2016). Multilevel Embeddedness: The Case of the Global Fisheries Governance Complex. *Social Networks*, 44(January), 281–294.

Hughes, H., and Paterson, M. (2017). Narrowing the Climate Field: The Symbolic Power of Authors in the IPCC's Assessment of Mitigation. *Review of Policy Research*, 34(6),744–766.

Kim, R. (2013). The Emergent Network Structure of the Multilateral Environmental Agreement System. *Global Environmental Change*, 23(5),980–991.

Marsden, P. (2005). Recent Developments in Network Measurement. In P. J. Carrington, J. Scott, and S. Wasserman, eds., *Models and Methods in Social Network Analysis*. Cambridge: Cambridge University Press, pp. 8–30.

Marsden, P. (1990). Network Data and Measurement. *Annual Review of Sociology*, 16(1),435–463.

Morin, J.-F., Louafi, S., Orsini, A., and Oubenal, M. (2017). Boundary Organizations in Regime Complexes: A Social Network Profile of IPBES. *Journal of International Relations and Development*, 20(3),543–577.

Morin, J.-F., Pauwelyn, J., and Hollway, J. (2017). The Trade Regime as a Complex Adaptive System: Exploration and Exploitation of Environmental Norms in Trade Agreements. *Journal of International Economic Law*, 20(2),365–390.

Paterson, M. (2019). Using Negotiation Sites for Richer Collection of Network Data. *Global Environmental Politics*, 19(2),81–92.

Paterson, M., Hoffmann, M., Betsill, M., and Bernstein, S. (2014). The Micro Foundations of Policy Diffusion Toward Complex Global Governance An Analysis of the Transnational Carbon Emission Trading Network. *Comparative Political Studies*, 47(3),420–449.

Pearce, W., Holmberg, K., Hellsten, I., and Nerlich, B. (2014). Climate Change on Twitter: Topics, Communities and Conversations about the 2013 IPCC Working Group 1 Report. *PLoS ONE*, 9(4), e94785.

Raustiala, K., and Victor, D. (2004). The Regime Complex for Plant Genetic Resources. *International Organization*, *58*(2), 277–309.

Robins, G. (2015). *Doing Social Network Research: Network-Based Research Design for Social Scientists*. London: Sage.

Sapinski, J. P. (2015). Climate Capitalism and the Global Corporate Elite Network. *Environmental Sociology*, 1(4),268–279.

Stadfeld, C., Hollway, J., and Block, P. (2017). Dynamic Network Actor Models: Investigating Coordination Ties through Time. *Sociological Methodology*, 47(1),1–40.

Thistlethwaite, J., and Paterson, M. (2016). Private Governance and Accounting for Sustainability Networks. *Environment and Planning C: Government and Policy*, 34(7),1197–1221.

Venturini, T., Laffite, N. B., Cointet, J.-P. et al. (2014). Three Maps and Three Misunderstandings: A Digital Mapping of Climate Diplomacy. *Big Data & Society* 1(2), 2053951714543804.

Ward, M., Stovel, K., and Sacks, A. (2011). Network Analysis and Political Science. *Annual Review of Political Science*, 14(1),245–264.

Widerberg, O. (2016). Mapping Institutional Complexity in the Anthropocene: A Network Approach. In P. Pattberg and F. Zelli, eds., *Environmental Politics and Governance in the Anthropocene: Institutions and Legitimacy in a Complex World.* London: Routledge, pp. 81–102.

Part IV

Implementing and Adapting

13

Experiences

Reflecting and Comparing Research on Negotiations

ARNE LANGLET, TIMO LEITER, INA TESSNOW-VON WYSOCKI, AND HARRIET THEW

13.1 Introduction

This book argues that understanding agreement-making requires studying the multiple sites, actors, and processes through which agreements are made and shape world order (see Chapter 1 and Hughes et al. 2021). This chapter outlines how we have studied (and continue to study) agreement-making in our PhD research projects using global environmental conferences as sites for empirical research and data collection. We share our experiences on how we designed, conducted and analyzed data collected through participant observation at negotiations under the United Nations Framework Convention on Climate Change (UNFCCC) (Harriet Thew and Timo Leiter) and through collaborative event ethnography at negotiations for an international legally binding instrument on the conservation and sustainable use of marine biological diversity of areas beyond national jurisdiction (BBNJ) (Ina Tessnow-von Wysocki and Arne Langlet) (see Table 13.1 for a comparison of the two agreement-making sites).

Table 13.1 *Overview of the two agreement-making sites*

Agreement-making site	UNFCCC	BBNJ
Cases	Harriet Thew & Timo Leiter	Ina Tessnow-von Wysocki & Arne Langlet
Issue	Climate change	Marine biodiversity beyond national jurisdiction
Agreements	United Nations Framework Convention on Climate Change (UNFCCC) (1994), Kyoto Protocol (1997), Paris Agreement (2015)	United Nations Convention on the Law of the Sea (UNCLOS) (1982)
Duration & location	Two weeks in May/June in Bonn, Germany and two weeks in November/December (location rotating annually between UN regional groups)	Four conferences for two weeks at the UN HQ in New York

Table 13.1 (*cont.*)

Agreement-making site	UNFCCC	BBNJ
Side events	Several hundred side events are held inside the venue and around; Several dozen countries represent themselves with on-site pavilions where further side events are held (see Chapter 7)	Normally three different side events are taking place simultaneously during the lunch break
Size	~20,000 at COPs (only a fraction are directly participating in the government negotiations)	~ 1,000 people (mainly negotiators)
On-site access	On-site participation requires accreditation via a party, an observer organization, a UN or international organization, or as a media representative (see Chapter 6)	On-site participation requires accreditation via a party or an observer organization with UN ECOSOC consultative status, a UN or international organization, or as a media representative
Online access	Plenary sessions and side events organized in dedicated side-event rooms are streamed and recorded and are publicly accessible. Due to COVID-19, all formal negotiation sessions at the COP in December 2021 were for the first time also streamed, but not recorded, and streaming was only accessible to accredited participants.	During the break of on-site negotiations due to COVID-19, online dialogue formats took place. One conference was held in-person with limited participants and online streaming for registered participants
High-level attendance	The COPs in November/December are usually attended by 50–100 heads of state or heads of government and by more than 100 ministers.	The BBNJ IGCs are not attended by heads of states or ministers

All four of us attended negotiation sessions and engaged in event ethnography (Campbell et al. 2014). The advantages of event ethnography are elaborated in Chapters 10 and 11. This chapter discusses how we applied ethnographic methods to different agreement-making sites from the perspective of four PhD students. We found commonalities and differences in how we prepared to access and navigate the agreement-making sites (Chapter 6), how we collected and analyzed data (Chapter 8 and 9) and how we reflected upon our positionality (Chapter 5). We discuss from a practical point of view how we dealt with these topics presented in other chapters of this book within our research projects. Recognizing that due to the COVID-19 pandemic, we had to adapt our approaches to increasingly study online events (Hughes et al. 2021; Vadrot et al. 2021; see also Chapter 14), we suggest that some processes and dimensions of global agreement-making can only be fully grasped by being on site.

In the following, we provide a brief background on the two environmental negotiation processes studied before outlining our PhD projects and analyzing their commonalities and differences.

13.2 Researching UN Climate and Marine Biodiversity Negotiations

13.2.1 The UN Climate Change Negotiations

Literature on climate change negotiations often disengages with the actual negotiation process, assuming that its outcomes could be predicted or explained through modeling based on countries' power and self-interests (Mandani 2013; Dimitrov 2012). Ethnographic research can address this gap by studying the processes and dynamics that shape the outcome of negotiations and that are essential to understanding agreement-making (Eastwood 2019; Hughes et al. 2021).

Climate change negotiations have become a large and complex undertaking, with many negotiation streams and events running in parallel, effectively creating multiple sites within the conference (see Chapters 6 and 7). In total, recent COPs have had more than 20,000 accredited participants, of which only a couple of thousand are directly involved in the negotiation sessions. The sheer size and complexity pose limits on what individual researchers can observe, requiring a focus on specific aspects such as the influence of nonstate actors (Hale 2016) or the impact of the conference organization and presidency (Dimitrov 2016). To date, only few ethnographic accounts of the UN climate change negotiations have been published (e.g., Eastwood 2019; Thew et al. 2020), which offers opportunities for upcoming PhD projects.

13.2.2 The BBNJ Negotiations Under UNCLOS

The international negotiations for a legally binding agreement on the conservation and sustainable use of marine biodiversity of areas beyond national jurisdiction (BBNJ) are a recent example of multilateral negotiations under the United Nations Convention on the Law of the Sea (UNCLOS). The new instrument seeks to govern marine biodiversity in areas that do not fall under the jurisdiction of states – areas that make up around two-thirds of the world's oceans. It is therefore not only an important part of global environmental governance, but is also connected to a number of geopolitical, economic, and social equity issues connected to the protection and use of a global good. Moreover, the BBNJ instrument seeks to complement the existing ocean governance framework, which makes the negotiations particularly complex and interesting to study from an institutional perspective.

The BBNJ negotiations provide an opportunity to study the early phase of agreement-making, when a new treaty is negotiated and a new regime emerges. With five two-week long intergovernmental conferences (IGCs) taking place between 2018 and 2022, this time frame was suitable for PhD students to undertake an in-depth analysis of the process. Compared to climate change COPs, the BBNJ agreement-making site is much smaller and less well studied, with around 1,000 state and nonstate delegates (see Table 13.1) and only a few researchers participating in the IGCs (De Santo et al. 2019; Tessnow-von Wysocki and Vadrot 2020). Thus, the five-year research project MARIPOLDATA (2018–23), funded by the ERC, where Arne and Ina were employed, provided a unique opportunity to be trained in the conduct of event ethnography at an emerging site and process of global environmental agreement-making (Campbell et al. 2014; Vadrot 2020). Future PhD projects may look at meetings of a resulting BBNJ COP or other emerging treaties as objects of study.

In the following sections, we introduce each of the four PhD projects before identifying shared aspects and issues that featured across our research projects and outlining how we addressed these.

13.3 The Four Cases

13.3.1 Youth Participation at UNFCCC COPs: Harriet Thew

My PhD, completed in November 2020, explored the lived experiences of youth participants in the UNFCCC negotiations (Thew et al. 2020, 2021, 2022). From 2015 to 2018, I collected longitudinal ethnographic data through participant observation at three UNFCCC COPs, as well as at the intersessional conferences in May/June each year. I also observed my case study organization, The UK Youth Climate Coalition (UKYCC), throughout the year as they prepared for, reflected on, and reacted to their experiences of UNFCCC participation. In addition, I conducted semistructured interviews with members of UKYCC (aged 17–29 years old), including interviews to investigate how their experiences and perspectives changed over time.

Prior to my PhD, I had engaged with youth participation in the UNFCCC as a practitioner, having led international delegations of young women to several UN conferences on behalf of the World Association of Girl Guides and Girl Scouts. This increased my understanding of intergovernmental processes, enabling me to navigate their complexity with far fewer challenges than I would have faced if it had been my first conference. My previous experience also made it easier to identify and approach a suitable “gatekeeper” within my chosen case study organization, and subsequently facilitated reciprocity with my research participants as I could share my understanding of the process with those who hadn’t previously attended.

I triangulated my observations and interview data with document analysis of formal documents produced by the UNFCCC’s Youth NGOs constituency (YOUNGO). I found that studying texts produced in different spaces was illuminating (see Chapter 8), particularly in identifying the role of power dynamics in shaping strategic speech events. For example, I analyzed the outcome documents of conferences of youth (COY) meetings, comparing young people’s justice claims articulated therein with justice claims made in UNFCCC spaces. COY meetings occur prior to each UNFCCC COP, with young people from around the world gathering to share knowledge and coordinate positions. This includes production of a publicly available outcome document, which is shared with high-level decision makers in government delegations, the UNFCCC Secretariat, and online. I found significant differences between the justice claims made in COYs as youth-led spaces and in COP spaces they share with other, nonyouth actors. This contributed to my argument that young people's true preferences are silenced by power dynamics in the UNFCCC and that the framing and claiming of justice is a power-laden process (Thew et al. 2020). This finding was initially reached *without* text analysis, captured during my interviews and participant observation. However, text analysis was invaluable in illustrating the extent to which this finding from my case study could potentially be representative of the broader experiences of youth participants from around the world.

13.3.2 Government Negotiations Under the Paris Agreement: Timo Leiter

My PhD is about climate change adaptation and how progress in becoming better adapted to climate change can be assessed (Leiter 2021a, 2021b; Leiter and Pringle 2018). Part of my research involves participant observation at the UN climate change negotiations to understand the debates and politics around what countries are asked to report regarding their adaptation actions. My engagement with the UNFCCC negotiations evolved from my previous job in climate policy at Germany's international development agency (GIZ), which included observing the negotiations and participating in side events. In 2018, when the negotiations of the rulebook that specifies details of the Paris Agreement went into its final phase, I became an advisor in the German delegation, which provided me with further insight into the government negotiations. I therefore already had a high degree of familiarity with the UNFCCC processes by the start of my PhD, which proved valuable. It would have otherwise taken at least two to four negotiation sessions to acquire a similar level of familiarity and to develop a sufficiently broad network of contacts.

As a country delegate, I had a level of access to the government negotiations that is unusual for researchers. Yet, when delegation sizes were reduced due to COVID-19, I had to shift again to observer status as part of my university's delegation. This shift also meant a change in my role from being a participant to returning to an observer without access to closed-door negotiations. Reflecting on my positionality, experiencing the negotiations through the delegation of a well-resourced European country is certainly a different perspective than is gained through the delegation of a small island development state or a least developed country. To balance this influence, I triangulated my observations with records from UNFCCC documents, NGO reports, and conversations with delegates from other negotiation groups. My previous work in international development cooperation, including having lived for several years in East Africa and having had frequent exchanges with developing country delegates, helped me to better understand their positions and perspectives.

My top recommendation for anyone aiming to study the UN climate change negotiations is to get acquainted with the common practices and processes before your first attendance (see Chapter 6), for example by watching recordings of prior plenary and negotiation sessions, and, where possible, talking to regular COP participants.

13.3.3 Social Network Analysis at the Marine Biodiversity Negotiations: Arne Langlet

In my PhD project, I research the institutional networks that underlie the BBNJ negotiations. I am interested in this because in order to fulfill the objectives of the future BBNJ agreement, it is necessary to monitor biodiversity as well as manage related databases and activities carried out in areas beyond national jurisdictions. Hence, the institutional setting of the agreement will be crucial for implementation. Currently, the draft text foresees the possible establishment of a conference of the parties, scientific and technical body, a clearing-house mechanism, and secretariat as principal organs for the institutional arrangements of the BBNJ Agreement.

A myriad of international institutions, such as the Convention on Biological Diversity (CBD), regional fisheries management organizations, and conventions under the International Maritime Organization (IMO) and the International Seabed Authority (ISA), already exist and manage certain human activities and their effects on marine biodiversity. For this reason, I thought that better understanding how the new treaty would relate to existing institutions would be an important topic of research. I was interested in network structures of the existing institutional framework and how the future agreement and its bodies would fit within them.

I understand the involvement of different institutions as competition for the authority to monitor high seas biodiversity, which is attributed to institutions by states. States appear to be using the negotiation of a new agreement to either redistribute or solidify the authority of existing IGOs in the field of marine biodiversity. In order to research this, I look at how the actors involved in the agreement-making process relate, refer, and interact with each other. This interaction creates links, which, in a network sense, are connections between actors (see Reflection Boxes 12.1 and 12.2). Hence, I use social network analysis to grasp the relational nature of the competition and distribution of authority.

When I started, I had some experience of conducting network analysis and found it fascinating to do this in ongoing UN negotiations. However, I was not prepared for the complexity of multilateral negotiations. My initial struggles to transform our ethnographic observations into usable network data stem from the fact that when you practice your coding and data analysis skills at university, the dataset is normally clean and put together with the purpose of being used for network analysis. However, we collected live ethnographic data during the negotiation sessions for multiple analytical purposes. This means that I spent a considerable amount of time deliberating how to transform the ethnographic data into usable network datasets and subsequently coding and data-wrangling. I recommend that anyone who aims to undertake a similar project starts getting into the "dirty" data work as early as possible.

13.3.4 Science–Policy Interfaces at Marine Biodiversity Negotiations: Ina Tessnow-von Wysocki

My PhD project, "Science–Policy Interfaces for Ocean Protection," studies the role of science in the ongoing intergovernmental negotiations for a legally binding instrument on marine biodiversity. These negotiations are supposed to be based on the *best-available science* because ocean protection requires knowledge of the stressors on ocean life and how environmental degradation can be reversed and prevented (Intergovernmental Oceanographic Commission 2020). However, it is often unclear in the process how science informs agreement-making, which actors are included, and whose voices are heard when negotiations on a global common take place. My research seeks to uncover the science–policy interrelations that are taking place within the negotiations that will lead to new legally binding measures for states on how to explore, exploit, and protect ocean space and life. Through this research, I aim to contribute to understandings of science–policy interfaces within UN processes by detecting gaps and opportunities in current science–policy practices.

My PhD examines different dimensions of science–policy interfaces within the BBNJ negotiations: science output, science input, science institutionalization, and science uptake. In this way, I can study the role science plays in the *negotiations*, in the *final agreement*, and what implications this holds for its *implementation*. Literature reviews are necessary to portray the "science output," namely how the diverse scientific community writes on the BBNJ negotiations, while a combination of collaborative event ethnography (CEE), interviews, and analysis of official documents offer valuable methods to study science input, institutionalization, and uptake.

There are two challenges that I experienced with studying ongoing negotiations. Firstly, the unpredictability of time schedules of negotiation outcomes can in some cases demand flexibility in adapting the research design, methodology, or the use of particular sources. My PhD project initially intended to evaluate the "uptake of science" in the legal treaty text after completion of the agreement. However, the postponement of the final intergovernmental conference by more than two years due to the COVID-19 pandemic required flexibility in my research design, including adaptation of the individual papers, as well as use of different data sources (digital ethnography data from online discussions instead of on-site ethnographic data).

Secondly, there is the difficulty of adjusting the timing of publishing academic papers to the negotiation schedules so that they inform and, potentially, normatively impact the negotiations, which is an opportunity that studying an emergent process offers. This can be challenging because of lengthy rounds of peer review. Even with close consideration of publication time frames and corresponding schedules of the negotiations, there is no guarantee that articles will be published "on time." Thus, one way to still communicate your research findings to conference stakeholders in a timely and more accessible manner is to publish blogs and policy briefs alongside journal articles.

13.4 Similarities and Differences Between the Four Research Projects

Commonalities and differences of the four PhD projects are shown in Table 13.2. The following sections discuss four aspects in detail: access and preparation, data gathering, data analysis, and positionality.

Table 13.2 *Comparison of the four PhD projects*

Negotiations	**UNFCCC**		**BBNJ**	
Researcher	Harriet Thew	Timo Leiter	Ina Tessnow-von Wysocki	Arne Langlet
Research aim	Increase understanding of youth participation in UNFCCC negotiations	Understanding government negotiations and politics around climate change adaptation	Understanding practices and actors in the science–policy interfaces in BBNJ	Understanding the actor network in the BBNJ negotiations
Role	Active participation in the NGO space	Active participation as advisor in the government negotiations, and as observer	Observer	Observer
Researcher mode	Individual researcher	Individual researcher	Collaborative team research	Collaborative team research
Attended sessions	COPs 21, 22, and 23 and intersessional negotiations; youth preparation meetings ahead of each COP	COPs 23, 24, 25, 26, and intersessional negotiations; meetings of constituent bodies	BBNJ IGCs 1–5 (four digitally; one on site), intersessionals	BBNJ IGCs 1–5 (three digitally, two on site), intersessionals
Data collected	Field notes, documents	Field notes about negotiation procedures, iterations of negotiation texts, country statements	Field notes, material collected on-site (e.g., publications, flyers)	Field notes, documents
Data collection method	Participant observation, semistructured interviews	Participant observation, informal interviews	Participant observation, semistructured interviews	Participant observation, semistructured interviews
Data analysis	Qualitatively, including longitudinal analysis, document analysis	Qualitative content analysis including thematic analysis	Qualitatively combined with document analysis	Quantitatively & qualitatively; quantitatively with R creating a network graph

13.4.1 Access and Preparation

To attend the negotiations, researchers need to be accredited under a country delegation, an observer organization, a UN organization, or as a media representative (see Chapter 6). Admitted observer organizations typically include academic institutions (the website of the respective negotiation secretariat contains a list of observer organizations). NGOs that have "Consultative Status to the United Nations Economic and Social Council (ECOSOC)" can attend open negotiation sessions under the United Nations. Depending on the negotiation forum, there may be access restrictions for certain stakeholder groups, such as observers (see Chapter 6). Different types of accreditations may also impact how you are perceived by others and affect your positionality, as discussed in Section 13.4.4. As part of a government delegation, for instance, politically sensitive matters might influence the research process. As PhD candidates, we managed to secure access to the respective negotiations through different channels.

Harriet was able to take part in the UNFCCC COPs through the University of Leeds, which is a UNFCCC-accredited observer organization. Timo initially participated as an observer for GIZ as part of his previous job, and in 2018 as a member of the German delegation as an advisor before shifting back to an observer accreditation through the London School of Economics. Timo's participation as a member of the German delegation enabled him to witness the negotiations first hand, but required more active involvement in the negotiation process.

Ina and Arne participated as part of the research team MARIPOLDATA, led by Alice Vadrot, who trained them in the preparation and conduct of CEE. They gained observer status through the International Studies Association, an organization with consultative status to the UN ECOSOC. The NGO badge provided them with access to the UN building and the formal sessions, but not to consultations between parties.

A common lesson from all four projects is that preparation prior to attending the negotiations is key. It is useful to familiarize yourself with the legal jargon used within negotiations (see Chapter 8), as well as the general structure of the UN system, with its complexity of actors and parallel negotiations (see Chapter 6). In Timo and Harriet's cases, they had already attended several UNFCCC negotiation sessions prior to commencing their PhDs, and Ina had participated in the Ad Hoc Open-Ended Expert Group on Marine Litter and Microplastics. Arne had not taken part in an international negotiation beforehand, but prepared by reading through key documents and getting familiar with the rules and procedures.

Being familiar with the processes and procedures of negotiations helps to navigate this complex and hectic environment. The multiyear observation and preparation period that was required to fully understand the inner workings of the UNFCCC negotiation process allowed Harriet and Timo to draw on an established network of contacts. Timo also benefited from years of experience as an observer for GIZ. Furthermore, having experienced different roles as an observer and a country delegate offered him a chance to witness the side-event space as well as getting a view into the actual government negotiations, which are often parallel worlds in the same venue (see Chapter 7).

We all found that it takes time to immerse ourselves in the processes in order to be able to understand how things operate and how actions shape the negotiations. Ina and Arne started as newcomers as they had not participated prior to 2019, but they felt that being part of a team which conducts CEE helped in overcoming possible challenges in data collection and analysis (see Chapter 11 and Campbell et al. 2014). The value of CEE lies in the diversity of individual researchers within the team, in terms of level of experience, gender, nationality, and scientific discipline (see Chapter 11). It is a great help if a more experienced senior researcher is part of the team.

Within MARIPOLDATA, Ina and Arne collectively prepared their attendance prior to the negotiations during a two-day preparatory workshop. They got acquainted with relevant literature (Campbell et al. 2014; Hughes and Vadrot 2019; Kawulich 2005), and exchanged practical guidance on how the negotiations work, how a negotiation day is structured, what the procedures for access are, and the customs on site. They also familiarized themselves with the specific contents of the negotiations, including the positions of main actors. Moreover, they prepared narratives and consent forms and identified and contacted potential interview partners prior to the conference (see Chapter 9). A division of work between attendance at formal sessions, parallel side events, and interviews further helped to organize their time more effectively.

Tips:

- Prepare by familiarizing yourself with the content of negotiation site(s), common practices, and jargon.
- Identify and contact interview partners in advance.
- Speak with people who have already participated in the respective negotiations to get insights prior to attending.
- Inform yourself about the different ways to access the negotiations (accreditation) and identify potential options available, for example through your university (if an observer organization), other NGOs, or a national delegation.
- Select, to the extent possible, your type of accreditation and your accreditation entity according to your research objectives.

13.4.2 Data Collection

We applied a mix of methods to collect the data needed for pursuing our particular research interests. Although all of us undertook some form of ethnography, we differed in our approach and use of ethnographic data collection methods (see Table 13.2).

Harriet found ethnography particularly appealing as it facilitates incorporation of participant experience into research design and because it enables, with reflexive application, reciprocity without compromising ethical concerns regarding participant–researcher power dynamics (Hammersley and Atkinson 2007; Madden 2010). It enabled her to experience climate governance spaces first hand, alongside participants, gaining greater understanding of their experiences without taking time away from their voluntary activities. In order to test her data collection methods, she went through a deliberative process and conducted a scoping study at a UNFCCC intersessional conference in June 2015. This allowed her to identify participants and to assess how her data collection methods – participant observation, interviews, and thematic analysis of publicly available documents – would contribute to gathering the necessary data for her study. Harriet discussed potential research questions with more experienced members of her case study organization and practiced observing participants as they engaged in the conference.

Participant observation was also used by Timo to understand how UNFCCC negotiations work and how the interests and positions of different actors lead to the agreed text. Part of his observations were undertaken as a member of a government delegation which enabled him to participate in both open and closed negotiation sessions, wherein he collected different types of data through observations, informal talks and exchange with other participants: (a) iterations of negotiation texts produced during the negotiations, (b) country statements, and (c) observations of the negotiation process.

Ina and Arne also built on ethnographic data collection methods through CEE (see Chapter 11). CEE helps in overcoming difficulties of comprehensively covering (parallel) sessions, conducting interviews, and taking field notes in a hectic and multi-sited environment. Furthermore, it enables joint collection and brainstorming on site – for example, through morning and evening briefings, and exchanges of experiences and impressions. Observing international negotiations as a team makes it possible to produce an exhaustive account of these international negotiations that is beyond the possibility of a single ethnographer. In contrast, Timo, as a lone researcher, had to focus on a narrower set of topics that were close to his area of expertise.

International negotiations are complex, intense and may take place simultaneously at different sites (see Reflection Box 11.2). A research team can more comprehensively cover relevant data collection of the event. Ina and Arne undertook field work as a research team to attend parallel sessions and make sense of the overall context of the negotiations and state positions throughout all topics. They prepared a data collection matrix for each session which allowed them to make and codify systematic observations of every session attended by one of the team members. The structure of the data collection matrix allowed them to quickly organize their data and provided comparability between negotiation settings among team members. The matrix consisted of standardized data-entry categories, including Date, Time, Actor, Negotiation Format, Agenda Item of the Negotiations, and Content of Observation. Thus, Ina and Arne were able to simultaneously take notes without having to specify a number of contextual factors for each observation and with the ability to combine the data each day and analyze the data jointly across the different negotiation settings.

Ina and Arne further supplemented their data with interviews they conducted with participants in the negotiations and textual documents that were produced by the delegates, as well as material that was handed out at the negotiation site. They realized that a combination of different methods can be particularly helpful to collectively understand the negotiations at hand. Working within a team and using a combination of approaches enables the creation of a more comprehensive data set, which is useful for conducting SNA (see Reflection Box 12.1).

Tips:

- Establish a field-note-taking technique tailored to your research questions (e.g., types of observations, content of statements, tone of voice, dynamics in the room, etc.).
- Organize your data by marking the date, time, place, and negotiation element under discussion.
- Record delegates' names and statements in the plenary to identify interviewees and questions.
- Set priorities according to your research interest (e.g., in case of scheduling conflicts – it may be worth conducting an interview over attending a side event).

13.4.3 Data Analysis

Whereas we all used similar ethnographic methods to collect data, our analysis methods differed. Harriet took a longitudinal, ethnographic approach to facilitate insights into participants' experiences and processes of meaning-making. This is a subjective process by which individuals and groups make sense of their experiences, with meaning described by Krauss (2000) as "the underlying motivation behind thoughts, actions and even the interpretation and application of knowledge" (p.763). Harriet used a case study approach, which can be particularly useful when studying a real-time situation wherein the researcher has limited control over the events under scrutiny (Yin 2011). She focused on a UK-based youth NGO to enable observation of and immersion in their preparatory activities and discussions throughout the year, in addition to participant observation during UNFCCC COPs and intersessionals. Harriet approached her intended case study organization through a gatekeeper, using purposive sampling, the most common approach in ethnographic research, determining a specific group to focus on and the particular context in which she was interested (Madden 2010). She treated consent as an ongoing process: regularly reminding participants of her research aims, checking whether they were comfortable with her observing their meetings and asking for feedback regarding her positionality.

A common critique of ethnographic and case study research is that, given the small number of participants, it is difficult to generalize results. Harriet found this to be a challenge when submitting articles for publication, with peer reviewers keen to know more about the extent to which her findings could be applied to the broader youth constituency of the UNFCCC (YOUNGO). Triangulating document analysis with her other research methods was particularly useful in this regard. For example, in her paper on young people's justice claims (Thew et al. 2020), she thematically analyzed documents produced by YOUNGO and found that there were similarities in articulated justice claims to those she had identified in her case study.

Ina used various qualitative methods to complement event ethnography, including participant observation and semistructured interviews with document analysis to make sense of the science–policy interfaces within the negotiations. Through this approach, the team could identify practices of agreement-making – in Ina's case science–policy interfaces – that are not found in documents or that can be studied through quantitative studies. This gave insights into the processes of decision-making and negotiation, the interactions among actors, the negotiation sites, and the dynamics, which tend to be neglected in international relations literature. Using event ethnography at these negotiations helped her to better understand the context, as well as to identify important actors, sites, and practices of science–policy interfaces within the process. Insights from semistructured interviews offered information on the informal processes and social relations that made up the science–policy interfaces prior to, during, and after the actual negotiations. Additionally, document analysis of UN treaty draft texts made it possible to compare negotiation texts at different stages of the negotiations (see Chapter 8). This was valuable for Ina's research on how stakeholders envisaged the science–policy interfaces for the implementation of the agreement, as well as to study the final uptake of scientific concepts within the legal text. The approach of combining different qualitative methods therefore enabled her to empirically study the role of science and knowledge in the BBNJ negotiations.

Arne took a more quantitative approach to analyzing the ethnographic data. While he used CEE to collect data, he applied computational data analysis to identify social networks. He used the bulk of recorded statements to find references to International Organizations (IOs) in order to uncover the underlying institutional network in global marine biodiversity governance (see Reflection Box 12.2). All the statements were computationally scanned for references to IOs, which were then coded to become links in the network of actors (states and IOs). He found that states refer to IOs in order to strengthen their position within the agreement-making process, and used these references to construct a network of institutions involved in global marine biodiversity governance.

Focusing on identifying the underlying networks of global agreement-making processes, Arne found that conducting social network analysis at international negotiations has great potential (Paterson 2019), as international politics are increasingly conceived as a network phenomenon (Kahler 2011). However, it also presents the researcher with substantial challenges in data collection and analysis (see Reflection Boxes 12.1 and 12.2). While CEE can help to address the limitations of the "lone" ethnographer (see Reflection Box 11.1), the interpretation of data depends very much on the composition of the research team (see Reflection Box 11.2). As SNA is primarily quantitative in nature, it strips the data of many nuances and dimensions. Therefore, he also used his ethnographic knowledge and contextual understanding to attach meaning to the networks that were constructed computationally.

Tips:

- Consider a combination of analytical methods.
- Triangulate between different data sources.
- Reflect on notes, data, and your interpretations with other colleagues.

13.4.4 Positionality

A traditional challenge of ethnography is keeping the balance between critical distance and engagement with the social context (Flick 2006). This requires pragmatic and reflective efforts from the researcher to position oneself within large-scale international negotiations.

As we reflect on our own position within the negotiations, we realize that we started with certain expectations but retained flexibility to adapt to the unfolding events.

For example, being part of the German government delegation provided Timo with access to spaces that nongovernmental observers could not access. This position gave him access to privileged information shared "behind the scenes," whereas in a youth activist meeting he would have been perceived as an outsider in that space. These experiences show that one particular type of accreditation is not better than another, but, where possible, the type of accreditation needs to match the social group and sites where the respective research question can be addressed.

It is also not uncommon for researchers in global environmental governance processes to "wear multiple hats," shifting between collecting data, advising governments and/or NGOs, engaging in activism, and speaking to the press. Timo and Harriet may wear suits in government meetings, but they don T-shirts and jeans to participate in a protest. This is a simplified visual representation of our agency as researchers to dynamically position ourselves, adapting to different occasions. As Kerr and Sturm (2019, 1139) put it, "assumed status, positioning and associated capital are never static." As such, reflecting on ones' own positionality cannot be static either.

Harriet used a method of close engagement and careful listening rather than pursuing a fixed hypothesis (Guba and Lincoln 1994; Krauss 2005). Being a critical realist researcher included acknowledgment that she was part of the social reality being studied and could not be separated from it, prompting continuous reflection on her positionality and the potential impact her actions could have. She reflected deeply upon her positionality, revising her behavior in the youth constituency which she had been involved in for a couple of years prior to her PhD and taking a step back from groups in which she had previously been very active to ensure that she didn't portray herself as a leader whom her prospective participants should feel obliged to speak to. Harriet sought to mitigate the power dynamics associated with being a researcher (Hammersley and Atkinson 2007) by engaging with group activities as much as possible whilst trying not to influence their discussions with her own perspectives. She slept on the floor in student houses, engaged in communal cooking and cleaning during group gatherings and was an enthusiastic participant in team-building exercises, icebreaker games, and songs around bonfires. She kept a reflexive diary throughout data collection to document her reactions to the data as the project went on. Whilst the diary contents were not used directly in the papers, this was an important tool to help her to identify ways in which her personal views and experiences may have shaped the research (Gaskell and Bauer 2000). She also reflected in the diary on how her perceptions changed over time, considering the impact of sociocultural trends, politics and ongoing exposure to climate change governance processes and the participatory spaces which operate around them (Madden 2010).

Researching the BBNJ negotiations, Ina and Arne felt that being an insider or an outsider is not a dichotomous choice; rather, one's position is along a scale of insiderness to outsiderness, supporting recent literature on this issue (Kerr and Sturm 2019). It became clear to them that they moved (and had to move) more toward the insider position when realizing how, after one to two weeks of attending the negotiations, their language had changed. They had by then largely adopted the vocabulary (including abbreviations) of the delegates, which helped them not only to communicate with participants but also to follow and understand the overall agreement-making process.

Applying a CEE approach, they found that working in a team not only meant increased coordination and data collection opportunities, it also provided them as researchers with a continuous "mirror" in which they could reflect upon their theories, approaches, and results. They did this by repeatedly presenting their (preliminary) findings and impressions to each other in the team, as well as to other academics and diplomats. Within their team, although all members were immersed in the same discipline and took part in the same fieldwork, they continuously challenged their understanding of the events and critically rethought how they had come to their results. When presenting to other academics and diplomats, they discussed their findings in light of other academic backgrounds or working experiences. This way, they continuously challenged their assumptions and approaches during different steps of the research process. This was particularly helpful in the case of SNA. When conducting SNA, the researcher must always check the empirics of whether his/her assumptions about the nodes and links in the network hold. For example, within the MARIPOLDATA research team, a common practice has been that Arne first visualized network graphs using the data from the ethnographic fieldwork before they interpreted them as a team based on common and individual experiences from the ethnographic fieldwork. Hence, CEE can help the researcher to come closer to "reflexive sociology," as practiced through everyday research (Bourdieu and Wacquant 1992). CEE has proven to be a valuable addition to SNA as it allows the researcher to reflect on one's (network theoretical) assumptions and to give meaning to the network positions and measurements.

Tips:

- Critically reflect on your role, your values and your type of access, and how this shapes the data gathering, interpretation, and knowledge you generate.
- Reflect on how preconceived views or ideas you hold before starting the research might shape your research hypothesis and perspective going into the study of the negotiations. Reflect, together with peers, on how this might shape your perceptions and observations.
- Go outside of the "bubble" of the group or spaces through which you access the negotiation sites (e.g., a particular constituency) and be open to other perspectives on how things unfold.

13.5 Conclusion

This chapter has presented experiences from four PhD projects that research global environmental negotiation sites from diverse angles, using a multiplicity of methods. Applying the methodological knowledge presented in this book to our studies, we highlight the broad range of questions that can be addressed when researching global environmental negotiations: from youth participation and social network analysis to science–policy interfaces and the processes and politics of negotiation sessions. While there is a diversity of ways to research intergovernmental negotiations, there are themes that link all four experiences: (a) access and preparation, (b) data collection, (c) data analysis and (d) positionality. This chapter takes the reader through all four PhD projects along these themes.

We recommend that early career researchers, regardless of which environmental negotiations they seek to study, familiarize themselves with the complexity of the UN system and the procedures and legal language used in the negotiations, and undertake basic preparations prior to attendance, such as arranging meetings with relevant stakeholders, preparing documents for ethnographic field work and becoming knowledgeable about the specific contents of the negotiations under observation. Overall, our experiences show that even when negotiation events are only two weeks in duration, they require a long preparatory period (in some cases up to several years) to be able to fully understand the processes, gain access, establish contacts, and produce high-quality research outputs. In this regard, studying global environmental negotiations is similar to traditional ethnographic research. We also emphasize the value of combining multiple research methods for data collection and analysis to gain a more complete and nuanced picture of events. Finally, we have gained insights from studying global environmental negotiations that broadened our understanding in ways that would not have been possible through document analysis alone. We therefore recommend that motivated students explore the possibility of researching UN negotiations and hope that the experiences outlined in this chapter are helpful in preparing new PhD projects.

Further Reading

1. Dimitrov, R. (2012). The politics of persuasion: The UN climate change negotiations. In P. Dauvergne, ed., *Handbook of global environmental politics*, 2nd ed. Cheltenham: Edward Elgar Publishing, pp. 72–86.

Emphasizes the important role of the dynamics and circumstances of the negotiation process and, consequently, the need to observe the negotiation sites in order to explain negotiation outcomes.

2. Bäckstrand, K., Kuyper, J. W., Linnér, B. O. and Lövbrand, E. (2017). Non-state actors in global climate governance: From Copenhagen to Paris and beyond. *Environmental Politics*, 26(4), 561–579.

Provides a good overview of the history of nonstate actor participation in the UNFCCC, and is a good introduction to a larger body of excellent critical work in this space.

3. Tessnow-von Wysocki, I., and Vadrot, A. B. M. (2020). The voice of science on marine biodiversity negotiations: A systematic literature review. *Frontiers in Marine Science*, 7, 1044.

Introduces the reader to the complex negotiations and highlights its relevance for future marine biodiversity governance by giving an overview of the current state of the art on the main topics identified in peer-reviewed literature related to the BBNJ process until 2020.

4. Paterson, M. (2019). Using negotiation sites for richer collection of network data. *Global Environmental Politics*, 19(2), 81–92.

Highlights the immense opportunities of negotiation sites for the collection of network data and pragmatically addresses issues researchers may encounter when sampling network data.

References

Bourdieu, P., and Wacquant, L. J. (1992). *An invitation to reflexive sociology*. Chicago, IL: University of Chicago press.

Campbell, L. M., Corson, C., Gray, N. J., MacDonald, K. and Brosius, J. P. (2014). Studying global environmental meetings to understand global environmental governance: collaborative event ethnography at the Tenth Conference of the Parties to the Convention on Biological Diversity. *Global Environmental Politics*, 14(3), 1–20.

De Santo, E. M., Ásgeirsdóttir, Á. , Barros-Platiau, A. et al. (2019). Protecting biodiversity in areas beyond national jurisdiction: An earth system governance perspective. *Earth System Governance* 2, 100029. https://doi.org/10.1016/j.esg.2019.100029.

Dimitrov, R. (2016). The Paris Agreement on Climate Change: Behind closed doors. *Global Environmental Politics*, 16(3), 1–11.

Eastwood, L. E. (2019). *Negotiating the environment: Civil society, globalisation and the UN*. London: Routledge.

Flick, U. (2006). *An introduction to qualitative research*, 3rd ed. London: Sage Publications.

Gaskell, G. and Bauer, M. W. (2000). Towards public accountability: Beyond sampling, reliability and validity. In G. Gaskell and M. W. Bauer, eds., *Qualitative researching with text, image and sound: A practical handbook for social research*. London: Sage, pp. 336–350.

Guba, E. G. and Lincoln, Y. S. (1994). Competing paradigms in qualitative research. In N. K. Denzin and Y. S. Lincoln, eds., *Handbook of qualitative research*, 2nd ed. Thousand Oaks, CA: Sage, pp. 163–194.

Hale, T. (2016). "All hands on deck": The Paris Agreement and nonstate climate action. *Global Environmental Politics*, 16(3), 12–22.

Hammersley, M. and Atkinson, P. (2007). *Ethnography: Principles in practice*. New York: Routledge.

Hughes, H., and Vadrot, A. B. M. (2019). Weighting the world: IPBES and the struggle over biocultural diversity. *Global Environmental Politics*, 19(2), 14–37.

Hughes, H., Vadrot, A. B. M., Allan, J. I. et al. (2021). Global environmental agreement-making: Upping the methodological and ethical stakes of studying negotiations. *Earth System Governance*, 10, 100121.

Intergovernmental Oceanographic Commission UNESCO. (2020). *The science we need for the ocean we want: The United Nations Decade of Ocean Science for Sustainable Development (2021–2030)*. https://unesdoc.unesco.org/ark:/48223/pf0000265198.

Kahler, M. (2011). *Networked politics: Agency, power, and governance*. Ithaca, NY: Cornell University Press.

Kawulich, B. B. (2005). Participant observation as a data collection method. *Forum: Qualitative Social Research*, 6(2), 1–28.

Kerr, R. and Sturm, D. (2019). Moving beyond "insider or outsider": The ethnographic challenges of researching elite sport facilities in New Zealand. *Qualitative Inquiry*, 25(9–10), 1137–1147.

Krauss, S. E. (2005). Research paradigms and meaning making: A primer. *The Qualitative Report*, 10(4), 758–770.

Leiter, T. (2021a). Progress in implementing adaptation: Insights from project proposals and scientific literature. In United Nations Environment Programme (UNEP), ed., *The Adaptation Gap Report 2020*, pp. 33–40. www.unep.org/resources/adaptation-gap-report-2020.

Leiter, T. (2021b). Do governments track the implementation of national climate change adaptation plans? An evidence-based global stocktake of monitoring and evaluation systems. *Environmental Science & Policy*, 125, 179–188.

Leiter, T., and Pringle, P. (2018). Pitfalls and potential of measuring climate change adaptation through adaptation metrics. In L. Christiansen, G. Martinez, and P. Naswa, eds., *Adaptation metrics: Perspectives on measuring, aggregating and comparing adaptation results*. Copenhagen: UNEP DTU Partnership, pp. 29–48.

Madden, R. (2010). *Being ethnographic: A guide to the theory and practice of ethnography*. London: Sage.

Mandani, K. (2013). Modeling international climate change negotiations more responsibly: Can highly simplified game theory models provide reliable policy insights? *Ecological Economics*, 90, 68–76.

Thew, H., Middlemiss, L. and Paavola, J. (2020). "Youth is not a political position": Exploring justice claims-making in the UN Climate Change Negotiations. *Global Environmental Change*, 61, 102036.

Thew, H., Middlemiss, L. and Paavola, J. (2021). Does youth participation increase the democratic legitimacy of UNFCCC-orchestrated global climate change governance? *Environmental Politics*, 30(6), 873–894.

Thew, H., Middlemiss, L. and Paavola, J. (2022). "You need a month's holiday just to get over it!" Exploring young people's lived experiences of the UN climate change negotiations. *Sustainability*, 14(7), 4259.

Vadrot, A. B. M. (2020). Multilateralism as "site" of struggle over environmental knowledge: The North-South divide. *Critical Policy Studies*, 14, 233–245.

Vadrot, A. B. M., Langlet, A., Tessnow-von Wysocki, I. et al. (2021). Marine biodiversity negotiations during COVID-19: A new role for digital diplomacy? *Global Environmental Politics*, 21(3): 169–186.

Yin, R. K. (2011). *Applications of case study research*. Thousand Oaks, CA: Sage.

14

Adapting

Responding to Unforeseen Research Circumstances

ALICE B. M. VADROT

14.1 Introduction

In order to conduct fruitful research on, or during, global environmental conferences, you need to be prepared for the unexpected. The complexity of multilateral negotiations (Chasek 2001), the performative nature and drama of large-scale events (Craggs and Mahony 2014; Death 2011), and the contingent struggle between states that may become visible in relation to specific parts or terminologies of the negotiation text (Hughes and Vadrot 2019, Tessnow-von Wysocki and Vadrot 2022) that nobody in the room could have anticipated demand a certain degree of flexibility from the researcher. Once on site, you may be forced to adapt your research focus, methodology, or data collection strategy to unforeseen circumstances, access conditions, and negotiation dynamics. There are many examples of situations that demand rapid reaction and adaptation strategies on the spot (e.g., denied access, sessions running in parallel, or lack of agreement). It is therefore advisable to think about such circumstances beforehand, and to prepare contingency and risk management plans. However, on-site adaptation to unforeseen developments is only one side of the coin.

Agreement-making has always been, and continues to be, shaped by gradual change, to which both participants and researchers must adapt. Although the principles of multilateral diplomacy do not seem to have changed significantly in the past fifty years, the stakes of global environmental conferences have become higher and practice has sharpened. Firstly, as environmental degradation accelerates – threatening the lives of millions of people, and severely affecting the living conditions of the poorest and most marginalized communities – participating in environmental conferences can no longer be considered an innocent activity. As scholars of agreement-making – its sites, actors, and processes – we are not only forced to adapt to both incremental and sudden change, it is also our duty to explain continuity and disruption, and to anticipate future changes and their consequences for how we design a political process that will ensure the health of our planet.

Secondly, more and more actors negotiate in a shorter time, thereby stepping up on-site pressure. The pace of talks has accelerated, with meetings becoming shorter, thereby rushing delegates into the rapid development of negotiation text. This leaves less time for the individual negotiator to become familiar with the complexity of the matter and to bargain over contested passages with other delegates. The image in Figure 14.1 exemplifies the gradual change over the past three decades. The UNCLOS III negotiations took place

Figure 14.1 February 27, 1981, Third United Nations Conference on the Law of the Sea, informal meeting of the Drafting Committee, at United Nations Headquarters, New York.
Source: Material obtained on 07.07.2022 from the website of the United Nations Audiovisual Library of International Law, located at www.un.org/law/avl.

between 1973 and 1982 in Montego Bay Jamaica, with negotiation sessions lasting for several weeks; participants traveled by ship and worked on the text for several weeks with pen and paper. The BBNJ Treaty (see Figure 14.2), which will be an implementing agreement of UNCLOS, is negotiated during five intergovernmental conferences lasting for two weeks each.

One factor that has contributed to these accelerations is the use of information and communication technologies (ICTs) and social media. ICTs facilitate text-based negotiations, as demonstrated by Figure 14.2, with screens showing the intervening party and the negotiating text. These gradual changes, which involve the adaptation of agreement-making to those technological innovations that have been reshaping diplomatic practice and text-based negotiations (also conceptualized by the term "track-change diplomacy"; Adler-Nissen and Drieschova 2019), need to be considered by researchers, along with changing actor constellations, power dynamics, issue linkages, and new types of actors joining the negotiation site (e.g., mayors of cities, youth movements, business actors, start-ups).

The COVID-19 pandemic provides a recent example of the need to adapt to the unexpected in the two aforementioned ways. In March 2020, the pandemic disrupted agreement-making by forcing conference hosts to indefinitely postpone scheduled meetings, since travel bans had been implemented and sites, including the United Nations

Figure 14.2 IGC 2 of BBNJ negotiations, *Earth Negotiations Bulletin*.
Source: IISD/ENB | Francis Dejon.

Headquarters, were closed. Treaty secretariats and organizers adapted to the situation by initiating digital meetings, implementing hybrid solutions, and strengthening on-site hygiene measures, as exemplified by the example of the COP26 of the UNFCCC and several other meetings (Allan et al. 2021). These developments have compelled many scholars to adapt their research projects and methodologies, either by conducting digital ethnography wherever possible or by refraining from negotiation site fieldwork. While a pandemic is an extreme case and may pass as quickly as it came, COVID-19 has been jeopardizing global environmental agreement-making for more than two years, forcing both actors and researchers to work out new strategies and practices to adapt to the new situation and its effects: in many cases, meetings were less transparent and inclusive, had fewer outcomes, and were much more difficult to navigate. This may well have long-lasting effects on both the conduct and the study of global environmental meetings.

This chapter provides guidance on how to cope with the unexpected, discusses specific situations that may occur on site, and shows how to make use of digital and hybrid sites in methodological and conceptual terms. Firstly, it will present a set of typical unforeseen situations that may arise at any point during the research process, especially during fieldwork, and identifies strategies for adapting to these kinds of unanticipated events. Secondly, it will illustrate how the methodology of an entire research project can be modified by using the example of an ERC research project, MARIPOLDATA, whose research team had to cope with the indefinite postponement of marine biodiversity negotiations owing to the spread of COVID-19. Thirdly, it will demonstrate that digital ethnography may be used to study virtual sites of agreement-making, and guide readers through the application of this research method. Fourthly, the chapter will discuss the future role of digital and hybrid meetings, before examining whether and how these might alter prospects for the study of global environmental agreement-making.

14.2 Typical Situations That Demand Adaptation

There are several types of situations that demand flexibility from the researcher; they should be anticipated through contingency and risk management plans when developing a research project. The first type regards restricted access to your research object. This includes the situation where several meetings you wish to attend take place at the same time and you need to decide which one to follow, as well as deciding whether to use your time for interviews or participant observation. The second type involves unforeseen negotiation developments and dynamics. For instance, the negotiation item might move into a completely different direction, thus challenging research assumptions, hypotheses, and the conceptual framework developed beforehand. The third and final type may occur after the fieldwork is over. You might realize that your data (interviews, field notes, or network data) are incomplete, meaning that you either have to complement your dataset, select a complete subset of data in the incomplete dataset, or triangulate. The following sections go into these issues in greater detail.

14.2.1 Adapting to Denied/Impossible Access

Although (as outlined in Chapter 2), on-site research is not a precondition for producing sound research on global environmental agreement-making, it might be difficult to modify your research project once you learn that, for whatever reason, you cannot gain access to the relevant negotiation site. A contingency plan should include all options to be explored to gain access (see Chapter 2) and how you will manage the risk of not being able to carry out your fieldwork. Adapting your overall methodology and exploring different methods of data collection become almost mandatory if you still wish to conduct your research without discarding your research interest and questions.

One possible strategy if you cannot access a meeting is to "follow" it as it takes place: to reserve as much time as possible during the time window of the conference and "pretend" that you are there while following what is happening on site "from a distance" (either "a distance" from home, or, as may also happen, "a distance" on site). If available and accessible, watch webcast plenaries and working group meetings online, read the daily *ENB* reports each morning as soon as they are published, follow the agenda, look for accessible documents online, track the proceedings by following the conference's twitter account or hashtag, ask attendees (that you will have contacted beforehand) to send you regular updates on specific issues you are interested in, and put together a list of potential questions that you would wish to ask your interviewees. You can collect and use most types of textual data (as described in Chapter 8), and reconstruct negotiation dynamics by triangulating data, for example, by complementing data from the *ENB* reports and available online government statements with semistructured interviews.

Videos of meetings made available by the UN greatly facilitate research at a distance; even when watched at a later stage, these records allow researchers to collect observational data through digital participant observation and ethnography (Pink 2013; Vadrot and Ruiz Rodríguez 2022). The MARIPOLDATA research project provides one example of ethnographic data collected on site that was complemented with data collected with the help of recorded sessions. Because project funding was received after the first IGC had already taken place, my team could only attend IGC 2 and IGC 3 of the BBNJ negotiations in New York. However, thanks to the efforts of one team member who collected data provided by the recordings of IGC 1 – through digital ethnography and the same data collection strategy that we had already used on site – we could at least complement our field notes of the plenaries and working group sessions (see Chapter 10 and Box 14.1).

14.2.2 Adapting to Changing Negotiation Dynamics

Imagine that you have secured access to the conference that you planned to attend; you have figured out where and when your negotiation item will be on the agenda; you arrive at the site and are given a seat in the negotiation room, from which you can observe the

Box 14.1 Collaboration between researchers participating on-site and "from a distance"

With the increase of online and hybrid formats, collaborations between researchers participating on-site and "from a distance" are becoming more frequent. It may be an advantage to collaborate with somebody "at home" who can, for instance, watch parts of the event online and jump in to take fieldnotes, which may be particularly valuable if the on-site person cannot access the negotiation room or has scheduled an interview in parallel. In turn, watching meetings online and conducting "digital ethnography" (see Box 14.2), reading the *ENB* reports and draft texts, and participating in regular meetings with a colleague or team of colleagues on site can allow a researcher to follow the event "from a distance" and engage in collaborative event ethnography (see Chapter 11).

While there are many advantages to this form of collaboration, it is of the utmost importance to reflect on the ethical and practical aspects of this kind of collaboration to avoid unequal distribution of work, misunderstandings regarding research and data collection priorities, and ownership. Therefore, the collaboration process should start before the actual fieldwork and involve clarification of and agreement on:

1. The purpose of the collective research (cooperation or collaboration, Chapter 10);
2. How to balance the research and data needs of all collaborators;
3. How to address institutional needs and expectations (e.g., data needed for a PhD thesis, authorship, ownership);
4. How to divide research tasks (data collection, management, analysis, writing).

proceedings. The chair introduces the negotiation item; they may point to specific brackets and options in the text that delegates should comment on when expressing their views; and governments start to make their statements, which you carefully listen to. While preparing your research stay, you had developed specific assumptions about issues that might become central or spark controversy, positions that might conflict, and the agreements that would be reached. As you listen to the speakers you notice that your prior expectations and assumptions do not match your empirical observation in the field, or that the talks are developing in a direction that you had not anticipated. Maybe an actor you planned to observe does not engage in the negotiation item at all – there has been a change in the delegation or in the government's priorities, leading to less engagement at the conference. Or, you were interested in a specific negotiation item or an element of the negotiated text that you specifically perceived as controversial and suitable for an analysis of major conflict lines between actors or between some of their negotiation strategies, yet the item is hardly discussed or is not even addressed.

A good example of such a situation is provided by the fourth plenary of the IPBES, which took place in February 2016 in Kuala Lumpur (Malaysia). The IPBES was adopting its first two assessments, which was considered an important milestone for the so-called "IPCC for biodiversity"; it was also a testing ground for its functionality as a global assessment body feeding knowledge into the CBD and other biodiversity-related conventions. This plenary attracted a handful of researchers concerned with the adoption of the first assessments; most of them assumed major conflicts in relation to a chapter on pesticides and diverging government views on how explicit the relationship between biodiversity loss and neonicotinoid use should be made in the summary for policymakers (SPM; i.e., the negotiation document summarizing the assessments' key findings). Many participants assumed that negotiations on pesticides would be difficult and would dominate the talks as a whole.

For my part, I attended the meeting as an observer mostly interested in "epistemic selectivities" (see Chapter 2) and conflicts arising during the adoption of the methodological assessment. I was less focused on the adoption of the thematic assessment on "Pollination, pollinators, and food production," where the pesticide issue would be addressed. I had planned to attend all plenaries (where overall progress was discussed) and working group meetings (where the methodological assessment was negotiated). In addition, I conducted interviews with several state representatives and assessment authors to better understand the assessment practices and processes that led to the SPM drafts.

On the second day, during a plenary session where the chairs of working group meetings were reporting on progress made in each group, I observed a series of interesting statements by several South American governments on why they wanted to support the concept of "biocultural diversity" in one of the assessment chapters (dealing with noneconomic aspects of pollination); they asked the chair not to delete the concept from the draft. The atmosphere in the room felt tense and the issue caught my attention. I reached out to scholars who attended the thematic assessments' adoption. Many of them had expected clashes between governments on the pesticides chapter; they were disappointed about the smooth negotiation process and could not understand why "biocultural diversity" had emerged as a key object of struggle that nobody had anticipated.

I decided to change my research strategy and attend the other working group meetings in order to be able to follow the conflict. I realized that its implications for state competition over the epistemic representation of biodiversity might be significant. Before doing so, I went through *ENB* reports to understand what had happened during the two days I had missed and spoke to other researchers "in the corridors," as well as Hannah Hughes, with whom I was in close contact during field work. We had started collaborating with the aim to compare the IPCC and IPBES. While I was on site doing ethnography for my post-doctoral research, Hannah observed the proceedings "from a distance." Regular talks enabled us to exchange our views on what was going on and make sense of the on-site dynamics.

In 2016, this strategy enabled me to quickly grasp the state of play and better situate the conflict within the broader IPBES setting. On the way back from the fieldwork, we used the collected material to reconstruct what had happened and identify relevant state and nonstate actors; we then reached out to them for interviews and slowly started to unpack the struggle and its meaning. We drew on Pierre Bourdieu's "act of naming" concept and developed our own approach: the "weighted concept," which allowed us to conceptualize the struggle over a specific term as a key element of agreement-making and the contestation of world order (Hughes and Vadrot 2019).

Negotiations offer many opportunities to collect data. However, if a specific event catches your attention and you decide to change your focus, be careful not to lose direction or control over your research endeavor. Key conditions for being able to adapt to changing on-site negotiation dynamics include:

1. Developing a solid knowledge base on the overall negotiation process before you arrive at the site (making yourself familiar with the agenda, all negotiation items, and the schedule);
2. Updating your knowledge base by collecting and reading information material (e.g., the *ENB* reports every morning), using negotiation apps if available, or holding conversations with other on-site researchers or actor groups on a regular basis (if you are part of a national delegation or NGO, you will have the opportunity to attend meetings where delegates update each other; see Chapter 13), If you are part of a team, make sure you regularly meet to update each other on what is going on (see Chapter 11);
3. Staying in control of your research work by carefully revising your schedule (see Chapter 2) and by adapting your data collection strategy;
4. Taking analytical and methodological field notes (see Chapter 2, 10, and11). *Analytical field notes* can include preliminary assumptions or observations that you consider relevant; they also outline your reasoning for changing the data collection focus. *Methodological field notes* should document contextual information, changes in methodology, incomplete data collection, and adaptation strategies.

The aforementioned example shows that researchers addressing actors, sites, and processes of agreement-making and who attend global environmental conferences need to be flexible enough to adopt a different research route if they do not come across what they had expected to "find." Being "on location" will inevitably shape your understanding of the research object; it may lead you to refine your research questions and focus. If negotiation dynamics change and you consider these changes to be relevant for your project and the specific phenomena you wish to explore, trust your intuition and follow the research avenue that these changing dynamics have opened up.

14.2.3 Adapting to Incomplete Data

Negotiation sites are comparable to large archaeological excavations. There are a lot of potential forms of data to collect and it is almost impossible to collect all data at once, even if you have a very clear research focus, and especially if you are a "lone" researcher. Thus, although data management is an important task that you should try to perform while still on site (see Chapter 2), you need to be prepared for the possibility that, once back at your office, you find out that your dataset is incomplete. There may be several reasons for this. You may have missed important parts of the talks because you could not be in the room or simply because you were not able to capture specific dynamics during field note-taking owing to the rapid pace of government interaction; or, it may have proved impossible to interview specific actors or collect a particular kind of survey data. A worst-case scenario is losing your laptop or other device where you stored your data, which is why using cloud-based storage, a shared folder, or an external saving device (e.g., a USB flash drive), and backing up your data after each day of fieldwork, is strongly advised.

Depending on the kind of data that is missing, you can complement your dataset by collecting data after your research stay or by using other types of data to triangulate (see Table 14.1).

Table 14.1 *Dealing with incomplete data*

Type of data	Collection site	How can it be complemented?
Interview data	On site	Conducting interviews after the event (telephone interviews, virtual interviews, face-to-face interviews at the office of your interviewee) (see Chapter 9) If you use interview data to reconstruct negotiation dynamics and the role of specific actors within the negotiations, you can also use *ENB* reports and other types of text (see Chapter 8).
Field notes	Plenary and working group sessions	You can use *ENB* reports and other types of text (decisions, reports, and minutes of meetings) to reconstruct negotiation dynamics (see Chapter 8) Interviews conducted after the event can be useful to interpret specific situations (see Chapter 9) If available, you can watch recorded sessions of plenaries and working group meetings and conduct "digital ethnography."

Table 14.1 (*cont.*)

Type of data	Collection site	How can it be complemented?
	"Informal informals"	Collecting data during informal informals is problematic. In many cases, for ethical reasons you are not supposed to use the data. If you gain access to informal informals, you may take field notes, but need to be careful with how you use them (e.g., in your publications). Check official information available in *ENB* reports and other text sources that confirm your observations. Conducting interviews with participants who took part in informal informals and asking them to confirm some of your observations is an option to obtain "valid" data.
	Side events	Descriptions of side events can be found online. Side events are also recorded and many of them are covered by *ENB* reports. Interviewing participants or organizers of these events may also be a way to complement your field notes. The names of organizers can be found in the online program.
	In the corridors	Observations of events outside of the negotiation room or side event location are difficult to reconstruct. *ENB* reports include an "in the corridors" section to capture the atmosphere of the conference and individual perspectives on progress made. Taking pictures may be a way to capture interesting situations.
Network data	All	Depending on your network data collection method (see Chapter 12), you can either use recorded sessions to take field notes of interaction between actors that you missed, or send an online survey to participants asking them to reconstruct their interaction with other participants or to list the "top ten" participants with whom they interacted on site.

14.3 Adapting Methodology During the COVID-19 Pandemic

All over the world, national lockdowns introduced by many governments in March 2020 as a reaction to the outbreak of COVID-19 affected our social and public lives in unforeseen and disruptive ways. Moreover, the pandemic affected both ongoing and scheduled talks, disrupting environmental diplomacy as we knew it (as described in other parts of this book: see Chapters 1, 5, and 6). In the following, I will use my research project, MARIPOLDATA, to illustrate how we adapted to new circumstances by developing and applying alternative methods that allowed us to continue our ethnographic research on marine biodiversity negotiations throughout the pandemic.

14.3.1 Indefinite Postponement of Meetings

At the beginning of March 2020, when the pandemic started to disrupt our lives, we – my two PhD students Ina and Arne (see Chapter 13) and myself, their supervisor – had already planned down to the last detail how to conduct event ethnography (CEE) at our chosen site of multilateral negotiation: the fourth intergovernmental conference (IGC 4) toward a new, legally binding instrument for the conservation and sustainable use of marine biodiversity beyond national jurisdiction (BBNJ) (Tessnow-von Wysocki and Vadrot 2020). The so-called BBNJ Treaty negotiations involve more than 100 governments and several observers – approximately 600 state and nonstate actors in total – meeting at the UN Headquarters in New York; their mandate is to develop and adopt the treaty in the course of four two-week-long IGCs. We had already attended the second and third IGCs, where we collected data through CEE, exploring the various roles of science in the treaty-making process; we expected governments to adopt the treaty at IGC 4 or, if a fifth meeting was needed, assumed that the talks would lead to an outcome by summer 2020 at the latest.

We had registered for IGC 4 – my PhD students as members of the International Studies Association (ISA, which is accredited as an observer to ECOSOC, grants access to several UN negotiations for its members, and provides special support to young scholars) and myself as a member of the Austrian delegation. Knowing that a large part of IGC 4 would be negotiated within the framework of "informal informals," implying restricted access for observers (only five representatives of nonstate actors were allowed in the room), I had reached out to the head of the Austrian delegation, who supported our research and invited me to join the delegation. We had booked our flights and accommodation (close to the UN Headquarters), prepared all documents required for our research (informed consent forms, interview guides, and project information sheets), and discussed hypotheses regarding the upcoming meeting, potential conflict lines, and expected developments.

During preparatory meetings in January and February 2020, we divided up the research tasks (participation in side events, interviewing, and participation in "informal informals"); each of us would focus on specific issues in the treaty text and on specific actor groups. We had also updated our matrix, which we used for field-note-taking, and identified potential interviewees by consulting IGC 3 participant lists and critically examining our sample (we had already conducted more than fifty interviews at IGC 2 and IGC 3). We went through our daily schedule for fieldwork (team meeting at 7:30 a.m.; accessing the building at 8:00 a.m.; securing seat in the conference room at 8:30 a.m.; time for conducting interviews, collection of material, recruiting interviewees, observing negotiations from 10 a.m. to 1 p.m. and 3 p.m. to 6 p.m.; and attending side events during lunch breaks). We had also developed an emergency plan in order to be prepared for restricted access and to be able to quickly adapt to unforeseen developments on the spot (see Table 14.1).

On March 5, I was informed about the cancellation of IGC 4 by the head of the Austrian delegation. At that time, COVID-19 cases were increasing ominously, people had started wearing masks, and disinfection devices were being installed in buildings. We had to cancel our accommodation and flights. Only one week later, on March 13, my team and I met for the last time in our offices and together watched the press conference where the

Austrian Chancellor announced a national lockdown. This meant that we would not be able to return to our offices. I developed an emergency plan to ensure that we could continue our research from home, including daily online project meetings where we discussed our work; thanks to these, we developed a new working practice and managed to continue our research. Fortunately, we had saved our scientific data and material in a shared university directory that was accessible to all team members, hence we were able to continue working.

14.3.2 Conducting a Survey

Now we were faced with the problem of not knowing if, when, and under what conditions BBNJ negotiations would resume. Would the COVID-19 pandemic make the talks redundant, drive environmental issues away from public and political consciousness, or reduce the likelihood that there would be a BBNJ Treaty at all, especially in view of the fact that some states, such as Russia and China, had opposed a new treaty quite strongly from the beginning? Not knowing how long the pandemic would continue to unsettle our lives – and definitely not expecting that it would rule the world for more than a year – I thought about ways to continue studying the process and find out how multilateral diplomacy would respond to such a crisis.

During the early days of the pandemic, when national lockdowns became the "new normal" in all parts of the world, I developed the idea of an online survey reaching out to diplomats and other stakeholders involved in the BBNJ process. I intended the survey to be both a route out of the impasse of a disappearing object of research and a project that the whole MARIPOLDATA team could be engaged with. I hoped that this would enable us to explore new ways of working collectively during the first phase of teleworking, which was entirely new and somewhat challenging for us.

When we started to discuss ideas and draft the survey, we noticed that many scholars were rushing to use survey methods to reach out to all kinds of audiences and target groups in order to assess the impact of COVID-19 on everyday lives. Would it be ethical to ask people to participate in our research during a time of crisis, and would the BBNJ community welcome our work? We saw that, after an initial state of shock, several NGOs and scientists started launching online webinars and circulating BBNJ-related content; this reassured me that there was enough momentum for initiatives seeking to keep the BBNJ Treaty negotiations high on the political and public agendas. Many people interested in the BBNJ process seemed to use the additional time released by global lockdowns to further engage in BBNJ-related issues – diving deeper into the various package elements of the treaty and debating outside of the negotiation room.

In order to capture these activities and their potential impact on the future agreement, we designed our survey around our research interest – that is to say, changing communication patterns and the potential of online tools for state and nonstate interaction. Furthermore, it was our ambition to contribute to maintaining momentum by widely disseminating the survey and selecting ideas on how to move on with the BBNJ process despite the pandemic. Our online survey ran in May 2020, was accessed by 709 persons, and was completed by

105 respondents, many of whom had participated in the talks either as national delegates or nonstate observers.

Our results suggested that the effects of online tools on participation and inclusiveness appeared to determine how participants perceived the suitability of virtual arrangements for continued formal negotiations of any sort online (Vadrot et al. 2021). When asked whether online negotiations made the BBNJ process more inclusive, state actors responded quite differently from nonstate ones. State respondents – who tended to answer "no" – argued that the process was "already quite" or "highly" inclusive. Nonstate respondents drew a different picture, pointing to the challenges of physically attending IGCs. Some mentioned that attending online negotiations might be cheaper and less time consuming. They also pointed to groups that might benefit, including delegations from developing countries, local communities and Indigenous Peoples, and marginalized communities with limited resources (Vadrot et al. 2021, 9).

14.3.3 Studying Emerging Digital Sites

We also learned about several online initiatives organized by various actors to maintain intergovernmental dialogue during the pandemic. Very quickly, the Informal Intersessional High Seas Treaty Dialogue started (April 2020); since then, more than 200 state and nonstate participants have exchanged views through this dialogue (using Webex). A few months later, in September 2020, the Virtual Intersessional Work of the Intergovernmental Conference was launched by the president of the negotiations to facilitate the written exchange of opinions among more than 1,000 registered participants (using Microsoft Teams platform).[1] These two digital sites were established to keep up the momentum of the talks and to provide both state and nonstate actors with a digital space wherein they could exchange views on various parts of the treaty draft.

I was very fortunate to participate in these virtual talks and decided to use the same field-note-taking method and matrix as developed for on-site fieldwork. I quickly noticed that online interaction was built on "old" practices from the diplomatic realm, although enacted through new digital ones. I concluded that diplomatic practice in the digital space was situated somewhere between continuity and change – it is detached neither from past treaty-making tradition nor from future diplomacy. Most participants in the High Seas Treaty Dialogue and BBNJ Intersessional Work gained access because they were registered for IGC 4, and many had followed the BBNJ process since the first IGC. There seemed to be a shared appreciation among participants of what constitutes "normal negotiation practice." This shared collective "background knowledge" on structural conditions for treaty text negotiation, the kind of practices that are considered meaningful, the sense of where one actor stands in relation to others, and the degree of success of strategies designed to influence the negotiation's outcome had all developed over time and through repetition (Adler and Pouliot 2011). Nonetheless, some BBNJ practitioners

[1] At a later stage, the Virtual Intersessional Work of the IGC also started to employ web-based tools to facilitate discussion between state actors (using Webex).

were already performing on virtual sites and had developed a collective sense of how to act online meaningfully.

These insights from practice theory allowed me to argue that online dialogues already carried meaning because they were built on "old" practices – though enacting new ones. This implied that we needed to think more carefully about the potential of online interaction (on digital sites and at hybrid meetings) in the context of multilateral negotiations. We should also reflect on the limitations of digital tools, the role(s) they might play in international negotiation settings, and their effect on agreement-making in the future (Chasek 2021; Vadrot et al. 2021). While the broad range of online initiatives and hybrid meetings, and the high degree of state participation since the outbreak of the COVID-19 infection, are clear indicators of the commitment to the global sustainability agenda and to multilateralism as a practice to agree environmental protection at the international level, current digital diplomatic efforts are still not designed for treaty-making.

This new research avenue implies a range of new research questions. Will we see extended use of digital tools in environmental negotiations after the pandemic has passed? What will be the impact on power constellations, inclusiveness, and trust relations? How can we make sense of the diverse (digital and hybrid) forms of interaction among states? Do new sites shape how marginalized actors influence treaty-making, or will they contribute to the exclusion of marginalized voices? How can we conceptualize these new forms of negotiation, and how will we approach digital or hybrid diplomatic practices? One route that we started exploring in our research is to adapt the methodology of digital ethnography to the specific needs of negotiation sites.

14.4 Digital Ethnography and Hybrid Futures

Suiseeya and Zanotti (2019) conducted an ethnographic study of how actors used digital sites to influence formal procedures during COP21. Yet, digital ethnographies capturing these emerging forms of influence – through social media, for instance – were not designed to investigate the new types of online meeting that appeared in response to the COVID-19 pandemic. Thus, digital ethnography meant to study, for instance, social media interaction alongside in-person environmental conferences (see Chapter 6) cannot easily be applied to situations where the virtual seems to become the (dominant) "new normal"; it needs to be adapted to the purpose of investigating digital and hybrid meetings (Adler-Niessen and Eggeling 2022;Vadrot et al. 2021; Vadrot and Ruiz Rodríguez 2022).

Approaches inspired by the Science and Technology Studies (STS) treat media technologies and the internet as socio-material complexes (Gillespie et al. 2014) or forms of "social shaping" (MacKenzie and Wajcman 1985) and field sites in their own right (Hine 2017). They appreciate the multiplicity of meanings that participants attribute to specific technologies and the multiple ways in which the latter are used (Mol 2002). The context determines a given form of use of digital space, which is constituted by "specific sets of practices through which digital spaces acquire meaning" (Hine 2017, 23). STS-inspired approaches consider how "the agency of users and the significance of practices [constitute] – in a thorough-going way – what a technology is" (Hine 2017, 23). This "offers a rationale for conducting ethnographic studies as a means to find out exactly what that technology becomes in each specific context of use" (Hine 2017, 23).

Thus, digital ethnography is a "way of doing ethnography that is part of and participates in a digital-material-sensory environment rather than simply ethnography about the digital" (Pink 2014, 420). In a digital context, defining a field's spatial and temporal dimensions "is equivalent to drawing its boundaries" (Tunçalp and Lê 2014, 60); gaining "access" to the field is "being able to capture interactions or behaviours of interest" (Beaulieu 2017, 34); and being in the field is reframed in terms of "experiential rather than physical displacement" (Hine 2000, 45).

Digital ethnographers can study a field that is purely online (a single online site or several) or that is both online and offline; they can observe real-time social phenomena and/or recorded social phenomena (Tunçalp and Lê 2014, 65). Finally, digital ethnographers must consider their participation level in the field and whether they should disclose their identity and presence (Tunçalp and Lê 2014, 65), for digital ethnographers can easily lurk in the background compared to traditional in-person ethnographers (Hine 2000, 48).

Scholars interested in digital sites of agreement-making thus need to explore how to apply digital ethnography to either virtual or hybrid negotiation sites, find ways to access them, and make sense of what can be observed in these "virtual fields." Furthermore, the increased recourse to hybrid arrangements – such as at the UNFCCC's COP26 and the CBD's COP15 – introduces new forces that are bound to shape both negotiation dynamics and research practices.

14.2 Reflection Box: You are not watching TV, you are collecting data!

By Silvia C. Ruiz Rodríguez

When working in the project MARIPOLDATA, I collected digital ethnographic data of the first session of the negotiations for a new treaty to conserve and sustainably use marine biodiversity in the high seas. I did this a year after this session took place by taking notes of the videos available on https://media.un.org/ as my colleagues were unable to conduct on-site ethnography during this session. From this experience, I would suggest that **digital ethnography** of recorded videos of international environmental negotiations **differs from on-site ethnography in the following respects:**

- **Temporal dimension:** Digital ethnography breaks "the linearity of time" (Tunçalp & Lê 2014, pp. 64–65) and enables researchers to experience and revisit the phenomenon of study in ways that on-site ethnography does not. It allows researchers to observe agreement-making sites as if they were part of them (Pink 2013) and as many times as the researcher would like.
- **Spatial dimension**: When conducting digital ethnography, the field site is bounded to the website where the videos are available; when conducting on-site ethnography, the field site is bounded to the physical negotiation rooms and related digital spaces (see Suiseeya and Zanotti 2019).
- **Bodily experience**: While it is true that you can experience the events of the site through your senses, in a "bodily way" (Gray 2016, p. 504) even when conducting digital

ethnography (Hine 2000). You can feel emotions and live experiences more strongly on site, increasing your understanding of the issues at hand, such as actors' "red lines"; polite, diplomatic language; among others.

On-site and digital ethnography present different advantages and challenges. Digital ethnography poses particular methodological and practical challenges to the researcher.

First, digital ethnographers of international environmental conferences do not take part in the community they research (Vadrot and Ruiz Rodríguez 2022). This implies that digital ethnographers do not perform practices that delegates perform on site, which may limit their understanding and their ability to interpret these. Furthermore, researchers cannot see how delegates interact informally because conference videos do not document these interactions. For instance, NGO delegates lobby in in-person international conferences by having casual conversations with representatives of state actors in hallways and other public spaces, or by distributing pamphlets and other printed material.

Second, it can be more exhausting to conduct digital ethnography than on-site ethnography, just as it is more exhausting to focus on an online lecture than on a face-to-face lecture. Additionally, you can look at a screen only for a (healthy) limited period during a day, hindering you from experiencing the "real pace" of negotiations, which often finish late at night due to extended sessions (Campbell et al. 2014).

These challenges do not decrease the quality of digital research, although it may mean you can answer different research questions, depending on the method you use. For instance, an on-site ethnographer might focus on how NGOs exert influence in-person in negotiations, while a digital ethnographer might focus on when and how states use NGO-developed concepts in their statements.

One important lesson from observing online interaction during the COVID-19 pandemic is that digital ethnography should explore both online and offline dynamics while assuming that digital practices will maintain routines and strategic behavior already developed in the physical negotiation room. In this regard, the "digital turn" in global environmental agreement-making contains both disruptive and gradual elements that practitioners and scholars alike will need to come to terms with. Different online and hybrid arrangements introduce different dynamics, especially in relation to the temporal and spatial dimensions, access options, issues of transparency, inclusiveness, and equality (Vadrot and Ruiz Rodríguez 2022). Methodological tools borrowed from digital ethnography have enabled scholars to quickly adapt to the emergence of new digital and hybrid sites; however, we do not yet know what the future of global environmental agreement-making will be.

Governments tend to resist the idea of negotiating in virtual space and argue for the need of face-to-face meetings (Vadrot et al. 2021). Hybrid solutions, for their part, introduce new dynamics by creating two types of sites and participants: those that are on site and those that "join in virtually," with fewer possibilities to intervene and shape the agreement-making process. For the study of digital or hybrid meetings, this may come with the advantage that scholars, especially those that cannot afford participation, can take part in their empirical study. However, it also means that we have to ask new research questions to assess how these dynamics shape the processes and sites of agreement-making and the strategies of actors to shape treaty text.

14.5 Conclusions

This chapter conceptualized methodological adaptation as a two-way approach. On the one hand, we need to be prepared to confront unforeseen situations at any point in the research process, especially during fieldwork, where changing negotiation dynamics, access restrictions, or incomplete datasets may challenge the validity of our research. On the other hand, we need to adapt to the gradual changes that have been reshaping actors, processes, and sites of agreement-making; this is exemplified by the increased use of ICTs in the context of global environmental conferences and treaty-making. Although digital tools had already started influencing negotiation practices, especially regarding their pace and scope, the COVID-19 pandemic introduced a new dynamic by disrupting traditional agreement-making and paving the way for new types of meeting and interaction – digital and hybrid.

These new objects of research and emerging field sites pose new challenges for both the practice and the study of global environmental agreement-making. Indeed, they question what it actually means to observe agreement-making by "being there" (O'Neill and Haas 2019), and what it takes to build trust and negotiate in a multilateral setting. Digital ethnography is one very promising methodology that helped me to adapt to the new situation ushered in by COVID-19. Yet, instead of losing its relevance after the pandemic has passed, it might well stay and, in the guise of "hybrid ethnography," become a key approach enabling us to examine the ways in which virtual and hybrid sites have become the "new normal" of agreement-making.

Further Reading

1. Vadrot, A. B. M., Langlet, A., Tessnow-von Wysocki, I. et al. (2021). Marine biodiversity negotiations during COVID-19: A new role for digital diplomacy? *Global Environmental Politics*, 21(3), 169–186.

One of the first papers to discuss the impact of COVID-19 on global environmental agreement-making and the study thereof; uses the BBNJ case and describes the results of a survey conducted to assess state and nonstate actors communication patterns and use of digital formats during the global lockdown in 2020.

2. Chasek, P. (2021). Is it the end of the COP as we know it? An analysis of the first year of virtual meetings in the UN Environment and Sustainable Development arena. *International Negotiation*, 12(3), 1–32.

Provides an overview on how different agreements adapted to COVID-19 and what the future of the COP might look like after the pandemic.

3. Vadrot, A. B. M., and Ruiz Rodríguez, S. C. (2022). Digital multilateralism in practice: Extending critical policy ethnography to digital negotiation sites. *International Studies Quarterly*, 66(3), 1–13. https://doi.org/10.1093/isq/sqac051.

Proposes a definition of digital multilateralism as a set of digital and physical diplomatic practices performed across space and time by state and nonstate actors engaged in a joint enterprise of simultaneous negotiation through physical and digital infrastructures in information-rich, highly interactive environments and illustrates how critical policy ethnography can be expanded to digital negotaiton sites using the BBNJ case.

References

Adler, E., and Pouliot, V. (2011). International practices. *International Theory*, 3(1), 1–36.

Adler-Nissen, R., and Drieschova, A. (2019). Track-change diplomacy: Technology, affordances, and the practice of international negotiations. *International Studies Quarterly*, 63, 531–45.

Adler-Nissen, R., and Eggeling, K. (2022). Blended diplomacy: The entanglement and contestation of digital technologies in everyday diplomatic practice. *European Journal of International Relations*, 28(3), 640–666.

Allan J., Soubry B., Rosen T. and Tsioumani E. (2021). The State of Global Environmental Governance 2020. Report, International Institute for Sustainable Development.

Beaulieu, A. (2017). Vectors for fieldwork: Computational thinking and new modes of ethnography. In L. Hjorth, H. Horst, A. Galloway, and G. Bell., eds., *The Routledge Companion to Digital Ethnography*, London: Routledge, pp. 29–39.

Campbell, L. M., Corson, C., Gray, N. J., MacDonald, K. I. and Brosius, J. P. (2014). Studying global environmental meetings to understand global environmental governance: Collaborative event ethnography at the tenth Conference of the Parties to the Convention on Biological Diversity. *Global Environmental Politics*, 14(3), 1–20.

Chasek, P. (2001). *Earth Negotiations: Analyzing Thirty Years of Environmental Diplomacy*. Tokyo: United Nations University Press.

Craggs, R. and Mahony, M. (2014). The geographies of the conference: Knowledge, performance and protest. *Geography Compass*, 8(6), 414–430.

Death, C. (2011). Summit theatre: Exemplary governmentality and environmental diplomacy in Johannesburg and Copenhagen. *Environmental Politics*, 20(1), 1–19.

Gillespie, T. (2014). The relevance of algorithms. In T. Gillespie, P. J. Boczkowski, and K. A. Foot, eds., *Media Technologies: Essays on Communication, Materiality, and Society*. Cambridge, MA: MIT Press, pp. 167–193.

Gillespie, T., Boczkowski, P. J., and Kirsten, A., eds. (2014). *Media Technologies: Essays on Communication, Materiality, and Society*. Cambridge, MA: MIT Press.

Gray, P. A. (2016). Memory, body, and the online researcher: Following Russian street demonstrations via social media. *American Ethnologist*, 43(3), 500–510.

Hine, C. (2000). *Virtual Ethnography*. London: SAGE.

Hine, C. (2017). From virtual ethnography to the embedded, embodied and everyday internet. In L. Hjorth, H. Horst, A. Galloway, and G. Bell, eds., *The Routledge Companion to Digital Ethnography*. London: Routledge, pp.21–28.

Hughes, H., and Vadrot, A. B. M. (2019). Weighting the world: IPBES and the struggle over biocultural diversity. *Global Environmental Politics*, 19(2), 14–37.

Mackenzie, D. and Wajcman, J., eds. (1985). *The Social Shaping of Technology*. Milton Keynes: Open University Press.

Mol, A. (2002). *The Body Multiple: Ontology in Medical Practice*. Durham: Duke University Press.

O'Neill, K. and Haas, P. M. (2019). Being there: International negotiations as study sites in global environmental politics. *Global Environmental Politics*, 19(2), 4–13.

Pink, S. (2013). *Doing Visual Ethnography,* 3rd ed. London: SAGE.

Pink, S. (2014). Digital–visual–sensory design anthropology: Ethnography, imagination and intervention. *Arts and Humanities in Higher Education*, 13(4), 412–427.

Suiseeya, K. R. M., and Zanotti, L. (2019). Making influence visible: Innovating ethnography at the Paris Climate Summit. *Global Environmental Politics*, 19(2), 38–60.

Tessnow-von Wysocki, I., and Vadrot, A. B. M. (2020). The voice of science on marine biodiversity negotiations: Systematic literature review. *Frontiers in Marine Science*, 7, 614282.

Tessnow-von Wysocki, I., and Vadrot, A. B. M. (2022). Governing a divided ocean: The transformative power of ecological connectivity in the BBNJ negotiations. *Politics and Governance*, 10(3).

Tunçalp, D., and Lê, P. L. (2014). (Re)Locating boundaries: A systematic review of online ethnography. *Journal of Organizational Ethnography*, 3(1), 59–79.

15

Conclusions

Reflecting on the Future (Study) of Global Environmental Agreement-Making

ALICE B. M. VADROT AND HANNAH HUGHES

15.1 Introduction

Global environmental negotiations unfold at complex sites and are shaped by multiple actors and processes. As outlined in the Introduction, scholarly interest in negotiation settings has steadily increased and led to new insights on *global environmental agreement-making* – a concept introduced to broaden understanding of what constitutes global environmental negotiations and to encourage critical thinking about the methodological and ethical stakes of studying this expanding set of sites, actors, and processes (Hughes et al. 2021). These sites may continue to proliferate in the years to come with the possibilities offered by new forms of digital participation, which have become more common since the outbreak of COVID-19 (Vadrot et al. 2021), and as efforts to collectively respond to the rapidly degrading natural environment increase. Although the multilateral setting, with its "old-fashioned" diplomatic practices and formalities, creates the impression of stability, routine, and immutability, there is change and the possibility to do global environmental relations differently. We understand critical scholarship to have a vital role in illuminating enduring power relations and revealing potential openings for change and transformation to ensure agreement-making enables better collective stewardship of the Earth. This aspiration nourished the objective of this book to problematize *how* and *why* we conduct research *at* and *on* global environmental negotiations and to evaluate and expand the concepts and methods available to further this study.

Conducting research on global environmental agreement-making is challenging. It involves multiple decisions throughout the research process, from delineating the puzzle to identifying the site of study, and from developing a research methodology to analyzing the different types of data collected on and off site. Practical issues such as access to a venue, getting familiar with a site, or finding a quiet place for an interview are as important as the selection and application of methods, particularly in a multilateral negotiation setting, which can, at first, be experienced as a hostile and impervious environment. The chapters of this book have aimed to make negotiation sites, in all their forms, more accessible. The book has taken the reader through the different stages of studying agreement-making, illustrating how theoretical and conceptual frameworks can be developed and methods for data collection and analysis can be identified, implemented, and combined. This step-by-step approach guides the reader through application, with authors drawing on multiple examples and lessons learned from their own research experiences at and on diverse negotiation settings. The fact that scholars working on different actors, sites, and processes share similar experiences suggests some degree of comparability between negotiation settings (e.g., COP, subsidiary bodies, etc.) and agreements (e.g., UNFCCC, CBD, BBNJ, CITES). This indicates that there is a shared agreement-making culture to interrogate, although it does not imply that we should neglect to study single events in relation to their historical, political, and institutional contexts. As other scholars concerned about the future of global environmental governance indicate (Burch et al. 2019; O'Neill et al. 2013), reflexivity is critical to advances in the study of environmental relations. Reflexivity is a central pillar of both the agreement-making framework and the design of the book, and the contributing authors encourage and identify methods for researchers to become reflexive of their own positionality and relationship with their "objects of research" and the implications of the methods they employ for data collection and analysis.

It is likely that most researchers have experienced moments when the endless battle over words observed during negotiations and often until late into the night – the theater, drama, and performance (Death 2011) accompanying diplomatic habitus and routines – dimmed hope in multilateral efforts. Once reached, can an agreement introduce the transformative change needed to address the multiple environmental crises and alter world order? Multilateralism has come under scrutiny for multiple reasons, and by researchers and practitioners alike. We do not consider agreement-making sites and multilateral negotiation practices in their current form the best institutional response. Voting procedures, conditions for participation, and possibilities to alter legal text and introduce alternative framings, epistemologies, or worldviews are far from ideal. However, there are signs of change, and there are always potential openings for more transformative shifts in agreement-making processes. This is why studying global environmental negotiations in terms of agreement-making implies the imperative to constantly and critically assess its practice and the potential to change in time and space. Why and how do powerful actors use agreement-making sites to become more powerful? What strategies do marginalized actors employ to contest world order and make their voices heard? How do different epistemologies have the potential to alter the meaning of words in a final negotiation text? Multilateral environmental negotiations are sites of struggle over the environment, how we know it and how we relate to it, and, as such, they are critical sites of study (Hughes and Vadrot 2019; Vadrot 2020).

This concluding chapter brings central elements of all chapters to the fore, reflects the need for critical thinking, and problematizes the future of agreement-making and the study thereof. In addition, it addresses critical questions that run through the book and its chapters: Why does it matter to "be there"? How to cope with closeness and emotion? Is data ever complete? What will "being there" mean in the future? It closes with a reflection on future research questions and themes.

15.2 The Critical Nature of Agreement-Making

The book offers the concept of agreement-making as a framework for conceptualizing and connecting the myriad actors, sites, and processes observed at global environmental meetings across space and time. A central aim of introducing this conceptualization is to bring to the fore the stakes in agreement formation, as a site of challenging and potentially remaking or revising the global order of social, economic, and environmental relations (Hughes et al. 2021). The framework intends to provide a way of connecting up diverse forms of scholarship within and across issue areas to explore the making of agreement, as well as what a given agreement creates in the form of new partnerships, networks, and initiatives. This connecting up of scholarship across space and time is critically important to keep up with collective attempts to address current levels of environmental degradation, to measure its effectiveness, and to identify and illuminate what else is being made alongside and in the name of environmental action.

The chapters of the book offer methodological tools for developing research projects into the study of environmental negotiations, as a broadened field of activity, by outlining ways of assembling an approach: from theory and concepts to the methods for gathering and analyzing information collected on and at sites of agreement formation. What becomes clear through the authors' reflections on conducting this research is that studying the myriad of actors, sites, and processes that constitute agreement-making is not just about assembling – the putting together of concepts and methods. To think in terms of the stakes involved, and to keep this in mind throughout the assembly process, also makes *unraveling* critical to the study of global environmental agreement-making. This is perhaps clearest in Chapter 5, where Marcela describes how she observed environmental negotiation in the Ashaninka territory before she arrived at a global intergovernmental meeting. It is in these moments in the study of agreement-making – when scholarly expectations don't fit with the scene viewed – that openings are created and there's a chance to see differently, reproblematize, and learn anew.

The necessity of allowing the unfolding research to unravel theories, concepts, and the conduct of research itself is evident throughout the book. In Chapter 3 on frameworks, Michele describes the back and forth between empirical observation of NGOs and the theoretical understanding of their significance in international relations. The discrepancy between theory and observation initiated the development of an analytical framework to demonstrate the influence NGOs can have on collective action. What is also clear from Naghmeh's discussion in the chapter, however, is that there is rarely a single model that can be stamped onto a new site of research. Each research problem requires adjusting the chosen approach, and when the limits of a framework are reached this can become the catalyst for developing new approaches. This includes the development of new concepts, which we explore in relation to the weighted concept and through which we aim to better explain the role of knowledge in upholding or challenging the making of order (see Chapter 4).

However, as the chapters also make clear, it is not only the theoretical approach that needs to be tailored to the research problematic; adaptability and a readiness to seize an opportunity or revise expectations are critical elements in studying the rapidly evolving sphere of collective environmental action. As Alice illustrates in Chapter 14, COVID-19 has perhaps been the most dramatic event to shape the conduct of research on negotiations in recent years, but every meeting, field trip, and interview requires an ability to respond, adapt, and change when circumstances do not present themselves as expected. The need to adapt and change at all stages of the research process brings into focus a core pillar of every chapter in the book: the significance of reflexivity in conducting research on global environmental agreement-making.

Reflexivity facilitates and enables change in research practice. This is clearest in Chapters 10 and 11 on ethnography and collaboration, as well as in Chapter 13, where reflection on research experiences is the central theme. As many scholars before us have identified (Bourdieu 2004; Burch et al. 2019; O'Neill et al. 2013), reflexivity is a critical tenet of providing new knowledge and insights on global environmental agreement-making and a practice that has strongly influenced the presentation of the book. As Kim and Laura outline in Chapter 12, reflecting on observations – both those taking place in the room and their inward effect – is built into the ethnographer's schedule and daily practice (see Table 10.3). This is a valuable form of data that cannot always be immediately processed, as we indicate in Chapter 4 on concepts: being struck by an observation – feeling the effect in the room of silence or nonresponse and not being able to explain its occurrence – can prove to be a key moment in the research process, presenting a puzzle that needs to be explored.

Thus, reflecting – looking back on ourselves and our observations – is critical to all stages of research, from problematizing to collecting data, and from analysis to write-up. It is certainly critical to learning and developing, which is why as a practice it has informed how we have written and presented the book as a collective of authors. Rather than directing the reader – telling them what to do, why, and how – as authors we have aimed to provide a methods book by recounting our experiences of conducting research. In the chapters we describe how we have done it, the mistakes we have made, and what these taught us so that the reader can learn with and through these experiences as relevant to their own research practice. Those in the midst of or having recently finished their PhD projects are perhaps the best equipped to translate their recent experiences into advice and tips to the reader embarking on a new project, which is exactly what Arne, Harriet, Ina, and Timo offer in Chapter 13 when they compare their research interests, sites of study, and approaches to fieldwork. This perspective is also offered throughout the book in the form of reflection boxes, which gives unique insights and practical application on the content of the chapter from those that are currently or have recently attempted to use a particular theory, method, or resource, or sought to access and observe new and different sites for the purpose of analysis.

The practice of reflecting is not important simply for producing more insightful analyses and developing new theories and concepts – the recognized "work" of scholarship – it also has a critical role to play in challenging the reproduction of order. It is through reflexivity that the scholar can become more aware of their positionality and the social, political, and economic order of relations produced in and through knowledge from that social location. This brings us back to the agreement-making framework and serves as a reminder that this is not just about the methods of conducting this type of research, but also the ethics (Hughes et al. 2021). A frequent observation made in the book is how the badge worn in a global environmental meeting has the potential to distinguish you from or connect you to other actors at the event. For Timo (Chapter 13) as part of the German delegation, and Yulia (Chapter 11) as a writer on the *ENB* team, their affiliation enabled unique and often behind-the-scenes access to the intergovernmental negotiating process. However, as Harriet identifies in Chapter 13, the badge can also condition how you are responded to by research participants, possibly leading to less of an insider perspective if, for example, your respondents are suspicious of the authority and motivations of government delegates, as in the case of youth activists. This highlights the varied positions that researchers can occupy within the world of environmental conferences and the potential to shape this world as it is being observed, studied, negotiated, and (re)created through environmental agreements.

An important method the researcher has to shape this universe is through knowledge produced and disseminated in publications. This brings us to the stakes in global environmental agreement-making. In the Introduction we highlighted that researchers of global environmental politics frequently share a stake – a growing concern – in the state of the environment and how to contribute to the collective response. However, researchers have their own individual stakes that operate alongside this because individual achievement and contribution to knowledge (within academia) is frequently measured by research outputs. As highlighted by Noella et al. in Chapter 12, the need to distinguish the individual researcher through publications as a measure for promotion and tenure puts pressure on collaborative relations and has to be sensitively managed to ensure that each researcher within the collaboration earns what they need to advance academically. This need to publish distinguishes the academic stakes from those of other actors invested in the process.

This focus and reflection on individual and collective stakes in global environmental agreement-making highlights both the shared and the unique aspects of these, but also perhaps cautions researchers to the effect that individual stakes in the process can have. With the pressure of time and achievement that academic measures produce, is there time to be attentive of and sensitive to the order of relations written into and through knowledge? Is there time to cultivate relationships with researchers in the Global South and North in a more precarious institutional setting and potentially with less (paid) time and financial resources for conducting research? Is there time to establish collaboration with authors in countries that are facing politically challenging circumstances that shape this institutional setting and the possibility (and safety) of working? Is there time to unravel and allow different, new shared stakes to emerge that might not have the same academic currency?

Authors of this book have taken this time. In Chapter 13, Harriet describes how she earned the trust of the youth participants she was researching through sharing their experience of climate activism at climate cops. At the same time, she reminded youth participants of her position and objectives as a researcher to enable renewed consent to their participation in her project. And she tested her observations and analysis with her research participants so that they could challenge her perspective and views on the process as she informed theirs. In Chapter 5, Marcela identifies the stakes for Indigenous negotiators, representatives, and researchers in agreement-making – the preservation of worlds and the possibility of realizing new worlds – and describes the research journey that has shaped her research practice as she engaged with, learned from, and supported Indigenous politics. These are self- and world-altering experiences, which reshape and change the stakes of engagement for the researcher. They highlight that while, as an institution, academia may measure individual influence and success by publication, there are more practical ways that researchers are engaging with and shaping agreement-making through the relations established and nurtured through cultivating different forms and practices of research.

15.3 Closeness, Completeness, Emotions, and "Being There"

All authors of the book have participated in global environmental negotiations – many of them in different capacities, for various research projects and purposes, as single researchers or as part of a team, with multiple stakes and research agendas. As we engaged with each other's research practices and methods at two book workshops, we drew on our own experiences and noticed how challenging it was to talk about research *at* and *on* negotiation sites without becoming emotional. This raised questions that we wanted to explore further here in the conclusion, as it is suggestive of new directions for more careful consideration in future work. Have we become too close to our research objects and participants? What does closeness in this context mean? How close do I need to be? Is it a precondition for good research, or can it interfere with the objective to produce a good research outcome? Last, but not least, what does "being there" change in this respect, and is it a requirement for conducting research on global environmental agreement-making?

We also noticed that the discussions of these topics amongst a group at different career stages and with different levels of experience and immersion in agreement-making processes raised concerns and insecurities around what is an appropriate level of contact and what amounts to sufficient knowledge of an institution or process. These are concerns that we wanted to acknowledge here as we felt they were likely shared by many readers. We also wanted to be clear that the book is not proposing one way to conduct research or "know" global environmental negotiations, but aims to encourage diversity and methodological innovation in all forms of research practice.

15.3.1 Closeness and Completeness

In the book, chapters and authors have emphasized the importance of familiarizing onself beforehand and immersing oneself on site, and many of the book's authors have had unique opportunities to do this as *ENB* writers and as activist researchers. However, starting research from a point of not knowing anything and not understanding the processes that you're observing remains equally valuable: it offers the opportunity to learn and be conscious of the changes to thinking that immersion in the field brings. It also identifies one of the central purposes of the book – to provide a practical guide to help all researchers navigate, especially the newly acquainted. Beth and Tracy provide exactly this in Chapter 6, as they walk the reader through the structure of a global environmental negotiation so that if you, as a reader, are new to the process, you can quickly orient yourself and your research on site. In Chapter 7, Jennifer expands out from the negotiating room to the nooks and crannies that constitute the range of agreement-making sites, identifying the locales that are currently understudied but that offer important potential for further exploring the varied sites, actors, and processes informing agreement-making. And in Chapter 8, Jen and Pam acquaint the reader with the range of texts available for the researcher to follow a given process on and off site, to fill in gaps, and to study the formation of an agreement, as they do through the example of the Sustainable Development Goals.

In Chapter 13, the authors emphasize the importance of being there and establishing relationships before starting the research – Harriet led delegations of young women at UN conferences before she undertook research on youth participation for her PhD, and Timo acted as an advisor to the German delegation. These levels of experience can be daunting to the newly acquainted and raise the question "Do I know enough of the process to start studying it?" Similar questions often arise during the research and write-up: Have I observed enough? Have I interviewed a sufficient number of participants? Have I got all the information and data I need to draw these conclusions? And what if you can't gain access at all? Can you still know, study, and analyze global environmental agreement-making? While Chapter 13 emphasizes the benefits of being there and being part of proceedings, this isn't the only way. Every researcher needs to be aware of, reflect on, and adapt to the limitations of their research practices, and this includes having unrivaled access and closeness to the process.

Familiarity with proceedings and close ties and affinities to the actors studied can raise its own issues. When the language of the process is learned it can be easy to forget the separateness and confusion that was felt in the beginning – and there's value in this distant vantage point that can be lost over time (Coleman and Hughes 2014). The closer a researcher becomes and the stronger the relationships formed, the harder it can be to maintain a critical view of an actor's participation, even when this may be upholding and reproducing hierarchies and power asymmetries that a researcher set out to illuminate. Suddenly, as a researcher, we can find ourselves in the position of questioning whether and how to write these insights when they could affect the relations cultivated during the research and/or criticize an actor or institution that has a pivotal, albeit imperfect, role in environmental action. All this to say, that closeness and being there are not the only or always the best ways to study agreement-making, and are also accompanied by their own set of tensions and questions. Watching from a distance, knowing no one, standing at the back of the negotiation room or watching on your laptop in your bedroom, if this is how environmental conference spaces are accessible to you, still hold the possibility to gain unique observations and insights that can contribute to critical understanding. There is no *one* way; there is the way the researcher seeks out and secures as an avenue for conducting research and addressing the questions and puzzles that arise along the study of agreement-making.

While closeness is not a precondition, it does occur over time. Time is the critical element here, enabling the researcher to gain deeper insight as well as an ability and a desire to capture and connect observations. In Chapter 5, Marcela highlights the importance of time in forming the necessary knowledge and gaining the understanding to conduct sensitive and ethical research on and with Indigenous diplomacies. We see the importance of time and closeness in other chapters as well. As a researcher spends more time studying particular actors and institutions, they learn more of their nature and the character of relations and interactions that constitute them, and new methods present themselves, such as SNA, that enable the researcher to capture these. A critical researcher is often looking for ways to evidence and demonstrate the existence of power asymmetries, how they operate, and their effects that become apparent over time, and Mat describes in Chapter 12 how SNA, as a research method, holds the potential to document these.

This time needed to become familiar with one site can be connected across sites through collaboration, and Noella et al. identify the value of this in Chapter 11. Collaboration can allow scholars to share observations and analysis across sites and connect diverse forms of scholarship. The chapter authors explore the stronger form of the collaborative relationship as developed through CEE. This highlights that it is not only the researcher's connection and closeness to the study objects that matter, but also the closeness cultivated with other researchers through collaboration. While collaboration brings its own tensions to be navigated, it offers incredible power and potential for expanding knowledge and understanding of the myriad actors, sites, and processes of agreement-making. Opening up and developing collaboration in more systematic and transparent ways through scholarship and its write-up has to be a critical element of future study and the collective shaping of global environmental negotiations.

Along with the question of closeness comes the issue of completeness – the completeness of data and whether it is sufficient to draw inferences and substantiate conclusions; the perennial questions: Do I have enough? Do I know enough? The notion of complete data is a particular consideration in Chapter 12, where Arne reflects on his process of data collection and "incompleteness" in Reflection Box 12.1. However, it is also evident in discussions of data collection in ethnography in Chapter 10. What dynamics does the researcher attune themselves to in their ethnographic practice? What materials and artifacts does the researcher collect, and how much of these? When is saturation (emotional, physical, and material) reached and data collection complete? In our own experience – and we can refer only to that – there is no such thing as completeness. We have never felt completely secure in the conclusions we reach, but have just felt that our observations are critical enough to be presented with the evidence collected and allow for other researchers to evaluate whether this is persuasive, sufficient or not. And perhaps, just perhaps, it's a fool's errand to think that it is possible to capture all and everything at global – or local – sites of agreement-making. Haraway tells us that the view is partial (Haraway 1988); best we accept that, acknowledge the limitiations, and connect up what we can through time and collaboration.

15.3.2 Emotions

Conducting research on global environmental agreement-making can be emotional. Emotions may come into play during fieldwork when attending a global environmental meeting or at any other research stage, especially with the stakes involved. The intensity of environmental negotiations, the drama and theater when no progress is made (Death 2011), and the joy when an agreement is reached can affect all participants, including the researcher. Fieldwork during global environmental negotiations is tiring, and the more tired we are, the more emotional we feel. Euphoria and anger are two types of emotions researchers conducting research during negotiation experience. Euphoria because of the feeling of being part of a big community, something significant that may alter how we know and govern the environment. Anger because negotiations can be slow, and any agreement, regardless of how progressive it is, is not forward-looking enough to make a real difference and induce the transformative change needed to stop environmental degradation. Although immersion in the field is a recognized component of ethnographic research, with its objective to become part of the community and practices under study, the deep emotional connection a researcher may have to the environment, its degradation, and the connection to others invested in this politics means that all researchers are, in some sense, immersed in the field and can experience its emotions.

This reveals that however we conduct research at and on negotiations involves closeness – closeness to ourselves as researchers and people that care, and closeness through personal connection with the object chosen to study. This makes demarcation – drawing boundaries around and staying distant from – unreal, unlikely, and imperfect. It also means that getting started for this type of research, as we have tried to inform and prepare the reader for in Chapter 2, isn't just these formal steps; it's also about taking a deep breath, diving in, and being prepared to perhaps lose oneself in the emotional ride of studying agreement-making. If following negotiations is diving in, when the "jamboree goes home" it's also about finding oneself again, as best one can, on the other side – picking ourselves apart from and recognizing how we have become connected to all that is seen and observed at the multiple sites, with the varied actors immersed in any given process of global environmental agreement-making.

However, it is not just the emotions experienced during fieldwork that are significant and which need to be acknowledged; it is the broader situations and structures in which we produce this research and live our lives as part of and beyond this work. Working together as a collective of authors on this book during COVID-19 lockdowns brought to light the structural dynamics that affect every aspect of academic work. Many of the authors lost childcare, and school closures meant that suddenly there was the additional need to support children's learning as well as undertake the "normal" workload of an academic job. The burden of this further increased as modules and courses were remade for the virtual learning environment, which student and teacher alike were attempting to navigate. The job market narrowed even further as many universities froze their hiring of new staff. The geography of authors was brought starkly into focus, as the politics in Brazil meant that the institutional environment that Marcela was working in became more precarious for staff and students; violence in society increased; COVID-19 took loved ones and strongly impacted on Indigenous communities. For many of us, the space is only just beginning to open up to reflect on the physical and emotional toll the pandemic has had on minds, bodies, family, work, and research relations.

Despite the effect of the situation that we found ourselves in, and the emotions we feel toward the planet and studying human and environmental exploitation, there often is not a place in scholarship for this to be expressed and acknowledged. Ethnography, as an evolving practice, clearly has an important role to play in bringing the affect – the feelings and experiences – of researching global environmental agreement-making into scholarship. However, if *how* we feel for the planet – love, fear, concern, anxiety for its beauty, degradation, and survival – motivates and animates the research and knowledge produced, then surely these emotions have an important place in all forms of scholarship and in becoming environmental stewards.

For our part, we want to acknowledge emotions here, and the very real struggle of staying invested in the study and practice of global environmental agreement-making. We want to thank the authors of the book for staying involved in and committed to providing their contributions during a pandemic; accelerating climate change and biodiversity loss; increasing plastic, chemicals and waste pollution; and the emotional toll these take on our physical and mental wellbeing. Each author has offered their experiences and, in doing so, revealed some of the lessons they have learned on this journey of studying collective action – in other words, they have revealed some of themselves to help others. Thank you for doing that.

15.3.3 "Being There"

Attending a global environmental meeting in person is a privilege. As outlined in Chapter 2, it satisfies multiple needs, especially of early career scholars: acquainting with multilateral environmental diplomacy, accessing interviewees, networking with other scholars working in your field, getting involved and engaged, and meeting key state and nonstate actors from all over the world that may become important connections in your future academic or nonacademic work. "Being there" at a global environmental meeting implies that you immerse yourself in a social world that offers multiple opportunities, including the feeling of being part of a vast, diverse community that meets to make the world a better place. Research into environmental negotiation processes and practices has strongly benefited from scholar participation in global environmental meetings. It is often said that the actual breakthrough happens "in the corridors" or "behind closed doors" and that you can get a better sense of these dynamics on site. Indeed, many studies draw on "insider perspectives" where, for instance, diplomats, activists, and *ENB* reporters turn their observations into research.

However, access to global environmental negotiations is unequally distributed and conditioned upon the availability of funding, institutional support, and successful accreditation. A researcher's economic and regional background can impede participation for formal reasons, often affecting researchers from the global South with less institutional support and funding opportunities. But this is not the only way in which access can be challenging. The very nature of global environmental negotiations and the study thereof can become an obstacle. A global environmental meeting, especially if it is a mega-event such as a UNFCCC COP, may be experienced as a hostile environment, especially by those who are not familiar with the formal and restrained culture of multilateral diplomacy or the sheer size of such a gathering. As described in many chapters of this book, attending a COP can be overwhelming, and even if a researcher gets the chance to "be there," they might constantly feel that the event remains inaccessible and almost impossible to study, especially as a single researcher.

The authors of this book have introduced the reader to different methods of data collection, including the analysis of different forms of text (Chapter 8), interviews and surveys *on* and *at* negotiation sites (Box. 3.2, Chapter 9), social network analysis (Chapter 12), and a variety of ways to conduct participant observation, including as a team (Chapter 11), as part of event ethnography (Chapter 10), and in the form of virtual participation (Chapter 14). Many methods do benefit from research on site, but can – as demonstrated in each of these chapters – also be applied "from a distance." The vast number of materials available once a UNFCCC COP or a BBNJ meeting has finished – including summaries, *ENB* reports, pictures, statements, and submissions – and the opportunities offered by data collection techniques such as interviewing and surveying, allows research on agreement-making from a distance. As described in Chapter 14, we can adopt research strategies that allow us to get immersed in a global environmental meeting even if we do not have the means or capacities to "be there." The more so, as the physical sites and digital lives of agreement-making perpetually converge.

As a collective, we saw that the pandemic might offer the possibility of new ways of researching, as many negotiations moved online, thereby offering state and nonstate actors digital spaces to continue multilateral dialogue (Vadrot et al. 2021, Vadrot and Ruiz-Rodríguez 2022). Many authors of this book have followed their research objects into virtual spaces and adapted their methodologies (Chapter 14) to critically assess continuities and disruptions between these new emerging sites and in-person meetings (Chasek 2021). Would this lead to a long-term trend toward virtual meetings? As a group of authors, this prompted us to ask whether being there might continue to be as important to advancing the study and understanding of global environmental negotiations and meeting sites? As we saw it, from an environmental perspective the increase in online events offered the potential to reduce the greenhouse gas emissions of research and increase access to more diverse forms of participation. From the expense of fieldwork perspective, this could indeed provide access to more students and early career researchers. And for parents and carers, it may have made it possible to attend more events and conferences without the bargains and complex arrangements of time away.

However, in reality, online meetings introduce new inequalities and challenges. As discussed in Chapter 14, although digital ethnography equips researchers with a reliable method to conduct fieldwork at digital negotiation sites, it cannot resolve inequalities related to the accessibility of technology (internet connection) and the effects of different time zones, making it almost impossible for some researchers (and actors) to follow a meeting (Vadrot et al. 2021). When attending meetings online, we have encountered several difficulties, but also new emerging opportunities to study agreement-making, especially if the meeting is hybrid in nature, as was the case with UNFCCC COP26, IGC 4 of the BBNJ process, and several CBD-related events. This new development implies that we need to challenge and broaden our understanding of what "being there" means, the forms it can take, and how it may look in the future.

15.4 Anticipating the Future

Global environmental agreement-making is in constant flux, and so is our research. The example of emerging digital and hybrid sites illustrates the constant need to be reflexive about agreement-making and the study thereof. Being close to our research objects and "being there" at global environmental negotiations, either in person or virtually, offers multiple insights into the practice of agreement-making and the actors, processes, and sites that have emerged in the past five decades to develop a collective response to increasing environmental degradation. We introduced the concept of global environmental agreement-making to challenge traditional conceptions of global environmental negotiations and broaden our understanding of what they are, how they work, and why they need to be studied and changed. Looking to the future of conducting research on agreement-making, we anticipate three major trends that call for further methodological innovation: new and proliferating sites (*research objects*), new relations and collaborations (*research methods*), and rising environmental stakes (*research ethics*).

15.4.1 Research Objects: New and Proliferating Sites

Global environmental negotiations are important nodes connecting multiple actors, sites, and processes for a specific period of time and within the particular practices of multilateral environmental diplomacy (Campbell et al. 2014). Although the network of existing agreements and conventions is already complex and dense (Mitchell et al. 2020), multilateral treaty negotiations continue to create new sites, such as the UN Treaty on Plastic Pollution or the new international legally binding BBNJ instrument, which extends marine biodiversity conservation to areas beyond national jurisdiction. The emergence and consolidation of new agreements creates new sites, actors, and processes that will require scholarly attention. In addition, studying agreement-making will increasingly imply that we will have to leave the in-person negotiation room and follow the actors and processes under study to other agreements-making sites, including the virtual space and digital life of a conference and the new and proliferating sites of action that all agreements create.

This may imply that we trace a process from the international to the national or local levels and follow our actors under study outside an event. As illustrated by Chapter 5, studying Indigenous Peoples' actions during negotiations has implied going beyond the negotiation site and starting research within the territory. Starting at the local site of the actors we follow is also an important research strategy for researching the practices and strategies of scientists and other knowledge holders seeking to influence negotiations with their knowledge. It is, for instance, not enough to ask what strategies experts adopt to shape agreement-making and exercise influence in the negotiation room. We also need to ask how agreement-making shapes their work – that is, (scientific) knowledge production, research practices, and entire scientific fields (Vadrot 2020; Vadrot et al. 2022). The MARIPOLDATA research project, for instance, studies how marine biodiversity science shapes the BBNJ negotiations in tandem with the emergence and development of marine biodiversity research and its practices.

In addition to broadening our research objects, we may see more and more research connecting agreement-making sites or comparing different actors, sites, and agreements-making processes across issue areas. As illustrated in Chapter 4, sharing expertise on climate change and biodiversity negotiations, IPCC participant observation, and IPBES ethnography has offered new analytical perspectives and nourished conceptual innovation. There is a tendency in the negotiation room for delegates to cross-reference agreement-making sites, sharing experiences of what has worked and failed, drawing explicit and creating formal links between conventions and their bodies. What we observe in practice can inspire research across environmental agreements and beyond the environmental field to connect environmental diplomacy to areas such as health, security, and trade.

In this regard, multisited ethnography may offer future research avenues connecting the multiple sites that matter in global environmental politics and agreement-making. Multisited ethnography, however, may have to increasingly include digital sites and virtual spaces to account for what has become more common: webcast negotiations, online participation, hybrid formats, and social media as a new form of influence and site of drama, theater, and performance. What we witness is an increased convergence between in-person meetings and virtual participation. The boundaries between what you can research and observe on site and what you can study and record as an observer of the digital life of a global environmental meeting are not clear cut and create new research objects and hybrid practices that are poorly understood. Although the final negotiation and adoption of an agreement will probably continue to be performed in person, it is very likely that parts of a conference and the intersessional work will increasingly be moved into online spaces. Many diplomats seem convinced that multilateral negotiations are about trust and that trust emerges in face-to-face relationships and bargaining behind closed doors (Vadrot et al. 2021, Vadrot and Ruiz-Rodríguez 2022). We know many things about state behavior and alliances, including the stages, casts, scripts, and drama of conferences and summits (Craggs and Mahony 2014; Death 2011), based on physical event observation, which will need to be revisited. This also goes for well-studied practices of nonstate actors, such as NGO influence (Betsill and Corell 2008), which will need to be critically reviewed in light of new emerging digital and hybrid sites. We need to restudy how nonstate actors will mobilize and reskill in order to navigate these sites and gain power and influence, initiate struggle and contestation, and challenge dominance as part of agreement-making in the future.

15.4.2 Research Methods: New Relations and Collaborations

Researching and connecting different sites and locales of agreement-making implies new forms of collaboration and new cultures of inter- and transdisciplinary research. Future research trajectories need to respond to the multiplication of sites that matter in agreement-making but are conditioned on methodological innovation and collaboration to expand our knowledge beyond what we can observe when conducting research on and at global environmental negotiations. One key challenge will be to adapt our methods to study the digital aspects of agreement-making and attribute meaning to the digital meetings, social media communication, and emerging forms of hybrid interaction that we have witnessed, especially during and after the COVID-19 pandemic. Here, we can learn from other disciplines, most notably the science and technology studies (STS), communication science, and branches of sociology, human geography, anthropology, and cultural studies that have problematized the study of digital life in the past. Media technologies and the internet have, for instance, been described as sociomaterial complexes (Gillespie et al. 2014) or forms of "social shaping" (MacKenzie and Wajcman 1985). However, the most important insight that can be drawn from these works is that technologies, infrastructures, or digital and virtual negotiation sites, as we call them, can be treated as field sites in their own right.

Methodologically, and as described in Chapter 14, digital ethnography (Beaulieu 2017; Pink 2013; Tunçalp and Lê 2014) may be the most promising method to help us to collect data online and unpack the meaning of emerging virtual negotiation sites. Moreover, scholars studying agreement-making have started to explore how cross-fertilization between digital ethnography and global environmental politics might look (Suyesay and Zanotti 2019; Vadrot et al. 2021; Vadrot and Ruiz-Rodrigez 2022). Nevertheless, this is just the beginning of a long research journey, through which we have to reflect on how digital and hybrid sites shape agreement-making and how they (may) transform the relations between researcher and research objects on the one side and research collaboration practices on the other side.

As described in Chapter 11, the complexity and size of agreement-making sites have inspired scholars to collaboratively study these sites and create large research teams to capture every aspect of a global environmental meeting. We already know that such collaboration demands a high degree of reflexivity to confront asymmetry, exploitation, and unhealthy work practices and relations. Many of the chapter authors have experienced different forms of collaboration and have learned how to create the conditions for respect and mutual recognition of each other's research skills, expertise, and epistemologies in collective research practices. However, and as discussed in Chapter 14, collaboration across in-person and virtual sites can create new imbalances between researchers, mainly because of the privilege associated with "being there" and the difficulties of getting immersed in the field when studying the process from a distance. In order to avoid digital participation being perceived as the "second best option," devalued as a research method and producing asymmetries in hybrid research teams, more methodological and analytical work needs to be done to understand the digital nature of agreement-making and unpack the meaning that these new sites and practices will produce as they unfold in the future.

15.4.3 Research Ethics: Rising Stakes

As a way of concluding, while continuing to look forward, we want to come back to the ultimate stake in the study of agreement-making: the planet. What does any of this matter if the Earth is lost? The concept of agreement-making is aimed at challenging the study of global environmental negotiations, including who is recognized as a participant of negotiations and the sites and processes that are acknowledged as constitutive of collective agreement. However, this is not simply or even mainly for scholarly purposes; it is because we care about the Earth, we care about the relations that degrade each other and the environment, and it is these relations that matter. Global environmental agreement-making, then, is also about practices that can be changed, relations that can be built, and orders that can be made that move care and stewardship for each other and the Earth to the center. By understanding what is taking place through the negotiations – the political order, interests, and forms of domination that are being maintained – and by identifying the sites and strategies that are contesting and challenging this dominance, maybe, just maybe, we (as scholars and as activists) can facilitate the realization of a different type of agreement-making: one that has the recognition, respect and care for all life at its heart.

References

Beaulieu, A. (2017). Vectors for fieldwork: Computational thinking and new modes of ethnography. In L. Hjorth, H. Horst, A. Galloway, and G. Bell., eds., *The Routledge Companion to Digital Ethnography*. London: Routledge, pp. 29–39.

Betsill, M. M. and Corell, E., eds. (2008). *NGO Diplomacy: The Influence of Nongovernmental Organizations in International Environmental Negotiations*. Cambridge, MA: The MIT Press.

Bourdieu, P. (2004). *Science of Science and Reflexivity*. Oxford: Polity.

Burch, S., Gupta, A., Inoue, C. Y. A. et al. (2019). New directions in earth system governance research. *Earth System Governance* 1, 100006.

Campbell, L. M., Corson, C., Gray, N. J., MacDonald, K. I. and Brosius, J. P. (2014). Studying global environmental meetings to understand global environmental governance: Collaborative Event Ethnography at the tenth Conference of the Parties to the Convention on Biological Diversity. *Global Environmental Politics*, 14(3), 1–20.

Chasek, P. (2021). Is it the end of the COP as we know it? An analysis of the first year of virtual meetings in the UN environment and sustainable development arena. *International Negotiation* 27, 1–32.

Coleman, L. M., and Hughes, H. (2014). Distance. In C. Aradau, J. Huysmans, A. Neal, and N. Voelkner, eds., *Critical Security Methods: New Frameworks for Analysis*. Oxon and New York; Routledge, pp. 142–158.

Craggs, R., and Mahony, M (2014). The geographies of the conference: Knowledge, performance and protest. *Geography Compass*, 8(6), 414–30

Death, C. (2011). Summit theatre: Exemplary governmentality and environmental diplomacy in Johannesburg and Copenhagen. *Environmental Politics*, 20(1), 1–19

Haraway, D. J. (1988). Situated knowledges: The science question in feminism and the privilege of partial perspective. *Feminist Studies*, 14(3), 575–599.

Hine, C. (2000). *Virtual Ethnography*. London: SAGE.

Hine, C. (2017). From virtual ethnography to the embedded, embodied and everyday internet. In L. Hjorth, H. Horst, A. Galloway, and G. Bell, eds., *The Routledge Companion to Digital Ethnography*. London: Routledge, pp. 21–28.

Hughes, H., and Vadrot, A. B. M. (2019). Weighting the world: IPBES and the struggle over biocultural diversity. *Global Environmental Politics*, 19(2), 14–37.

Hughes, H., Vadrot, A., Allan, J. I. et al. (2021). Global environmental agreement-making: Upping the methodological and ethical stakes of studying negotiations. *Earth System Governance*, 10, 100121

Mackenzie, D. and Wajcman, J., eds. (1985). *The Social Shaping of Technology*. Milton Keynes: Open University Press.

Mitchell, R. B., Andonova, L. B., Axelrod, M. et al. (2020). What we know (and could know) about international environmental agreements. *Global Environmental Politics*, 20, 103–121.

O'Neill, K., and Haas, P. M. (2019). Being there: International negotiations as study sites in global environmental politics. *Global Environmental Politics*, 19(2), 4–13.

O'Neill, K., Weinthal, E., Marion Suiseeya, K. R. et al. (2013). Methods and global environmental governance. *Annual Review of Environment and Resources*, 38, 441–471.
Pink, S. (2013). *Doing Visual Ethnography,* 3rd ed. London: SAGE.
Suiseeya, K. R. M., and Zanotti, L. (2019). Making influence visible: Innovating ethnography at the Paris Climate Summit. *Global Environmental Politics*, 19(2), 38–60.
Tunçalp, D., and Lê, P. L. (2014). (Re)Locating boundaries: A systematic review of online ethnography. *Journal of Organizational Ethnography*, 3(1), 59–79.
Vadrot, A. B. M., and Ruiz-Rodríguez, S. C. (2022). Digital multilateralism in practice: Extending critical policy ethnography to digital negotiation sites. *International Studies Quarterly*, 66(3), 1–13. https://doi.org/10.1093/isq/sqac051.
Vadrot, A. B. M., Ruiz-Rodríguez, S. C., Brogat, E. et al. (2022). Towards a reflexive, policy-relevant and engaged ocean science for the UN decade: A social science research agenda. *Earth System Governance*, 14, 100150.
Vadrot, A. B. M., Langlet, A., Tessnow-von Wysocki, I. et al. (2021). Marine biodiversity negotiations during COVID-19: A new role for digital diplomacy? *Global Environmental Politics*, 21(3): 169–186.
Vadrot, A. B. M. (2020). Multilateralism as a 'site' of struggle over environmental knowledge: The North–South divide. *Critical Policy Studies*, 14(2), 233–245.

Index

For EU product safety concerns, contact us at Calle de José Abascal, 56–1°, 28003 Madrid, Spain or eugpsr@cambridge.org.

www.ingramcontent.com/pod-product-compliance
Lightning Source LLC
LaVergne TN
LVHW060055220926
848484LV00006BA/1340

* 9 7 8 1 0 0 9 1 7 9 4 4 7 *